The Transformation of Nomadic Society in the Arab East

Martha Mundy and Basim Musallam bring together an international team of contributors consisting of archaeologists, geographers, historians, anthropologists and agronomists in a penetrating interdisciplinary account of the transformation of nomadic society. The chapters provide an integrated analysis of the changing relations of ecology, economic and socio-political organisation in the steppes of the central Middle East, documenting the *longue durée* of history alongside the more rapid transformations of the twentieth century. A series of maps and figures illustrates the narrative while a bibliographic essay analyses the existing literature. This is an accessible and interactive book which provides a comprehensive overview of a fascinating and complex society. It will attract readers from a variety of disciplines, including those interested in contemporary environmental and development issues.

MARTHA MUNDY lectures in Anthropology at the London School of Economics. Her publications include *Domestic Government: Kinship, Community and Polity in North Yemen* (1995).

BASIM MUSALLAM lectures in Islamic Studies at the University of Cambridge. His publications include *Sex and Society in Islam* (1989) and *The Arabs* (1983).

University of Cambridge Oriental Publications 58

The Transformation of Nomadic Society in the Arab East

A series list is shown at the back of the book

These essays constitute the final volume of *Arabian Studies* to be published under the auspices of the Faculty of Middle Eastern Studies, University of Cambridge. The Faculty is grateful to the following members of the Editorial Committee for their contributions to the volume:

Riccardo Bocco: Institut Universitaire d'Etudes du Développement, Geneva
Ronald Jaubert: Institut Universitaire d'Etudes du Développement, Geneva
Françoise Métral: Centre National de la Recherche Scientifique, Lyons

The Faculty also wishes to thank Dr Mundy and Dr Musallam for their work as executive editors.

Gordon Johnson, Chairman of the Publications Committee of the University of Cambridge Oriental Faculty

The Transformation of Nomadic Society in the Arab East

EDITED BY

MARTHA MUNDY

London School of Economics

AND

BASIM MUSALLAM

University of Cambridge

CAMBRIDGE
UNIVERSITY PRESS

CAMBRIDGE UNIVERSITY PRESS
Cambridge, New York, Melbourne, Madrid, Cape Town,
Singapore, São Paulo, Delhi, Tokyo, Mexico City

Cambridge University Press
The Edinburgh Building, Cambridge CB2 8RU, UK

Published in the United States of America by
Cambridge University Press, New York

www.cambridge.org
Information on this title: www.cambridge.org/9780521770576

First published 2000

A catalogue record for this publication is available from the British Library

Library of Congress Cataloguing in Publication data
The transformation of nomadic society in the Arab East / edited by Martha Mundy and
Basim Musallam.
p. cm.
Includes bibliographical references.
ISBN 0 521 77057 2 (hb)
1. Bedouins – Arab countries. 2. Nomadism – Arab countries.
3. Bedouins – Relocation – Arab countries. 4. Bedouins – Economic conditions – 20th century.
5. Bedouins – Social conditions – 20th century. 6. Bedouins – Government policy – Arab
countries. I. Mundy, Martha. II. Musallam, Basim.
DS36.9.B4 T73 2000
909′.0974927–dc21 99-045363

ISBN 978-0-521-77057-6 Hardback

CONTENTS

ILLUSTRATIONS

Figures

Maps

TABLES

PREFACE

Society and environment in the great arid and semi-arid zones of the Arab World have dramatically changed over the past century. This transformation is the subject of this volume which brings together specialists in geography, archaeology, history, anthropology and agronomy. For three thousand years pastoral nomadism was the main form of human adaptation to this harsh and fragile environment, which covers over 70 per cent of the Arab Middle East. Common to all the contributions to this volume, and the source of their strength, is a vision of pastoral society not as a world apart but as one bound up with the wider structures of economy and polity.

Most of the chapters were first presented as papers to the symposium on 'The Evolution of the Steppe in Arabia and Bilâd al-Shâm' held at the Institute of the Arab World, Paris, in April 1991. The symposium proceedings, which differ substantially from the present publication, were edited by R. Bocco, R. Jaubert and F. Métral (*Steppes d'Arabies, Etats, pasteurs, agriculteurs et commercants: le devenir des zones sèches*, PUF/IUED, Paris/Geneva, 1993). Alison Betts wrote a joint chapter especially for this volume with Kenneth Russell, who died in May 1992, before its completion. It is to the memory of Ken Russell that we would like to dedicate this volume.

We are grateful to several institutions whose support made this volume possible: the Groupe de Recherches et d'Etudes sur le Moyen-Orient Contemporain (GREMO), Maison de l'Orient Méditerranéen, Lyons; the Institut Universitaire d'Etudes du Développement (IUED), Geneva; the Institute of Archaeology and Anthropology, Yarmouk University, Irbid; the Institute of the Arab World, Paris; the Ford Foundation, Cairo; the International Center for Agricultural Research in the Dry Areas (ICARDA), Aleppo; the Centre for Studies and Research on the Contemporary Middle East (CERMOC), Amman; the Centre National de la Recherche Scientifique (CNRS), Paris; the French Ministries of National Education and Foreign Affairs; and the Centre of Middle Eastern Studies, University of Cambridge. We also wish to thank C. Beamish and E. Tampier for their translations of some chapters from French.

The system of transliteration adopted for Arabic terms is that of the *International Journal of Middle Eastern Studies*. However, in the case of some place and personal names, not in italics, it was not always possible to standardise the transliterations of all vocalisation. Where this differs from the *IJMES* system, it follows the author's style. All maps except those accompanying the article by Jörg Janzen (chapter 13) were drawn by Yves Montmessin of the graphics department of the Maison de l'Orient Méditerranéen, Lyon.

The bibliography brings together the references from all the chapters in this volume to form, with the bibliographical note by Riccardo Bocco, a comprehensive overview of the literature on the steppes of Arabia and geographical Syria, and the current state of knowledge.

ABBREVIATIONS

ACSAD	Arab Centre for the Study of Arid and Dry Lands
AGS	American Geographical Society
ASFEC	Arab States Fundamental Education Centre
BAR	*British Archaeological Reports*
BSOAS	*Bulletin of the School of Oriental and African Studies*
CERMOC	Centre d'Etudes et de Recherches sur le Moyen-Orient Contemporain
CHEAM	Centre des Hautes Etudes Administratives sur l'Afrique et l'Asie Modernes
CNRS	Centre National de la Recherche Scientifique
FAO	Food and Agriculture Organisation
IBRD	International Bank for Reconstruction and Development
ICARDA	International Center for Agricultural Research in the Dry Areas
IFEAD	Institut des Etudes Arabes de Damas
IJMES	*International Journal of Middle East Studies*
ILO	International Labour Organisation
IPC	Iraq Petroleum Company
MAE	Ministère des Affaires Etrangères
MRT	Ministère de Recherche et Technologie
PEF	Palestine Exploration Fund
SEDES	Société d'Etudes pour le Développement Economqiue et Social
UNESCO	United Nations Educational, Scientific and Cultural Organisation
UNDP	United Nations Development Programme
WHO	World Health Organisation
ZDPV	*Zeitschrift des Deutschen Palästina-Vereins*

The Arabian Peninsula, Syria and Jordan

Introduction

The transformation of nomadic society

Pastoral nomadism was the classical form of human adaptation to the harsh yet fragile environment of the dry steppe lands and so, although this volume is mostly about its waning, it opens with reflections on the conditions of its emergence. At the beginning specialised pastoralism grew out of agriculture, and throughout history pastoralists have belonged to the societies about them, exchanging their products with agriculturalists and the cities, and serving the systems of empire and trade. Indeed, we should not think of the inhabitants of tents simply as pastoralists: all evidence from the past reveals that they also engaged in cultivation, trade and military pursuits. The bedouins (*badw*) are people of the *badiya* (the open country) who may live by more than one strategy. This book explores how their different activities were bound into wider systems of rule, trade and production. And it demonstrates that the forms of leadership and social solidarity expressed in an idiom of descent (which we know as tribes) were also not confined to pastoralists.

From the turn of the twentieth century bedouin movement and control over territory in the *badiya* came to be challenged by new and more powerful forms of central administration and law. The restriction of bedouin autonomy was hastened by the division of the former Ottoman lands into separate states under European control after World War I. The Ottomans built the first railways through the *badiya*, and the decades after the fall of the empire were to witness the still deeper revolution in the structure of space brought by the automobile. During these years appeared a vision that declared nomadic pastoralism a backward way of life antithetical to social and national development. This was to be institutionalised as policy in the independent states of the area after World War II. As this view of national development gained adherents the pastoral economy was penalised by agricultural policies which, from the 1960s onwards, would concentrate efforts on the zones of higher rainfall and irrigated agriculture.

Today rapid population growth, agricultural deficits and increasing demand for meat, all spurred by the oil affluence, have returned the dryland areas to the centre of debate. Since the 1970s agriculture and meat production have sharply expanded throughout the *badiya*, taking on forms perhaps best described as 'mining'. The steppe scarcely presents a common aspect today, as some areas are given over to mechanised cereal production, others to the mining of hydrocarbons and phosphates, and yet others to construction, ubiquitously in cement. That these evident transformations with their dangers of environmental degradation are accompanied by deeper changes in the societies of the *badiya* is itself a central topic of this book.

In the first chapter Paul Sanlaville invites us to place a simple observation in context: nature does not set fixed bounds for pastoral production or for agriculture. Quite different areas appear propitious for pastoral or agricultural exploitation every year. What is most striking on the ground is not what the map suggests – gradually declining isohyets of average rainfall – but the variability of rainfall, both annually and between micro-regions. Given the mobility enjoyed and capital possessed by rural populations of the Near East today, this variability invites them to redraw the boundaries of cultivation and sheep-herding dramatically.

But the recent extension of cultivation and sheep-herding into ever more arid areas rests on a much longer integration of pastoral production within the wider economy. The archaeologists' contribution to this volume serves to remind us that such integration has been true from the beginning. Thus Jacques Cauvin considers the emergence of pastoral nomadism within the general framework of the development of agriculture and animal husbandry. As is well known, animal husbandry began in association with settled agriculture well before the emergence of pastoral nomadism. On present evidence pastoral nomadism appears not, as so long believed, a subsidiary adaptation by people forced to exploit less promising lands, but rather a broad social movement entailing, through pastoralism, exploitation of wider territory.

Alison Betts and the late Kenneth Russell examine the issues involved in the domestication of pastoral animals in greater detail, and for periods well after the beginnings considered by Cauvin. Their study closes with the importance of the camel in restructuring relations between 'the desert' and 'the sown' in the Near East. Betts and Russell argue that whereas the important changes in nomad–state relations that occurred in the first millennium BC have often been explained on the grounds that 'the camel, and more specifically a particular design of riding saddle, permitted the rise of "warrior nomads" who could threaten the settled lands from the security of the desert', the more fundamental factor was the 'greater trade activity throughout the Arabian Peninsula' and the new roles this offered to nomads. In other words, change in the wider economy, not a single technical development, appears to have been very important.

Work on the steppe is particularly rare for the central periods of Islamic history, a silence which we hope may some day end. The documented history of the steppe begins in earnest only with the nineteenth century, and remains more political than economic. Norman Lewis continues his study of the extension of settled agriculture in nineteenth-century geographical Syria by focusing on two regions, the southern Hawran and the Palmyrena (on the latter see also the chapter by F. Métral). He demonstrates how the extension of settlement in the second half of the nineteenth century was matched by Ottoman regulation of bedouin movement. But radical curtailment of bedouin migration was finally to succeed only after World War I as political authorities were able to restrict movement across the newly imposed state borders.

The principles used by the post-World War I states to claim dominion over bedouin territory are discussed by John Wilkinson. In negotiations over borders between the British and the rulers of Arabia, primarily Ibn Saʿud, several levels of right were invoked: that of the bedouin to wells and hence to territory about the wells; that granted by the bedouin to the Saudi rulers through the payment of *zakat* (often reciprocated by gifts to tribal shaykhs from the Saudi ruler); and that claimed by the British, usually simply a general undertaking signed with a local ruler, but in the case of South Arabia sometimes also principles recognised locally. Whatever the details of the negotiations, the imposition of new state boundaries after World War I, and the introduction of automotive transport, spelt the end of large nomadic movement between the Arabian Peninsula and geographical Syria, and everywhere marked the abandonment of camel-pastoralism for sheep-herding.

The three chapters by Christian Velud on north-east Syria, Ugo Fabietti on Saudi Arabia and Tariq Tall on Trans-Jordan discuss the impact of government policies on the society of the steppes after World War I. In each case, government policy encouraged the bedouin to settle (on Trans-Jordan see also the chapter by Bocco). In the Syrian Jazira, Velud shows how the Mandate authorities allowed certain bedouin leaders to register ownership to vast tracts of land. Here the 1920s saw not only the closing of borders to bedouin movement, but also the settlement of important new refugee populations. These populations were encouraged to settle in the recently developed zones of irrigated agriculture and the small towns of the Jazira. These developments, while they spelt wealth for the shaykhs, rendered a pastoral life more difficult for the common bedouin who increasingly sought work as agricultural labourers.

Fabietti notes that in Arabia, although the Saudi rulers had negotiated boundaries on the basis of tribal 'territories' (*dira*) and possessed close links with bedouin leaders, by 1925 the Saudi state formally abolished the right of any tribe to regulate access to its *dira*. In so far as management of territory was central to the very identity of the tribe, this spelt the death-knell of the tribe as an effective social unit. From then on the only unit for economic management of bedouin resources became the household, the very character of which was thereby transformed.

The analysis of Trans-Jordan by Tall reveals both parallels and differences to the Syrian and Saudi Arabian cases. On the one hand, government policy, particularly from the time of Glubb Pasha, privileged links with bedouin leaders and, like Saudi policy, incorporated men from the bedouin tribes in the army. Nevertheless, according to Tall, such political privilege does not entail support for the local economy of the 'tribes'. Quite the contrary: economic policy is made by an urban commercial and bureaucratic elite which has little interest in small-scale rural production. It is noteworthy that Tall's usage of the term 'tribe' differs from that of other authors. Tall does not restrict the term to former nomadic groups but applies it to all Trans-Jordanian rural society in a manner suggesting a more general political 'tribalisation' of the East Jordanian population.

In Jaubert's chapter on the arid regions of Syria since 1930 the drama and the actors are the same but their roles appear reversed. Far from the state simply remaking the rural economy according to its wishes, government policy appears quite as often as not simply reactive to the dynamism of productive systems in the steppe.

The chapters of the anthropologists Sulayman Khalaf, Françoise Métral, and Donald Cole and Soraya Altorki explore different dimensions of the interplay between local economy and public policy. Khalaf traces the story of one prominent family whose role shifted from that of local shaykhs who gained title to land developed for cotton production and so acquired the way of life of landlords, to that of politically marginalised 'feudalists' in the years of land reform and peasant unions, and finally back – through the avenues of education and the ruling party – to a position of regional prominence as professionals and members of the new political establishment.

The continuity of familial and social identity in the face of important political and economic change appears equally clearly in Françoise Métral's study of Sukhna. Métral's analysis allows us to understand, at the intimate level of partnerships, family and kin, the calculations permitting today's dramatic and ecologically corrosive extension of barley cultivation and sheep-herding deep in the arid zone.

Like Sukhna, the Najdi city of 'Unayzah described in the chapter by Cole and Altorki served as a market centre for trade with the bedouin. The change in 'Unayzah has proved yet more radical than that at Sukhna. Sukhna's economy still depends primarily on pastoral production, however transformed, whereas every aspect of 'Unayzah's economy appears reworked by the priorities of the political economy of petrol production. Métral writes of Sukhna's sophisticated marketing networks that allow producers of pastoral and agricultural goods to negotiate between the 'free market' and the powerful state purchasing agencies (see also the chapters by Jaubert, Treacher and Jones). But in 'Unayzah the marketing for what remains of local animal and vegetable production appears primitive by contrast with the sophisticated marketing of imported goods (compare likewise the study of Janzen). In a manner yet more dramatic than Tall's Jordanian case, government policy appears to reflect priorities of a commercial and bureaucratic elite for whom 'development' has another meaning than the development of a local vegetable or meat market.

The last section considers 'development' in the steppe today – its institutional discourse, the dilemmas of its technical solutions, and the environmental degradation entailed in the financially rewarding forms of exploitation dominant today. Jorg Janzen presents a case study from a very different ecological zone, that of Omani Dhofar in south-east Arabia. In spite of the uniqueness of the monsoon-mist environment and the cattle-herding way of life, the broad lines of transformation he describes will by now be familiar: unrestricted access by trucking to pastures once distant, destruction of vegetation as the former pastures become feed-lots, incorporation of bedouin groups into the safety net of the state through military subsidy, failure to develop marketing structures for local animal production, and dominance of the local economy by an urban bureaucratic and commercial elite. Janzen forcefully emphasises the threat to the environment and to long-term productivity that lies in present systems of production in the more arid zones.

Michael Jones and Timothy Treacher's chapters, when read alongside the earlier ones of Jaubert and Métral, provide a sharp picture of the interrelation of systems of barley production and sheep-raising in Syria today. They are aware of the unsustainable nature of contemporary productive systems, but by analysing the complex determination of these systems, they eschew the notion of an easy solution. Gone are the days when agronomic work could proceed in isolation from the economy and society in which it is to be introduced. But, as Jones notes, information on the productive systems in the more arid zones remains very poor, and although the funders of development work now pay lip-service to ecological sustainability, they still require their investment to produce quick results in a manner that will surely render the introduction of ecologically less destructive systems very difficult.

Finally, Riccardo Bocco reviews the discourse of development experts concerning nomads in the Arab Middle East since the 1950s. He demonstrates an unacknowledged continuity with Mandate policies and, more generally, the poverty of information and imagination that has permitted thinking to remain static for so long. It is only quite recently, after hardly a nomad was left to be 'settled', that the experts began to invoke the very principle that their predecessors sought to annul, namely tribal regulation of access to pastures – the native institution of *hima* or protected pasture, as a solution to the crisis of mounting ecological degradation. As Bocco points out, the existence, let alone the character, of this institution has not been documented by the experts. The magnitude of the difficulty in reversing the principle of free access to territory should not be underestimated.

The bibliography brings together the references of all the chapters in this volume to form, with Riccardo Bocco's bibliographical note, a comprehensive overview of the literature on the steppes of Arabia and geographical Syria, and the current state of knowledge.

1
Environment and development

PAUL SANLAVILLE
Centre National de la Recherche Scientifique, Lyons

Most of the studies in this volume concern the steppe on the inner edge of the Fertile Crescent, adjoining the Arabian desert. Others, however, consider areas right in the heart of the Arabian Peninsula, where conditions differ quite markedly, and for which the term 'steppe' is not appropriate.

The latitude and annual temperature variations of the Arabian Peninsula make it a tropical area, in spite of the fact that winters can be cold, particularly at high altitude. Most of the peninsula is desert, with very low rainfall, generally below 100 mm except in certain mountainous regions. These less arid regions are: (a) the western edges of ʿAsir and Yemen, where rainfall on high ground exceeds 200 mm (sometimes even 500 mm); and (b) the mountains of Oman (see map 1.1). Rainfall occurs in winter and is caused by cooler air masses. Rain also falls in summer (June–July) on the mountains in the south, when the intertropical weather front moves northwards. These are monsoon rains. This area is perceptibly more arid than the inner edge of the Fertile Crescent. Summer temperatures are very high indeed and rainfall occurs only a very few days a year and varies greatly from year to year. As a result the local vegetation looks very different: the climate is Saharo-Sudanese and is favourable to trees but not to grasses. Rather than being steppe, the landscape consists of very open scrub jungle, mainly acacias and thorn bushes concentrated in the wadis. This strip of desert margin within the Arabian Peninsula is fairly narrow and extends between the mountainous zones stretching through the Hijaz, ʿAsir, Yemen, Hadramawt and Oman and the vast dune-covered depressions in the centre, the Nufud and the Rubʿ al-Khali. The strip consists of sand and pebble foothills traversed by a dense network of wadis, whose sporadic outpourings quickly disappear into the sand (see map 1.2). These inner foothills are used as thoroughfares by nomads but, except in exceptional cases, agriculture is confined to the oases and is always irrigated.

The inner edge of the Fertile Crescent, on the northern border of the Arabian desert, presents quite a different picture. It covers a great arid and semi-arid arc extending right through Jordan, Syria and Iraq. Lying as it does between the desert, used by the nomads as pastureland, and the areas occupied since neolithic times by settled agriculture, this inner border is difficult to

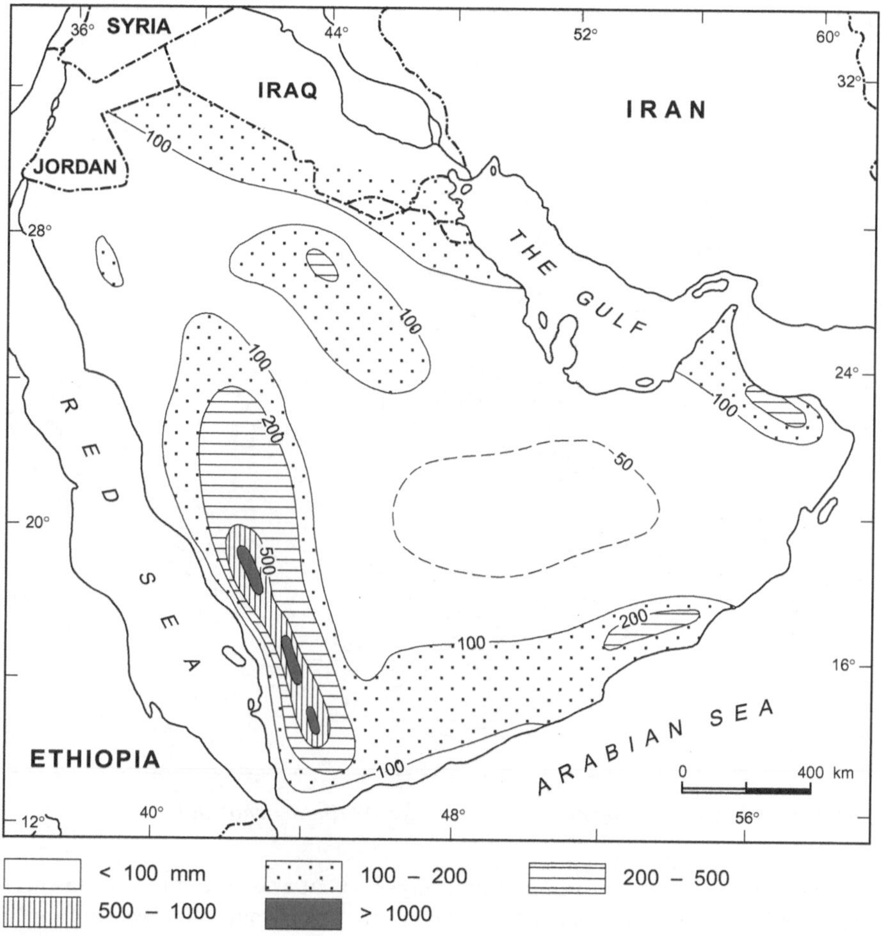

Map 1.1: Average annual precipitation in the Arabian Peninsula

demarcate exactly. In appearance the area consists of vast plains and plateaux broken by limestone hills (the mountains of the Palmyrena and Jabals Bishri, ʿAbd al-ʿAziz and Sinjar) or volcanic outcrops (the Druze mountain); a dense network of wadis covers the plain, which dips gradually southwards in Iraq and northern Syria, less gradually eastwards in southern Syria and Jordan. The vegetation best adapted to local climatic and soil conditions is steppe grassland, comprising a rich variety of species. In well-watered areas this steppe also supports oak and pistachio trees. Very early exploitation of the steppe by mankind has caused progressive damage to the vegetation and has led to the almost total disappearance of trees.

During the most recent glacial period in the northern hemisphere the

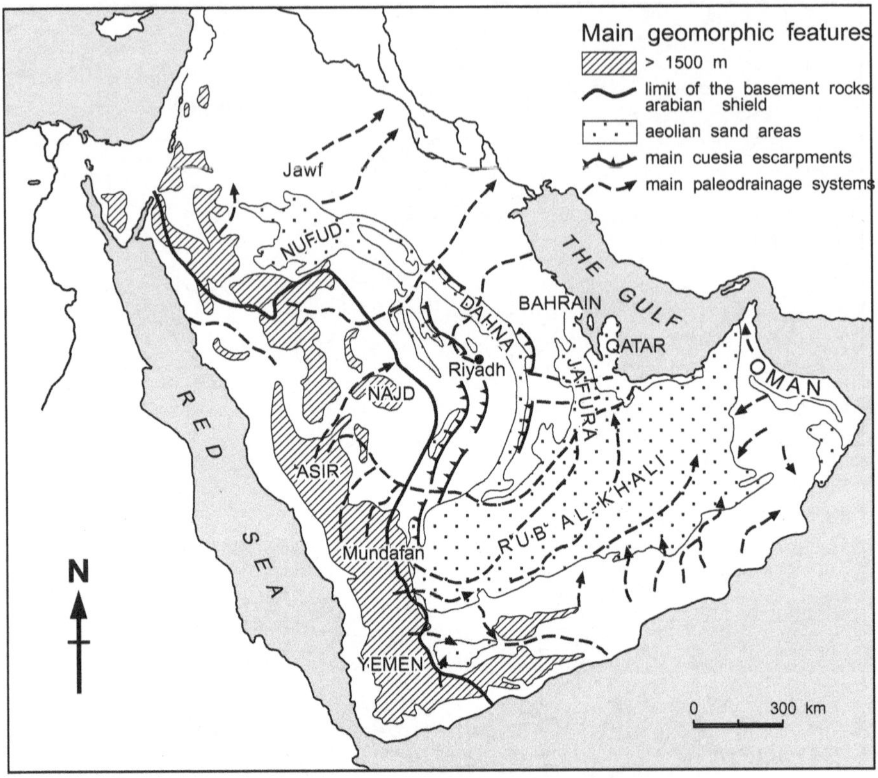

Map 1.2: Main geomorphic features of the Arabian Peninsula

climate of this region was one of extremes of heat and cold, but this has gradually changed over the past 12,000 years into the climate that we are familiar with today. As the climate there grew warmer, the Fertile Crescent played host to the neolithic revolution; the population adopted a settled way of life and began progressively to domesticate both plants and animals, growing crops (wheat, barley and pulses) and raising sheep and goats. From the fourth millennium BC the region witnessed the birth of the urban revolution. It is a region that has played a key role in the history of mankind. Land occupancy and land use in this transitional area have changed quite radically over the millennia, keeping pace with climatic changes and political and economic vicissitudes.

Climatic uncertainty

The steppes on the northern border of the Arabian desert enjoy a Mediterranean climate with two principal seasons. The rainy season extends over a seven-month period, from October to April, with the maximum rainfall in December, January and February. The summers are extremely hot and dry, and their length increases the further south one goes. Rainfall varies both

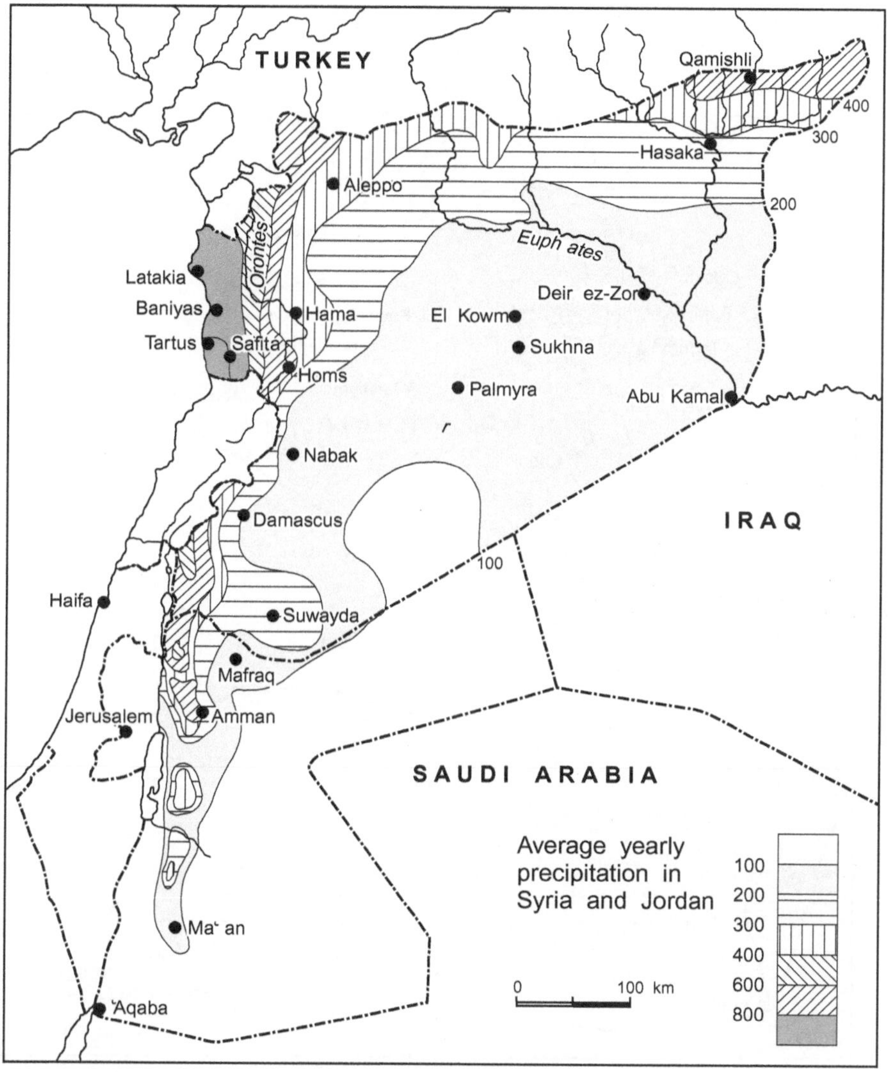

Map 1.3: Average annual precipitation in Syria and Jordan

in annual quantity and in its distribution throughout the year. It is not easy to describe this transitional zone, between the cultivated belt and the desert, in statistical terms. The data available on climatic matters are inadequate because statistical records are too recent and rainfall observation stations too widespread; the data that do exist have never been properly interpreted, and the readings available are marked by great irregularity, both temporal and spatial. Some idea can be gained from a series of statistics which emphasise the irregularity of the annual rainfall and its general unpredictability (see map 1.3).

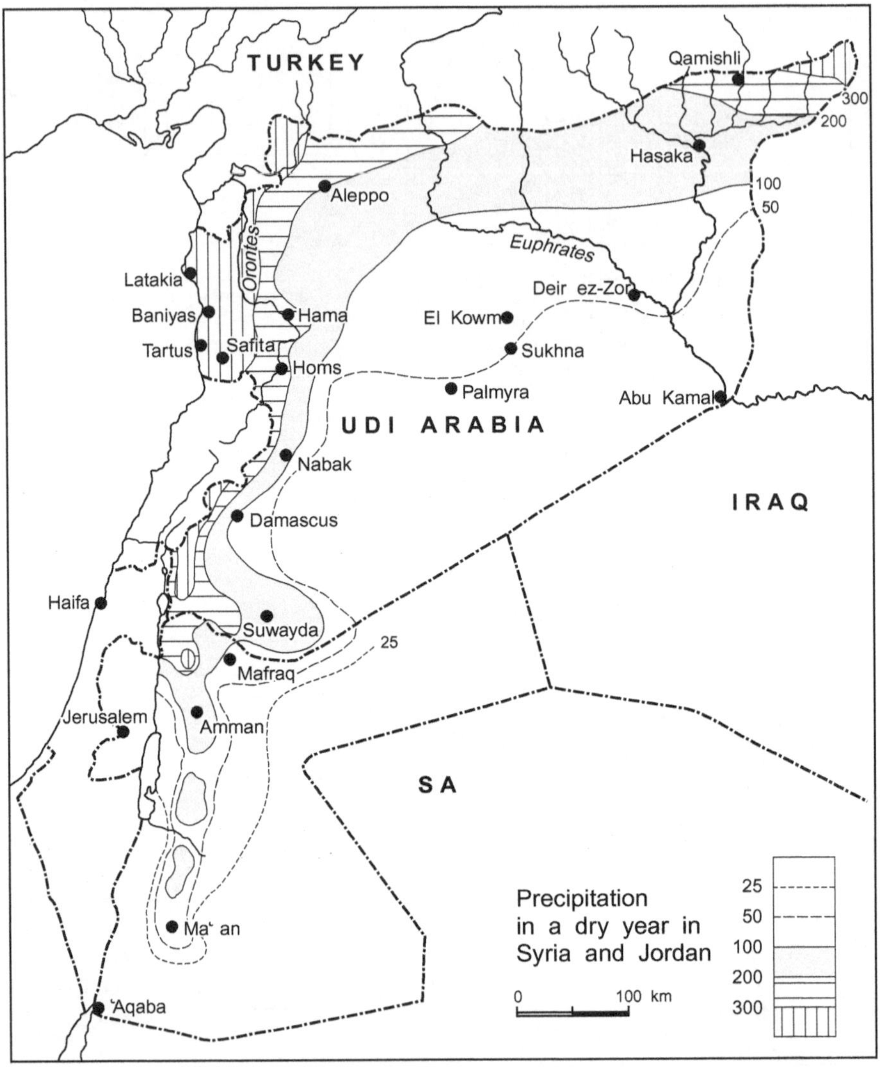

Map 1.4: Precipitation in a dry year in Syria and Jordan

Schematically, the zone falls between the curves representing twenty-five and forty days rain per annum, and between the isohyetal lines representing 100 mm and 250 mm average annual rainfall, i.e. well short of what is needed for growing normal cereal crops. Harvests in this area, when crops are sown, are extremely risky. In fact rainfall varies extremely from one year to the next and can be as low as the desert norm (less than 100 mm) or relatively high (300 mm, sometimes more); the latter figure allows cereal crops to prosper, but the variation in rainfall gives rise to some terrible disappointments in drought

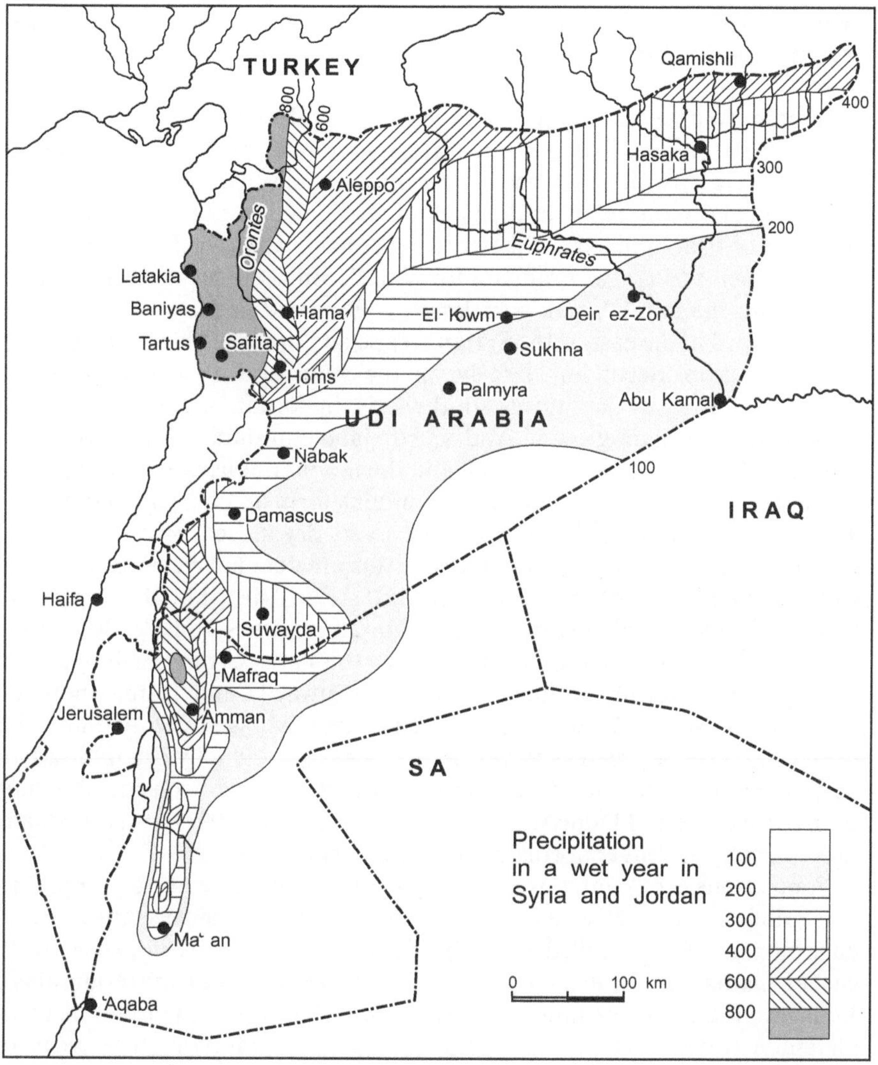

Map 1.5: Precipitation in a wet year in Syria and Jordan

years. The northern border of the steppe could be said to correspond approximately to the 150 mm isohyet in a dry year and the 350 mm isohyet in a wet year (see maps 1.4 and 1.5).

It is estimated in Syria, therefore, that over a period of ten years, the occurrence of years in which the rainfall is too low for any crops to grow is three in areas where the average rainfall is 300 mm, and nine in areas where the average annual rainfall is less than 150 mm. The irregularity of this pattern of rainfall can be expressed by a calculation of average variability across a number of years, i.e. by the average departure from the norm. This variability is in the region of 45–50 per cent, higher still in zones where the average rainfall is lower.

In order to understand the steppe one has to take a certain number of variables into account. These include, first, the number of days of rain and the irregularity with which they occur, year by year or even month by month. The most irregular months fall at the beginning and end of the wet season, i.e. at the most critical moments in the growing season, when the first shoots come up and when the ears of grain are formed. Second, the seasonal distribution of rainfall: the rainfall peak is in January–February in the west but shifts to March–April in the east of the Syrian steppe and in Iraq. Third, transpiration by evaporation, depending largely on the wind and on temperature: this increases sharply as one moves southwards, in Jordan, and accentuates the water deficit for plant growth. And fourth, land contours also play an important role. Altitude increases rainfall and the mountainous areas feed the aquifers under the wadis. The hills and mountains form an obstacle to the humid winds and their eastern foothills are often very dry indeed.

The enormous regional differences in this area cannot be emphasised too strongly. Many showers are caused by local storms, distributed in completely random fashion, and this may make rainfall statistics completely different from one monitoring station to the next, as the statistics on year-by-year variability at monitoring stations in Palmyra, Suwayda and Hama show. For example, the year 1975 was slightly wetter than average in Hama, and even wetter in Palmyra, whereas the same year was exceptionally dry in Suwayda. In 1987 Hama experienced the average rainfall, Suwayda considerably more than the average and Palmyra much less. The winter of 1991–2 was very damp in western Syria, but abnormally dry in the steppe.

Populations exploiting this arid margin have to put up with very unpredictable rainfall, and to survive the consequences of this upon vegetation and the environment. The so-called Fertile Crescent is very narrow in places: to the east of Damascus, for instance, where the double barrier of the mountains of Lebanon and anti-Lebanon brings the desert right up to the foothills of the Qalamun range; and in the southern part of Jordan. In other parts the Crescent is relatively wide: nearly 200 km on either side of the Euphrates at Raqqa in Syria, or on the eastern side of the Jabal Druze. Here the transition to desert is much more gradual; the isohyetal lines vary widely from year to year.

Although rainfall is the most important factor determining agricultural potential and the high level of climatic risk typical of the region, it is not the only factor. Agricultural potential is also closely linked to temperature and soil quality. In winter, water loss through evaporation is low because temperatures are relatively low, and in areas receiving more than 200 mm of rain per year water needs are generally met. On the other hand, as soon as spring comes, temperatures rise quickly and drought conditions reappear very quickly. Because temperatures vary enormously year by year the development cycle of barley can vary by three or four weeks, according to the temperature prevailing in the cold season. The effects of lack of water are even more of a threat when the temperature shoots up in the spring. In order to complete their development cycle the plants depend heavily on water that has accumulated during the winter.

The water available at the end of the growth cycle depends on rainfall and also on the ability of the soil to conserve excess. Pedological conditions are not on the whole very favourable. The soils are generally thin and therefore not very suitable for the practice of dry farming, which is based on the accumulation of water from one season to the next. When the depth of the soil is less than 60 cm, only a portion of excess rainfall can be utilised by the plants to complete their development cycle. In addition, the soil is mainly calcareous or gypseous, and therefore lacking in nutritive elements – particularly in phosphates, nitrogen and organic matter. Furthermore, the soil is structurally unstable and therefore fragile; in the least well-watered areas it deteriorates very easily.

The threat of desertification

Several chapters in this volume consider the damage being done to the environment and to natural resources, in cultivated areas as well as in the grazing lands. The observations made by their authors leave no room for any doubt about the serious nature of the problem, and the urgency of finding solutions. In some areas the damage has become virtually irreversible, and the land is becoming desert. Scientists engaged in studies of the area have given a clear picture of the stages leading up to the present situation.

Traditional pastoral practices, where the flocks visited the pastures twice a year, in spring and in autumn, took into account the fragility of the steppe environment, giving it time to recover between grazing. The flocks would leave the steppe during the latent season, to go and crop the stubble in the cultivated areas (in summer) or to retreat into the desert (in winter). Since the end of the nineteenth century, however, and at an ever-quickening pace, pressure on the steppe has increased. The reasons for this are manifold:

- The advent of motor transport has played a decisive part by reducing distances and by permitting the rapid transport of water, foodstuffs and animals to any area. Motor transport has made possible the rapid expansion of cultivated areas, and has allowed flocks to graze areas that were previously difficult of access, where now they can remain even during severe droughts.
- The increase in population, dramatic urbanisation and a general rise in the standard of living have brought about a growing demand for meat, particularly lamb and mutton.

- Agricultural policy has, directly or indirectly, encouraged intensification in the use of resources, without imposing any controls. Political and economic crises, frequent in the recent history of the region, have often had a direct effect on the desert areas, which have been used as overspill areas. In Jordan, the wave of emigration triggered by the Israeli occupation of the West Bank in 1967 was followed immediately by an expansion of land under cultivation into the desert regions of Jordan. In Syria the considerable increase in barley production between 1986 and 1990 is the direct result of the economic crisis that afflicted the country after 1985; it is detrimental to the steppe. These two examples demonstrate how the dry regions are used as pressure valves or outlets during times of crisis, but unfortunately this exploitation damages their longer-term prospects. In Syria, barley-growing has spread into the steppe, reducing the land available to nomadic herdsmen. Barley is now grown below the 100 mm isohyet, in what is termed zone 5 (and even beyond), well beyond the theoretical limit of rainfed culture; 15 per cent of barley cultivation now lies outside this limit. The steppe thus plays a considerable role in barley-growing and sheep-rearing, but the flocks only receive a small proportion of their nourishment from this locally produced barley, the major part nowadays being provided by pellets and straw purchased by herders.
- These developments have been accelerated by the authorities, who have done their best to settle the nomads while rushing through measures to suppress tribal property rights and to prohibit the fallowing of land. They have authorised the cultivation of drier and drier areas.

The environmental consequences of such developments are very serious. Flocks that are too large stay too long in one place and take no account of the latency periods required for plant growth. Herds of livestock trample the plant cover and cause great circles of desert to appear in areas where they are herded together. Motor traffic builds up. Land is often cultivated on perpendicular slopes, which destroys local vegetation and exposes bare soil to the danger of erosion by wind and by water.

Archaeological and geographical research has revealed how the agricultural colonisation of the region advanced and retreated by turns over the centuries. During periods of dense, intensive occupation the number of villages and the population of each village increased; the inhabitants penetrated further into the arid margin, which was itself occupied at the time. There were also periods of decline, when the settled areas were more or less abandoned to the nomads and their flocks. There were phases of dense occupation during the Halaf and Obeid periods (sixth and seventh millennia), then during the chalcolithic period and the Bronze Age (fourth and third millennia) and finally round about the beginning of our era, peaking during Roman times. Other periods, however, show a marked decline, for example the more recent Bronze Age (middle of the second millennium AD) or from the seventeenth century on; it is not clear to what extent the changes are attributable to environmental modifications or to historical, political or economic factors.

Such a vision of *la longue durée* helps to put into perspective the problems that we observe today, which form part of a cycle that began when agriculture was first developed in the region. Nevertheless, pressure on the land has never been so strong nor the disequilibrium so great since pastoral and agricultural exploitation began. In the past the low population made the temporary abandonment of deteriorated lands quite feasible; this is no longer the case today, however, as population growth in the Middle East is one of the highest in the world and pressure on the land is extreme.

Signs of the deterioration of basic resources are increasingly in evidence, although the economic and social consequences cannot compare as yet with those affecting other parts of the world, in particular the Sahel, where such developments have been studied in detail. Although periodic droughts cause a damaging decline in productivity in the Near East, their effects are not as dramatic as the effects of drought in the Sahel. In the Near East aridity is less extensive, the cycle of drought much less prolonged and, most important of all, the economic and social consequences are mitigated because the states are richer, their economies more diversified and the populations affected have access to more varied resources.

The increasing desertification cannot be ignored, however: plant cover has been considerably reduced, interesting species are disappearing, to be replaced by plants not attractive to livestock. Soil fertility has decreased enormously since fallowing was abolished, and the drop in the quantity of nutrients in the soil (phosphates and nitrogen) has the effect of lengthening the growing cycle and thereby increasing the risk of plants being scorched when the hot weather starts.

Some spectacular examples of soil erosion have been reported: ravines being hollowed out or large bodies of earth carried away by water running off the hills. Wind erosion, perhaps the most spectacular of all, creates mobile sand dunes (barkanes) that sometimes block roads or cut off railway lines. Unfortunately we do not possess many details of this erosion, either statistical or cartographical, but it has been estimated that wind erosion could account for the loss of 10 to 50 tonnes of soil per hectare per year. Sand travels through the air across short distances and is soon brought to a halt by obstacles in its path (usually hills). Dust is raised by the wind and is transported in suspension at relatively high altitudes, sometimes for a long way, and this accounts for the definitive loss of a considerable volume of fine soil particles from the area. Water erosion is the greater threat in zones where rainfall is higher, wind erosion the greater in drier zones with sandier, less structured soil.

Soil erosion is bound to increase as the plant cover deteriorates and becomes more sparse. The history of the region shows that periods when the population pressure was heavy have always been followed by periods when erosion was bad; the regeneration has taken a long time afterwards, and often seems to have remained incomplete. We can learn from the examples above, always bearing in mind that the pressure imposed by man on the environment has never been as great as it is today.

Rational development

Thanks to the presence of two international research agencies in the region (ACSAD and ICARDA), large sums of money have been spent on research and on the application of technical improvements. The various research programmes are producing promising results, but these results have not, as yet, been very widely applied. The implementation of the results has come up against a number of obstacles, political, economic and social. Agricultural policy appears to pay no heed to the results or to the proposals put forward by the research bodies; one wonders what kind of relations must exist between the research bodies and the policy makers.

The proposals made by the research organisations raise a few questions themselves. On the one hand some of the proposed improvements run the risk of missing their objective and of contributing to the destruction they are designed to avert. A case in point is the application of fertilisers, proposed for the semi-arid zones as part of a package of measures centred round the introduction of leguminous fodder crops. Used on their own, fertilisers compensate for the chemical deficiencies of the soil and thus make it possible to maintain cultivation in sensitive areas for a longer period; this may simply serve to hasten the physical degradation of the soil. Study of the problems of soil degradation has only recently begun, previous agronomic research having principally (if not exclusively) focused entirely on the application of technical solutions. Basic phenomena such as the physical and chemical deterioration of cultivated land are still little understood.[1] It is difficult to forecast whether or not the projected improvements will lead to the long-term stabilisation of productivity.

Collaboration between politicians, practitioners and academics (from the natural as well as the social sciences) is essential for the production of a mini-series of thematic and deductive maps. This could cover selected areas of Syria and Jordan, in places where geographers and anthropologists have already started work and which are already well known to archaeologists and historians. In this way an effective dialogue could be set up, the first and indispensable step towards the drawing up of the integrated development plans that so many people have requested.

[1] For further research on these issues, see Sanlaville, 2000.

2

The emergence of agriculture, animal husbandry and pastoral nomadism in the Near East

JACQUES CAUVIN

Centre National de la Recherche Scientifique, Lyons

The subsistence strategies we see today have not always existed. They are as much the result of climatic imperatives (and climate in the Near East as elsewhere has its own history) as they are of economic and cultural initiatives which over time modify man's relationship with his environment. Since the emergence of hominids about three million years ago, the earth's climate has been characterised by an alternation between cold periods, known as glacial ages, and periods of higher temperatures, or interglacial ages. Because of its latitude, the Near East region remained beyond the furthest extension of glaciers, and therefore never experienced the extremely cold periods that marked Europe's temperate zone.[1]

Apart from this climatic advantage, the region of Bilad al-Sham also benefited early on from human habitation due to its location at a point of junction between the African continent, where *Homo erectus* and then *Homo sapiens sapiens*, our most immediate ancestor, appeared, and the rest of the ancient world. Both species of early man passed through the Levant in their expansion towards Europe and Asia. The first occupations by palaeolithic hunter-gatherers in this region go back about one million years, but it is between 600,000 and 150,000 BP (before present) that sites increased in number, during what is known as the Acheulian culture.[2] This area includes today's arid steppic regions as well as the coastal areas; however, as dry periods alternated with wetter ones, we find prehistoric artefacts scattered along wadis which are dry today or else concentrated near sources of water.

Between 150,000 and 40,000 BP, cultures native to the northern Levant (Yabrudian, Hummalian) or found between the Euphrates and the Sinai (Levalloiso-Mousterian) can also be found in oases. Japanese excavation results from Duara near Palmyra, for instance, allow us to reconstitute for the Middle Palaeolithic (between 80,000 and 40,000 BP) a wooded countryside of wild hackberry and plum trees difficult to imagine today.[3]

For the Upper Palaeolithic (40,000 to 14,000 BP), the Levantine Aurignacian culture, usually found in coastal regions, has recently been discovered in the oases of El Kowm and Palmyra. All these cultures give

[1] Rognon, 1987. [2] Hours, 1985. [3] Gordon Hillman, personal communication.

indications of a thriving human population, and are often more technically advanced than their European contemporaries. In particular we notice the early appearance here of flint microlithic bladelets, probably used to arm composite tools – a development occurring in western Europe only much later, during the Magdalenian. The harsher ecological conditions characterising the Near East today began to come into existence progressively, beginning about 20,000 years ago. Concerning these climatic conditions, it is perhaps the scarcity of water more than high summer temperatures that constitutes the major problem of the steppic regions.[4]

Since the end of the ice ages the earth's climate has become progressively warmer, but the Near East showed a peculiar version of this general transformation, primarily through changes in its rainfall levels. The Middle East was already a very arid zone long before 20,000 BP, lacking then, it would seem, the precious monsoon rains off the Indian Ocean, as well as today's Arabian Gulf with its permanent reserves of humidity, which was formed only 6,000 years ago.[5] This eastern desert expanded progressively westwards: by 20,000 BP Lake Palmyra had dried up, followed in 16,000 BP by Lake Damascus and before 12,000 BP by the immense Lake Lisan in the Jordan Depression, of which only a few remnants subsist today (Dead Sea, Sea of Galilee). Only the Mediterranean coast with its regular sea breezes was spared this increased aridity. A general but temporary return of greater humidity marked the period between 14,000 and 12,000 BP when epipalaeolithic hunter-gatherers of the Geometric Kebaran were scattered in their dense encampments over what are now desert or semi-desert zones such as the Sinai, Negev, Syrian and Jordanian deserts.

It is only beginning with a progressive return of dry weather from 12,000 BP that climatic conditions comparable to those we know today definitively spread throughout the Bilad al-Sham. For nearly two thousand years the Natufian civilisation, known for its geometric microliths in the form of segments of a circle, covered the entire Levant. The Natufian civilisation extended from the Euphrates to the Mediterranean Sea, but very different subsistence strategies were adopted in accordance with the ecological zones in which they were found. It was in climatic zones with rainfall exceeding 200 mm a year, from the Middle Euphrates to the Negev, that the first sedentary villages were established. These villages, with circular houses partly dug into the ground, were pre-agricultural but had a sufficiently broad-based predatory subsistence strategy (fishing, hunting, gathering) to enable their populations to stay year-round in one place.[6] The best known of these villages are Abu Hurayra and Muraybat on the Euphrates and Mallaha in the Jordan Valley. The characteristic vegetation predominant then was the 'steppe-forest', land sparsely covered with pistachio, almond, and perhaps a few oak trees, often associated with wild cereals. If these trees have today largely disappeared, except for some rare remnants found in mountainous areas, man rather than climate is responsible for their destruction. In the arid zones of the interior, only small-scale

[4] See Métral and Sanlaville, 1982. [5] Sanlaville, 1989. [6] Cauvin, 1978.

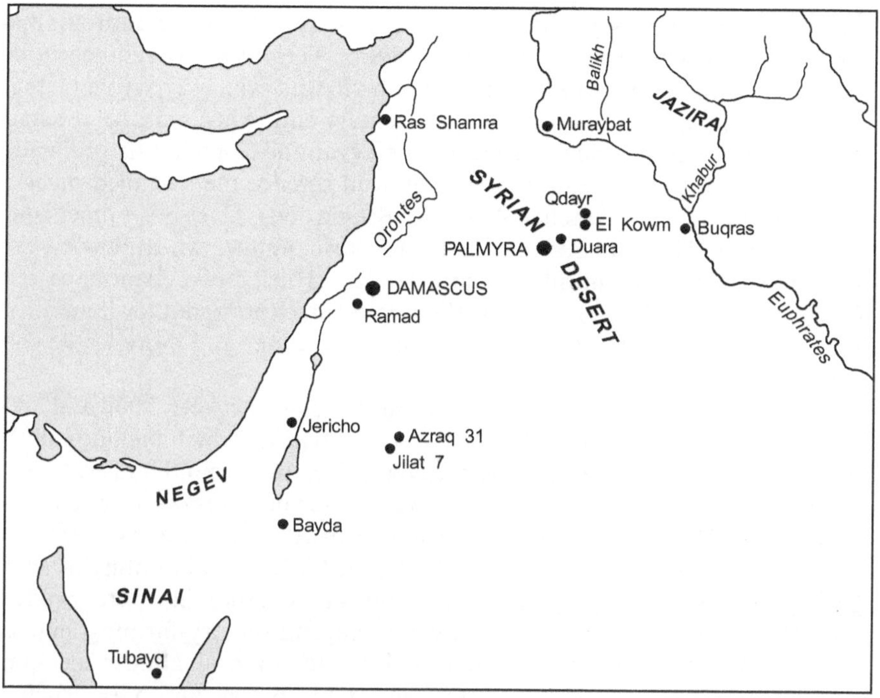

Map 2.1: Principal archaeological sites

Natufian campsites are found, indicating smaller and definitely more mobile populations than in the higher-rainfall areas. Tools utilised for gathering (sickles) and processing plants (grinding stones and mortars) are much less numerous than instruments used for hunting, contrary to what we find in Natufian sedentary villages.[7] Already at this time then, these nomadic hunter-gatherers lived more from animal than from plant resources.

At the end of the Natufian, that is, in the eleventh millennium BC,[8] the steppic regions were almost completely abandoned by man. With the beginning of the Holocene and the invention of agriculture, a new episode emerged in which the arid zones had no part to play.

Beginnings of agriculture and animal husbandry in the 'nuclear zone' (9500–7500 BC)

Agriculture first came about, as we now know, in the Near East, or to be more precise, in what is known as the Levantine Corridor. This is a narrow crescent-shaped strip of land extending from the Middle Euphrates to the Jordan

[7] Byrd, 1989.

[8] The BC dates used from here on have all been calculated according to calibrated C14 chronology.

Valley and encompassing the oasis of Damascus; almost the entire human population was concentrated in this corridor.[9] This strip covered nearly the same area as the previous zone of Natufian villages, which by virtue of their increased population density and their sedentary nature in a sense set the stage for the beginnings of food production. The Levantine Corridor also coincides fairly closely with the natural habitat of wild cereals, the so-called 'nuclear zone' (according to the archaeologist R. Braidwood), or else is immediately adjacent to it. These indigenous cereals (einkorn, emmer wheat, barley, rye) grow more commonly in hilly country (Judean Hills, anti-Lebanon, eastern Taurus and upper Jazira), whereas the first farmers preferred lowland areas, in alluvial valleys or the Damascus basin where flatter and more fertile soils were more suitable for agriculture.

These very first cultivators belong chronologically, between 9000 and 8800 BC, to the 'Pre-Pottery Neolithic A (PPNA) horizon', which includes all the neolithic cultures derived from the Natufian. They built round houses in large villages which could cover as much as two to three hectares (as in Jericho and Muraybat). Findings from Muraybat show them as being more selective about their food sources: they more or less abandoned fishing and hunting of small game in favour of larger animals (wild equids and cattle), but were 'producers' only of plant foods and did not yet go beyond the dry-farming climatic zones. Eight species of plants came under cultivation at almost the same time:[10] cereals such as einkorn, emmer wheat and barley, and pulses such as peas, lentils, broad beans, chick peas and vetches. According to new findings, we could probably add rye to this list.

The civilisation which followed, the Pre-Pottery Neolithic B (PPNB, from 8800 BC on), was very different both in tool types and the rectangular architectural structures that began at this time. This culture was also confined to virtually the same geographical limits as its predecessor, at least until halfway through its history, around 7500 BC. Villages were more numerous and all were agricultural. Domestication of the goat appeared for the first time in a very few places, notably Abu Hurayra, Jericho and Baydha. It is important to note that animal domestication in the Levant took place within sedentary populations. There is no trace at this time of pastoral nomadism.

Late and final PPNB and the reconquest of the steppe (7500–6500 BC)

In the middle of the eighth millennium the PPNB civilisation was still developing and would continue with its characteristic tools, architectural forms and religious practices for several centuries. What did change completely around 7500 BC was the relationship of human populations to space. There would appear to have been movements within the nuclear zone itself; most of the old villages were abandoned, many more new ones were built, often not far from

[9] Cauvin, 1989. [10] Zohary and Hopf, 1988.

their predecessors. Farming improved and new species of cereals appeared (durum wheat, six-row barley), as well as the first cultivation of flax (at Ramad, near Damascus). Animal husbandry became widespread, with sheep being raised as well as goats. At the beginning of the seventh millennium the first domesticated cattle appeared (Ras Shamra), again in a sedentary context.[11]

More important still, we find that after 7500 BC neolithic civilisation was no longer restricted by climate to the nuclear zone. PPNB sites from the late and final periods, before and after 7000 BC respectively, are found in quantity in semi-arid steppe regions abandoned by humans since the end of the Natufian: in Syria, along the Euphrates and in the oases of El Kowm and Palmyra, in Jordan in the Azraq oasis and in the Black Desert, and also in northern Arabia and the Sinai.

How did human populations adapt to new and much harsher environmental conditions than those in territories to the west where they originated? Several solutions seem to have been found to this problem.[12] Some groups founded sedentary villages with a combined farming and herding economy, as for instance at Buqras and El Kowm 2. Dry farming was theoretically not possible due to insufficient rainfall, but could be compensated by cultivation in specific micro-environments such as the low terraces subject to flooding along the Euphrates, as at Buqras, or the more or less humid lowlands on the edges of *sabkha*s near oasis springs, as at El Kowm 2. Farmers at El Kowm 2 engaged in agriculture that was by no means rudimentary: they planted four different types of cereals as well as pulses. We cannot exclude the possibility that they used a primitive form of irrigation by gravity based on the fact that Vauclusian springs in the basin of El Kowm gushed to the plains from the summit of mounds created through wind action. Here too they bred a large number of ovicaprids, supplemented at Buqras by cattle and perhaps pigs, as well as hunting a significant amount of large game (gazelles, equids, wild cattle) which provided up to 30 per cent of their needs in animal protein.

The second solution found to the harsher climatic conditions of the region was pastoral nomadism. Its most ancient traces are indeed found in the Bilad al-Sham. The sites uncovered by excavations reveal no built structures, except in rocky terrain such as the basaltic Black Desert in Jordan and in the Sinai, where low circular walls for consolidating tents have been found. Fauna remains of domesticated animals have been found in only a few sites: Qdayr 1 in the El Kowm basin and Azraq 31 in Jordan. What herding there was involved mostly sheep, and hunting remained a major activity. Other sites such as Jilat 7 and Dhuwayla in the Black Desert and Wadi Tubayq in the Sinai yielded only wild game remains, justifying speculation as to whether a real economic regression occurred, leading PPNB populations temporarily to abandon all subsistence production. In fact, as mobility had become the rule

[11] Helmer, 1992. [12] Cauvin, 1990.

for these groups, it was possible that a single group could have left behind 'prehistoric stations' of diverse natures varying according to the particular activities practised in each, be they campsites, flint-knapping workshops or simple hunting stations from which sheep would normally be kept.

Research is now in progress concerning the territory covered by these first nomads. We know for certain that the El Kowm basin and the mountains around it show traces of numerous surface stations belonging to the PPNB facies known as the 'Qdayr facies'. A British team is doing analogous research in Jordan's Black Desert. What does seem probable, if we are to believe the evidence of the first plant remains discovered at the Qdayr 1 dig, is that some cultivation occurred during longer halts, and that we therefore see here a type of semi-nomadism where pastoralism was the dominant but not the only source of livelihood.

Yet the question remains: why pastoral nomadism? For many years the answer seemed simple: nomadism in arid zones was traditionally interpreted[13] on the basis of later evidence, as resulting from population expulsions, usually of demographic surplus, from more clement zones. In this view, pastoral nomadism appeared to be a successful adaptation to difficult but imposed climatic conditions. It allowed food producers to move their 'provisions', i.e. their herds, over space in accordance with seasonal variations in the natural vegetation cover of the land – which was in any case sparse in this climate. Lee and Bates have also defined pastoral nomadism in the Near East in these terms.[14]

Do the older data now at our disposal confirm this model? Not really. First, it seems not altogether wise to speak of surplus of population at a time when human habitats were sparsely distributed. More significantly perhaps, we see evidence of nomadism increasing at the same periods in the coastal regions themselves. This evidence has been little studied, as a neolithic nomadic campsite – whose presence is often shown only by a concentration of flint on the ground – rarely leaves stratigraphic deposits that can be excavated.[15] It is nevertheless clear that a Late PPNB village such as Ramad, in the oasis of Damascus, witnessed the arrival around 7000 BC of nomadic populations who settled in the village, interrupting its traditional architecture by digging rudimentary round pit-houses.[16] We know that these nomads came not from the desert but from the coast, because they brought with them the burnished black pottery known as DFBW (dark faced burnished ware) characteristic of the neolithic of the Amuq, whose western origin has been confirmed by chemical analysis.[17] Other examples show the same phenomenon. This could mean that pastoral nomadism was originally not linked to any specific environment. We should not overestimate the role played by ecological pressure in creating this

[13] See e.g. Lattimore, 1967; Service, 1989. [14] Lee and Bates, 1974.

[15] From this point of view, it is easier for archaeologists to study nomadic groups in more arid zones, where wind-borne deposits have contributed to sealing the remains of even temporary human habitations. [16] Contenson, 1971. [17] Le Mière and Picon, 1987.

new way of life, of which the bedouin in the Bilad al-Sham are the present-day descendants. It may be that cultural initiative – for example a specific ideology favouring mobility, of which today's bedouin do in fact give evidence – also played a role in bringing about this change.

3

Prehistoric and historic pastoral strategies in the Syrian steppe

A. V. G. BETTS AND K. W. RUSSELL

University of Sydney

The aim of this chapter is to discuss the nature of pastoral strategies in the Syrian steppe, the processes that may have been involved in domestication and early animal husbandry, and the archaeological and historical evidence for nomadic pastoralists.

Nomadic pastoralism is one of the mainstays of the economy of people who use the lands of the Syrian steppe, but herders rarely rely exclusively on pastoralism as a means of support. Early food-producing strategies usually involved a mix of subsistence options. Ethnographic and ethno-historic records show that this has also been the case in more recent periods.[1] Pastoralists often forage for wild plant resources, hunt wild game, and seasonally plant cereals. Similarly, agricultural populations frequently keep livestock, collect wild plants, and hunt. 'Pure' or 'specialised' food-production strategies, in the sense of an exclusive dependence on either pastoral or agricultural products, occur only very rarely, if at all. However, control and breeding of animals is a year-round occupation, and animals require daily attention. Other means of subsistence must take second place to animal management. Planting or harvesting can be delayed for some days, but animals must be fed and watered regularly.

Pastoral strategies can take a variety of forms, depending on the physiological needs of the animals herded, and the economic priorities of the herdspeople. Methods of keeping and breeding of domestic animals fall into two basic classes: extensive and intensive husbandry. Intensive husbandry involves a strategy in which humans not only control the animals involved, but also procure or produce the forage resources those animals consume. Intensive husbandry practices are predominantly, though not exclusively, associated with sedentary agricultural populations. Extensive husbandry relates to pastoral strategies in which humans control the animals involved, but regulate

Kenneth Russell died suddenly in May 1992, before this chapter was completed. We discussed the preliminary outline of the article together in 1991, and on the basis of these discussions, Ken wrote a draft MS for his section. The final text is based on his draft MS, which I have edited and incorporated with my own section. I am grateful to Martha Mundy for her encouragement, and for asking us to contribute to this volume. *Alison Betts*

[1] For pastoralists see Lancaster, 1981; Fabietti, 1990.

their feeding by moving herds to available forage. The two systems are not mutually exclusive. Various combinations of extensive and intensive strategies are sometimes practised, often on a seasonal basis.[2]

The domestication process

Much scholarly debate surrounds the initial domestication of herd animals, a process which has sometimes been seen as unnecessarily complex. It is often perceived as a radical, and long-term, development, involving genetic manipulation of wild stock to produce the ideal domesticate. While highly controlled selective breeding has resulted in the great variety to be found in modern breeds of domesticate, this degree of change was not necessary to produce tamed animals which would respond to human control and provide basic supplies of primary and secondary products. With few exceptions (e.g. tail carriage in domestic dogs), there is little evidence to suggest that the basic behaviour patterns of domestic ungulates and carnivores have significantly diverged from those of their wild progenitors.[3] That numerous changes do occur in the behaviour of animals under the altered ecological conditions produced by human husbandry is undeniable. However, these seem primarily to result from such factors as imprinting, effectively inducing the animal to behave towards humans as a member of its own species, or from conditioned responses and learned adjustments as a result of the frequency and duration of their association with humans.[4]

The length of time required for the domestication process is important in determining how domestication was accomplished. If wild animals raised in close contact with humans can be treated much as animals from established domesticated stock, then the move from hunting to herding could be a short and relatively simple one, requiring only the ability to make the animals respond positively to human stimuli. Pastoralists primarily control herd movements by exploiting their general responses to acoustic and visual signals.[5] Similar signals have been found effective in manipulating the movements of a variety of domesticated, feral and wild herd animals, including caribou, yak, bison and moose. This might suggest that pastoral herding techniques were derived from the knowledge and experience of animal behaviours acquired by prehistoric hunting populations exploiting herds of gregarious animals.[6]

The control of females and young in herds may be achieved by exploiting general patterns of mother–infant behaviour.[7] Caribou cows and their calves seek to reunite if separated from one another,[8] and in many herd species, dam and offspring will return to the place where the last suckling took place if they are subsequently separated.[9] This behaviour is frequently exploited among

[2] Sweet, 1974, p. 96; Watson, 1979, p. 104. [3] Cf. Clutton-Brock, 1981, p. 55.
[4] Russell, 1988, p. 20. [5] Ibid. [6] Baskin, 1974; 1976. [7] Russell, 1988, p. 20.
[8] Lent, 1974, p. 28. [9] Baskin, 1974, p. 539.

both camel and sheep/goat herders in the Syrian steppe as a means of controlling milking herds. For general herd management such as regulating the breeding of females, minimising conflicts between males in the mating season and adjusting grazing to maximise productivity, pastoralists herding sheep, goats, cattle and camels seasonally subdivide their herds into smaller groups. These subdivisions are quite similar in their age–sex composition to the natural seasonal divisions observed among all herds of gregarious bovids.[10]

Yields of secondary products can also be quite easily enhanced through a close understanding of animal behaviour. Even by such simple processes as providing stimuli beyond their usual period or intensity, certain productively significant behaviours can be prolonged. For example, egg-laying may be encouraged in numerous species of birds by removing eggs as they are laid.[11] A similar result may be obtained in the quantity and length of lactation in certain species through milk extraction by humans.[12]

Overall, many of the changes normally assumed to be associated with early domestication may be attributed to extant plasticity in behavioural traits among specific animal species living within ecological constraints imposed by humans. Presumably, prehistoric hunters adopting pastoral strategies would have been able to exploit and manipulate behavioural tendencies already present in certain herd species. Further, those species exhibiting such traits might have been preferentially chosen for husbandry over alternative species in which such traits were either absent or less pronounced. Finally, it seems reasonable to suspect that those animals in which desired behavioural traits were most strongly marked would have been selectively favoured as founding members for early pastoral breeding herds, and that these traits would have been maintained and reinforced in subsequent generations through selective breeding and preferential slaughter practices.

Reasons for domestication

A key issue of debate is whether animals were initially exploited only for meat, or also for secondary products such as milk and wool.[13] Calculations of the returns on energy expended for meat pastoralism alone suggest that this option is unlikely.[14] A balanced strategy involving use of meat, milk and other secondary products is more efficient and more plausible. Such a strategy would also fit best with the socio-economic structure documented among the bedouin today, a highly efficient pattern which may be, in very general terms, of great antiquity.[15]

Evidence for milk processing in the archaeological record is scant and ambiguous. While some scholars suggest that milk production was an essen-

[10] Russell, 1988, p. 21. [11] Hale, 1962, p. 36. [12] See Cowie et al., 1980.
[13] See Sherrat, 1981, 1983; Ryder, 1969, 1973, 1983. [14] Russell, 1988, pp. 152 ff.
[15] Lancaster and Lancaster, 1991a.

tial attribute of the domestication process, at least for goats and cattle,[16] others suggest that wild species in general produce only sufficient quantities of milk to rear their own young, and that increased milk production and dairying were necessarily the result of post-domestication selective breeding.[17]

While the suggestion that lactating females in wild herds only produce sufficient quantities of milk for their immediate offspring is generally correct, the factors that regulate this must be understood. During the course of lactation, the mammary glandular cells modulate both the composition and yield of milk to comply with the changing requirements of the young,[18] and an increase in the number of offspring can result in increased levels of milk production.[19] Further, it is known that both the quantity of milk produced and the duration of lactation may be favourably altered in specific herd species through human milking activities. Sheep, goats, camels and cattle have inherited an evolved functional anatomy of lactation which involves a milk-storage system composed of large cisterns, quite distinct from the more prevalent system of alveolar storage found among other mammals such as pigs.[20] With goats, for example, up to 80 per cent of the total milk yield may be stored in capacious udder cisterns, while in most species alveolar milk probably accounts for roughly 70–90 per cent of the stored volume.[21] Among species with capacious udder cisterns, the milk-ejection reflex serves to fill the cisterns, from which milk extraction can be achieved at any time through a pumping action on the teat, whether by offspring or by humans. This reflex is triggered by the recognition of offspring, usually by sight and/or smell. Among species lacking capacious udder cisterns, the ejection reflex must be induced before adequate quantities of milk can be extracted. Stress can easily inhibit the milk-ejection reflex. While the stress created by human attempts to extract milk from species with alveolar storage might inhibit the required milk ejection reflex, this would not be so with species possessing capacious udder cisterns. If the reflex had been previously triggered through the presence of the offspring, milk could be extracted regardless of any consequent stress on the animal.

A second argument put forward against the use of milk by early pastoralists is the problem of lactose intolerance in adults.[22] Among many populations, weaned infants cease to produce lactase, the enzyme necessary for breaking down and digesting lactose, the sugar present in milk. Drinking milk results in diarrhoea, cramps and flatulence.[23] However, processes involved in preventing milk from spoiling have the added advantage of breaking down the lactose, and so making a more easily digestible food. Milk may be stored for short periods by various methods of controlled fermentation, and for longer

16 See Banks, 1984, p. 237; Wendorf and Schild, 1980, p. 278.
17 See Bökönyi, 1976, p. 22; Harris, 1977, pp. 219–31; Sherrat, 1981, p. 276.
18 Hollman, 1974, p. 4. 19 Tucker, 1974, p. 315.
20 Cross, 1977, pp. 194–5; Grosvenor and Mena, 1974, p. 236. 21 Cross, 1977, pp. 194–5.
22 See Sherrat, 1981, 1983. 23 Simoons, 1979.

periods by dehydration. In general, the fermentation of fresh milk appears to be universally practised by both pastoral and agricultural populations in the Near East.[24] While fermentation increases the labour costs of dairying, and diminishes caloric returns, it has the benefit of reducing lactose levels to a point where dairy products can be more easily digested by lactase-deficient adults.

Hair and wool can only have been incidental by-products of pastoralism in its early stages. Available evidence suggests that the true wool fleece was not developed until the historical periods. Ryder believes that little change in coat structure took place for 3,000 or 4,000 years after initial domestication.[25] The moufflon, wild progenitor of the domestic sheep, has a long hairy coat, with short soft underwool. Selective breeding has produced the modern domestic sheep with almost pure wool fleece. It is likely that with early domesticates the hair was used for certain products, but sheep were clearly not domesticated with the primary aim of wool production.

The beginnings of domestication

A major difficulty facing the archaeologist is to determine when domestication of animals first took place. Changes in animal morphology under conditions of human control have been the primary focus of extensive archaeological and zoological attention. It has been argued that early in the evolution of animal husbandry, distinct morphological changes took place in herd animals. These included changes in horn size and shape among cattle, sheep and goats, absence of horns in female sheep, changes in skull size and shape among cattle, and changes in coat coloration in sheep and cattle.[26] However, there is some doubt as to the significance of these proposed morphological indicators of domestication, as there is considerable variation in such traits among wild populations. Several scholars have concluded that most of the morphological criteria by which domestication is claimed for cattle, sheep and goats could equally occur as a result of processes unrelated to domestication.[27] Evidence for morphological changes in the camel during the process of domestication is apparently absent. Neither Bactrian nor dromedary camels appear to have been modified by domestication.[28]

There are also problems in using the study of herd composition as a criterion for identification of domestication. It might be assumed that under herd-management strategies for food production, pastoral faunal deposits should be dominated by relatively young males and older females.[29] Young male animals not required for breeding would be killed off at about a year old, while

[24] Russell, 1988, p. 31. [25] Ryder, 1983.
[26] See Bökönyi, 1973; Clutton-Brock, 1981; Jarman, 1969; Perkins, 1969; Ryder, 1969.
[27] Berry, 1969, p. 214; Jarman and Wilkinson, 1972, p. 96.
[28] Zeuner, 1963, pp. 339–40; Clutton-Brock, 1981, p. 126; Compagnoni and Tosi, 1978, p. 100.
[29] Davis, 1987, p. 150.

females would be slaughtered when they were no longer efficiently reproductive.[30] However, animal bones are rarely recovered in sufficient quantities and in a suitable state of preservation for detailed slaughter patterns to be measured reliably. In addition, it is possible that hunter-gatherer predation practices may produce similar patterns to those postulated for herding groups. The faunal record can also be deceptive. Herders wishing to maintain high productivity often supplemented their diet by hunting, with only limited slaughter of domestic stock. Thus, the frequencies at which herd animals are represented on early pastoral sites may be inversely related to their true economic significance.

However, although evidence for the earliest stages of the domestication process is ephemeral, it is clear from changing proportions of species in the archaeological record that by the late seventh millennium BC sheep- and goat-herding formed an important part of the mixed hunting/herding/agricultural economy of the Near East. In the key period of the early Neolithic when plants and animals appear fully domesticated on archaeological sites, the pattern of development is one of village settlements in well-watered regions, usually lying close to permanent water with access to woodland and open grassland. Thus, sites such as Jericho grew up near springs in the Jordan Valley, with a floodplain below the site and wooded hills behind.[31] ʿAyn Ghazal, on Wadi Zarqaʾ near modern Amman, was sited close to the woodland/good steppe interface,[32] and the occupants of Abu Hurayra on the Euphrates had access to the steppe behind, the floodplain of a tributary stream beside the site and the river and river marshes to the north.[33] The neolithic villagers supported themselves on a mixed economy combining agriculture and limited animal husbandry, together with the traditional exploitation of wild resources, both plant and animal.

Early pastoralism

The first half of the seventh millennium BC saw the establishment and growth of numerous village settlements with related cultural traditions throughout the Levant along a line which stretched from southern Jordan to the Taurus mountains. The second half of the seventh millennium BC saw changes to this pattern. Many sites were abandoned, while others continued to grow in size. In addition, groups now moved out into the steppic regions, areas apparently very little used in the earlier part of the Neolithic period. With only a few exceptions, sites of this period in the steppe have faunal remains consisting exclusively of wild animals.[34] In the early sixth millennium BC the last Early Neolithic villages were abandoned, although some were reoccupied in the Late Neolithic. In the steppe, there is continued evidence for use of even the poorest

[30] Lancaster and Lancaster, 1991a, p. 129. [31] Kenyon and Holland, 1981.
[32] Rollefson and Simmons, 1988. [33] Moore, 1975. [34] Baird et al., 1992.

areas, with sites along the wadis running across the whole of the Syrian steppe from the Levant to the middle Euphrates. However, while the earlier steppic sites were used by hunter-gatherers, these new sites, from the evidence of their faunal remains, were used by herder/hunter-gatherers.[35]

Again, there is speculation over the reasons for these changing patterns of settlement, and for the development of nomadic pastoralism out of village-based agro-pastoral systems. It has been suggested that environmental degradation in the intensively exploited environs of the Early Neolithic villages prompted economic adjustments which included wider ranging herding patterns.[36] In addition, goats, the main Levantine domesticates, thrive best on rough ground with shrub vegetation, and are prone to disease if kept on soft, over-grazed ground.[37] Cauvin emphasises the generally wider range of economic adaptations in this period, which included not only pastoral nomadism, but also expansion into differing environments, and an increasing variety of domesticated plant and animal species.[38] The reasons for the changes that took place at this time may lie in a combination of factors which included both the necessity to find new land, and an increasing ability to adapt basic farming practices to new conditions.

Management of sheep and goats in the *badiya*

While animals could be herded around the Early Neolithic villages in verdant areas all year, pastoralism in the Syrian steppe must have involved seasonal movement in and out of the more marginal zones. Much of the Syrian steppe is semi-arid, with vegetation consisting mostly of salt-tolerant perennial shrubs, with a spring bloom of grasses and flowering plants. Rainfall varies from around 200 mm to less than 50 mm a year, falling mainly as localised erratic storms. There are few permanent water sources, but winter floods fill rainpools in the wadis which may hold water well into the dry season. Under such unpredictable conditions, the amount of water and grazing varies greatly each year.[39] Sheep and goats differ in their feeding habits and responses to adverse conditions. Sheep prefer to graze annuals, although they will browse, while goats prefer to browse shrubs, although they also graze. Thus goats fare better than sheep in dry years where annual growth is restricted. Optimal grazing for sheep is in spring, while goats are better adapted to more extended seasonal use from the autumn dew-fed perennial growth through to the drying of perennial vegetation in early summer. Goats are generally more tolerant than sheep of extremes of heat and drought, although they are more susceptible to cold and wet. In cold, wet weather goats are usually penned at night, and grazed on sheltered slopes.[40]

Under the erratic environmental conditions of the *badiya*, mobility is an

[35] Ibid.; Betts et al., 1990, 1991; Cauvin, 1990. [36] See Köhler-Rollefson, 1988. [37] Ibid.
[38] Cauvin, 1990. [39] Lancaster and Lancaster, 1991a. [40] Ibid., p. 130.

important factor in herd management. Flocks must have access to both grazing and water, which do not necessarily occur together. The normal grazing range for sheep and goats is around 10 km a day, but when not grazing, herds can be moved up to 40 km to new sources of water and pasture. On average, in the winter months the distances between grazing and rainpools will be less than this over a fairly extensive part of the Syrian steppe, permitting fairly unrestricted access for herders along the wadi systems. In poor years it would be more difficult, and in the summer months almost impossible to maintain more than a very small herd of animals close to a permanent or semi-permanent water source.[41]

Archaeological data are as yet insufficient to establish the annual cycle of prehistoric herders in the *badiya*, but given the nature of the environment, and the requirements of the flocks, there must have been a seasonal cycle involving penetration into the deep steppe in winter and spring, and a retreat to the verdant fringes, or to oases and permanent water sources, during the summer months. It is also possible that the *badiya* herders comprised a mixed population of village-based semi-nomadic groups and fully nomadic hunter-herders.

The Syrian steppe in the proto-historic and historic periods

From the Late Neolithic period onward, the steppe appears to have been used regularly by herder/forager groups. There is evidence from lithics, pottery and structural remains that the major wadi systems were used as routes, as 'grazing corridors' for the movement of flocks across the steppe in the fourth and third millennia BC.[42] By the second millennium BC, archaeological evidence can be backed up by historical data. Some of the most detailed information comes from texts recovered in excavations at the ancient city of Mari (modern Abu Kamal) on the middle Euphrates.[43] Semi-nomadic shepherd/farmers lived in villages along the Euphrates and the Khabur, and herded their flocks across the Jazira and the Syrian steppe. The system must have been very similar to that recorded by Charles for the ʿAqaydat in the early years of this century.[44] When Charles visited the middle Euphrates area, he found a mixed pattern: farmers (*fallahin*) who lived in mud-brick houses; semi-nomads who lived in more flimsy shelters for the part of the year spent in the river valleys, and in tents while herding sheep and goats in the steppe; and fully nomadic bedouin who herded camels in the deep steppe, and only came up to the valley occasionally to trade, particularly for grain. While fully nomadic camel-herders were not present in the second millennium BC, the existence of more or less nomadic shepherd/farmers is clear from the texts. Lack of grazing and water in the *badiya* during the summer months meant that the traditional herding pattern involved a spell in the verdant zones during the hottest and driest months of the year. This move was in most cases linked to the agricultural cycle, so that

[41] Ibid., p. 131. [42] Betts, 1992. [43] Luke, 1965; Matthews, 1978. [44] Charles, 1939.

the flocks could be grazed on the stubble after harvest. Pastoralists might own land and cultivate it, or have a reciprocal arrangement with village communities to obtain fodder or access to grazing in return for herding village sheep with their own flocks or providing pastoral products.

The Mari pastoralists would have remained in obscurity, were it not for their dealings with the state. The archives recorded attempts to conscript troops from the villages, raids by the herders on royal flocks, and more peaceful relationships which included herding contracts and casual labour.[45] It is significant that these echo more recent nomad–state relationships where military service, occasional raiding and herding arrangements with settled farmers were an integral part of the socio-economic pattern in the region.[46] However, it would be a mistake to draw close parallels between recent patterns and those of much earlier periods. Unfortunately, there is little in the archaeological record to give a more detailed picture of the pastoralists of the second millennium BC. Broad comparisons may be drawn with more recent groups, but there were certainly differences in the social and economic structure which cannot be identified on available evidence.

While shifts in political and economic patterns must have caused variations through time to the pattern of agro-pastoral subsistence in the Syrian steppe, the most radical change came with the introduction of camel-herding around the early first millennium BC. Until relatively recently, the introduction of camel-herding was seen as the catalyst for a major shift in the power politics of the steppe.[47] This view was based largely on the assumption that the camel, and more specifically a particular design of riding saddle, permitted the rise of 'warrior nomads' who could threaten the settled lands from the security of the desert. While there were major changes in nomad–state relations during the first millennium BC,[48] these were largely related to greater trade activity throughout the Arabian Peninsula. It is likely that interest in camel-breeding developed in part as a response to new demands for riding and pack animals, and that increased political power wielded by the nomads was as much created by their control of trade routes as by the military potential of the camel.[49]

[45] Matthews, 1978. [46] See Marx, 1978; Gellner, 1991, p. 111.
[47] Caskel, 1954; Dostal, 1967; Bulliet, 1975; Knauf, 1985, p. 41. [48] Eph'al, 1982.
[49] Helms, 1990, pp. 21 ff.

4

The Syrian steppe during the last century of Ottoman rule: Hawran and the Palmyrena

NORMAN LEWIS

Centre for Lebanese Studies, Oxford

In the first half of the nineteenth century nearly all the Syrian steppe and the country adjoining it was uncultivated, and its population was sparse and largely nomadic.[1] Today a considerable part of the steppe itself and most of the border areas have been ploughed and the whole region is relatively densely populated by human beings – few of them nomadic – and their millions of sheep. The developments that led to this situation began in the nineteenth century, as I have attempted to show in previous publications.[2] Thus I will give here only the briefest resumé of developments in and near the steppe in the country as a whole in the century before 1914, and will discuss in more detail changes that took place in the Hawran and the Palmyrena.

First, then, very briefly, generalities, nearly all of which should be qualified if space allowed. At the beginning of the nineteenth century Ottoman government in Syria was ineffective, the economy stagnant, the population sparse. Ottoman forces were weak and hardly contributed to the safety of the countryside. Nearly all of the steppe was beyond the control of the government. Most of the country east of the road from Aleppo to Hama, Homs and Damascus was uncultivated, and there were very few villages in it. The same was true of Trans-Jordan south of the River Zarqa'. Nomads frequently raided within settled areas and also took *khuwwa* from villagers.

During the second half of the century government became more effective, and the armed forces were strengthened, communications and economic conditions improved, the population increased. Trans-Jordan, the Palmyrena and the Euphrates valley were brought within the administered area; officials, soldiers and gendarmes were stationed in those areas. The bedouin were subjected to various forms of interference by the government. Much land that had

[1] A widely accepted, rule-of-thumb definition of the Syrian steppe would restrict it to the area that receives an average annual rainfall of between 100 and 200 mm per year (and the desert to the area with less than 100 mm per year). If more sophisticated definitions were used extensive areas adjoining and merging with the area that receives 200 mm but which themselves receive heavier rainfall could also be said to have a modified steppe climate, or, as Wirth termed it, a 'West-Syrian steppe climate' (Wirth, 1971, pp. 100–4). Such areas, which include Hawran, therefore merit consideration in this chapter, but in view of the important differences between them and the 'steppe proper' or 'semi-desert' I have preferred to call them here the 'fringes', 'borders' or 'margins' of the steppe.

[2] Lewis, 1987, 1988, 1991; Douwes and Lewis, 1991.

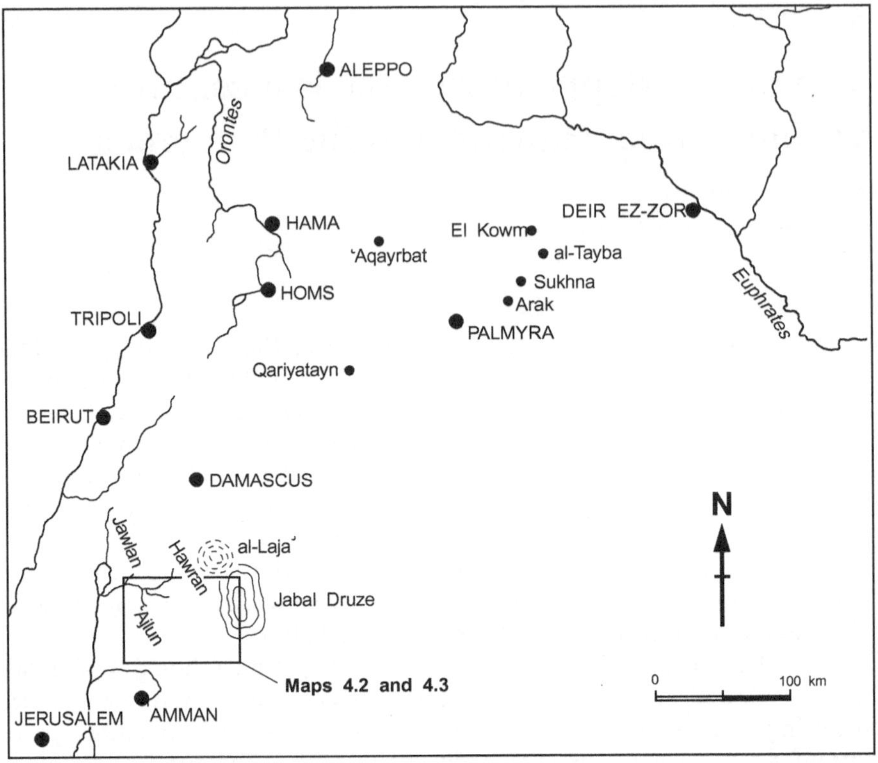

Map 4.1: The Palmyrena and, to the south-west, Hawran

been uncultivated and inhabited by nomadic or semi-nomadic people was taken over by peasants, or tribesmen turned cultivators, or their shaykhs, or city-based land owners. Many villages grew up along the borders of the steppe.

It would be possible to substantiate and amplify these brief statements by examining almost any part of the country, but I have chosen illustrative examples from only two areas, southern Hawran and the Palmyrena (neither of which was discussed in my earlier publications). The first example concerns the relationship between a major bedouin tribe and the government in Hawran, the second the extension of cultivation and settlement in southern Hawran, and the third developments in the central steppe, around Palmyra.

Hawran in the first half of the nineteenth century

The two most important tribes in the area at this time were the Wuld ʿAli and the Rwala, both of whom were ʿAnayza. They usually spent the winter in the desert and moved north to Hawran in the spring to find water and grazing for the summer, to sell their produce and to buy what they needed for the coming winter. The Wuld ʿAli had been coming to the area since the beginning of the eighteenth century or before and had developed a working relationship with the Ottoman authorities in Damascus. They were supposed to keep the peace in the area, to provide men and camels to the Hajj caravan and to protect it, for all of which their shaykhs received payment or subventions. The Rwala seem to have begun to come to the area towards the end of the eighteenth century and were not yet assured of the right to do so on a regular basis.[3] They wanted this, and their shaykhs coveted the advantages the Wuld ʿAli shaykhs enjoyed. Throughout the first half of the nineteenth century the shaykhs of the two tribes vied for government favour, and the tribesmen frequently raided and skirmished with one another. At first, government troops, if they intervened in tribal 'battles' at all, usually took the side of the Wuld ʿAli, but as Rwala strength gradually increased and their shaykhs became more adroit at dealing with officials, they were more often favoured.[4]

A number of local nomadic or partly nomadic tribes lived in the Jawlan and al-Lajaʾ, but most of the people in the central plain were village-dwelling farmers. The villagers were subject to onerous taxation and in addition often had to pay *khuwwa* to the bedouin. They suffered from Ottoman soldiery, from sporadic strife with the Druze of Jabal Druze, from disputes amongst themselves, from occasional raids by bedouin or other tribes and from incursions by flocks and herds into their fields. Such conditions had impelled many Hawranis to leave the district altogether before the nineteenth century. The plain was now underpopulated, most of the villages were very small, and many were partly or intermittently deserted or altogether abandoned. The southern part of the plain was the driest and most frequently overrun by bedouin. Better land and half-empty villages were available in the north, and people had been moving northwards for generations. The result, as map 4.2 shows, was that the south was now almost entirely deserted by villagers; only Busra, Darʿa and al-Ramtha survived, and they were in poor straits.[5]

Hawran, 1850–1914

The bedouin

The years 1858–63 marked something of a turning-point in the relationship between the Wuld ʿAli and the Rwala, and in the relationship of both of them to the government. The sporadic strife between the two tribes which had gone on during the first part of the century came to a climax in the years 1858–62,

[3] Seetzen, 1809, pp. 281 f.; Burckhardt, 1831, vol. I, pp. 1–9, vol. II, pp. 2–4.

[4] Consuls' reports, particularly those of 1844, 1845 and 1847–8 in FO 195/226 and 291.

[5] The general statements in this paragraph and the specific information embodied in map 4.2 are derived from Burckhardt, 1822, pp. 51–120 and 211–309; Robinson and Smith, 1841, vol. III, pp. 148–62; Seetzen, 1854, pp. 37–128; other contemporary travel literature; consuls' reports, particularly in the 1840s.

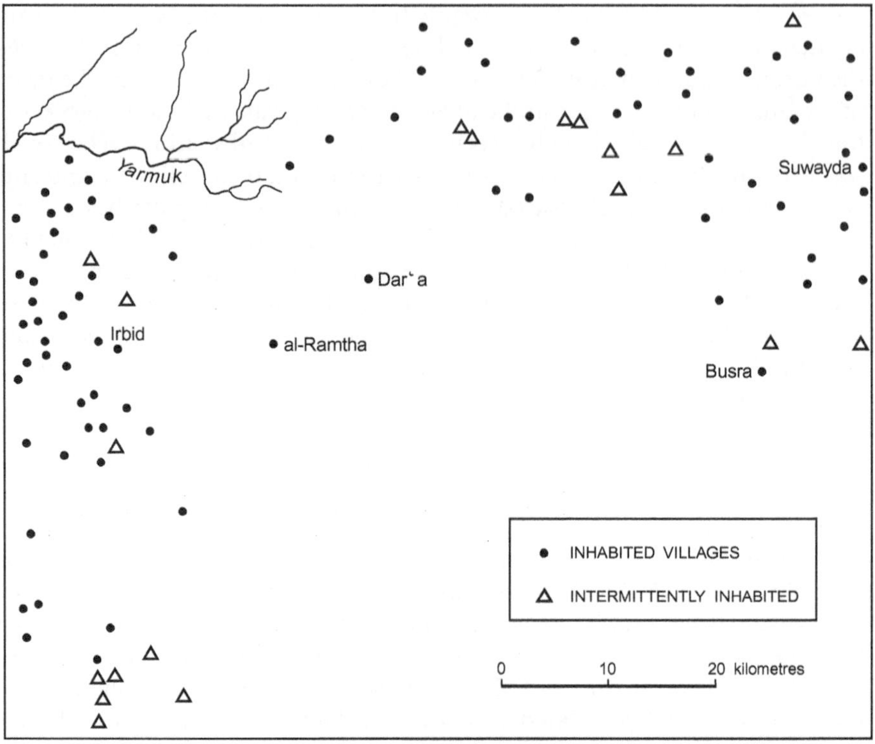

Map 4.2: The villages of southern Hawran at the beginning of the nineteenth century

with the advantage to the Rwala, and in 1863 the tribes were driven to alliance and short-lived 'rebellion' when they were attacked by government troops, apparently without good cause.[6] After that the two tribes generally lived at peace with each other while they were in Hawran; the Rwala were now the stronger tribe.

During the next few decades the bedouin were subjected to an increasing measure of government control while they were in Hawran. Their movements were restricted, they were only allowed to camp and graze in certain areas, and had to pay for so doing.[7] They were also liable to pay taxes. Raiding and taking *khuwwa* were forbidden. Compounding all this was the capricious nature of official policy; in some years the bedouin were met and escorted to the summer grounds by troops, in others they were left much to their own devices, and in

[6] On the events of 1858–63 see Wetzstein, 1860, pp. 138–50; Guarmani, 1938, pp. 100–1; Musil, 1928b, pp. 57, 581; FO 195/601, 3 Aug. and 19 Oct. 1858; FO 195/677, 13 June ff. 1861; FO 195/727, 10 July ff. 1862; FO 195/760, 16 Sept. ff. 1863; Oppenheim, 1939, pp. 94–5; Schilcher, 1981, pp. 167–70. [7] FO 78/2985, 16 Aug. 1879.

others again were prevented from entering the settled country at all. Officials tended to regard them with hostility and suspicion, and bribery was often the only way for them to obtain favourable treatment. Government dealings with them were not infrequently marred by bad faith and treachery.[8]

In these conditions, the Rwala were fortunate in being led from 1877 to 1901 by Shaykh Sattam al-Shaʿlan. He decided that co-operation with the government, within limits, would serve his own and his tribe's interests better than continued defiance. He tried to maintain good relationships with governors in Damascus and with other officials, bribing the venal ones when he had to, negotiating with them on behalf of the tribespeople and occasionally persuading them to make troops available to help the Rwala in their conflicts with others.[9] He, in turn, could assist the army if it suited his own purposes to do so.[10] The government was glad to deal with such a man and to bolster his authority; in 1892 he was bidden to an audience in Istanbul with Sultan Abdul-Hamid II, who gave him a decoration and the title of pasha.

Despite all this, Sattam could never be sure of good treatment, for the Rwala were often in trouble, particularly when they and their great herds of camels moved northward and westward in spring or summer. In 1897, for example, they seem not to have secured permission to enter settled country but were in great need of water for their camels. In July, many of them came to springs on the edge of cultivation near al-Zarqaʾ and Jarash, where the Bani Sakhr opposed them in a series of bloody skirmishes, and where their camels damaged village crops. Schumacher, who was there at the time, was told that Sattam had tried to persuade the *mutasarrif* of Hawran to let them water their herds there; he argued that with waterless desert behind them, and harassed as they were by the Bani Sakhr, they had no alternative but to come into the settled country, even though they were confronted there by the guns of villagers and soldiers. He hoped that the sultan would forgive him (for having allowed this incursion).[11]

It seems that his pleas were ineffective, for about 14 July a conflict took place with government troops near al-Ramtha as some of the Rwala tried to force their way into cultivated land which was 'prohibited by Imperial order'. Sattam was then invited to discuss the matter with the *mutasarrif*, but he got wind of a plan to arrest him at the meeting and to send him as a prisoner to Damascus.[12] He did not fall into this trap and even after this he continued his efforts on behalf of his tribespeople. Earlier in the year he had written to Mirza Wasfi, commander of gendarmerie in central Trans-Jordan, asking for his help, and on 25 July he wrote again asking for respite or delay – it is

[8] For examples, see FO 195/368, 12 May 1852; FO 78/2243, 28 May 1872; note 6 above, notes 12–18 below. For an opinion of Ottoman government widely shared by bedouin see Musil, 1927, p. 399.

[9] Blunt, 1879, vol. I, p. 62; vol. II, pp. 89, 140–4; FO 78/2985, 16 Aug. 1879; Lees, 1895, p. 5.

[10] FO 195/1940, 3 Sept. 1896. [11] Schumacher, 1897b. [12] FO 195/1984, 23 July 1897.

reasonable to suppose that Mirza Wasfi had ordered him to get his bedouin out of the area – and begging him to allow them continued access to water because they were 'perishing from thirst'.[13]

Bedouins were most likely to cause damage after dry, cold winter and spring seasons, for then they often moved north and west before the villagers' crops were harvested; 1909 was such a year. In March H. C. Butler stood on one of the towers of Qasr al-Hallabat in the Trans-Jordanian desert and watched a great number of ʿAnayza moving northwards with their tens of thousands of camels. He wrote that the compact mass of camels 'extended to the eastward as far as the eye could see, and field glasses failed to discover the eastern flank, which must have been miles away . . .The solid dark brown creeping stream . . . flowed steadily past the castle hour after hour . . . the rear guard went by eight hours after we had first seen them.' A few days later he came to Summaqiyat, the southernmost village of the Hawran plain, and found that 'the Anezeh had come and gone, leaving not a trace of green in the fields, for the hungry camels had eaten every blade and spear down to the ground'. Further north the fields 'looked as if fire or a pest of locusts had passed over them'. Soldiers from Busra were only able to harass, not divert, the bedouin – and to take a mere 100 camels from them.[14]

On 27 April 1909, Sultan Abdul-Hamid was deposed and the Young Turks took over. Almost immediately it became obvious that the new government was determined to subjugate unruly elements in Syria, notably the Druze and bedouin. Rumours, some of them later confirmed, circulated to the effect that payments to bedouin shaykhs would be stopped, that taxes would be increased and that bedouin (and others) would be disarmed and made subject to conscription.[15]

In 1910 the resolve of the new government was demonstrated by its ruthless suppression of a Druze uprising and by action taken against rebels at Karak. There was much unrest amongst bedouin, and Rwala elements were believed to have been involved in various acts of violence. Many tribesmen were punished after these outbreaks and new and stricter bedouin control regulations were published.[16] Nuri al-Shaʿlan, the then shaykh of the Rwala, took the precaution of leaving for the desert, fearing that Sami Pasha, the general commanding operations against the rebels, might punish him for the alleged misdeeds of some of the Rwala. In May 1911, however, Sami wrote to him guaranteeing immunity of life and property.[17] The two men began to negotiate about a settlement for outstanding matters, Sami calling for the surrender of

[13] Letter no. MW 5/12 in the collection of Mirza Wasfi papers in the Department of National Archives, Amman. Cf. nos. MW 5/7, 5/19, 5/22 and 5/23. I am very grateful to Dr Eugene Rogan for providing me with these and other papers from the Mirza Wasfi archive, which throw much light on relations between government and bedouin in the 1890s.

[14] Butler et al., 1930, pp. 90, 92. Cf. Musil, 1927, pp. 110, 194, 314, 321, 353.

[15] Musil, 1927, p. 327. Cf. FO 195/2370, 29 March 1911.

[16] FO 195/2370, esp. 27 May 1911.

[17] FO 195/2370, 27 May 1911.

2,000 of the rifles in the hands of the Rwala. Nuri later claimed that he had also paid Sami large sums in gold. Then, in a sudden act of treachery, Sami arrested Nuri when the latter went to Damascus to continue discussions. Nuri was 'threatened with the gallows' and remained a prisoner for two years.[18]

During the reign of Sultan Abdul-Hamid the bedouin had been obliged to accept a certain amount of government interference, but had never had to give up their weapons or to serve in the Turkish army. If the new government had seriously attempted to disarm or conscript them they would undoubtedly have resisted to the utmost, but in the event these policies were not seriously pursued in the short period before World War I.

The villages

In the 1850s increasing quantities of grain began to be grown in Hawran to satisfy the Damascus market and the new and growing export trade. The amount of wheat and barley grown in the next half century varied enormously from one year to the next, but was very large in years of good rainfall. The expansion of cultivation first became noticeable in the 1850s, when the population of Busra, for example, began to increase and, although vast areas of land around the villages were still uncultivated 'each year the people exploited a greater quantity'.[19] The reoccupation of deserted villages and the reinforcement of underpopulated and intermittently inhabited places followed. As early as 1858 a Rwala shaykh observed to Wetzstein that high grain prices were causing the colonisation of deserted villages and that grazing was becoming scarce. In the same year Wetzstein found the village of Darʿa busy and its elders in continuous consultation because they had just established two 'colonies' nearby, at Nuʿayma and al-Turra.[20]

Agriculture was further stimulated by the auctioning of government land in and after 1869, when many landlords and merchants from Damascus bought land and invested in farming and the grain trade. As more places were garrisoned by troops, better armed and controlled than in the past, and as bedouin raids became less frequent and less serious, 'the fellahin began to feel themselves more protected and began to risk further settlement'.[21] They moved out from villages in the Jawlan, from the hill country of Irbid and ʿAjlun and from old-established villages on the Hawran plain. Sayda, for example, which was in ruins in 1858, was subsequently occupied and had 250 people by 1895.[22] Schumacher wrote that an enterprising farmer from Tafas 'expropriated' land at ʿAmrawa while the village was still a ruin and the area unsettled. After difficulties with the bedouin he settled down and eventually registered the land

18 FO 195/2371, 30 Sept. 1911; Musil,1927, pp. 377, 398, 429; Oppenheim, 1939, p. 105.
19 Delbet, 1877, pp. 306–7, 322, 380, 393–6.
20 Wetzstein, 1860, pp. 85, 138. The Nuʿayma referred to here is 4 km east of Darʿa.
21 Schumacher, 1886, p. 22. 22 Schumacher, 1897a, p. 70.

in his own name, becoming the shaykh of the village whose inhabitants were his ploughmen.[23] Occasionally villages were settled or reinforced for reasons that were not purely economic; for example Nuʿayma, south of Irbid, was reinforced in 1868 by a group of families who had been involved in serious disputes in al-Husn and who were ordered by the governor of the district to leave al-Husn and to go to Nuʿayma.[24] Other villages north and south of Nuʿayma, which had been recorded as uninhabited in the first half of the century, were reinhabited in the latter years of the century.

In 1884 there were still wide stretches of uncultivated land between villages in western Hawran and in the Jawlan, but by the mid-1890s 'no hectare of good land was without its owner'. In the south, the whole area between Busra and Darʿa was cultivated by 1895, and the villages that had been reoccupied about 1858 had become quite big places, each with several outlying farms or hamlets. Darʿa itself now had 4,000 inhabitants and Busra about 850, apart from its garrison.[25] An indication of the size and distribution of the villages is given by map 4.3; the contrast between map 4.2 and this map is striking, especially in the south.[26]

Land hunger had developed as the central plain filled up. The area south of Busra was not tempting: the rainfall was light and erratic, the land often overrun by bedouin, and in the east of the area Hawrani peasants had to compete with Druzes. Despite all this the southernmost fringe of the plain attracted a few settlers in the 1880s and 1890s, if only because the rest of the Hawran was now full of people. When, about 1896, Schumacher asked the Christian inhabitants of Summaqiyat, 'who were leading a miserable existence in the parched Hamad, oppressed by Druzes and Bedouin', why they didn't improve their lot and go and join their fellows further north, they said they couldn't because there was no more land left there. Summaqiyat had been uninhabited as late as 1890, but there were eleven families there in 1895 and twenty-five in 1905. In 1909 they suffered when bedouin overran the area.[27]

In such an area the villages are widely spaced. Summaqiyat's nearest neighbour is al-Mutaʿiya, 12 kilometres to the north-west. It was in ruins until 1892 when it was bought for 1,000 Turkish gold pounds by an energetic shaykh named Khuntush. He built cisterns and brought in people and in 1895, when there were 150 inhabitants, he set about getting more ploughmen. There were 200 people in the village in 1905.[28]

Shaykh Khuntush made a success of al-Mutaʿiya but failed at Umm al-Surab, 10 kilometres further to the south. This place was several times reoc-

[23] Schumacher, 1886, p. 117 and 1889, p. 14.
[24] Abu Jaber, 1989, pp. 163–76. The Nuʿayma referred to here is about 20 km south-southeast of Irbid. [25] Schumacher, 1897a, p. 70.
[26] Main sources of information in map 4.3: Schumacher, 1897a and his map published in 1913–21; Steurnagel, 1925, esp. pp. 137–44.
[27] Schumacher, 1897a, pp. 70, 150; Butler et al., 1930, pp. 33, 91.
[28] Schumacher, 1897a, pp. 140–1; Butler, 1919, p. 87; Butler et al., 1930, p. 32.

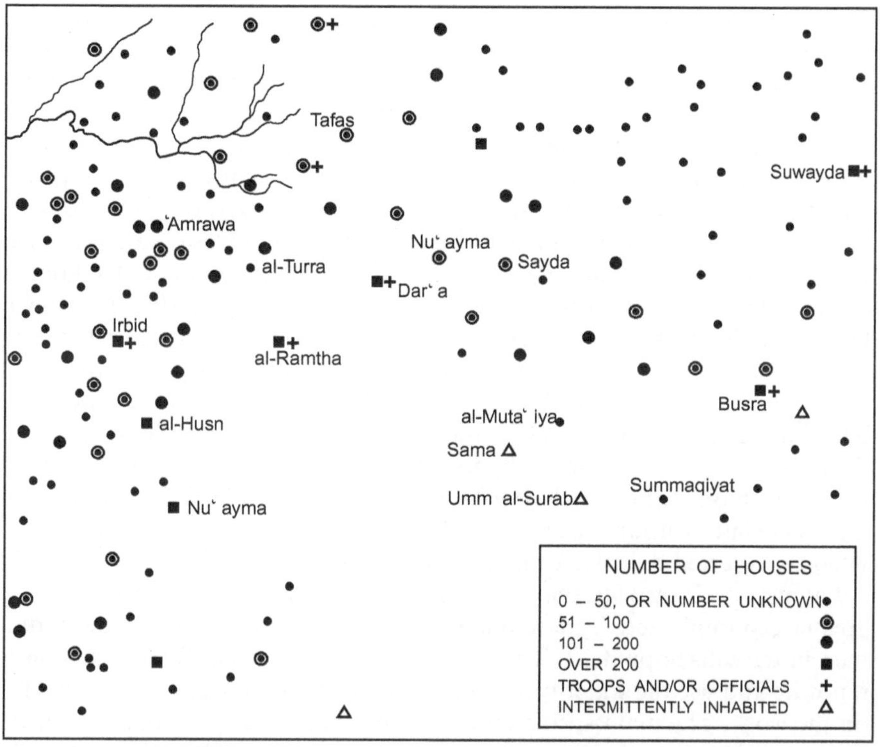

Map 4.3: The villages of southern Hawran around 1900

cupied and deserted towards the end of the nineteenth century and Shaykh Khuntush put people into it about 1894, but the ʿAnayza camels drank all the water and the place was abandoned again. In the 1890s a few people from al-Mutaʿiya also went 7 kilometres south-west to Sama, another hamlet which was several times occupied and then deserted again. In 1905 it was 'partly inhabited'.[29]

These southernmost villages were, then, in a truly marginal zone, one of competition between settlers and nomads for land and water. South of these poor and scattered little places the steppe and desert were as yet uncluttered and free for the tribes.

The Palmyrena

The effects of a slight improvement in local security were felt even in the heart of the north Syrian steppe. In or about 1870 military posts were set up at

[29] Schumacher, 1897a, pp. 143, 163; Butler, 1919, p. 83; Butler et al., 1930, p. 33.

Palmyra and at other places in the steppe and on its fringes, and from then onwards some sort of military presence, albeit usually feeble, was maintained in the area. Most of the posts were very small and often the bedouin merely 'made fun of them',[30] but settlers sometimes responded remarkably quickly when given even a minimum measure of protection. The village of al-Tayba, for example, had been deserted since the eighteenth century when its people had dispersed to Sukhna and other places. In 1870 a descendant of one of the families that had gone to Sukhna obtained permission from the governor of Deir ez-Zor to resettle al-Tayba. He moved there with ten or twelve families and a second group went to another deserted site nearby, El Kowm. Gendarmerie posts were built at both places; that at El Kowm consisted of an NCO and four gendarmes. The villages managed to survive until they were sacked during disorders at the end of the 1914–18 war (and were reoccupied later when French protection was assured).[31] Arak, another little oasis village, demonstrated the same sensitivity to the presence or absence of protection, in reverse fashion. A post or barracks was sited there in the 1870s but the soldiers were later withdrawn and when bedouin pressure became intolerable the villagers deserted the village and took refuge in Palmyra.[32]

Palmyra itself also felt the effects of slightly improved security as well as of greater economic activity elsewhere in Syria.[33] In 1885 three of the leading men in the village paid 50 Turkish lira to the government for permission to renovate and use the water of one of the ancient conduits, and spent 200 lira on the work. The main spring and two others were cleaned out at about the same time. Despite this, the price of water rose as the population increased; by 1912 there were an estimated 350 houses, some of them built *outside* the walls of the great temple, within which the people had previously sheltered.[34]

By this time Deir ez-Zor had become a busy trading centre and Palmyra and Sukhna both lost some trade to it. Furthermore, their merchants and caravaneers who used to provide camels for the annual pilgrimage caravan suffered as demand collapsed in the first decade of the twentieth century when the Hijaz railway was opened. With local resources insufficient to sustain all the population, some people had to try their luck elsewhere.[35] A number of traders from Sukhna went to the cities or to Deir ez-Zor, and in 1900 a group of Palmyrene farmers moved over 100 kilometres north-westward to break entirely new ground, at ʿAqayrbat. Their new village, with its gendarmerie post, became the centre of a developing agricultural area where, in the twentieth century, many former nomads settled.[36]

The phase of expansion of cultivation in and near the steppe which began a century and a half ago has continued until the present day, and during the

30 Musil, 1928a, p. 86. 31 De Boucheman, 1937, pp. 101 f.; Lewis, 1991.
32 Cernik, 1875, pp. 11 and 14; Bischoff, 1881, p. 363; Musil, 1928a, pp. 85–6.
33 Blunt, 1879, vol. II, pp. 42–59.
34 Post, 1891, p. 34; Hill, 1891, pp. 72–3; Musil, 1928a, p. 145.
35 Oppenheim, 1899, vol. I, p. 317. 36 Local informants and observations.

same period the human and ovine population has enormously increased. Expansion and growth have now gone very far, with results that are examined in other chapters in this volume. It was difficult to begin and sustain the process of expansion in the conditions that prevailed in the middle of the nineteenth century, but it is evident that it will be even more difficult to solve the problems to which unrestricted expansion has finally given rise.

5

Nomadic territory as a factor in defining Arabia's boundaries

J. C. WILKINSON
University of Oxford

The emphasis in this chapter is on the importance Ibn Saʿud attached to tribal territory as a basis for defining state boundaries, and why Britain played it down. The British had found themselves dealing with Ibn Saʿud in a series of stages in Saudi state development: first as quasi-vassal of the Ottomans, then after 1915 with themselves as a sort of protecting power, then, after signing the Treaty of Jedda in 1927, as a notional equal in the eyes of international law; by the end of World War II the British had lost all influence with him and the independence of his state was firmly established. This was reflected in disputes over the frontiers of the Saudi state. In 1935 Ibn Saʿud was still prepared to compromise his principles over the frontier, but in 1949, partly encouraged by Aramco, he gave vent to his old rancours about what he considered deliberate British dishonesty in trying to trick him out of his rights. The British had rejected the genuine concession he had made in the interest of settlement in 1935, and he now based his claims on the principles of international law, that is, his rights to claim territory occupied by his subjects, over which his government had jurisdiction and in which its writ ran. The principle on which Ibn Saʿud had based his claims, that is sovereignty over the nomads, had not changed; only the list of tribes he was prepared to concede had altered. If the British could show evidence of rival authority in the contested areas then Ibn Saʿud was delighted to have a commission to help ascertain what the facts were. In other words Ibn Saʿud continued to claim the territories of all the frontier tribes, leaving to the protégé rulers only the settled cores of their domains. In the case of Abu Dhabi that would have removed all its western coastline and virtually all its hinterland including Buraymi and the Dhahira, where its claims and those of the sultan of Oman overlapped. In the end the dispute became so envenomed that all attempts to arbitrate it were abandoned and the British used force to impose a unilaterally declared frontier. That frontier was inherited by its protégé states when they achieved independence.

Notions of sovereignty

The essential problem in defining frontiers in Arabia was the nature of the sovereignties involved and the law applicable. Three sets of criteria were at issue: tribal, Islamic and international.

Traditional tribal notions of territory were expressed in terms of the *dar* or *dira*. The nature of control and degree of exclusiveness involved stemmed not only from the needs of the tribes to regulate rights in the exploitation of scarce natural resources (notably water, grazing, pearling and fishing), but also to secure access to the grain-producing area of rain-fed farming in Syria and parts of Yemen, and the intensively irrigated date-producing oases within the Peninsula, notably in Oman, Yemen and greater Bahrain (that is, Hasa province of eastern Saudi Arabia and the archipelago state of modern Bahrain). Exchanges between groups and movements between territories were generally regulated through alliances, clientage, protection and good-neighbour customs which found expression in a tribal code. This code did not necessarily exclude obedience to a supra-tribal leader operating a complementary law system, and that might be sanctified in Islamic and tribal notions of private property rights, notions also shared by the sedentary groups. Generally it was held that land could only be owned when it had been improved by labour; unimproved natural resources (such as pearl beds, grazing and, to some extent, rain-fed farming areas) had a notion of *res communis* attached to them: it was membership of the group (tribe, village etc.) that defined the community exercising these rights. Exclusive rights regulated only areas of intense cultivation in which major investment in irrigation and tree crops had been necessary for their development. Goods, livestock, buildings, some types of wells, fish traps, boats and the like were also generally privately owned property (*mulk* or *waqf* in Islamic law).

The role of the ruler was not confined to mediating between the tribes, but also in securing certain key urban nodes and access to communal resources by land and sea. These required the population to rise above tribal factionalism and to unite under some common leadership. In this way a sense of regional identity and a higher degree of central government power developed in the more densely populated areas of Oman, Yemen and Bahrain. The degree of attachment of groups living in the surrounding 'marchland' areas to these core areas of settlement varied. In the desert 'frontier' areas loyalties tended to be divided between different cores, while attachment to the government of one or other regional core tended to be opportunistic. The loyalties of nomads and semi-nomads were liable to be highly ephemeral, and were strongly affected by the benefits to be gained and the coercive pressure a ruler could exert.

Among camel-herding groups the small size of the population and the large areas they used meant that their notions of territorial (in contrast to group) exclusiveness were less well marked than those of the mixed herding and sedentary tribesmen whose sense of a defensible territorial space was highly developed. One of the anomalies of the Arabian frontiers disputes was the fact that Ibn Saʿud claimed the camel-herding bedouin who traditionally counted among the poorest inhabitants of the Peninsula, but whose *dar*s were the largest, yet least well defined, and often overlapping with other groups.

Traditional notions of sovereignty (*imara*) depended on two aspects, personal acceptability as a leader and physical command of resources and population. Such position could be reinforced, albeit also greatly circumscribed, by Islamic authority. Ibn Saʿud, for example, expressed his rights in purely Islamic terms, namely that he ruled by the laws of Islam (the *shariʿa*), and that submission to his government was evidenced by the fact that his subjects obeyed his call to *jihad* and paid the *zakat*. The imams of Oman and Yemen would have claimed likewise. *Jihad* is legal warfare, but *zakat* has a number of connotations. Strictly it is the personal contribution made by a true Muslim in the form of a tithe (*ʿushr*) on certain forms of 'revenue' and is destined for the upkeep of the government of the Islamic community (*umma*), and to help its poor. The sums are generally small and among non-sedentary populations rarely worth collecting unless paid voluntarily. But the payment is of great symbolic importance.

International law as applicable to our area stemmed from the law of the dominant European powers, particularly as elaborated in the Congress of Berlin (1884–5) and it was largely concerned with notions of *res nullius* and what constituted effective occupancy. The Ottoman government and Great Britain were members of the 'family of nations', and after World War I Yemen and Saudi Arabia emerged as recognised sovereign states. Britain held the sovereignty of the Mandated territories of Iraq and Palestine and effectively that of its protégé states in Arabia, which had stretched in unbroken continuity around the coast from Aden ('South Yemen') to Qatar and Kuwait. In the absence of a permanent and definitive treaty that determined the common boundaries between independent members of the 'family of nations', any land not under their jurisdiction was deemed *res nullius* and was subject to whichever state first established government (tribes as such did not have international status). And even if a treaty had been properly concluded, claims to sovereignty could be bettered by a continuous and peaceful display of sovereignty appropriate to the nature of the terrain, and it did not need much in the way of proof of jurisdiction to establish authority in sparsely populated districts.

The territorial position before World War I

For most of the nineteenth century, Britain was the sole external power in the Peninsula. During this period the only serious challenge it had to face was the expedition of the Ottoman viceroy of Egypt, Muhammad ʿAli, to suppress the Wahhabis, which it countered by firming up its treaty relations with the Omani ruler of Muscat, by developing the Trucial System within the Gulf and by occupying Aden at the entrance to the Red Sea.

That left only the Wahhabi al-Saʿud state, which was finally re-established after the Egyptian expedition by Faysal b. Turki in 1843, to deal with. Since the interests of the two powers were essentially complementary, understanding over control of the maritime and terrestrial domains was reached in flexible sovereignty arrangements. The British protégé rulers paid Danegeld, euphemistically described as *zakat*, in return for which the Wahhabi amir left them to run their own affairs. While the British acknowledged, on occasion, that Faysal notionally recognised the supreme suzerainty of the Ottoman sultan, they did not consider that this amounted to an admission of Ottoman territorial sovereignty, even in the Hijaz. They also denied that the Egyptian expedition had re-established Ottoman *de jure* rights (which they deemed had lapsed in the seventeenth century) anywhere in the Peninsula.

Britain thus recognised no other international power in Arabia and the issue of bounding territorial sovereignty did not exist. This situation changed radically in 1871 when the Ottomans intervened in the civil war that broke out over Faysal's succession, occupying Hasa and also placing a garrison at Doha in the Qatar peninsula. At the same time the opening of the Suez canal helped the Ottomans bring forces to occupy Yemen, and the British had to reach an accommodation with them. In 1908 the *modus vivendi* reached began to be upset as the Young Turks' government started asserting jurisdiction in its frontier areas. Since the Ottoman Empire was recognised as a member of the 'family of nations', Britain had to appear to deal with this changing situation within the norms of international law. In fact Britain used coercion and the economic privileges of the Capitulations to interpret the rule book. Eventually the British and Ottomans came to terms, and in July 1913 signed a provisional convention concerning the Gulf and particularly the issues of sovereignty in Kuwait, Qatar and Bahrain. In Kuwait, two semi-circular boundaries delimited different degrees of territorial authority exercised by its shaykh, an inner boundary where he had full autonomy under British protection, and an outer boundary where he controlled the tribes. In the south, Ottoman coastal authority terminated at the island of Zakhnuniya, just below 'Uqayr, and a 'Blue Line' was drawn due south from it to define the limit of the Ottoman sanjak of Najd.

A second Anglo-Ottoman convention (1914) covered Aden territory. There the boundary delimitation Britain had more or less forced on the Ottomans between 1902 and 1905 to separate the Yemen vilayet from the 'nine cantons' of the British protected amirs was confirmed, and now extended by a straight 'Violet Line' from the Wadi Bana to meet the Blue Line in the middle of the Empty Quarter (see map 5.1). Nothing was said about what either line separated the Ottoman domain from (except for the Qatar peninsula in the 1913 convention), and no recognition was made of the fact that Ibn Saʿud had driven the Ottomans out of Hasa before the 1913 convention was signed. The reason was quite simple: neither line had the slightest relevance to any past or present geographical, social or political entity. They were simply straight lines drawn to determine the sphere of influence of two 'colonial' powers. Since the 1913 convention formed part of a complex set of arrangements involving the other European powers it was never ratified, whereas the local understanding over Aden was.

Early delimitations of Saudi territory

Ibn Saʿud's principal preoccupations, after he refounded the Saudi state with the recapture of Riyadh in 1902, were to hold the loyalties of tribes that had

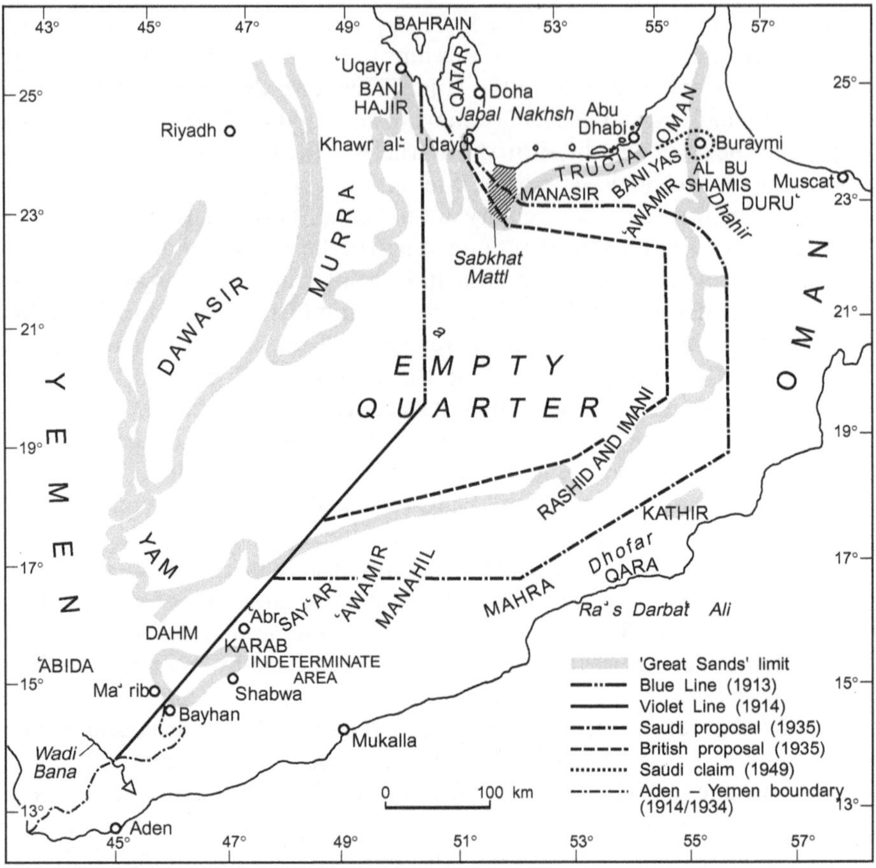

Map 5.1: Boundary agreements (1914)

already submitted; to expand his state by pursuing his successes against the Ibn Rashid confederation to the north; and to open his territory in the Najd to Gulf trade by re-establishing control in the coast of Hasa, which also had a sizeable tax-paying agricultural population. Such ambitions also raised the problem of how to deal with the Ottoman government which not only claimed to be his suzerain, but also retained a physical presence of sorts in Hasa, and supported his two principal local rivals, the Ibn Rashid (amirs of Ha'il), and the Hashemite sharif of Mecca.

As with the original foundation of the Wahhabi state, it was essential that Ibn Saʿud first consolidate his hold in central Arabia, and that involved breaking the power of the Ibn Rashid confederation which, at its height, included the Shammar, Dhafir, Mutayr and Rwala. It was not until he won a convincing victory over a Shammar–Ottoman force in 1906 that he began seriously to turn the tables. This gave him control of the Qasim region, while in the north the inhabitants of the Jawf switched their 'allegiance' back again to the Shaʿlan of the Rwala ʿAnayza, thus reducing Ibn Rashid's power more or less to the Ha'il area. Of great significance also was the change in loyalty of the Mutayr, for in due course the Mutayr and ʿAjman Ikhwan groups were to become the fiercest warriors in the Wahhabi cause. Even so, it was not until 1922 that Ha'il was finally subdued, and even then the Shammar continued to resist from the refuge of Iraq.

The Saudi rivalry with the Hashemites also had deep roots. The capture of the holy places by the Wahhabis in 1805 had been intolerable to the Ottomans and precipitated a series of campaigns by the Egyptian viceroy which finally led to the capture and execution of the Saudi amir in Istanbul (1819). In re-establishing the Wahhabi empire, Faysal b. Turki showed that he had learnt his lesson by leaving the Hijaz alone and accepting Ottoman suzerainty. This was far from nominal so long as Muhammad b. al-ʿAwn was sharif of Mecca, for he exacted tribute from Faysal on behalf of Istanbul, using force when necessary. So just as Muhammad b. al-ʿAwn had considered himself Faysal b. Turki's superior, so his grandson, Husayn b. ʿAli, who was sent by the Young Ottomans in 1908 to govern the Hijaz, became a thorn in the flesh of Ibn Saʿud, Faysal's grandson. Clashes first developed as Husayn tried to extend his influence in the Qasim in 1910. In 1915 a fight occurred over control of the important ʿUtayba confederation, but it was in 1918 that serious hostilities broke out over the border of the two putative states: the Ikhwan forces inflicted a severe defeat in which Husayn's son ʿAbdullah lost 5,000 men. Until then the British had not been greatly concerned about tribal manoeuvrings in the interior of Arabia. However, the 1918 fighting seriously threatened the survival of the Hashemites who had led the 'Arab Revolt', so the British put pressure on Ibn Saʿud. Since he was still dependent on their subsidies he subscribed to a sort of truce over the Hijaz which lasted the next four years.

Until World War I it was only in the Gulf that Ibn Saʿud really impinged on British interests. His first appearance there was in 1905, when he arrived at the base of the Qatar peninsula to settle trouble between the ʿAjman and neighbouring tribes, notably the Bani Hajir. Fear that he was also going to reappear in the Oman region caused some furore and excited old animosities in Trucial Oman which the India Office took seriously. The British were able to contain the situation by warning the shaykhs not to get involved with Ibn Saʿud and requesting Shaykh Mubarak of Kuwait to restrain him.

By 1911 Ibn Saʿud was seriously considering how to take possession of Hasa. His problem was not the size of the small Ottoman garrisons, but that removing them would be a direct attack against the Porte, unlike earlier moves which had been directed against vassals. Since he knew the British would dearly like to see the whole coast under their control, and hoping to do a deal something along the lines of Shaykh Mubarak's treaty over Kuwait, he offered to renew friendly relations 'in the same way as it existed between you and my ancestors', as he told Captain Shakespear in 1911. The India Office was in favour, but the Foreign Office had begun a much wider set of negotiations with the Ottomans and these reached a crucial stage from the beginning of 1913 which led them to veto all approaches to Ibn Saʿud. Ibn Saʿud decided to act regardless and in May easily took Hasa, a change of political control that was studiously ignored in London when the Anglo-Ottoman Convention of July 1913 was signed. Ibn Saʿud made his own peace with the Ottomans by a new special agreement recognising Ottoman suzerainty.

After the outbreak of World War I Ibn Saʿud was not prepared to co-operate with Britain without a clear treaty defining relations. On their side the Ottomans approached him as part of a general plan by which Ibn Saʿud would move north to protect Mesopotamia while Ibn Rashid would join the Rwala and other north-western tribal leaders to move on Sinai and Egypt. Ibn Saʿud, who was not concerned with the aims of either power, stalled the Ottomans by raising the issue of Ibn Rashid, against whom he in turn mobilised the ʿAnayza, representing this to the British as repelling the aggressions made by Ibn Rashid on behalf of the Ottomans.

For Britain it was sufficient that Ibn Saʿud did not come in on the side of the enemy, and so only essential problems were dealt with in negotiating his treaty. Here, however, lies the nub of the problem: what Britain and Ibn Saʿud considered essential matters differed radically. For Ibn Saʿud it was recognition as hereditary ruler of an independent territory defended by Britain which would also recognise him as absolute ruler of its tribes. He also wanted assurances that British protégés should give no refuge to fugitives, and if nomads entered their towns and problems arose concerning territory the differences should be decided according to ancestral rights of ownership. It is in the light of these expressed *desiderata* that the wording of the Darin Treaty signed on 26 December 1915 should be read.[1] Britain on the other hand was not worried in the slightest by such territorial matters and indeed was happy enough simply to have Ibn Saʿud formally promise to leave its protégés alone. Boundaries would be 'hereafter determined', the treaty stipulated. In return, Ibn Saʿud posed no problems about the British terms and the only matter of importance over which there was a degree of difference concerned the extent of the British commitment to defend him and how far they might have some role in approving his successor. It was after the war that these differences in essentials came to the fore.

After World War I: Defining the boundaries of the Hashemite states and Kuwait

After World War I the divisions between the British and French Mandated territories in the Fertile Crescent cut across tribal territory and involved special Anglo-French agreements to regulate nomads' trans-border migrations. Ibn

[1] Cf. Wilkinson, 1991, chap. 5.

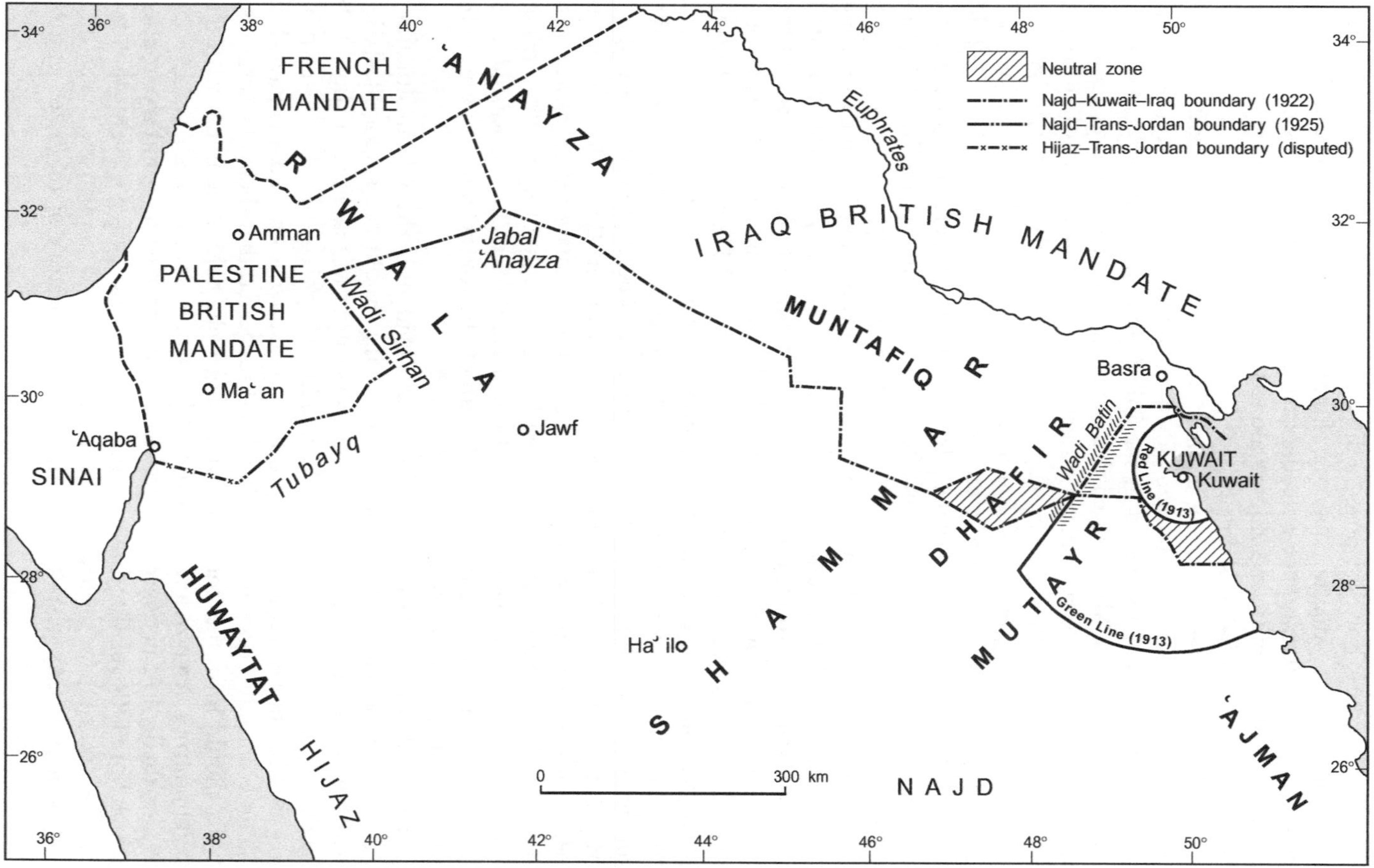

Map 5.2: Northern boundaries, after World War I

Sa'ud's boundary, however, posed a different problem since desert confederations such as the 'Anayza, Shammar, Dhafir, 'Ajman, 'Awazim and Mutayr depended for their existence on economic links with settlements and towns stretching from Kuwait and Zubayr along the Euphrates to Aleppo and the Orontes, or so Ibn Sa'ud claimed.

Tribal issues first arose in connection with Kuwait where the old Sabah–Sa'ud alliance had broken down as a result of the 'Ajman rebels finding asylum from Ibn Sa'ud in the Sabah domain. Matters were exacerbated when Salim b. Mubarak tried to enhance his authority over the outer ring of Kuwait territory, recognised as under his control according to the unratified 1913 Anglo-Ottoman Convention, by populating it with 'Ajman and Shammar refugees. When Ibn Sa'ud mobilised the Mutayr against him Salim appealed to the British to enforce his territorial rights, only to be told that the 1913 convention was a dead letter and that Sir Percy Cox would arbitrate: so much for the relevance in 1920 of the convention that Britain subsequently invoked to define Ibn Sa'ud's southern boundary.

In the meantime events in Iraq had intruded. Following the major uprising against the India Office's administration in 1920, Sir Percy Cox was appointed high commissioner to set up a new administration which was to accept the Sharif Husayn's son, Faysal, as king and obtain for the new state as large a defensive perimeter as possible. Influenced by H. R. P. Dickson's idea of using tribal criteria for determining the territory of the new states, Cox proposed that the Amarat, 'Anayza, Muntafiq and Dhafir should be Iraqi and the Shammar Saudi. Ibn Sa'ud was prepared to concede the semi-sedentary Muntafiq of the mid-Euphrates region, but claimed that unless the main bedouin tribes were recognised as his he could never guarantee the peace with the new Hashemite states. And indeed he was rapidly bringing these tribes under his control. In the west he had taken Ha'il from the Ibn Rashid, and then added the Jawf when Nuri al-Sha'lan of the Rwala came to terms with the French and abandoned the area.[2]

The vacillations of tribal loyalties, already evident in the Kuwait situation, increasingly persuaded Cox that the boundary should be 'geographical', by which he meant strategic. So in new discussions at Muhammara (May 1922) he decreed the allocation of tribes he had first proposed and laid down a provisional boundary. At a conference held at 'Uqayr a few months later, Ibn Sa'ud eventually conceded the Dhafir and suggested that their southernmost wells should form the boundary with Iraq: wells held in common with the neighbouring 'Anayza and Mutayr should form a neutral zone.

Cox finally lost patience with Ibn Sa'ud and decreed an arbitrary frontier which bore little relationship to tribal territories, accepting however the idea of a neutral zone for the area Ibn Sa'ud suggested. To compensate Ibn Sa'ud's losses in Iraq Cox gave him a fair chunk of territory in the outer ring of

[2] Lancaster, 1981.

Kuwait territory, justifying his action by stating that Shaykh Ahmad had not the same authority as his grandfather, Mubarak: he also set up another neutral zone, notionally to protect pasturing rights for the Kuwaiti tribes.

In Trans-Jordan the situation was even more complicated. It was not until August 1924 that ʿAbdullah had come sufficiently into line for Britain fully to back him.[3] By this time Ibn Saʿud was in no mood to compromise. British subsidies had stopped and a final attempt to regulate boundaries had failed, with Ibn Saʿud wanting to know whether or not Hashemite Hijaz, Trans-Jordan and Iraq formed one country. He now dealt with the Sharif Husayn, sending diversionary raids into Iraq and Jordan while the main Ikhwan forces moved on the Hijaz where they attacked and slaughtered the population of Ta'if. Abandoned by the British, Husayn abdicated. To ensure that Maʿan and ʿAqaba were not lost the British unilaterally transferred them to Trans-Jordan, which formally proclaimed their sovereignty under the 1928 Nationality Law.[4] Thus started a boundary dispute in the Hijaz section of the Jordan border that has never been entirely settled, although a major improvement in the situation occurred in 1965 under an agreement whereby Saudi Arabia exchanged territory around ʿAqaba for land in the Tubayq triangle.

As the fall of the Hijaz kingdom became imminent, Britain's primary concern became how to safeguard the now compliant ʿAbdullah and ensure that Ibn Saʿud did not establish a common frontier with the French at Jabal ʿAnayza to breach not just the Hashemite states, but also a zone of post-war British influence that extended from the Cape to Singapore. To that end Sir Gilbert Clayton concluded two agreements in September 1925 with Ibn Saʿud, the Hadda agreement on a Najd–Trans-Jordan frontier which preserved the desired corridor linking Iraq and Trans-Jordan, but ceded the much-disputed Wadi Sirhan to Ibn Saʿud; the Bahra agreement patched up some of the outstanding differences with Iraq concerning tribes. Both agreements outlawed giving refuge to groups involved in raiding or subverting tribal loyalties and confirmed the nomads' peaceful right to cross boundaries: the Hadda agreement specifically referred to grazing in the Wadi Sirhan, where lay the most easterly wells before the Euphrates and which was used by the Bani Sakhr, Huwaytat and Rwala. But in practice this did not stop the Ikhwan incursions, nor prevent taxation being claimed on both sides of the frontier. So, in reality, the bedouin did not dare cross it, even though an ensuing period of drought placed them under considerable stress. Effectively the tribes were 'encapsulated'.[5]

Thus in all these arbitrary solutions about Saudi Arabia's boundaries in the north, Britain took little cognisance of the traditional structures of tribal territory and determined the frontiers primarily on strategic grounds. Ibn Saʿud never really accepted the decisions that had been forced on him and he continued to believe that the British were promoting Hashemite interests. He also

[3] Dann, 1984. [4] Leatherdale, 1983; Dann, 1984. [5] Hiatt, 1981.

believed that they encouraged their designs on Kuwait: it was the renewal of an Iraqi claim to sovereignty in 1938 that more or less led him to drop his quarrel with the Al Sabah ruler and lift his economic blockade to allow the nomads to visit Kuwait territory.

Southern Arabia

A very different situation, however, existed in the southern part of the Peninsula. Although at ʿUqayr Cox had drawn a line running south from Salwa Bay and told Ibn Saʿud that Qatar had nothing to do with him, its shaykh in fact paid him tribute, while in Trucial Oman Ibn Jiluwi, Saudi governor of Hasa, took the ʿAwamir, Al Bu Shamis and Duruʿ under Saudi protection against the Abu Dhabian Bani Yas and Manasir tribes. He also sent expeditions to collect *zakat* from the Dhahira tribes.

The British were not desperately worried by this spread of Saudi influence in eastern Arabia. The focus of attention in the mid-1920s still lay in the west and north of the Peninsula, and after Ibn Saʿud captured the Hijaz Britain decided to puts its relations with him on a new footing. However, in the course of negotiating the definitive Treaty of Jedda (1927) it became clear that Ibn Saʿud was in no mood to recognise that Britain had a formal protection relationship with the Gulf territories, any more than with Trans-Jordan, and he raised the issue of the frontiers. To avoid such thorny issues intruding, the 'hereafter determined' clause of the old 1915 treaty was dropped and the new article VI of the Jedda treaty modified so that 'His Majesty the King of the Hejaz and Nejd and its Dependencies' simply undertook 'to maintain friendly and peaceful relations with the territories of Kuwait and Bahrain, and with the Shaikhs of Qatar and the Oman Coast, who are in special relations with his Britannic Majesty's Government'. Najd, it should be noted, still had its unspecified 'dependencies', while the shaykhs of Qatar and Trucial Oman were still not deemed to have territorial status: nor in 1927 was any mention made of the sultan of Muscat and Oman, nor the Aden territories, any more than it had been in 1915.

Ibn Saʿud's interest in south-east Arabia then subsided, for he had plenty of other problems to deal with. He had asserted his influence with the tribes there and the awesome reputation of Ibn Jiluwi, his governor in Hasa, was quite adequate to keep control of the nomads. In the course of worrying about Ibn Saʿud's intentions in the Oman region, however, the British departments in question began to formulate the claim that the Najd sanjak boundary of the Anglo-Ottoman Convention devolved on Ibn Saʿud. The British hoped through this legal device to keep Ibn Saʿud at bay without any further cost. So when eventually the question of oil concessions came up in connection with the boundary between Qatar and the eastern part of Ibn Saʿud's kingdom the British sprung the Blue Line on him (1934). The outcome was the Saudi frontier proposal of 3 April 1935. That was quite specific about border locations around the base of the Qatar peninsula, for it was based on detailed knowledge of the political affiliations of places and peoples there. Further east it became vaguer and finally ended up with straight lines in the Oman and Aden hinterlands. The Saudis knew little more of the precise topography of these areas than did the British, but the suggested lines were still meant to be approximations to tribal territories. Discussion then revealed that the essential tribes that the Saudis were claiming were the Murra, for whom a list of 161 wells they reputedly owned was provided, and a series of other tribes comprising the main nomadic tribes of Qatar, Abu Dhabi, Oman and Mahra–Dhofar hinterlands, all of which Ibn Saʿud claimed had submitted and paid *zakat* to him. However, in the interest of settlement the Saudi king was prepared to renounce his rights over certain groups and he would not push his ancestral rights in Qatar, Buraymi, Dhofar and al-ʿAbr.

In the ensuing negotiations British attention was almost entirely confined to the base of the Qatar peninsula where Britain had committed itself to Qatari sovereignty over Jabal Nakhsh, and Abu Dhabian sovereignty over Khawr al-ʿUdayd. The Foreign Office was playing with the idea that, while geographic and strategic considerations should be used to define the boundary near the coast, inland it might be possible to create a 'Desert Zone' where Ibn Saʿud would have personal rights over the inhabitants but not territorial rights. This, however, largely begged the issue of what constituted territorial rights in a desert if it were not the exercise of jurisdiction over its inhabitants. After its legal adviser explained some of the facts of international law, a more realistic view soon prevailed in the Foreign Office and it was suggested that whilst fixed boundaries were essential for the protection of Iraq and Trans-Jordan, here it was possible to see the Saudi point of view and base boundaries on tribal criteria. Unfortunately, the tribal criteria approach could not be used to British advantage in the Qatar peninsula dispute where in fact neither the shaykh of Doha nor the shaykh of Abu Dhabi could point to any exercise of jurisdiction, so the British stuck to their 'geographical' boundary guns to get what they wanted under cover of the Blue Line. Since they made no concessions here, Ibn Saʿud rejected out of hand the British frontier proposal of November 1935 (the so-called Ryan or Riyadh Line).

Further sporadic negotiations did take place before World War II, and the British did concede, 'without prejudice' to their legal case, Murra territory to Saudi Arabia, except in the Qatar area to protect Abu Dhabi's rights in Khawr al-ʿUdayd. Discussion then concentrated on the list of wells the Saudis had produced. To the British the list seemed infinitely extendable, and at one point an exasperated negotiator declared: 'If the Saʿudi Government always claims as a Murra well the next well beyond the last well we had conceded, there would be no reason why they should not eventually claim Muscat town' (Rendel–Yasin exchange, March 1937). In fact the British were often wrong because the Saudis, partly due to oil company surveys, had come to know the precise locations of wells rather better than the British.

On the south coast, however, the shoe was rather on the other foot, for the

Aden authorities came to know their territory, even in the desert hinterland where no central government exercised control. The fact was that Ibn Saʿud's rule extended only to the northern fringe of the Empty Quarter, meaning that he did collect *zakat* from the Murra who ranged southwards across it, but only occasionally from groups of southern bedouins when they moved northwards into the range of his seasonal tax-collecting expeditions.

The Empty Quarter had always been a formidable barrier to movement, and only in their first expansion had the Wahhabis established any sort of control towards the southern coast. Subsequently they had never reached beyond the borderlands of Oman, and it was not until Aramco started exploring the 'Great Sands' in 1954 that the issue of 'effective occupancy' came to the fore. In 1935 Ibn Saʿud had been enough of a realist to drop his claims to Sayʿar and Manahil, as also to the Kathir and Mahra sub-tribes, even though he knew that the Quʿayti–Kathiri and Mahra Sultanates exercised no jurisdiction over their desert hinterlands, and that the jurisdiction of the sultan in Dhofar did not extend beyond the Qara mountains.[6]

Thus the Aden government decided that the 'Great Sands' would indeed make an effective boundary, corresponding roughly to the territorial line separating the nomads who used the sand desert; militarily it also formed a barrier for patrolling. But they were determined to make the boundary well within the sands while Ibn Saʿud pushed his claims into the steppe – where the main wells used by the nomads were often located. The Aden government countered by claiming that many of these wells were held by the tribes in common. Certainly there was an element of doubt about rights, particularly over ancient or re-excavated wells, hence some of the British reserve about using the tribal criterion on the fringes of *dira*. In the end the British, in their 1955 unilateral declaration of frontier, simply reaffirmed the 1935 Riyadh boundary which approximated the edge of the Great Sands by a series of straight lines.

Legal principles used to determine boundaries

The break-up of the Ottoman Empire after World War I left only local powers to challenge Britain's authority in Arabia. All, except Yemen, were absorbed into the domain of Ibn Saʿud. Almost inevitably war broke out between these two states, but under the generous settlement made in Ta'if in 1934, Ibn Saʿud formally recognised Imam Yahya's state, keeping for himself only the *casus belli*, ʿAsir. A specific boundary was agreed in the north, but in the east it was simply agreed that the basis of settlement should be that the Yam were a Saudi tribe, and the Dahm and ʿAbida Yemeni.

Imam Yahya had refused to recognise British rights to what he considered as 'South Yemen' and had to be bombed out of the Adeni frontier area.

[6] Thomas, 1932, p. 9.

Profiting from his growing conflict with Ibn Saʿud, the British more or less forced him into signing the Treaty of Sanaa (February 1934) by which he recognised the status quo for the treaty's forty-year period. The boundary laid down was effectively that of the 1914 Anglo-Ottoman Convention, demarcated up to the Wadi Bana, but that agreement was not referred to in the text of the treaty. In fact British political authority was non-existent in the frontier areas, while the notional rights of the sharif of Beihan (Bayhan) and the amir of Daliʿ, and the supposed unity of the Yafaʾi confederation were so questionable that when an Aden government administration did begin to be extended to the area it cut across commercial and tribal relations, thus further exacerbating relations between the two sovereign powers.

Underlying the imam's position was the anti-colonialist argument that neither the Ottomans nor the British had established any permanent right in the area. Ibn Saʿud was more ambivalent about Britain's position but certainly would have agreed with the imam that any Ottoman rights had lapsed. He and the imam had another feature in common which affected their position in international law, that is, unlike the ex-colonial countries or Mandated territories, they did not have to negotiate their independence: that process generally required agreeing to the 'colonial' boundaries before acceptance as an independent member of the international 'family of nations'. Britain did not dispute Yemeni and Saudi independence, but it did maintain that they were Ottoman successor states and that therefore the 1913 and 1914 Anglo-Ottoman Conventions devolved on them. On his side not only did the imam reject this thesis, but also claimed that the British had established themselves by conquest and that traditionally 'South Yemen' had formed part of the Zaydi imams' domain: all he had agreed to in the Treaty of Sanaa was a provisional status quo, and that applied to both parties. Hence he objected to the sovereignty changes brought about by the Colonial Office after 1937 and after World War II when the British started to create a federation. He continued to protest, forcibly, against what he considered as frontier alterations in the Bayhan area, and also to Britain's claim to the Sayʿar and Bal ʿUbayd tribes.

The British argument consisted of the purely *de jure* thesis that the 1914 Anglo-Ottoman Convention devolved on the imam, and according to international law laid down a permanent and inviolable frontier. In the case of Ibn Saʿud the devolution issue was complicated by the fact that the 1913 convention was never ratified or implemented. In negotiating any possible concessions from these legal frontiers, Britain always played down historical claims other than its own, generally considering them to derive from acts of conquest (i.e. the re-establishing of Ottoman power in the nineteenth century, the Zaydi occupations of South Yemen, the Wahhabis in Buraymi), and refused to countenance any claim based on Islamic legitimacy, whether by Ottoman caliph, Zaydi or Ibadi imams, or the Wahhabi amir.

The British also tried to play down tribal loyalties as personal and not sovereign. That however was a more difficult issue, for they themselves had invoked tribal affiliations to force the Aden boundary on the Ottomans. After World War I citing such tribal authority became very much a two-edged weapon and the only place the British invoked it was in the East Aden Protectorate for al-ʿAbr and Shabwa. In contrast, it was the principal argument used by Ibn Saʿud. So, since the British could not deny the fact of his influence with the tribes, they defended themselves through legalistic arguments about the Blue and Violet Lines – until they were forced by the corollary in international law, that their claim could be bettered unless they could provide evidence of 'effective occupancy' on their side of the frontier. They then began to realise that all they had really agreed to with the Ottomans was a defining of respective spheres of influence. In international law spheres of influence had no recognition: what mattered was a peaceful exercise of jurisdiction. Only in Aden were the British prepared to give effect to their claim by furthering administration and consolidating control of territory, by force if need be. In the Gulf and Oman they were neither prepared for the cost of military defence nor prepared to reinforce their treaties by proclaiming formal protectorates.

Ibn Saʿud's own position was much more straightforward, and legally sounder. He maintained that by the Treaty of Darin in 1915 Britain had recognised his hereditary territories and agreed that the boundaries between the two domains would have to be negotiated. Furthermore, under the terms of this treaty the British had accepted an amendment to their draft so that Kuwait and Bahrain were designated as territories, but Qatar and (Trucial) Oman were downgraded to simple shaykhs, since everyone knew that their authority did not extend beyond their coastal trading centres.[7] Ibn Saʿud also strongly maintained that his hereditary rights, recognised by the treaty, included the nomadic tribes who had reaffirmed his sovereignty after he had refounded the Wahhabi al-Saʿud state in 1902, by paying *zakat*, obeying calls to *jihad* and submitting to the *shariʿa* law administered by his government. To agree a boundary, the Saudis continued to argue, the starting-point must be Ibn Saʿud's conquest of Hasa in 1913, and that delimitation should be based on the evidence of the bedouin, a great many of whom had acknowledged Saudi authority over a long time, and the criteria used should be the levying of *zakat* and the extent of the tribes' grazing rights, i.e., tribal *dira*.

Saudi attitudes to the nomads

To understand why Ibn Saʿud attached such importance to the bedouin it should be realised that the Wahhabis had always treated them differently from other populations. During the period of their first empire, about three-quarters of the state taxes came from the sedentary population, but the *zakat*

[7] For the evolution of article VI in the 1915 and 1927 treaties see Wilkinson, 1991, pp. 134–9, 152–4.

from the bedouin went direct to the amir, who himself redistributed it. Most of the Wahhabi state's revenue in fact came from settlements they made with the rulers of the areas they conquered, with by far the largest sum deriving from the oases of eastern Arabia. The Arab tribesmen themselves paid little. In Oman in the 1820s, for example, the sultan paid the Wahhabis from revenue that virtually all derived from overseas trade: almost none came from the interior where the villagers were considered the equals of the tribesmen and strongly resisted all exactions, except payment of the *ʿushr zakat* which all Muslims paid to a properly constituted imam. Virtually the sole source of wealth of the shaykhs of the small coastal centres up the Gulf was dues paid by merchants in the pearl trade. In the agriculturally rich centres of Bahrain, the Al Khalifa revenue derived from the commerce of the main ports, but the exploitation of the population for pearling was left in the hands of the Arab tribes, and the only income the ruler derived from pearling came directly through taxes on the merchants involved in financing pearling expeditions and trading in pearls. The quasi-sedentary Arab tribesmen living in the areas under British protégé rulers only paid indirectly to the Wahhabi amir through a protection tax (Danegeld) agreed from time to time by their nominal rulers. Payment of this agreed '*zakat*', which in fact was the equivalent in Islamic law of the sums paid under a peace treaty, was accepted by the Wahhabi amir as an adequate act of submission by the rulers of the main coastal centres.

The nomads living on the borderlands of the settled areas, on the other hand, paid proper *zakat* and its remission direct to the Saudi amir was notionally a recognition of his constitutional responsibility for the military side of the Wahhabi Muslim state. So there was a special relationship between the Wahhabi amir and the nomads that did not exist with respect to the rest of the population. When therefore in the frontier dispute Ibn Saʿud insisted on having his sovereignty over the bedouin tribes recognised, he was emphasising the historic continuity of his kingdom, a continuity to which he attached the greatest importance from the time he first started negotiating with the British before World War I. We can also perhaps understand why the Saudis argued subsequently that the only true *zakat* paid in the areas claimed by the British protégé rulers was that which Ibn Saʿud collected on the nomads' camels: what people such as the shaykh of Abu Dhabi collected were either illegal taxes or customary payments and presents. In fact, the shaykhs of the small coastal centres up the Gulf were incapable of extracting taxes from their bedouin followers: on the contrary, their position largely depended on the distribution of largesse to the tribesmen.

The importance attached to the bedouin by Ibn Saʿud was almost entirely due to their special historical relationship with his family who originated in an area where nomads were of particular importance. By embracing the religious reform of ʿAbd al-Wahhab the Al Saʿud rose above local amirs, but it took some forty years before they could consolidate the fragmented areas of Najd and break out of local politics. It was as warriors and manipulators of tribal alliances that the Al Saʿud acquired their position as defenders of the faith, and it was during this early phase that the importance of the bedouin became such that they were treated as directly subject to the amir. Today that same personal attachment can be seen in the family relationship with the tribesmen of the national guard.

The Wahhabi amir remained a tribal leader and the nomads became his personal followers, and although the relationship was rationalised in terms of Islamic legitimacy, the discipline of having to pay *zakat* was more apparent than real. The costs to the bedouin could be more than repaid in honorific presents (*ikramiyya*) and in patronage benefits. In the pre-oil days however, it was very much a two-way relationship. When World War II broke out, Ibn Saʿud worried that he might not be able to subsidise the tribes with food, clothes and cash, because the Pilgrimage revenue, along with his first oil royalties, more or less dried up. Without money he feared that he could not hold his kingdom together, for it was a personal rule, not an institutional state. It is because the British also shared the same understanding that they rejected tribal loyalty as a basis for drawing frontiers. They believed that whereas their own position in Arabia was permanent, Saudi Arabia would collapse when Ibn Saʿud died. Unfortunately for them, Ibn Saʿud lived a great deal longer than they expected and when he did die in 1953 his state did not fall apart.

After World War II

Before World War II the Empty Quarter was not of the slightest interest to anyone, and it was recognised that concessions there would not impress Ibn Saʿud. In so far as the Saudi southern boundary entered the scene before the war it was because of the Aden government's 'forward policy' after 1937, which also strongly affected relations with the imam of Yemen. Because the Yemeni dispute came under the same umbrella of the 1914 Anglo-Ottoman Convention as the Saudi border, the Foreign Office was determined not to offer any concessions until absolutely necessary, and in fact that situation was never to arise. The pre-war negotiations remained bogged down around the base of the Qatar peninsula, with Ibn Saud claiming that he had made his maximum concession in his 1935 claim, and he meant it. He never budged an iota until 1949 when he dropped his 1935 claim only to replace it with one that included the western half of the Abu Dhabi coastline and virtually the whole of its hinterland. He justified this new claim on the grounds that the Manasir and the nomadic elements of the Bani Yas recognised his authority. The new Saudi statement of frontier proclaimed that Buraymi and southwards, including the lands of the imam of Oman, were occupied by shaykhs who were not in treaty relations with the British and that Ibn Saʿud would deal direct with them.

This was essentially the case at that time with respect to Trucial Oman and the Dhahira. Although Saudi *zakat* collection in the disputed area had more or less stopped after 1935, the Saudi governor of Hasa was undoubtedly the force in the land, still collecting some tax from the western nomads who certainly tended to refer disputes to his *qadi*s (judges). Meanwhile Saudi influence was greatly expanding because of oil wealth and the patronage it made possible. The British knew that the loyalties of the tribes were to none of their protégé rulers, except perhaps around the Buraymi oasis where some of the tribesmen supported the ruling clan of Abu Dhabi. If tribal loyalty was going to be the criterion for determining boundaries the British were to face a no-win situation.

There was another feature which also contributed to the British finally abandoning the tribal criterion for settling with the Saudis after 1949: the fact that the poorer the tribal group the greater its territory. Five to ten thousand Murra tribesmen had given Ibn Saʿud some quarter of a million square miles. With some groups like the Rashid, estimated by Thesiger to number about three hundred, and the Bayt Kathir with perhaps twice that number, the tribesmen wandered so widely over such poor terrain that they could scarcely be considered as owning a *dar*. Yet no one could deny that a group like the ʿAwamir were just as independent a tribe as the Murra. So when the issue of the main nomadic tribes, ʿAwamir, Manasir, Hawamil (Bani Yas bedouins) and Duruʿ, came up after 1949, the British refused to discuss their loyalties and tribal territories as criteria for settlement.

Instead the British fell back on their defensive legal stance which was based on the validity of the Blue and Violet Lines. When negotiations broke down after the abortive Dammam conference in 1952, the Saudis occupied the sultanate part of the Buraymi oasis to give further substance to their claims of sovereignty over the Dhahira tribes (Kaʿb, Balush, Naʿim, and Al Bu Shamis) which had been more or less outside the pre-war discussions; and when the old imam, who had strongly resisted the Saudis, died in May 1954, the new imam switched sides. The British responded at the end of 1955 by using force to evict the Saudis from Buraymi and the imam from Oman, and declared unilaterally a modified Riyadh line as the Saudi boundary with Abu Dhabi and reunited Oman.

Conclusion

Despite the way it was enforced, there was some tribal sense to the 1955 *de facto* boundary in the Aden and Oman hinterlands. Unlike the arbitrary decisions of 1922 in the north, the incorporation of the tribes in the northern Oman hinterland into the political units which made up Greater Oman did make some geographic sense, for these tribes did not consider themselves as belonging to the 'tribes of the west' (*ahl al-gharb*), and the limits of their territory did lie in what was traditionally considered as the common frontier area between ʿUman (Greater Oman) and Bahrayn (Greater Bahrain).

Certainly, in the west the boundary declared was fairly arbitrary. Here the

British gave their protégés the benefit of the doubt. In due course that left a wide negotiating margin for Shaykh Zayid of Abu Dhabi to agree a new boundary with the Saudis for the United Arab Emirates when that was being formed. Although this boundary has still not finally been settled in all its detail, there is general understanding on where it lies. This is also true of the boundary between Qatar and Saudi Arabia. In the 1980s discussions took place over the Saudi–Omani frontiers with agreement based on the 1955 boundary line. The inter-Yemen boundary problem has disappeared with the union of north and south, and there is now understanding on the Dhofar (Oman)–Yemen frontier.

In southern Arabia only the Saudi–Yemeni boundary is still seriously in dispute. This boundary falls into two parts, the line between the former Aden Protectorate and Saudi Arabia, and that between Saudi Arabia and North Yemen where the eastern boundary still remains undefined and simply based on the allocation of tribes to one or other party. The continued tension might well be exacerbated by the spectre of a frontier dispute between Yemen and Saudi Arabia, precisely in that province where the newly discovered oil fields in the Ma'rib district of Yemen are at last producing the oil vital for the development of this much-neglected country, which has more people than the rest of the Peninsula countries put together.

6

French Mandate policy in the Syrian steppe

CHRISTIAN VELUD

Institut Français d'Archéologie Orientale, Cairo

The French and British occupation of the Arab provinces of the Ottoman Empire immediately after World War I could be described as the climax of nineteenth-century political and economic supremacy over Middle Eastern territories. Alternatively, it could be described as the continuation of the traditional power struggle between the two rival European colonial powers, France and England. The official granting to France by the League of Nations of an international Mandate over Syria and Lebanon, at the San Remo Conference on 25 April 1920, aggravated the rancour and disillusion that had been building up since the ending of hostilities in the Middle East. First, the transfer of French troops to the Levant was made extremely difficult by the absence of material support and manpower. For economic reasons, France was refusing the credits and military reinforcements that were required to counteract the widespread and growing hostility of the Syrian people, to which the only exception was the Lebanese Christian community.[1] It was only by force of arms, and with the greatest difficulty, that the French were able, between 1920 and 1921, to vanquish resistance and to seize power in Damascus (after the battle of Khan Maysalun), around Aleppo, in the Jabal ʿAlawi and the Jabal Druze, and in the Euphrates area.

The other great disappointment was the gradual loss of territory acquired by the French to Britain and Turkey. The irrecoverable loss of Palestine and the area around Mosul in December 1918, and Cilicia in 1921, dashed hopes of a 'Great Mandatory Syria' roused by the Sykes–Picot agreement in 1916. Following World War I, the Quai d'Orsay was prepared to forfeit in the Middle East what they hoped to hold on to or to regain along the Rhine in Europe. The Syrian Mandate was soon to become very unpopular with central government. After four years of costly and destructive war in Europe, was Syria seriously worth so much extra expense? What benefits could accrue from this Syrian adventure?

[1] The resolutions passed at the Arab Congress in Damascus on 2 July 1919, and the conclusions reached by an enquiry into Palestine and Syria by the American King–Crane Commission, published in August 1919, both carry a clear warning of the problems attendant on the proposed establishment of a French mandate in Syria.

In order to answer these questions, and thereby to justify the French presence in the Middle East, those in favour of the Mandate, led by the military, set out to make it economically viable by exploiting the territories under their control. Two-thirds of the territory, however, on either side of the Euphrates (called Shamiyya on the right bank[2] and Jazira on the left bank) was steppe (Badiyat al-Sham), peopled by nomads and semi-nomads; of these the majority were Arabs, but Kurds and Circassians were also to be found on the eastern borders.

Any plan for the economic exploitation of the steppe region therefore required a sound plan for management and development. The region was traditionally divided into two parts, the *maʿmura* and the *barriyya*, or so-called 'tchol'. The *maʿmura* is the name given to lands bordering the steppe proper, which receive between 200 and 250 mm of rain per annum, enough rain to support a settled population and dry agriculture. The *barriyya* is the central steppe, able to support only intermittent nomadic culture. There was never a clear dividing-line between the two zones, more of a grey transitional area tacked on to one side or the other according to local political circumstances, or sometimes in recognition of a strong and highly respected central authority. The last decades of Ottoman administration were marked by the encouragement and expansion of the bedouin economy at the expense of the traditionally settled region.[3]

Bearing this state of affairs in mind, and strengthened by their colonial experience in North Africa, the Mandate administration adopted towards the bedouin a policy whose objective was to establish law and order in the steppe before any attempt was made to develop the region economically. It was essentially in the east of Syria, in the regions of the Euphrates and the Jazira that, from the 1920s, the greatest efforts were to be made, leading over the period of twenty-five years to seemingly irreversible political and economic change for all the people in the Syrian steppe.

The pacification of the steppe and the subjugation of the bedouin

Between December 1920 and summer 1921 order was restored by military means in the Druze mountains and in the north of the country, from the Orontes to the Euphrates. Peace-keeping forces were sent to the area. Military strength was used next to enforce the occupation of the Euphrates valley and the Mesopotamian territories returned to Syria after the treaties of Angora and London (at which the eastern boundaries had been drawn). In 1920 the

[2] According to Ahmad Wasfi Zakariyya, the Syrian Shamiyya comprises the steppe area bordered on the east side by the valley of the Euphrates, and on the south side by a line joining Damascus and Anah, in the Euphrates valley south of Abu Kamal.

[3] An exception should be made here with regard to the plains of the Hawran and the Jabal Druze, in the area south of Damascus, where apparently the Ottoman authorities and local powers managed to keep tighter control over the tribes from the nineteenth century on. See Lewis (1987) and his chapter in this volume.

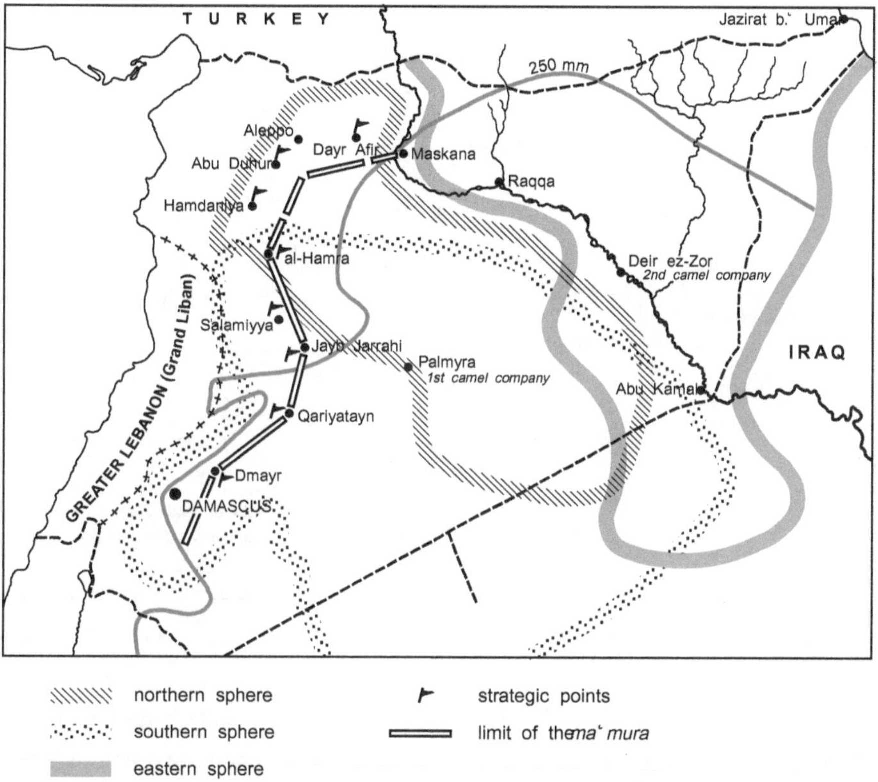

Map 6.1: Design for the establishment of a bedouin state in Syria

French Trenga mission took up residence in Deir ez-Zor unopposed; in September 1921 orders were given to send troops to Deir ez-Zor, under Colonel Debieuvre, to put down the insurrection of the ‘Aqaydat tribes of the Euphrates. Several battalions were sent to the Jazira too, between 1921 and 1923, to quell rebellion among the Arab and Kurdish tribes. The resounding defeat at Bayandur in the Jazira, in July 1923, against a coalition of Arab and Kurdish forces, forced the French to withdraw to the Khabur, and delayed the definitive French occupation of the upper Jazira by several years.

A further means of restoring order in the steppes was through the creation, in 1921, of two mounted camel companies, one stationed in Palmyra and the other in Deir ez-Zor; these crossed and re-crossed the *badiya* in pursuit of plundering and rebellious tribes, from Damir Qabu on the Turkish border to Dmayr, at the gates of Damascus.[4]

In general this peace-keeping campaign produced good results for French

[4] A third company was created in Dmayr in October 1927.

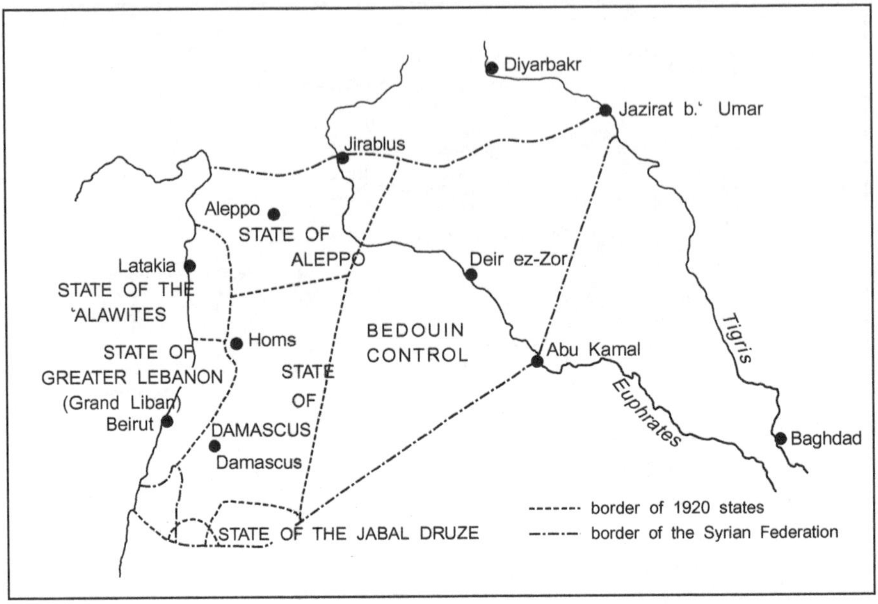

Map 6.2: The Levant in 1920

rule. Two points are worth making, however. The first is that in 1925 the Druze revolt broke out and spread rapidly towards Damascus and the north of Syria. Had this incited all the Syrian tribes to revolt (as the nationalist leaders of the insurrection fervently hoped that it would) the French would have been in serious trouble. In the end the nomads mostly stood back. The French interpreted this as evidence of the success of their policy of pacification of the nomads. But it is also, no doubt, a reflection of the long-standing divisions and mistrust between the world of the steppe and the urban and rural worlds of western Syria. The rallying calls of nationalists, which moved crowds in Aleppo and Damascus, found a less receptive audience in the encampments of Palmyra and the Jazira.

The second point is that the official (if tardy) recognition of the eastern borders of Syria, by Turkey in 1929 (for the stretch between Nusaybin and Jazirat b. 'Umar) and by Iraq in 1933, marked a decisive step towards a policy of tribal control. The existence of national boundaries was to prove fatal to the freedom of movement of bedouins and to their traditional migrations. With no trans-border escape routes in case of conflict with the occupying authority, the nomads had no alternative but to rally and to come to terms with central authority. This rallying of the nomads, however, whether spontaneous or not, was definitely encouraged by the Mandate. From the beginning of the French military occupation General de Lamothe, a veteran of Morocco and commander in chief of the army in Aleppo and the borders of the steppes, implemented a policy of the 'great chiefs'. The general implemented his policy by selecting the most influential bedouin chiefs, for example Amir Nuri al-Shaʿlan, chief of the Rwala tribe in the south and Amir Mujhim b. Muhid, chief of the ʿAnayza of Aleppo in the north. Tribal policy was to revolve mainly around the second of these two men. In February 1920, as a reward for his services in 1919, and for his continuing political support, the shaykh received the sum of one million francs. In July 1920, when French troops entered Aleppo assisted by the tribes, Mujhim was made Chevalier de la Légion d'Honneur. Finally, on 4 September 1920, he signed an alliance with de Lamothe. This recognised the amir of the ʿAnayza as head of the desert police, and charged him with assisting in the peaceful installation of the French in the eastern territories. Mujhim was also detailed to exert his influence northwards in an attempt to achieve agreement with the Kurdish Milli and the Arab Shammar (two of the most important tribes in the Jazira) thereby creating a buffer zone of bedouin allies who would support the Mandate cause.

This very demanding policy soon proved a failure and was abandoned. Apart from the amir al-Shaʿlan in the south, there was no prominent bedouin chief in the Syrian steppe; a multitude of tribes and sections of tribes jockeyed for power, each headed by a jealous chief. The decision was taken to adopt an overall bedouin policy, a kind of bedouin state, rather than to privilege a particular tribal leader, selected for his power and influence. The allied tribal chiefs were to negotiate directly with the military authorities. Why was such a decision taken?

First, the very first contact of the Mandate authorities with the Syrian nomadic tribes convinced them that control must be handled by a separate administration. There were various reasons for this, the primary one being the sheer number of nomads. Statistics published at the beginning of the French occupation of Syria, though probably far from accurate, recorded about 500,000 bedouins; more detailed studies, particularly the one carried out in 1924, put the figure at a total of 225,000 nomads, of whom 125,000 were truly nomadic and 100,000 semi-nomadic, out of a total population of 1,520,000.

In 1930 the bedouin population was estimated at about 130,000 individuals, divided between 23,000 tents. Although numbers had not increased, the nomads nevertheless remained a human force to be reckoned with, not least because they possessed a considerable arsenal. In fact tribesmen of the steppes possessed firearms, either looted from the Turkish and German armies during World War I or smuggled in from elsewhere. In 1923 a report on Shaykh Mujhim's tribe, which comprised 3,000 tents, estimated the number of soldiers armed with Mausers at the shaykh's disposal as 3,000. Obviously any tribal policy that ignored such a state of affairs would do so at its peril.

The plan also aimed at keeping the nomadic populations apart from the nationalist fervour prevailing in the western region, particularly in the towns. Taking advantage of the traditional enmity between the settled, urban population in the west and the bedouins in the east, France sought to control any influence in the steppe that might work against their interests. To this end they emptied the political prisons in Deir ez-Zor and Hasaka of all their nationalist detainees, hoping thereby to prevent ideological contamination of the inmates. The army had decided to retain exclusive administrative power over the steppe borderlands; they planned to turn the areas into a closely supervised military zone, directly under the authority of the commander in chief of the Levant forces.

The plan to set up an autonomous bedouin state was just one of various steps taken by the Mandate towards the division of Syria into several different states.[5] In 1922 a report by Commandant Labrue, head of the Service de Renseignements (SR or Intelligence Service) in Aleppo, and General de Lamothe, proposed the creation of a military border zone in the Jazira and Shamiyya which would incorporate the border areas of the states of Aleppo and Damascus, making a single region under the control of the SR, whose officers would be in charge. The area would have its own budget; although this would derive from the High Commission, it would be managed entirely by the army. This plan was very similar in concept to existing arrangements in the south of Algeria, where the territory was under a Service d'Affaires Indigènes (Native Affairs Commission). The plan was rejected as being too military in concept, and difficult to render compatible with the system and demands of the Mandate. A few years later further attempts were made to promote the idea of an autonomous bedouin territory, but once again they were rejected by the High Commission. From December 1925 onwards civil and military authority were more clearly differentiated from each other by the appointment of a senator, Henri de Jouvenel, to the post of high commissioner. The new commissioner was swift to react against the military plan to take over exclusive administration of an area as vast as the steppe. This disagreement over bedouin policy was to persist right through the Mandate, and made itself felt at local level through continuing rivalry between the SR and the Contrôle Bedouin (the Bedouin Control Commission).[6]

[5] Under the pretext of protection for religious and ethnic minorities, and of consideration for the different stages of development reached by the people of Syria, France divided Syria into three distinct political divisions: in September 1920 a state of Aleppo (with special regulations for the sanjak of Alexandretta), a state of Damascus and an ʿAlawi territory (which became a state in 1922) were created, and in March 1921 a state of Jabal Druze. Syria, recently separated from Palestine and Greater Lebanon, was thus divided into four distinct entities. The break-up was so exaggerated in fact that in 1922, on the suggestion of Catroux, the representative of the High Commission in Damascus, a Syrian Federation reunited Damascus, Aleppo and the ʿAlawis, but only for a brief period. In 1924 the ʿAlawi state was again separated from the state of Syria. Cf. Andre Raymond, 'La Syrie du royaume arabe à l'independence (1914–1916)', in Raymond, 1980, p. 69.

[6] Another reason for the High Commission's suspicion of the plan for a bedouin state, and then condemnation of it, was certainly fear. After the political and military upheaval of the Druze rebellion and its repercussions in the western part of Syria, the High Commission was wary of allowing unified groups, liable at some later date to rise up against the Mandate, to build up in sensitive border areas. Bearing this in mind, the unification of bedouin communities inspired distrust and reticence more than anything else among French officials in the Middle East, particularly after 1926.

The Service de Renseignements du Levant (Levant Intelligence Service), set up in June 1921, soon came to play a vital role in the control of marginal areas such as Latakia, Jabal Druze and the tribal areas, where it was in fact the only effective authority. Officers of the service were allowed a free hand by the military authorities and wielded direct rule which took none of the local administrative structures into account. They were like a separate militia, on the fringes of the other functions of the High Commission and not answerable to the civil authorities. After repeated complaints from the Syrian authorities, the High Commission and the League of Nations,[7] Paris decided to reorganise the service in 1930, creating the Service Spécial du Levant (SS, or Levant Special Service); its brief now was essentially administrative and it came directly under the High Commission. As things turned out, the regional situation never developed further: until the end of the Mandate it was always the officers of the SR who represented military authority – the only authority to carry any weight.

The officers of the Bedouin Control, former members of the SR, were deputised to lead the Camel Corps. It was their responsibility to look after the tribes and to maintain law and order in the steppe. From 1925 onwards the High Commission made use of this organisation, using the head of the Syrian Bedouin Control as intermediary to make good losses sustained in the steppe region. A silent power struggle ensued, with continual strife between civilians and military in the Bedouin Control and the SR. The SR were clamouring for the Bedouin Control to be disbanded, and insisting that its member officers should rejoin their original regiments.

From the 1930s on, the success of the peace-keeping force and the steady growth of the settled population meant that the continued presence of troops specially trained for the supervision of the nomadic population could no longer be justified. In 1934 the High Commission drew up a plan for the reorganisation of the bedouin administration which proposed the replacement of officers in the Bedouin Control by Syrian officials, and the replacement of the Camel Corps by a desert police force, under the authority of the regional representatives of the High Commission.

In spite of all this, and even though the High Commission had managed to curb the creation of private military hunting-grounds in bedouin territory, it was still primarily the military authorities who oversaw political and administrative affairs in the region.

The desire of the Mandate to 'protect' the bedouin world was evident in the way it dealt with the Syrian authorities and French civilians, and also in its

[7] In August 1930 Rappart, secretary-general for Syrian affairs at the League of Nations, expressed surprise at the continued presence of the SR in a country that since May 1930 had enjoyed independent status. 'In my opinion', he declared, 'there is a conflict between the continued existence of this service and the independent status aimed at liberating the country from the administrative supervision of the Mandate.' Nantes, Fonds Beyrouth, inventory 18, box 1565, letter from M Ponsot to the Quai d'Orsay, 17 Nov. 1930.

treatment of the tribes and governments in neighbouring countries. Generally speaking, all meetings of bedouin chiefs, from Syria or from abroad, were discouraged in order to avoid the risk of a bedouin union being formed in Syria, or elsewhere beyond the Syrian border. Two methods of avoiding such risks were recommended: the first was to turn a blind eye to the rivalries that existed between the great bedouin chiefs of the three spheres of influence, Damascus, Aleppo and the Euphrates, and to lend strong support to the conflicts of interest that kept them apart, thereby encouraging the individualism of each tribe; and to take care that minor rivalries thus generated should not degenerate into major conflicts.[8] The second was to act prudently at the many bedouin conferences set up between 1921 and 1934 to sort out inter-tribal territorial squabbles centred on the Syrian border with Iraq. Judging by reports of the conference sessions, it would appear that France deliberately kept a low profile, never taking any political stance that might eventually work against her own interests. This may explain the lack of progress made at these meetings. The French were deeply suspicious of the British, and were aware of the danger of bringing the tribes closer together.

The repopulation of the steppe: Kurdish and Christian immigration

Pacification of the tribes was more or less achieved by 1930 when the boundary problem was settled; however, a further major handicap to the economic development of the steppe had become obvious in the 1920s, namely the very small indigenous population.

In 1925 research in the sanjak of Deir ez-Zor by the agricultural department of the High Commission showed that it would be possible, if the irrigation network were extended, to increase the area under cultivation by 300,000 hectares. The manpower needed to farm such an area amounted to some 300,000 agricultural labourers, or 5 times the agricultural population of the sanjak in 1925. The engineer wondered if it was logical to try and assess the number of decades – or even centuries – that it would take to achieve such a result by the natural growth of the local population.[9]

The High Commission proposed three solutions to this problem: (1) the urgent development of medical aid to the local agricultural and bedouin community in order to reduce the appalling infant mortality prevailing in the region; (2) the encouragement of bedouin settlement, bearing in mind however that it was generally estimated to take several generations for a nomad to become a farmer; and (3) the speeding up of immigration and the organisation of reception facilities and housing assistance for refugees. Definite preference was to be given to Christians, i.e. Assyrio-Chaldeans from Iraq and Armenians and Syrian Christians from Turkey.

[8] Nantes, Fonds Beyrouth, inventory 6, box 552, note no. 182/K3, 15 March 1927.

[9] Nantes, Fonds Beyrouth, inventory 6, box 506; report of 10 August 1926. The report was also published in the *Bulletin Economique Trimestriel des Pays sous Mandat Français*, 1926, 3rd term: C. Achard, 'L'avenir de l'irrigation dans l'Etat de Syrie', pp. 1082–8.

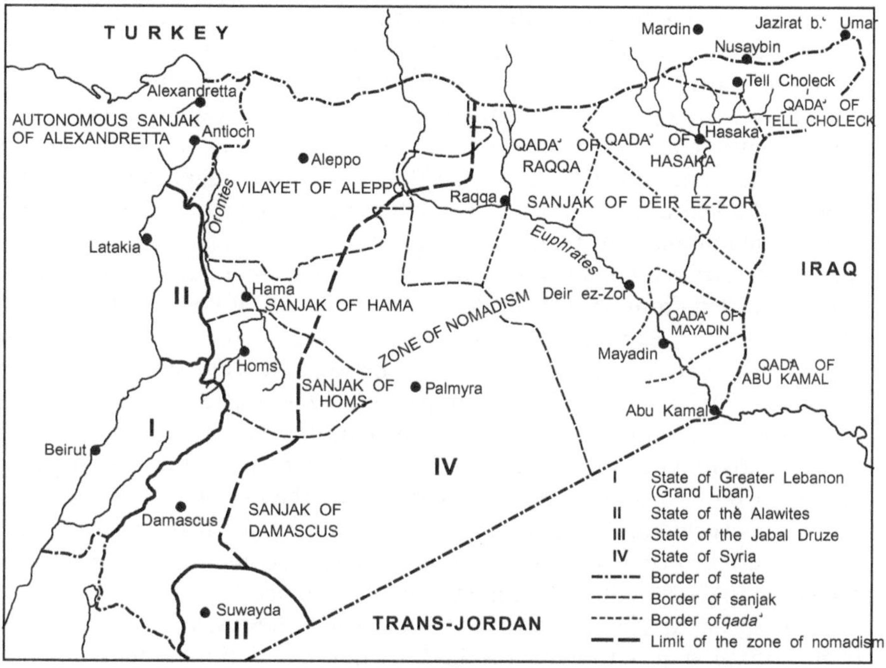

Map 6.3: The Levant in 1925

The refugee groups seeking asylum in the Levant throughout the 1920s were predominantly Armenian. On 1 January 1925 some 100,000 immigrants from Anatolia and Cilicia were registered, the great majority of them Armenian. In the state of Aleppo alone 49,600 refugees were counted on the same date, 44,700 of them Armenian. The reasons for the mass departure of the Christian population of Turkey for Syria, which was occupied by a Christian militia, and a French one at that, can be explained by their need for protection following the wholesale massacre of the Armenian community during World War I. France had pulled out of Cilicia in 1921, causing a flood of tens of thousands of refugees. A directive from Ankara ordering the reduction of the proportion of Christians in the area to 5 per cent between 1922 and 1926 caused ceaseless harassment of the bewildered Christian communities by the Turkish authorities, innumerable arrests and deportations and a deliberate purge of Christians in the main cities of Cilicia and Anatolia.[10]

After 1925 the situation improved quite markedly. The years of great influxes of immigrants had passed. After the initial shock of 1923–5 the

[10] General Weygand, high commissioner in the Levant from May 1923 to January 1925, exchanged letters almost daily with the Quai d'Orsay. He describes the scope and speed of the expulsion of Christians by the Turkish authorities during 1923–4; as a result the city of Aleppo was smothered by this influx of refugees. MAE, Series E Levant, 1918–40: Turkey, vol. 258 on Christian immigration in the Middle East.

Mandate was able to exploit the presence of this population on Syrian territory to better effect. They avoided concentrations of refugees in overcrowded reception centres such as Aleppo, and used the refugees' agricultural and craft skills in developing regions like the steppe, where manpower and experience were urgently required. The immigrant areas were mainly along the border with Turkey, and along the rivers Balikh, Khabur and JaghJagh and, after 1930, in the Jazira region as well. The latter region benefited from the arrival of Christian immigrants from Turkey (Syrian Christians and Chaldeans) and from Iraq (Assyrio-Chaldeans). There was also a large number of Kurdish tribes, expelled from Turkey by Kemalist repression following the Kurdish revolt of Shaykh Saʿid in Anatolia in 1925. These peoples settled for preference in villages along the Turkish frontier between Ra's al-ʿAyn and Jazirat b. ʿUmar. In 1927 out of a global population of refugees estimated at 10,000 persons in the Jazira region under Mandate authority,[11] about 6,000 were of Kurdish origin. Generally speaking the Christian communities coming from Turkey in the 1920s made up the backbone of the population of the small towns constructed under the Mandate after 1922.[12] The Christian immigrants were essentially urban and were to be found later in commerce, in craft industries, or employed in the local military auxiliary units.[13]

In the spring of 1931 a note from the Information Service in Hasaka to the High Commission put figures on the Christian population of these regional centres. These figures show how much the Christian population had grown since 1927. Over a period of four years more than 20,000 people had arrived to swell the small community recorded in 1927, in other words an average annual increase of about 5,000 people:

Refugee centres	*Total population*	*Christian population*
Ra'ʾs al-ʿAyn	3,000	2,000
Dirbasiyya	1,500	1,000
ʿAmuda	2,800	2,000
Qamishli	12,000	8,000
Dayrik	1,900	900
Qubur al-Bid	3,000	2,000
ʿAyn Diwar	1,000(?)	600 (?)
Hasaka	9,000	8,500
Tell Brak	500	500
Total	34,700	25,500

[11] In 1927 this comprised the two *qada*'s of Hasaka and Karu whose eastern boundary did not extend over the meridian of Damir Qabu. Approximately two-thirds of the Jazira was still under Turkish rule.

[12] These were the smaller towns of Hasaka, Qamishli, Ra's al-ʿAyn, Dirbasiyya, ʿAmuda, Qubur al-Bid, Dayrik and ʿAyn Diwar.

[13] The local auxiliary peace-keeping forces in the area were formed mainly of Assyrio-Chaldeans and orthodox Syrians (Jacobites). The Syrian Legion, which in 1930 became the famous Eighth Levant Battalion, and was garrisoned in all the main towns in Jazira, was composed of Christian troops and commanded by Christian officers.

The other source of Christian immigrants was Iraq, with Assyrio-Chaldean groups arriving from 1930 onwards, culminating in the settlement of more than 9,000 people under the League of Nations in the upper Khabur valley, between Hasaka and Ra'sal-ʿAyn. They were responsible for the agricultural development of this part of the Khabur valley. Mention should also be made of an influx of Jewish immigrants, mainly from the town of Nusaybin in Turkey. Although not very numerous, they became a very important element in the economic and commercial life of the towns.

When the High Commission published a survey of the population of the Jazira in 1941 the Kurdish, Christian, Arab (i.e. Arab Muslim) and Jewish communities were as follows:

Qada'	*Kurds*	*Christians*	*Arabs*	*Jews*
Hasaka				
Rural	5,720	9,600	27,480	0
Urban	59	6,922	2,070	59
Qamishli				
Rural	38,470	2,400	11,910	0
Urban	1,200	13,213	3,109	1,663
Tigre				
Rural	12,150	1,480	4,180	0
Urban	400	1,330	–	0
Total	57,999	34,945	48,749	1,722

Compared with the figure of 141,390, given by the High Commission for the total population of the Jazira in 1939, it is clear that, fifteen years after the real beginning of the Christian exodus, Christian refugees from Turkey and Iraq, from all rites, accounted for some 24.8 per cent of the population, or about one inhabitant in four. The Kurds, who had taken advantage of the massive immigration that took place at the end of the 1920s, accounted for about 41 per cent of the population of the sanjak, by far the largest ethnic group.

The French decision to repopulate the borders of the steppe with Kurdish and Christian immigrants to the country broadened the traditional composition of the population of the area and complicated it enormously. The immediate, irreversible consequence of the decision was the emergence of a multi-confessional and ethnically very diverse society. The policy for agricultural development favoured by the French had to be planned and implemented, bearing in mind the fact that the steppe border area round the Jazira had become a great melting-pot of communities.

The colonisation and settlement policy in the steppe region

The aim of the Mandate in the border areas was to fix on the land both the recent immigrant population and the nomadic population (the latter becoming progressively more settled anyway). The land policy adopted by the

Mandate was much better tailored to meet these objectives than it had been during the Ottoman period; in particular in respect of giving access to property rights to the greatest possible number of people. Now the question arose of statutory rights to possession of the land where people were to be resettled, and the methods of distribution and acquisition of the land.

The great majority of the land in Mandated Syria was *amiriyya*, i.e. government owned, but the state would transfer the ownership (*tasarruf*) either free of charge or for payment to anyone who could prove that he had been cultivating it for ten years or more. In 1858, when the government registry (*daftar khana*) began recording land ownership, the first title deeds (*sanad tabu*) were granted. Land in the steppe area was recorded as dead land (*mawat*) in the 1858 register; as it was uncultivatable it was regarded as belonging to no one. It could also be classified as 'free land' (*mubah* or *khalya*) which had never been privately owned within living memory.[14] The cultivation of this land restored the right to private ownership; once the land had been brought back under the plough it inevitably became *amiriyya.* However, the government had the right to declare *mahlul* (without owner) any land allowed to lie fallow for five years or more, or if not released, thereafter the land would be declared *mawat* again.

It appears that Ottoman law held the cultivation of land to be the official basis for acquiring legal rights to land, and so theoretically behind the large estates subsequently formed. In reality things were somewhat different. In the bedouin areas the occupation of a certain region, i.e. grazing of natural pastures by the flocks belonging to the tribe, conferred authority over that land which amounted almost to ownership. The tribe might have been living there for a long time or might have just arrived: the land had no written history and the guarantee of rights of any particular tribe depended usually on the strength of that tribe and the weakness of its competitors. In some cases tribes had been officially installed on named tracts of land by the Ottoman authorities.[15]

As a general rule the possession of land by nomadic tribespeople was never permanent, and depended on the continuing strength of the group. Claims and counterclaims by different groups were skilfully played off against each other in such a way that each group had a living and a grazing area of its own. The boundaries were set by tradition and mutual agreement. According to tribal customary law the land belonged collectively to the tribe, but in fact the government claimed ultimate legal title. This explains why nomadic land, held in either common or government ownership, could not be legally sold or transmitted.

In general a nomad in the process of settling, who wanted to take over some apparently free land in order to bring it back into cultivation with a view eventually to claiming possession of it, would encounter various problems. On one hand, the land in which he showed an interest could without warning be

[14] Once again, it was the bringing back of this land into cultivation that made it possible for it to be classed as *amiriyya* and taken into private usufruct ownership.

[15] The best-known example of this in the Syrian Jazira is the Chechen 'tribe', the Shashan, expelled from the Caucasus after the Russian conquest and settled on huge estates in the upper Khabur valley by imperial decree in 1876.

claimed by the tribal chiefs on the customary grounds of previous occupation. Or he might be met by claims from interested parties, often from the towns, who held an ancient and not very convincing *tabu* for the land. Whether awarded on the grounds of tribal occupation or possession of Ottoman *tabu*s (themselves usually forged), claims on *amiriyya* land were frequently improper and illegal. In order to further their plans for agricultural colonisation and urban development in the border zone, the French made detailed alterations to the existing land laws and intensified their policies aimed at encouraging settlement. To facilitate the gradual process of settlement and the cultivation of hitherto uncultivated land, the Mandate adopted a policy conceived in Istanbul and went straight to the shaykhs, making them their representatives and spokesmen. By relying on the tribal chiefs the Mandate authorities hoped to maintain law and order in the steppe. For the shaykhs, faced with the disappearance of many traditional aspects of tribal life (thanks to the process of settlement), there was a real danger of being gradually superseded by the new rising class of *mukhtar*s, or by other minor local chiefs. This gradual dilution of their power encouraged the tribal chiefs, with the support of French policies, to appropriate vast tracts of land in order to buttress their social and political position. Henceforward it was the amount of land owned that determined whether a bedouin chief could retain his prestige and social status.

The Mandate encouraged this development by persuading the chiefs to farm any of their land that could be cultivated as a condition for ownership. The chiefs traditionally despised agricultural labour and delegated the work to tenant farmers from outside the tribe, usually Kurds or Christians. In this way the shaykhs could be declared legal owners of the improved land and the area under cultivation continued to increase. The novelty was that legal recognition of the tribal chiefs' rights made them into land owners; the law relating to *tasarruf* ownership of state-owned land had been developing continuously since the turn of the century and now finally accorded usufructory possession the same status as ownership.

In order to win the loyalty of the tribal chiefs to an even greater extent, the Mandate rewarded their willingness to become progressively settled in various ways: they were given compensation and various legal measures were adopted that worked to their advantage. Two decrees, no. 132 of 1940 and no. 141 of 1941, allocated to the tribes government land that had never been registered; this land was in the desert south of Hasaka, on the dividing-line between the cultivated area and the area reserved for nomads. This procedure would not have been possible without two decrees, passed in 1925 and 1926, concerning public and private ownership of state land.[16] The traditional distinction

[16] Two orders, the first (no. 144/S, 10 June 1925) concerning public government land and the second (no. 275, 5 May 1926) concerning private government land, established the distinction between land registered in the name of the government and at the disposal of the director of the government estates, and land over which the state claimed legal ownership. The latter category included all occupied but unregistered land, and all land that was unoccupied and uncultivated.

between *mulk*, *miri* and *matruka* land was no longer respected. From now on the distinction was made between registered land over which full rights of ownership was established and unregistered land, like the *mawat* land of the steppe, where the government claimed legal ownership. Two consequences of this were (1) that the government thus built up land reserves which it would be able to dispose of as it pleased; and (2) that decrees 132 and 141 were partly responsible for the consolidation of huge estates in the border area, recognised officially as being privately owned (by the tribal chief). The system of large, privately owned estates which was so characteristic of this region, particularly just after World War II, stemmed from these two decrees.

The process of division of urban housing plots also allowed the French authorities to take advantage of local opportunities and benefit from the general slackness of land-registration policy. They thus achieved their objective, which was to construct refugee centres in the area.

One fundamental explanation for the fragility of the refugee centres was the problem of keeping peace (always precarious) in the area. The only solution was a series of well-organised and well-serviced garrisons. For this, sufficient land to garrison the military auxiliaries and reservists was required, particularly in Hasaka, the provincial capital. Once again the French in Syrian Mesopotamia appeared to take their inspiration from ancient history. What more natural than that Father Antoine Poidebard, crowned with glory following his successful research into the Roman boundaries of Mesopotamia, should have been their spokesman?

> The security question is of fundamental importance to the stability of the refugee centres. From a military point of view, Hasaka is indispensable as a centre for the policing and defence of the Upper Jazira, and also as a recruiting station. Here Assyrio-Chaldean mountain people, and mountain people from the Jabal Tur, immigrants to French Mandated territory, can be recruited for the Syrian Legion. To encourage these excellent recruits, their loyalty should be rewarded with generous pay. Experienced officers and professional soldiers, who know the area, should be retained, and each company should be well provided with local reservists. To this end it will probably be both advisable and necessary to grant land, in one form or another, to military families. This method of guarding the border lands would echo what took place in the same area under the Roman Empire. From the middle of the third century AD surveillance of the frontier, previously carried out by the entire imperial army, was entrusted to a special division which comprised both soldiers and settlers. Land had been granted to them in the border area and they were responsible both for cultivating it and for defending it. It was hoped that they would serve the empire with greater loyalty if at the same time they were defending their own personal property.[17]

In fact this project had twin objectives: to install military personnel and their dependants right in the centre of towns such as Hasaka by building

[17] Nantes, Fonds Beyrouth, inventory 6, box 571, report by the Reverend Father Poidebard on 'the refugee situation in the Upper Jazira in October 1927', p. 11.

new residential areas, and to build new refugee villages on the outskirts of towns, preferably on the banks of the rivers Khabur and JaghJagh. How could these development projects be realised, and on whose land, without provoking hostile reactions from the local population and the existing Syrian administration?

As a first step the decision was taken to allocate gardens and small fields to married members of the Syrian Legion, as well as to veterans of the legion who had to serve as reservists for a period after retirement. This land would be included in their living quarters. To implement the project it was necessary to find sufficient available land. Anxious to show consideration for the Syrian civil authorities and the local inhabitants, the Mandate made use of local legislation. The allocation of plots of *mahlul* land was based on a decision taken by the administrative council of the *liwa*ʾ of Deir ez-Zor (399 of 15 August 1922), with the approval of the *mutasarrif*, the *qadi* and the *mudir*. This decision declared as *mahlul* thirty-seven large plots of land around the neighbourhoods of Hasaka and Raʾs al-ʿAyn, and in the valley of the Khabur and its tributaries. In order to prevent this very important order being invalidated by the administrative tribunal, the military authorities acted quickly. A first step was to allocate small plots of land on the outskirts of the municipalities of Hasaka and Raʾs al-ʿAyn to members of the Syrian Legion and their families. A commission proposed by the *Qaʾim-Maqam*, nominated by the representative of the High Commission in Deir ez-Zor and presided over by the local SR representative, was appointed to examine applications. In reviving the order of 1922 it was decided to give it the force of law, thereby making it unassailable in court.

To a certain extent these official, legitimate measures for the recovery of land exploited the incoherence and vagueness of the land legislation; they were backed, moreover, by more directly political measures aimed at the recovery of land and the building up of land reserves. For example, the military authority could rightfully lay claim to a certain amount of urban land for military purposes, either for building barracks, landing strips, or for residential building plots. Although this fact is referred to on several occasions in the documents it has not proved possible to discover more about how such claims were enforced. Some of the land may have been registered in the name of organisations such as, for example, the Central Refugee Committee (Comité Central des Réfugiés), which was very active in bringing assistance to Armenian refugees in Syria throughout the 1920s. Father Poidebard was one of their most respected officials. These organisations regularly allocated plots of land to needy applicants, keeping legal ownership for themselves however. The Central Refugee Committee was to play a very important role in the Jazira, especially in Hasaka, but also in Qamishli and Raʾs al-ʿAyn as well. Their assistance in the creation of areas or villages for Armenian refugees had already been of central importance in Beirut, Aleppo and the north of Syria.

The success of the policy was soon evident in Hasaka, for instance, and in other main garrison towns of the Jazira such as Qamishli, Ra'sal-ʿAyn or Dayrik. In Hasaka a new military cantonment with accommodation for up to 1,250 people was constructed, the land used forming part of the plot given to the army by the municipality, near the military headquarters on the banks of the River JaghJagh.

Three refugee villages were constructed in the immediate neighbourhood of Hasaka, one beside the JaghJagh and the other two beside the Khabur. In each village an area of land was allocated to the families of two or three ex-soldiers who were to form the nucleus of the village. The village headmen, all former NCOs, were responsible for gathering other refugee families around them. Large tracts of land seem to have been given to them. It has not however been possible to obtain more information on the exact extent of the land allocated to them, nor on the organisation of the villages. What can be affirmed however is that the foundation of these villages foreshadowed an even more ambitious project. The military authorities were planning to divide up the land allotted to them along the banks of the Khabur. The idea of exploiting the upper Khabur valley, frequently reiterated by the military in justification of their refugee policy in the Jazira, had first been suggested by Father Poidebard after two fact-finding visits to the area in 1927 and 1929. It was his opinion that the land bordering the Khabur, upstream from Hasaka, should be confiscated.

A number of proposals aimed at the economic revival of the region were then put forward:

1. The use of lift pumps to irrigate much larger areas. In 1929 both banks of the river were irrigated by the traditional method, the 'noria', but the water raised from the river by this method could only extend between 10 and 300 metres away from the river. According to Poidebard traces of the ancient irrigation canals should assist the rapid construction of a new system for transporting water, and this would benefit the whole region. Poidebard reconstructed the configuration of the ancient canal system for his archaeological map by means of aerial photography, and thus had a rough idea of what the ancient network must have looked like. Until the relief map was completed this was the only map that showed the different levels of the landmass.
2. More manpower was a vital requirement for the exploitation of the Khabur basin. The influx of immigrants from Turkey and Iraq had to be maintained or stimulated, as the case might be. The arrival at the end of the 1920s of financiers willing to invest in the exploitation of huge tracts of land had to be preceded by the rapid creation of a local agricultural population, dedicated to the cultivation of small or medium-sized holdings which would provide the wealth of the region. Large-scale farming would inevitably push up the price of land and therefore prevent the development of an agricultural population. A

survey commission was urgently needed if plots were to be grouped together properly and land titles verified.[18]

3. Finally, to make the land redistribution measures less unpopular despite the number of expropriations the project would inevitably entail, former land owners would be compensated for their losses along the banks of the Khabur. Title deeds which would be beyond dispute were to be allocated to them by the survey commission. They would also be granted the right to use the new irrigation system of canals and water elevators to be installed by the new villages. In conclusion, Poidebard's report made clear that the land thus made available by confiscation should be reserved exclusively for smallholdings and for the creation of new refugee villages; this was the only way of bringing the required agricultural population to the Jazira.

Interestingly enough, the project presented in 1929 was partially implemented six years later when the Assyrio-Chaldean communities arrived from Iraq. The land survey and register of the whole territory of the Jazira and Shamiyya was postponed until much later, both for lack of funds and because it was not considered a high priority.[19]

Conclusion

French plans for populating and developing the Syrian steppe, particularly the eastern borders of the Jazira, raised problems more urgent than straightforward questions of land and law and order in the region. The economic and political survival of the bedouin was under threat. The French military authorities obviously regarded the repopulation of the steppe, officially rationalised in terms of development and appropriate exploitation, as a way of modifying for the better traditional power relationships between the indigenous nomadic population, viewed with suspicion because of their mobile and independent way of life, and the non-native settled population, subservient and therefore reliable.

Military records from the years between the two world wars, however, clearly illustrate the limitations and risks of applying the different sections of this policy. The influx of Kurdish and Christian immigrants, agricultural

[18] The land consolidation was considered necessary because there were narrow strips of farmland all along the banks of the Khabur. The commission was required to redistribute land in such a way that holdings would be perpendicular to the river rather than parallel. This would release large tracts of river frontage which could be allocated to new owners. The perpendicular reorganisation of the land would free the water for irrigation purposes, thus allowing cultivation further from the waterside.

[19] 31 December 1938. The Syrian survey covered 3,083,384 hectares, or a quarter of the whole area, and was confined to land that could be farmed. Mountains or arid areas were not included. The steppe region on the borders of the Jazira had still not been registered when the Mandate ended. Neither survey nor title deeds (apart from the Ottoman *tabus*) existed.

colonisation and the settlement of the nomadic tribes are constantly recurring themes. Justified in terms of security, the settlement of the tribes in specifically designated areas in fact destroyed the authority of the tribal chiefs, thereby threatening to destabilise traditional tribal organisation, as well as removing a means of keeping an eye on the highways of the Jazira, pending the formation of a well-trained and loyal territorial army. In addition, from an economic point of view, the policy deprived the area of pastoral produce, an important source of income. Finally, the oft-repeated saying that a forcibly settled nomad generally makes a very poor farmer should not be forgotten.

The security problem in the Jazira could have been solved if the centres of the new areas of settlement and colonisation had been planned as headquarters of the projected territorial armies, i.e., as economic centres with the capability of defending themselves and of providing sufficient personnel for the enforcement of law and order. The centres would thus have had nothing to fear once the tribes had settled in their designated tribal areas, or 'tribal territories', under the control of their traditional leaders whose authority, outwardly at least, would have been confirmed and reinforced. In fact, the authority of these leaders was virtually demolished. In political terms the retention of a tribal chief as head of his tribe became subject to the whim of the Mandate authorities. The creation of new national boundaries which restricted their freedom of movement left the bedouin and their leaders with no other course of action but to comply with the regulations imposed by the authorities.

An assessment of twenty-five years of Mandate rule in the Syrian steppe reveals tremendous contrasts. In eastern Syria, for example, the combined effects of land distribution, the settlement of the tribes and colonisation led immediately to a new relationship between town, steppe and countryside. As the nomadic population retreated southwards, under pressure from Kurdish and Christian immigrant farmers, the new urban centres began to flourish and the area under cultivation to increase accordingly.[20] But alongside this 'far-eastern' economic miracle an ever-growing proportion of the nomadic population was becoming progressively poorer, a process to which the exceptional series of devastating droughts in the 1930s also contributed.[21] All these developments led the Syrian as well as the Mandate authorities to a new understanding of the Syrian steppe and the political problems faced by a society in

20 The expansion of the settled cultivated area, spectacular in the years after 1926–7, reduced the area of pastures for the herds of the nomads. The resulting loss of income was in part counterbalanced by the increased value of lands the nomads owned and on which settled cultivation paid rent. But losses and gains were not equally distributed: rent on cultivated land, registered in principle in the name of the tribe, went entirely to the tribal chiefs. The shaykhs thus obtained economic compensation for their precarious and uncertain political status under the Mandate.

21 At the Bedouin Conference of Palmyra held in 1933, after several years of drought, the Syrian steppe was declared a disaster zone and the High Commission took measures to alleviate the sufferings of the population. See the articles in *Oriente Moderno* concerning these emergency measures during the years 1933, 1934, 1935 and 1936.

the throes of fundamental change. Civil and military observers of 'the bedouin question' had to acknowledge two irreversible trends at the beginning of the 1940s: first, the progressive decline of the bedouin tribes, now needing economic assistance as well as political protection; and, second, the economic emergence of a much more advantaged and dynamic area on the eastern borders of the country and steppe.

On the eve of independence, the future of pastoral societies and economies in the economic order of modern Syria appeared, to politicians and the military alike, primarily a matter of whether the nomads would survive. The Mandate had succeeded in 'solving' the military side of the nomad question in Syria, but this left the newly formed Syrian state with the very delicate problem of integrating the various populations of the Syrian steppe into one nation.

7

State policies and bedouin adaptations in Saudi Arabia, 1900–1980

UGO FABIETTI
University of Milan

The relations between the state and the bedouin in Saudi Arabia cannot be interpreted simply within the context of development policies concerning nomadic populations. Rather, these relations – whose most significant stages we shall outline below – fit into a pattern of control over bedouin tribes adopted by a centralised authority whose power was gradually consolidated in the course of the twentieth century. The focus of our study, the sedentarisation of nomadic groups, has been a very important phenomenon during this century and the Saudi state has employed considerable means to further it. To clarify the continuities and changes in its interventions, we have identified four principal historical phases.

Wahhabite Islam: strategies of sedentarisation and political mobilisation, 1900–30

The religious dimension 'incarnated' in the Saudi state from its inception allowed the Saʿud to mobilise the bedouins under the banner of holy war or *jihad.* In 1913, when the struggle against the Rashid of Haʾil entered its decisive stage, the Ikhwan (literally, 'brothers') were set up as a confraternity aimed at co-ordinating the action of the supporters of the Saʿud's cause. In that same year, following military actions led by ʿAbd al-ʿAziz b. Saʿud, the Ottomans were pushed out of the Hasa region. Indeed, if territories that had belonged to the Saudi emirate at the beginning of the nineteenth century, then at its peak, were to be 'reconquered', a much more effective military apparatus was needed than the one that had brought about the first victories around the small town of Riyadh. That force was made up primarily of farmers from oases and villagers, the majority of them small shopkeepers.[1] It became necessary thereafter to turn to the bedouin and back them up by an organisation capable of providing them, in addition to mobility, with the military qualities of the settled populations of central Arabia: loyalty to the amirs, regularity and immediate availability for call-up.[2]

[1] Rosenfeld, 1965. [2] Habib, 1978, pp. 14–15.

If we analyse Wahhabite discourse, we see the importance that *jihad* played in the process of sedentarising the bedouin. The notion of *hijra* (literally, 'migration'), central to the doctrine of the Wahhabite movement, refers on the one hand to abandoning the nomadic life, considered contrary to the teachings of the Prophet, and on the other, to the villages (*hijra*, pl. *hujar*) established for the 'converted' bedouin. Thus the bedouin who by enrolling in the Ikhwan became converts to Wahhabism and took up the cause of the Saʿud were also expected to give up nomadism, sell their herds and settle in one of the new *hujar*. Sedentarisation here took on a marked 'mystical' character. According to the founder of the Wahhabite movement, the word *hijra* designated 'the movement of the earth away from polytheism towards the land of Islam'. In this sense the bedouin became Ikhwan by settling on the land in order to place all their forces at the service of Islam. This decision was furthermore experienced as a 'ritual revival' of a decisive episode in Muslim history. As Habib, the eminent historian of the Ikhwan movement, maintains: 'Simulating the Prophet Muhammad's flight from Mecca to Medina which signalled the dawn of the Islamic Era, the Bedouin's *hijrah* symbolises the irrevocable break with the nomadic past.'[3]

The co-optation of bedouin elites and the policy of subsidies, 1930–45

In the years following the dismantling of the Ikhwan,[4] the new Saudi state abandoned its policy of mobilising the tribes under the slogan of *jihad*, preferring new means of controlling the bedouin. Between the end of the 1920s, when the territories held by the Saʿud had reached the approximate extension of the kingdom's present borders, and the end of the 1940s, when oil revenues began to flow into state coffers, the government adopted new attitudes towards bedouin groups. These strategies, which indeed recur throughout the history of relations between political organisations of sedentary origin and nomadic tribes in Arabia, have been summarised by Niblock:

[3] Ibid., p. 17. Interest in the establishment and development of the Ikhwan movement came late to the bedouin tribes of northern Arabia. At the beginning of the century these tribes maintained privileged relations with other emirates, in particular with that of Ha'il, governed by the Rashids (shaykhs of the Shammar tribe), and of Jawf, controlled by the Shaʿlan (shaykhs of the Rwalas). In 1921, when the Rashidite emirate fell, part of the Shammar tribesmen rallied to the Saʿuds. This can be explained, on the one hand, because certain clans from this bedouin tribe had long wanted to free themselves from the control of the Rashids, according to a logic typical of 'segmentary' societies (Fabietti, 1988). On the other hand, the reforming and unifying character of the Wahhabite ideology was able to channel the aggressivity of nomadic groups into a fight against the *kuffar* ('infidels').

[4] The end of the Ikhwan movement can be dated from the late 1920s and coincides with the period of revolts by some tribal chiefs who, contrary to the orders of ʿAbd al-ʿAziz b. Saʿud, pursued military actions against the 'infidels' beyond the frontiers established with the English Mandatory authorities. Furthermore, according to Kostiner (1991, p. 235), the demise of the Ikhwan can be explained by the 'tribal nature' of their milieu, with which the Saʿud were not willing to share state power.

. . . in return for the subsidies provided by the public treasury and the recognition given by Abd al-Aziz to their leadership and administrative authority within their own areas . . . the tribal leaders secured and maintained tribal (especially bedouin) loyalty to the regime. The assurance of direct and frequent access to the King reinforced the tribal leaders' involvement with the Al Saʿud, and the strong loyalties engendered provided the basis for drawing bedouin tribesmen into the White Army (later the National Guard). Links were further strengthened by intermarriage between the Al Saʿud and the tribal leadership: Abd al-Aziz himself took wives from the leading families of each of the major tribal groupings.[5]

The attitude adopted by the central authorities towards nomadic groups was not, however, uniform. Indeed the policy of co-opting tribal leaders concerned only those groups that had actively supported the Saʿud during their struggles against their main rivals, notably the Hashemites and the Rashid. The generosity of the central authorities was not extended to formerly hostile groups until the 1970s.

The logic of co-opting tribal elites as utilised by the Saʿud was not a new phenomenon in the history of relations between proto-state formations and nomadic tribes in the Arabian steppe. But this strategy, formerly used sporadically, became from the 1930s onwards an instrument of political domination on a grand scale, or even an essential element in the make-up of the Saudi state. This means of ensuring the allegiance of the nomads, who at that time made up more than half the kingdom's population, also led to the establishment of a complex and massive system of subsidies. The greater part of these subsidies consisted of special privileges accorded to tribal elites, as well as gifts in kind, given either to the shaykhs or to members of their tribes.[6]

The special treatment accorded the shaykhs underpinned a series of new measures concerning bedouin communities. These measures no longer aimed directly at sedentarisation – a policy temporarily abandoned following the revolts of the Ikhwan and the failure of the *hujar* – but were more concerned with modifying the system of resource management that had up to then characterised Arabia's nomadic communities.

In 1925 the practice of razzias (*ghazw*) was officially outlawed and the rights of bedouin groupings on their tribal territories (*dira*) were simultaneously abolished. It can be assumed that the bedouin welcomed the outlawing of razzias, since this practice had become increasingly violent and deadly due to the spread of firearms. In contrast, however, the abolition of tribal *dira* rights was only accepted after the mediation of bedouin leaders and the setting up of the system of subsidies.

[5] Niblock, 1982, p. 90.

[6] The subsidies (*al-ʿatiyat*) were of four different kinds: *al-sharha*, financial aid to the tribal shaykhs who periodically pledged allegeance to ʿAbd al-ʿAziz b. Saʿud; *al-barwa*, gifts in kind distributed by government agencies in different localities of the country; *al-muʿawnah*, financial aid given on demand and often in response to special needs (purchase of animals, construction of a house, marriage expenses); *al-qaʾidah*, annual gifts of money to those registered in the king's accounts. This last type of subsidy was suspended when the Ikhwan was dismantled.

On the basis of the 1925 provisions, each bedouin could in theory have access to resources outside his traditional tribal territory. Apparently this measure did not have a practical effect on the movements and use of resources of pastoral nomads, already accustomed to going beyond their territorial limits on the basis of inter-tribal agreements. The 1925 provisions did however bring a new dynamic to relations between the state and bedouin tribes, for they brought to an end the political autonomy of nomadic groupings. They effectively withdrew from the tribes all power of decision making concerning rights to their resources.

Oil revenues and sedentarisation policy, 1950–70

The coming of oil revenues at the end of the 1940s marked a new turning-point in the history of the bedouin and the state. The recruiting of bedouin into state institutions, in particular through the creation of the national guard and the religious police, became more and more widespread and helped to propagate among the nomads the image of the state as a redistributor of wealth. Oil revenues in effect allowed the growth of a national economy based on imports and characterised by large-scale consumption, which in turn aided in accentuating state intervention and discernibly modified the economic system of the bedouin tribes.

During the 1950s, and in accordance with a modernising ideology very different from that underlying the *hujar*, the capacity to acquire up-to-date technical equipment led the government once again to promote sedentarisation for the nomads. Agricultural development projects in the steppic zones, initially conceived with the aim of transforming the economic bases of nomadic pastoralism, were thus launched in Wadi Sirhan in the north-east of the country, and at Harad, in the eastern part of the kingdom. These projects did not aim at settling different tribes together in the same locality. On the contrary, it was thought that tribal homogeneity would further enhance the chance of success of these programmes.

However, the lack of technical preparedness, due largely to the absence of prior training which might have directly and effectively linked the bedouin to a particular project, was considered to be the principal cause of failure of the sedentarisation projects. The truth is that, apart from technical questions, the main problems arose from conflicts caused by the passage from one traditional system of access to resources to another. Writing about the Harad project, which was started up in the 1960s for the benefit of the Murra bedouin tribe, Cole noted that some clans of the tribe resisted participating in the project because members of other clans had prominent roles in it, which gave them better access to the new system of resource distribution.[7]

The collapse of the major sedentarisation programmes in the steppe led the

[7] Cole, 1975, p. 157.

Saudi government to seek indirect legal strategies of intervention and in particular to adopt a policy of attributing land ownership to individuals on a private basis.

Land redistribution policies and modifications in the system of access to resources, 1970–80

In order to understand this latter phase, we must return to the legal measures adopted in 1925 which aimed at abolishing the rights of bedouin tribes on their traditional territories. These measures, which had never been revoked, constituted the legal basis for redistribution of land to the bedouin.[8]

The application of the law on privatisation of land directly concerned only the regions of the kingdom where, with the help of modern technology, very ancient underground phreatic water tables permitted irrigated agriculture. One of the effects of land redistribution on an individual basis was the tendency of domestic bedouin units to turn themselves into small enterprises based on the combined exploitation of farming and herding, the land being used to produce forage for animals sold on the market. This tendency led almost everywhere to a differentiation of wealth between those domestic units able to benefit from land ownership and the subsidies necessary to start up forage production, and the other units excluded from the redistribution system. The line of demarcation between the two depended on the relative success enjoyed by different sections of the tribes, through their shaykhs, in maintaining good relations with the authorities. This system of land redistribution and of access to subsidies nevertheless only partly corresponded to the traditional logic of resource management. We do not here propose to serve up once again the stale image of a traditionally 'egalitarian' bedouin society,[9] but rather to stress that the new legislation brought about the passage from collective rights of access to resources to private land ownership, and that this transition necessarily led to an ever more accentuated socio-economic differentiation between domestic units within the different tribal groups.

Apart from the inequalities between those groups that became land owners and those that did not, another major difference arose between those who could reinvest outside the pastoral sector and those who could not. At the beginning of the 1980s, the region of Ha'il in northern Arabia offered significant examples of this tendency. The attribution of land to the bedouin had provoked the mobilisation of individuals belonging to the domestic units who benefited from it. The labour of women, children and even of the very old was fully utilised in the context of a new market-oriented logic of production.

Other researchers who studied the same region during the same period as

[8] Hajrah, 1982. [9] Ibid., 1982.

I did[10] believe that these transformations mark the beginning of a class society with, on the one hand, a few wealthy individuals able to manage large herds and, on the other, a 'proletarianised' mass of bedouins with very few animals, who represent a reserve labour force.[11]

Our view is that the domestic group, by mobilising its available manpower, is able to resist effectively the process foreseen by Fernea. Though we do not question the existence of social differentiation between domestic groups, we believe it would be unwise to view bedouin communities as totally defenceless against the menace to their system of social organisation.[12] The mobilisation of domestic manpower, which represents in effect a new form of production, marks a decisive turning-point in the history of the bedouin tribes, bound up with their integration in a system of commercial herding. This tendency also confirms the 'flexible' character of bedouin society.

In other words, we attribute to the domestic bedouin group a role different from that assigned to it by some experts on nomadic societies.[13] These experts consider isolation and underproductivity to be fundamental characteristics of bedouin domestic units. We prefer, on the other hand, to stress their flexibility and adaptability to 'cultural ecology'. Indeed, the perspective that sees the domestic group as an underproductive social body derives from the notion that its members' labour cannot be completely absorbed in the pastoral economy. This hypothesis is based on a postulate, usually implicit, that sees bedouin society as a society of pure pastoralists. This premise is untenable, however, since the economy of bedouins has never been exclusively pastoral. Furthermore, the whole notion of underproductivity of domestic bedouin units should be re-examined. If productivity is evaluated only in terms of pastoral activities, we come up against a major paradox: bedouin society, which according to archaeological, historical and ethnological data has never been composed of 'pure' pastoralists, would therefore be underproductive in terms of what never was.[14] As Khazanov effectively proved, the bedouin, ever since they appeared in the Fertile Crescent in the nineteenth century BC, have been integrated into a complex economic system based on exploiting multiple resources.[15] Within that system, mobility, flexibility and exchange have 'structurally' always played an essential role.[16]

Given that there is no evidence that bedouin communities were ever based on a pure and exclusive form of exploitation of pastoral resources, the domestic group within these societies is best seen as a flexible social unit managing a number of resources produced by 'mobile' individuals. Considered in this way, the domestic group would appear to be the social unit most capable of providing effective responses to the changes affecting nomadic groups. The recent

[10] I carried out several field trips in the Greater Nufud between October 1978 and March 1980, in the context of a study financed by SEDES in Paris. [11] See Fernea, 1987.
[12] Lancaster, 1980a, 1980b, 1981. [13] Cole, 1981b; Ibrahim and Cole, 1978.
[14] Fabietti, 1990. [15] Khazanov, 1984. [16] Kupper, 1957; Lancaster and Lancaster, 1988.

changes that have affected bedouin tribes of northern Arabia confirm our hypotheses.

The state and the bedouin: the sedentarisation process and detribalisation policies

If we look at state intervention during this century from a broad perspective, the political logic orienting Saudi policy towards the nomads appears clearly in the legal measures adopted by the authorities between the 1920s and 1940s.

Some researchers maintain that these measures were designed to put an end to the frequent conflicts between bedouin tribes over access to resources.[17] Our view, however, is somewhat different. By depriving the bedouin communities of their traditional rights, state intervention on the legal level, beyond its 'pacifying' character, aimed at denying the right of nomads to control and manage their resources in an autonomous fashion. The objective was to replace intertribal agreements in force before that time, and simultaneously to weaken one of the most important factors of cohesion of bedouin societies.

The 1920 laws were not immediately effective, but their consequences appeared only several decades later, following the spread of modern means of transport. This increased the mobility of herders and led in several regions of Arabia to a veritable destructuring of traditional pastoral territories. Thanks to motorised transport, nomadic movement became less organised and the social control that groups exerted over their territory weakened. It had in effect been through the management of its territory that a tribe reaffirmed, in various contexts, its identity. The model of territorial management was premised upon the irregular distribution of rainfall and plant resources, while the movement of herds was negotiated by agreements between the different tribal clans according to the system of priority rights to wells exploited by the different groups.

Beginning in the 1960s, the traditional pastoral nomadic model disappeared. In the course of the 1970s, following the proliferation of wells dug with modern techniques, huge concentrations of animals became possible in areas where rain had been most abundant. No attention was paid to the excessive pressure on pasturelands which thus became overgrazed and condemned to degradation.

Since the decline in the functions of the tribe as a unit managing communal resources resulted from legal measures adopted by the state, we would argue that the 1920s measures were part of a detribalisation project, more or less explicit, carried out by the Saudi state towards the bedouin groups. On another level, these legal measures replaced the objectives pursued by the Sa'ud during the period of the Ikhwan, through the association of different tribal groups in the *hujar*.[18] It seems important to us to establish a close link

[17] Cole, 1981b. [18] Farra, 1973.

between sedentarisation and detribalisation policies in order to bring out the common thread in state strategies towards nomadic groups during the historical phases described above. Furthermore, wherever sedentarisation conditions coincided with a new means of access to resources – i.e., the private appropriation of land – tribal links were more thoroughly weakened than where sedentarisation was encouraged though subsidies, as had been the case before the 1970s. State policy adopted prior to the promulgation of laws on individual land distribution appears therefore as qualitatively different from policy carried out afterwards. Until the end of the 1960s, sedentarisation and detribalisation had been pursued through the mixing of different tribal groups, a strategy carried out by subsidies inciting the bedouin to abandon the pastoral way of life which the authorities viewed as responsible for the permanence of the tribal system. During the past thirty years, on the other hand, with the introduction of new legislation governing access to land ownership, we have witnessed the decline of the tribe as a 'corporate group'.

Private appropriation of land is not an unknown phenomenon among the bedouin of Arabia. When the bedouin emirates were first formed during the nineteenth century, the drift away from the tribal system among certain lineage groups and their acquisition of political power resulted from the fact that their leaders had succeeded in controlling agricultural production in the oases. The essential difference between their earlier situation and that of today lies in the fact that private appropriation of land has not only become widespread but is also encouraged by the state.

In conclusion of this discussion of Saudi policy towards the nomads, we would like to stress two fundamental tendencies: on the one hand, a gradual intrusion of the state in tribal affairs, and on the other, an ever more market-oriented utilisation of resources. These two tendencies are not fortuitively linked. If it is true that the interference of the state has brought with it a slow decline in bedouin communities as bodies capable of administering tribal territory in the political sense, it is also true that the active maintenance of nomadic groups seems only to have been possible where bedouin have been able to adopt market-oriented production. It is in this perspective that we should interpret the mobilisation and reorganisation observed of the labour force of domestic bedouin units. While it is true these units have become veritable small enterprises, the mobilisation and reorganisation of the available labour force seem to be the primary solutions found by the bedouin world to counter state intervention and to respond to the disappearance of tribal practice of managing pastoral resources.

8

The politics of rural policy in East Jordan, 1920–1989

TARIQ TALL

Centre d'Etudes et de Recherches sur le Moyen-Orient Contemporain, Amman

Jordan has been called the 'classic example of a Middle Eastern tribal state'.[1] Even a casual acquaintance with the academic literature on the country reveals a near consensus on the importance of the East Bank tribes for the stability of the Hashemite regime. The bedouin tribes[2] in particular are seen to have been crucial in ensuring the support of the military and to have had a continuous representation at the highest levels of government. This has led Marius Haas to argue that the 'bedouin elite represents a power factor, the negligence of which would have far reaching consequences for the domestic politics of the country'.[3]

Paradoxically enough, this political salience has not brought commensurate socio-economic reward. The tribal hinterlands have suffered from relative governmental neglect, and the urban areas have received the greatest share of government expenditure.[4] The bedouin in particular lagged behind other social groups in income levels and social welfare.[5] Although individual members of the bedouin tribes have been the recipients of special favour, this has been not so much as a result of their tribal status as of their relationship to the state as clients of urban politicians or members of the bureaucracy and security forces.[6]

The disparity between the tribes' political importance and socio-economic status is symptomatic of a long-term bias against traditional agriculture and herding that has prevailed since the 1950s. In the following pages, I will try to make a case for a historical explanation of the bias of rural policy in Jordan, tracing its roots to the transformation of the nomadic economy, land taxation and land tenure wrought by the colonial state between the late 1920s and 1946. The following pages sketch the relationship between tribe and state under Mandatory rule, before going on to discuss more recent developments.

1 Jureidini and McLaurin,1984, p. 7.
2 'Tribal' is a contested term in Jordan (Layne, 1989). It is used loosely here to refer to the descendants of the nomads and peasants who inhabited the East Bank before 1920. For convenience sake only 'bedouin' refers to the camel-breeding tribes and their descendants.
3 Quoted in Hamarneh, 1987, p. 4. 4 Malkawi, 1978. 5 Abu Jaber, 1989.
6 Hamarneh, 1987.

The evolution of Trans-Jordan

During the last decades of Ottoman rule, tribal society in East Jordan witnessed major changes as the frontier of settlement was extended and wheat exports expanded. As a result, an unstable elite emerged from the bedouin aristocracy and the larger merchant families who accumulated sizeable estates in ʿAjlun and the Balqaʾ.[7] The takeover of Trans-Jordan by the largely tribal forces of the Arab revolt in 1918 put this nascent landlord class in jeopardy. Contemporary observers speak of the flight of the educated and the propertied and of crowds burning the land registries and tax offices in an effort to rid themselves of fiscal obligation or debt.[8] Even under Faysal, the Bani Sakhr encroached on merchant estates in the Balqaʾ, and British reports speak of Circassian settlers around Amman living in fear of massacre by the bedouin.[9]

Once the French had expelled Faysal from Damascus, the threat of further upheavals from below drew tribal chiefs, minorities and merchants into co-operation with Herbert Samuel's attempt to stabilise Trans-Jordan through the establishment of local governments in the summer of 1920. However, the elite proved unable to cohere even at a regional level, and political authority in the country fragmented along essentially tribal lines. Reduced to a shadowy authority in the towns, the local governments were eclipsed by ʿAbdullah's arrival in Maʿan in November. Self-interest as much as nationalist sentiment pushed the local notables into co-operation with the amir, and he was able to obtain British support for a central administration based in Amman a few months later.[10]

The endemic factionalism of the tribes allowed the Amman government to contain local revolts sparked by the reimposition of taxation. The most serious outbreaks were that in the Kura in 1921, and that of the ʿAdwan two years later. However, ʿAbdullah's financial profligacy, and the anti-French bent of the Syrians who dominated his first cabinets, soon ran foul of Britain's concern to ensure stability along Palestine's eastern frontier. Lacking financial means, and increasingly in need of RAF protection from Ibn Saʿud's Ikhwan, ʿAbdullah was inexorably drawn into the imperial embrace. He was forced to acquiesce in the transfer of administrative authority to a dependent elite composed of seconded officials from the Palestine government, and in the Clayton Mission's abandonment of the Wadi Sirhan in exchange for a secure land route to Iraq.[11]

British financial and administrative control was formalised in the 1928 Anglo-Jordanian agreement (the perfect expression of ʿAbdullah's 'relationship of dependence on Britain'[12]). Opposition to the treaty crystallised around

[7] Abu Jaber, 1989.
[8] Biographical fragments, Peake Papers; Imperial War Museum, London. [9] Kazziha, 1972.
[10] Wilson, 1984. [11] Ibid. [12] Ibid., p. 102.

the five Jordanian congresses convened between 1928 and 1933. Although most figures of influence in Trans-Jordan, whether tribal shaykhs or members of the minuscule intelligentsia, involved themselves in the movement, the congresses failed to extract more local representation in the administration. In the end, the opposition fell apart over the issue of Jewish land purchases,[13] leaving the executive virtually unchallenged.

Thus the events of the early 1920s reveal that the Trans-Jordanian elite lacked the means of cohesion for indigenous state formation. At first ʿAbdullah provided a rallying-point for its diverse segments, but lacking the means to distance himself from the British he ended up lending a veneer of sharifian legitimacy to an essentially colonial enterprise. Once localised tribal resistance had been contained, the Mandatory administration was able to operate with a high degree of autonomy from local society. Trans-Jordanians were reduced at best to a subaltern role in a 'collaborating elite' composed of the palace circle, bureaucrats, merchants and tribal shaykhs lubricating colonial control.[14]

Tribe and state under the Mandate

The autonomy of the Mandatory authorities allowed Britain to impose its strategic priorities on state finances. Despite regular calls by the opposition for expenditures that would promote the welfare of the inhabitants, administrative costs consumed three-quarters of budget allocations between 1924 and 1944.[15] In similar vein, the greater part of the British grant in aid was spent on strategic road building and defence.[16] The result was a kind of 'military Keynesianism' which financed an import surplus largely consumed in the towns which grew up around the military bases and lines of communication.[17]

Given the slant of state expenditure, and the fact that Trans-Jordan held no attraction for foreign capital, little was done to encourage productive development before the mid-1930s. The terms of the Rutenberg concession prevented any meaningful development of irrigation, and the promotion of dryland farming was confined to a few seed distribution schemes and the limited provision of credit to landlords.[18] Nonetheless, the conviction of local officials that the tribes held the key to stability, and the spectre of unrest in the wake of drought, locust invasion and famine in the late 1920s,[19] forced rural welfare onto the political agenda. The perpetual concern with economies meant that the approach taken was piecemeal, and until 1939 aimed at little more than guaranteeing minimal sustenance for the bedouin and the poorer cultivators.

The nomadic economy was already suffering from the loss of the market for camel meat in Egypt, and from the steady replacement of camel transport by

[13] Wilson, 1984. [14] Robinson, 1972. [15] Hurani, 1976.
[16] Report on the Political Evolution of Trans Jordan, Tripe Papers, St Antony's College, Oxford.
[17] Hurani, 1976. [18] Hamarneh, 1985. [19] Ibid.

the motor car.[20] A more fundamental problem was posed by the loss of free access to winter grazing grounds in the Wadi Sirhan once Ibn Saʿud began imposing *zakat* on tribes entering the area in 1927.[21] This effectively doubled the burden of taxation on the tribes as they faced Mandatory impositions at the other end of their range during the summer. By 1930, the extra burdens imposed by the new colonial borders had been magnified by environmental disaster in the form of drought and locust invasion, and by the escalation of raiding during the Ikhwan rebellion.[22]

Even after the suppression of the Ikhwan, mass raids continued to terrorise Trans-Jordanian tribes as Ibn Saʿud attempted to wrest the hinterland of ʿAqaba and Jabal Tubayq from ʿAbdullah. The result was a major transfer of livestock and wealth to the Saudis, and even greater losses from the flights and forced marches that accompanied the Wahhabi raids.[23] British mediation in the form of the McDonnell Commission failed to restore the loot,[24] and by the early 1930s this failure had left sections of the Huwaytat, the Bani ʿAtiya, and practically all of the Sirhan on the brink of starvation.[25]

The averting of widespread famine, and an upheaval involving the mass defection of the southern bedouin to Ibn Saʿud, was largely J. B. Glubb's doing. He ensured that the effective burden of the animal tax was lightened by centralising its collection and cutting out tax collectors.[26] Subsidies to tribal shaykhs curtailed raiding and brought nomadic migrations firmly under Glubb's control.[27] Together with income from relief work, and from enlistment in the Desert Patrol, the subsidies provided the tribes with the means to survive the drought years[28] while perpetuating their dependence on the state.

The Mandatory authorities gave special encouragement to bedouin cultivation, viewing it, however fitfully, as a harbinger of permanent settlement and therefore a means of drawing the tribes away from the frontiers and the influence of Ibn Saʿud. The substitution of sheep for camels had the same effect since (in the absence of trucks) their range was confined to the western part of the steppe. Glubb supervised the administration of seed loans and the leasing of state land to the bedouin, taking care to ensure that needy bedouin received priority, and to prevent the land from becoming the exclusive property of the shaykhly families.[29] The security brought by Glubb to the desert encouraged the semi-nomadic tribes, and even the *fallahin* to graze sheep in pastures previously the exclusive preserve of the camel herders east of the Hijaz railway.[30]

The steady integration of desert and sown was accompanied by the growth of Glubb's stature in Trans-Jordan's affairs after 1936, culminating in the use of the 'Desert Mobile Force' (DMF) to contain the spillover of the Palestine rebellion into ʿAjlun during 1939.[31] The DMF's task in ʿAjlun was greatly

20 Hurani, 1976. 21 PRO:CO831/11/6. 22 Ibid. 23 Ibid. 24 PRO:CO831/12/2.
25 St Antony's College, Glubb Papers: Report on the Administration of the Deserts of Trans Jordan, February 1932. 26 Ibid., June 1932. 27 Ibid., Dec. 1931.
28 Ibid., Nov. 1932, Jan. 1933. 29 Elphinston, 1945. 30 Glubb, 1938. 31 Glubb, 1948.

facilitated by the local peasantry's failure to support the rebels. This inclination to side with the government was in part a result of the prosperity of the region after three excellent harvests,[32] but was also the fruit of the land settlement nearing completion in ʿAjlun by the time of the rebel invasion. By dividing *mushaʿ* (shared village land) into individual holdings, the land settlement weakened village solidarity and therefore the capacity to mobilise in support of the rebels.

The Mandatory authorities took care to safeguard smallholder interests in the settlement process. This was done partly in the hope that owner-occupiers would show more interest in land improvement than absentee landlords, and partly out of a belief that a prosperous peasantry would best serve stability in the villages. The bias in favour of local smallholders is clear from land-settlement records which show few absentee holdings until the late 1940s. In contrast to Palestine, landlessness was never a serious problem in Trans-Jordan during the Mandate years.[33]

Land settlement was accompanied by a tax reform involving the commutation of the Ottoman tithe into a monetary tax on agricultural land.[34] The new land tax was more progressive, being levied as a percentage of the value of gross production, whereas previously no distinction was made between rich and poor holdings. Moreover the burden of the new land tax fell on a minority of large landlords: 70 per cent of cultivators were paying less than one Palestinian pound a year in 1943.[35] As with the animal tax, collection was rationalised, eliminating various intermediaries who had previously added as much as 30 per cent to the total burden.[36] The new land registers allowed individual as opposed to collective assessments which facilitated routine tax remissions after crop failures.[37] This in turn allowed tax impositions to vary with the cultivators' ability to pay.

The war years saw Trans-Jordan become one of the linchpins of Britain's security system in the Levant, and provided the means and resources to consolidate the progress achieved during the 1930s. The Arab Legion was expanded fivefold; the fact that it was now under Glubb's command ensured that the bulk of the new recruits were bedouin.[38] The loyalty and cohesion of the bedouin regiments allowed their inclusion in 'Habforce' during the suppression of the Gailini revolt in Iraq.[39] Glubb's hold on the nomads was such that the British could afford to imprison and publicly humiliate the Bani Sakhr shaykhs who tried to dissuade their kinsmen from joining the expedition.[40]

The development of ʿAqaba, army construction projects and migrant work in Palestine raised the demand for rural labour during the war years.[41]

32 PRO:CO8311/53/11. 33 Walpole, 1948. 34 Ibid. 35 Konikoff, 1946.
36 Walpole, 1948.
37 Cf. Reports by his Britannic Majesty's Government on the Administration of Palestine and Trans Jordan, various years. 38 Vatikiotis, 1967. 39 Ibid. 40 PRO:CO831/58/2.
41 Ibid., PRO:CO831/58/3.

Shortages of workers at harvest time appeared for the first time since the late nineteenth century.[42] Wartime smuggling provided a more unusual source of outside earnings, enriching the tribesmen who moved the goods as well as the traders who owned them.[43] Even camel portage saw a recovery due to the chronic shortage of vehicles and parts, and the number of camels enumerated rose for the first time since 1930.[44] Grain became a valued alternative to a currency much depreciated by wartime inflation, and the smuggling of grains into Syria and Palestine was commonplace.[45] The rise in cereal prices reduced the real burden of taxation, thus assuring the farmer of a secure income after meeting the burden of impositions.

Yet beneath the patina of wartime prosperity both bedouins and villagers were becoming increasingly dependent on external means to sustain their unaccustomed living standards. The 1940s saw a steady rise in mortgages at the Agricultural Bank facilitated by the possibility of using private lands as collateral after its registration and settlement.[46] The rise in peasant indebtedness was perhaps inevitable given the growth in demand for liquidity after the monetarisation of land-tax payments, and the severity of wartime inflation. However, it was also indicative of the underdevelopment of the rural economy, and its continued vulnerability to climatic fluctuation. In 1947 the authorities had to issue a decree cancelling farm debts as drought threatened to drive the majority of cultivators into bankruptcy.[47]

It seems clear therefore that the Mandate bequeathed an ambiguous legacy of economic underdevelopment and political cohesion to independent Jordan. The military bureaucratic 'enclave economy' in the towns kept the country financially dependent even as its chief beneficiaries, the bedouin, grew ever more reliant on welfare handouts under Glubb's control. The villages were left fragmented and their inhabitants weighed down by debt. On the other hand, the economic decline of the bedouin was balanced by the privileges they enjoyed as the praetorian elite of the regime. Compared to Syria or Iraq, class antagonisms in the countryside were muted by the prevalence of smallholdings[48] and access to supplementary earnings from outside work. For the individual cultivator, the relaxation of the real burden of taxation during wartime marked an improvement by the lights of a 'subsistence ethic' which measured exploitation by the residual left after meeting external impositions.[49] This served to reduce hostility to the encroaching state and to legitimise the authority of its Hashemite figurehead.

Tribe and state in contemporary Jordan

The solidity of its rural base, and the loyalty of an army largely composed of tribesmen in uniform, allowed the monarchy to survive the waning of

[42] PRO:CO831/60/2. [43] PRO:CO831/58/2. [44] Konikoff, 1946. [45] PRO:CO831/58/3.
[46] Walpole, 1948. [47] PRO:FO371/68849. [48] Gerber, 1987. [49] Scott, 1976.

'Britain's moment' in the Middle East and the upheavals induced by the absorption of central Palestine into the Jordanian state. Jordan was the only country of the Arab Levant to traverse the first turbulent decades of independence with the elite that had co-operated with colonial rule intact. Freed of the impediment of direct British control, and reinforced by elements of the Palestinian notability and American patronage, the old coalition of bureaucrats, merchants and landlords maintained a dominant influence over economic policy. Together with the palace circle, this coalition became the chief beneficiary of the development plans financed by the inflow of aid from the USA and the Gulf.[50]

In addition to enriching this 'bureaucratic bourgeoisie' the flow of aid financed the steady growth of public employment, not least in the army which witnessed two decades of rapid growth after 1950.[51] Given the chronic unemployment induced by the flow of refugees, military service continued to attract bedouins throughout the 1950s and 1960s and spread to encompass East Bank villagers drawn by the prospect of steady pay. Army salaries compensated for the loss of seasonal work in Palestine and rapidly made the Arab Legion as central to the livelihood of the villagers as it had been for the bedouin since the 1930s. By the late 1950s, 10 per cent of the male inhabitants of a typical village in the Kura were soldiers, and army pay formed the chief means of supplementing farm incomes.[52]

During the 1970s Jordan's privileged position as a 'subsidised economy perched along the . . . circulation channels of direct or indirect oil revenues'[53] was the catalyst for a sustained boom that transformed a chronic labour surplus into shortage and produced an import surplus of unprecedented dimensions. The growth of imports stimulated service industries in cities already swollen by successive inflows of refugees.[54] Together with earnings remitted from the Gulf, this inflated land prices and encouraged a pattern of 'charity urbanisation'[55] marked by the encroachment of urban areas onto agricultural land in the vicinities of Amman and Irbid. Although irrigation expanded in the Jordan Valley, the contraction of the cultivated area in the uplands and the drain of labour to the tertiary sector reduced the relative weight of agriculture in the economy as a whole.[56]

Initially, the boom in land prices produced the phenomenon of 'peasant investors, rural people made suddenly rich and looking for ways to invest their money'.[57] After 1989 the activities of such investors were complemented by those of rural migrants (often ex-army personnel who had worked in the Gulf) who invested their savings in rural housing, or in gaining access to the service sector where economic returns and the demand for their skills appeared highest. These parallel processes led to an increasing 'suburbanisation' of the agricultural areas in the north-west of Jordan and the growth of a

50 Ameri, 1982. 51 Vatikiotis, 1967. 52 Antoun, 1972. 53 Chatelus, 1987, p. 204.
54 Mazur, 1979. 55 Findlay, 1986. 56 Ameri, 1982. 57 Day, 1986, p. 101.

commuter belt around the Amman and Irbid conurbations.[58] In the wake of these developments urban consumption patterns spread to the rural areas, and by the early 1980s interviews revealed an increasing substitution of purchased commodities for food formerly produced at home.[59]

The intermeshing of the rural and urban spheres should make one wary of drawing broad contrasts between impoverished villages and prosperous cities. More localised studies within the rural areas reveal a complex typology embracing both highly capitalised farms with urban or emigrant finance, often owned by absentee landlords and reliant on wage labour, and more 'traditional' farm households pursuing multiple strategies (including livestock herding) using family labour.[60] Ownership patterns provide little guidance to the two types of farm; however, outside the Jordan Valley the second type appears to be associated with a high degree of fragmentation,[61] a result of the introduction of individual holdings in the context of partible inheritance and population growth.

State policy played a major role in producing the dualistic pattern outlined above. By the early 1980s the main recipient of public investment, the East Ghor irrigation project was dominated by absentee land ownership and an input-intensive type of horticulture oriented towards the Gulf market.[62] Subsidised irrigation water and concessionary government credit encouraged the diffusion of new technology in the valley and its spread to the irrigated sector in the uplands.[63] A stable and, after 1982, overvalued dinar was crucial to the whole process as up to 60 per cent of the new inputs were imported.[64] However, the high exchange rate eroded competitiveness and, by encouraging a marketing glut as production expanded, ensured that middlemen and commission agents emerged as the chief beneficiaries of the new agriculture.[65]

In a similar vein, high grain prices stimulated the development of commercial wheat cultivation using pivot irrigation near Disi and Sahl al-Suwwan in the south.[66] The price subsidies were justified by the need to increase food security, and represented a reversal of previous policy which had fixed prices in favour of urban consumers from 1974 onwards.[67] The new pricing structure subsidised both consumers and producers and was supposed to encourage the diffusion of better practices among small farmers of 'traditional' outlook. However, production showed little response to prices between 1980 and 1986,[68] and the subsidies were of little benefit to smallholders whose grain was largely used for family consumption or for animal feed.

The transparent bias of policy in favour of the modern capitalised sector is explained in part by the benefits this conferred on commercial farmers, merchants and middlemen: groups well integrated into the ruling elite. This well-defined interest group encouraged bureaucratic interventions in its favour; in return it offered support in other areas of policy making or factional

[58] Seccombe, 1987. [59] Basson, 1981. [60] Mundy and Saumarez-Smith, 1990.
[61] Qasem, 1986. [62] Musa, 1987. [63] World Bank, 1989. [64] Musa, 1987.
[65] Tarawneh, 1989. [66] Shepley, 1988. [67] Mazur, 1979. [68] Shepley, 1988.

politics.[69] At the same time the group's commercial orientation promoted specialisation and therefore the achievement of clear gains from a specific measure such as a wheat subsidy. This group possessed the means and resources to impress its viewpoint on the bureaucracy and to lobby effectively in its own interest.

In marked contrast, the traditional farmers had to cope with both the intrinsic difficulties facing collective action by any group of smallholders,[70] and a historical legacy that left them fragmented and dependent on non-agricultural activities. The multiple strategies to which they resorted in order to survive on the margins of the modern sector divided their interests and reduced the impact of a single subsidy or price change. These difficulties were exacerbated by the fact that policies favouring small farmers required sustained intervention going against the grain of market outcomes. For example to improve traditional wheat cultivation comprehensive packages were required to increase the scale of operation, to insure farmers against risk and to address complementary farm activities such as herding.[71]

Unable to exert sustained influence on policy through lobbying, the rural tribes were also for a long time reluctant to protest against state policy through collective action. The resort in 1983 by Bani Hasan tribesmen to 'collective non-compliance' or 'voice' to protect tribal land rights in eastern Amman[72] highlights the main obstacles to concerted action in the rural areas. One obviously exceptional circumstance in the case of the Bani Hasan was the fact that urban land was at a premium, and therefore people had an obvious incentive to defend it. More importantly, the insistence of the authorities on applying their own 'legal' definition of property left the Bani Hasan with no legitimate economic channel through which to act.

Yet it was precisely such a channel, or 'exit' option,[73] that the steady expansion of employment and earning opportunities in the army or the towns since Mandatory times provided for the rural tribes, leaving little incentive or need for collective action. As a result, it was only after rising levels of unemployment and a collapsing currency began to close off this avenue that mass protest erupted. In the spring of 1989 price rises decreed by the IMF sparked riots in Maʿan that quickly spread to encompass most of the tribal hinterlands of the East Bank.[74] The riots were unprecedented in being centred in the areas traditionally considered to be the heartlands of loyalty to the regime and proved instrumental in inaugurating the present process of democratisation. It remains to be seen, however, whether these protests will provide the catalyst to close the gap between the political and economic statuses of the tribes.

[69] Along the pattern described by Bates, 1981 for tropical Africa. [70] Ibid.
[71] Mitchell, 1986. [72] Razzaz, 1989. [73] Hirschman, 1971. [74] Hurani, 1989.

9

Government policy and productive systems in the arid regions of Syria since the 1930s

RONALD JAUBERT

Institut Universitaire d'Etudes du Développement, Geneva

In the nineteenth century steppic vegetation covered virtually the totality of the arc of arid and semi-arid land where average annual rainfall is below 350 mm (see map 9.1). This region, which during the last century was the domain of nomadic tribes, has in the past one hundred years undergone profound changes. Caravan transportation and camels have disappeared, replaced by sheep-herding. Cereal production has greatly expanded, to the detriment of the steppe. The nomads have progressively settled in the villages that sprang up as the margin of cultivation advanced.

The arid zones, which were of secondary priority in the 1960s, are today of vital economic importance. They are the principal source of mutton, for which public demand has increased significantly over the past twenty years. This intensification in production has in turn brought about a rapid deterioration in natural resources.

State intervention played an important role in initiating the process of sedentarisation and extension of cultivation which is still continuing today. Relations between the state and the bedouin tribes were for many years characterised by either conflict or alliance. To consolidate their political control over these marginal populations, the authorities at times used coercion, at other times offered incentives. Since independence, state intervention of all types has multiplied in the arid zones but the authorities' objectives have been divergent and sometimes contradictory.

In this chapter we shall analyse the evolution of the policies adopted and their effects in transforming the farming and herding systems and the management of resources. Let us begin by giving an overall sketch of this evolution, focusing on the changes in farming and herding systems and on the consequences of these changes for the physical environment.

Extension and transformation of farming systems

The movement towards sedentarisation in the arid regions of Syria began in the 1860s. Historically some of these areas had been cultivated, only to be abandoned later by sedentary populations.[1] Until the end of the 1940s

[1] Lewis, 1955; 1987.

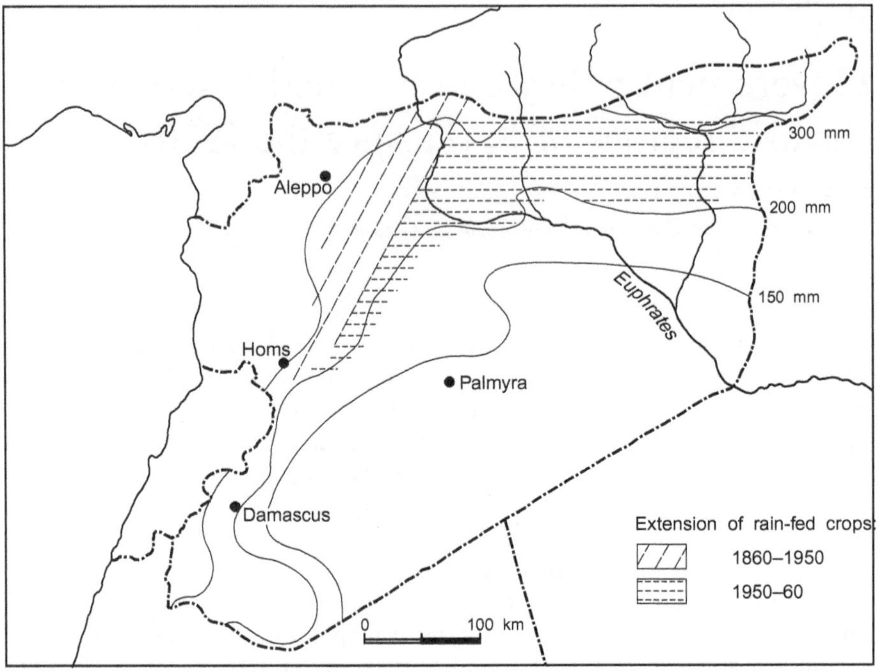

Map 9.1: The extension of rain-fed crops in northern Syria (1860–1960)

sedentarisation and the extension of cultivation advanced relatively slowly and were limited to a movement westwards along the Damascus–Aleppo axis (see map 9.1). Norman Lewis's article in this volume (chapter 4) on the Hawran plain south of Damascus provides an illustration of the sedentarisation process in the latter half of the nineteenth century. The cultivated arid zones to the south-east of Aleppo were also colonised during this period. Studies carried out in this area showed that where today there are villages there had formerly been groupings of tents. Permanent dwellings, the 'sugar loaf' cones characteristic of the Aleppo region, became common only from the 1930s on. Until the end of the 1950s, cultivators used very extensive farming methods. Herds remained more than six months in the steppe. At the end of the 1950s fallows still covered more than 50 per cent of the cultivable surface. Wheat, which together with milk products constitutes the basic diet of the local population, was the major crop planted. Barley took up only about 10 per cent of the land given over to cereal cultivation. From 10 to 15 per cent of the cultivated area was planted with forage legumes, mainly common chickling (*Lathyrus sativus*).[2]

The extension of the margin of cultivation accelerated suddenly following

[2] Jaubert and Oglah, 1985.

the introduction of mechanisation at the end of the 1940s. Within a few years several tens of thousands of hectares came under the plough, particularly in the Jazira plains between the Turkish border and the Euphrates river. By the end of the 1950s, most of the natural pasturelands in the semi-arid zones (with annual rainfall between 350 and 200 mm) had disappeared, replaced by cereal crops. This period, characterised by a rapid development of agrarian capitalism and large estates owned by bedouin shaykhs, is described in Sulayman Khalaf's article in the present volume (chapter 10). The very rapid development of cereal production was made possible by investment from private entrepreneurs. The latter, often merchants from Aleppo who had bought stocks of agricultural machinery, financed the new cultivation. They rented land controlled by nomadic tribes and carried out all stages of the operation, from tilling the soil to harvesting the crops. The biggest entrepreneurs had individual plots covering several thousands of hectares.[3] The bedouin owners, the shaykhs, in fact, received a share of 20 to 30 per cent of the harvested grain, as well as the straw and stubble left on the fields. The great camel-owning tribes at this time began to face profound changes in their economic activities. The rise of motorised transport had effectively accelerated the decline in caravan traffic, already under way since the 1930s, and camel-herding had in consequence virtually disappeared.

Cereal cultivation spread at the expense of the best pasturelands. Greater availability of water, from well-drilling and in particular from the widespread use of water tanks which could be hauled by tractors or mounted on trucks, reduced the constraints linked to water shortages. As a result, herders were able to exploit the steppe areas to the south of the Euphrates which had formerly been difficult for grazing due to lack of water.

In the areas where sedentarisation had begun in the nineteenth century, mechanisation developed later, in the course of the 1960s. There cultivation expanded rapidly, taking the place of fallows. The retreat of the steppe, and the need to purchase a water tank and a truck or tractor to follow the herds into the steppe, led many herders to abandon the practice of seasonal migration. Barley planted to provide feed for the herds became the principal cultivated crop. However, wheat production, though less adapted to local climatic conditions, continued. Surveys carried out in the Aleppo region show that wheat production is generally limited to the surfaces necessary to supply a family's domestic needs.[4] Though less profitable than barley, wheat production covers the food requirements of families in all but drought years. Forage legumes are today planted on only 2 to 3 per cent of the cultivable surface. The very limited area planted in legumes can be explained primarily by the fact that these crops cannot be mechanically harvested, due to a problem of seed shattering. Costs of agricultural labour are today so prohibitive that agro-industrial by-products such as cottonseed cakes provide a cheaper source of

[3] Hannoyer, 1980. [4] Tully, 1984; Jaubert and Oglah, 1985.

Table 9.1 *Farm size, land use and flocks in the western and north-western zones of barley production*

Farm size and land use (1)	**North-east**	**West**
– Number of farms	84	69
– Average surface per family (in hectares)	148	47
– Rotation as % of farms:		
– barley/barley	56	20
– Barley/barley/fallow	25	11
– Barley/fallow	18	60
– Other	1	8
Livestock (2)		
– Number of villages	38	41
– Average herd size (number of sheep)	171	52
– % of transhumant flocks	57	13

Sources:
1. Somel et al., 1984 (survey carried out in 1981 on a sample of 153 farmers located within the 350–200 mm rainfall zone).
2. Jaubert, 1987 (survey carried out in 1984 on a sample of 79 villages located with the 200–350 mm rainfall zone).

protein than forage legumes if the labour necessary to harvest the latter must be remunerated. Surfaces planted with forage legumes generally do not exceed what family members can harvest unaided.

Comparisons between the western region, where colonisation began in the nineteenth century, and the north-east region, where cultivation started only in the 1950s, show significant differences in farm size and farming system (see map 9.1, table 9.1). The average surface of north-eastern farms is three times larger than that found in the western regions, where population density can reach or even exceed fifty inhabitants per km^2, as in Aleppo province. In the most heavily populated western areas, the average farm is under 15 hectares. Here non-agricultural employment and short-term emigration have become important sources of income.[5] Indeed, agriculture in these villages is tending to become a secondary source of income utilising the labour of family members who cannot be employed off the farm.

At the beginning of the 1980s the two regions also differed markedly in patterns of land use and herding. Less than 20 per cent of farmers in the north-east practised a barley–fallow rotation, which was still the prevailing custom in the west. Since that time, fallowing has declined in both the north-east and the west. The average size of herds is also distinctly larger in the north-east,

[5] Tully, 1984; Jaubert and Oglah, 1985.

where more than half of the herds continue their seasonal migration to the steppe to graze on traditional rangelands in the arid zones. Migration is not limited to movement between the barley-producing zone and the steppe; it now includes a stop in the autumn for grazing on irrigated land or in the coastal region. For a deeper analysis of interregional relations based on the movement of livestock, readers should consult the article by Timothy Treacher in this volume (chapter 15).

The trend towards expansion of barley cultivation continued gradually until 1987, when there occurred a sudden acceleration of the phenomenon. These recent developments, which can be linked to modifications in the land-use laws, are discussed in the article by Françoise Métral on the Palmyra region (chapter 11). In general, the surface planted in barley throughout the country went from 1.5 to 2.9 million hectares.[6] This doubling of the surface for barley took place at the expense of steppe pasturelands and fallows. By cross-checking observations from field studies we can estimate that virtually the entire zone where annual rainfall is between 150 and 200 mm and 60 per cent of the zone where it is between 100 and 150 mm have been put under cultivation between 1987 and 1989. Since then, three years of drought leading to a decline in the stock of seeds have lessened the area cultivated. In the absence of any study on land use, it is difficult to estimate the current surface cultivated. The extension of cultivation that occurred between 1987 and 1989 was comparable in scope to that following the introduction of mechanisation in the late 1940s. Again it was largely due to private initiative. Entrepreneurs took from 50 to 70 per cent of the harvest or of the rent paid for grazing the plot, the latter being the more common practice. In areas with an average annual rainfall of 150 mm, it has been estimated that harvesting is possible in only one out of every ten years. In these extremely unfavourable circumstances, barley cultivation may seem surprising. But apart from its speculative nature, this planting can be explained by the severe degradation of the rangelands. Herds now graze mostly on barley, as the biomass produced by barley exceeds natural vegetation the disappearance of which has been accelerated by ploughing. The extension of cultivation in the driest zones inevitably raises the problem of loss of soil fertility.

Soil deterioration

From an agro-ecological perspective, we can divide the region under discussion into two major zones: one where rain-fed cultivation is considered possible and the other where it should be prohibited. The border between the two zones was fixed in 1970, and until 1987, by a decree forbidding rain-fed cultivation in areas where average annual rainfall is less than 200 mm. Such a precise limit always has something of the arbitrary about it. Land that can be

[6] Cooper and Bailey, 1990a.

considered cultivable without risk of deterioration is dependent on factors such as rainfall, the quality of the soil (which may vary within each zone) and the method of exploitation. Soils in the cultivated semi-arid zones where average annual rainfall is over 200 mm also show signs of deterioration. The results of a survey carried out in 1982 in the 200–350 mm rainfall zone show that farmers in twenty-seven out of the fifty-one villages studied estimated that yields had fallen by 50 per cent or more over the last twenty years.[7] A pedological study carried out south-east of Aleppo indicated reductions in levels of soil nutrients and in organic content in cultivated plots in comparison to uncultivated plots in the same vicinity.[8] If we look at the farming systems utilised, it is hardly surprising that soil fertility has fallen following the intensification of planting. Barley is usually grown without the benefit of any organic or mineral additive. Fertilisers are almost never used in rain-fed cultivation.[9] Manure left by grazing herds is used as fertiliser for irrigated plots now found in many villages or is sold in the irrigated perimeters. Except for the roots, the totality of the biomass produced is removed from the land. Following the harvesting of the grain and straw, sheep graze the remaining stubble right down to the ground.

How are cultivated soils being modified? This question has not been the subject of any precise study. In soils cultivated over several decades, it is likely that soil nutrients and organic content diminish less rapidly than in the first years of ploughing or that they stabilise at a lower level. However, observations made in the 1980s at ICARDA's experimental sites show a definite phenomenon of fragilisation in soil structure. In particular crust formation limiting water penetration has been observed.[10] This phenomenon causes problems for germination and multiplies the risks of water stress at the end of the growing cycle. In effect, for three-and-a-half months, from mid-November to February, rainfall in average years is slightly higher than the need of plants for water. Crops reach their optimum development with water stored in the soil during this period. Any reduction in water penetration or in the capacity for water retention may cause a significant decline in yields. The risks of water stress rise rapidly after mid-February. Furthermore, the alteration in soil structure aggravates water and wind erosion. In comparable zones in Jordan, losses due to wind erosion have been estimated at as much as 10 to 50 metric tons per hectare per year.[11]

The first effect of cultivating rangelands is the destruction of natural vegetation. Ploughing is the last phase of the process begun by pulling up bushes for firewood and overgrazing.[12] The effects of the recent extension of cultivation on soil have not yet been the subject of detailed pedological study. Given the magnitude of the displacement of fine soil particles in the arid zones since 1988, it would appear that physical deterioration of soils must be occurring very rapidly.

[7] Jaubert, 1986. [8] Cocks et al., 1988. [9] Somel et al., 1984. [10] Cooper et al., 1988.
[11] Jaradat and Abu Mushrif, 1988. [12] Bahhady, 1981.

Development policies since independence

State intervention has played an important role in the evolution of the arid zones and in the subsequent deterioration of resources. The expansion of the cultivated area at the end of the nineteenth century was closely linked to the active policy of sedentarisation pursued by the Ottoman authorities.[13] During the French Mandatory period, the authorities attempted to turn the opposition between settled and nomadic populations to their advantage to consolidate their position. Hamidé notes that 'the officers in the Bedouin Control Force were guided by the fixed idea that the bedouin is firmly wedded to a wandering life and considers working on the land to be degrading', and consequently accorded them some measure of respect.[14] As Christian Velud demonstrates in his contribution to this volume (chapter 6), sedentarisation projects primarily concerned the irrigated areas. The rise in grain prices during World War II and the establishment by the Allies of a crop-purchasing bureau encouraged the development of cultivation. The landholding rights accorded by the French authorities to bedouin shaykhs also played an important role in the development of agrarian capitalism at the end of the 1940s.

With independence came a change of policy towards the nomadic population. The programme of the Baʿth Party in 1947 called specifically for the settling of the bedouin.[15] The goal of sedentarisation was expressed again in the Syrian constitutions of 1950 and 1953.[16] The special development budget approved in 1955 allocated 10 million Syrian pounds to a seven-year sedentarisation programme.[17] The Agrarian Reform Laws of 1951 also called for the expropriation of the large estates granted to bedouin shaykhs during the Mandate, but these laws ran up against opposition from large land owners and shaykhs strongly represented in parliament and were therefore not enforced. The instability and political dividedness characterising the 1950s hampered the implementation of national policy for economic development.[18]

Political unification of Syria and Egypt within the United Arab Republic marked a turning-point in economic and social policies. One result was the abrogation of the special legal privileges enjoyed by the bedouin since the Bedouin Laws of 1940. Agrarian reform laws began to be applied, a process that was to intensify when the Baʿth Party came to power in 1963.

The agrarian reform is often considered to be one of the factors, or even the major factor, leading to the disappearance of the traditional system of rangeland management based on the tribal organisation of bedouin society.[19] In fact, the picture is rather more complex. On the one hand, as Sulayman Khalaf indicates, social and political relations among the tribes were already evolving well before the reforms. On the other, water shortages and drought conditions which periodically decimated the herds reduced the pressure on rangelands.[20]

[13] Lewis, 1987. [14] Hamidé, 1959. [15] Seurat, 1980. [16] Lewis, 1987.
[17] Mahhouk, 1956. [18] Hopwood, 1988. [19] Masri, 1991. [20] Tleimat, 1991.

And there is evidence of deterioration of the vegetal cover and cultivation of the steppe from long before the reform.[21]

After having played an important part in increasing agricultural production in the 1950s, the arid zones were relegated to the bottom of the pile in state priorities, with attention going instead to irrigated zones. In the 1960s the primary aim of agricultural policy was to reduce the agricultural deficit by promoting import-substitution. This led to efforts being concentrated on the production of wheat, milk and sugar. Giving priority to the development of irrigation, the government adopted the plan proposed several years earlier by the World Bank.[22] In the early stages efforts were concentrated on small- and medium-scale projects and after 1976 on the Euphrates Valley project. The risk of degradation of the steppe and the cultivated arid zones was well known, however, and the Ministry of Agriculture attempted during a ten-year period to limit pressure on these areas and to improve rangeland management.

Attempts at resource conservation

In 1964, with the help of the World Food Programme, the ministry initiated a project to develop nomadic sheep-herding. This entailed the creation of sheep and range co-operatives so as to distribute feed and organise the use of rangelands. The project had at its disposal $4.5 million earmarked for loans to build warehouses and buy supplemental feed. The establishment of a feed-supply system had the dual objective of reducing grazing on the steppe so as to allow regeneration of its natural vegetal cover and of helping to alleviate food shortages in periods of drought. The export of fodder and concentrates used to feed livestock was outlawed at the beginning of the 1970s.

The first sheep-and-range co-operative was established in 1968. Each co-operative was responsible for a specific territory where grazing rights were restricted to members. This part of the plan was presented as a reintroduction of the traditional system of collective management of rangelands and followed the recommendations of Omar Draz.[23] Sheep-and-range co-operatives were linked to co-operatives to fatten lambs for the market, the objective being to restrict use of the steppe to ewes and lambs needed for restocking the herds. Between 1968 and 1973, forty-six herding co-operatives and fifteen fattening co-operatives were set up. Their role was restricted to distributing supplemental feed and supplying credit. No significant measure was enacted to protect the rangelands.[24] The reintroduction of the traditional system posed a number of problems, however. The co-operatives had no legal or material means to control access to the steppe. The very notion of reinstating a traditional system also led to controversy. Omar Draz's recommendations had been based on observations made in Saudi Arabia. The few regions of rangeland control he noted in Syria were not located in the steppe.[25] According to Muslim law,

[21] Bahhady, 1981. [22] IBRD, 1955. [23] Draz, 1980. [24] FAO, 1984. [25] Draz, 1980.

access to the steppe is said to be free to all. The ownership of wells may provide an indirect means to control grazing, but the strategic nature of wells was greatly reduced once mobile water tanks began to be widely used.

The creation of co-operatives was backed up by a law passed in 1970 outlawing rain-fed cultivation in areas where annual rainfall was under 200 mm. More specifically, the law limited cultivation to 10 hectares per family, for those families who had cultivated in this zone prior to 20 July 1970. According to regulations adopted during the 1970s, farmers in the 250–350 mm rainfall zone were obliged to rotate crops and fallow every second year, while those in the 200–250 mm zone could grow crops only one year out of three. These measures were intended to reduce pressure on the arid zones but their effects were in fact slight.

Table 9.1 shows just how slight they were. To our knowledge, no serious attempt was made to carry out these restrictions on cultivated land. The technical services required to enforce them were, and still are, virtually absent in these areas. Having no input to offer – fertilisers were distributed only in the wetter areas and in irrigated zones – the technical services were in any case deprived of any means of pressure.[26]

The law prohibiting cultivation in the steppe was just as ineffective. Studies made in the early 1980s on two villages in the 150–200 mm zone in Aleppo province showed that nearly 70 per cent of the villagers' land was illegally cultivated.[27] In the Raqqa region, according to other studies, the law was similarly ignored.[28] A few attempts to apply the restriction took place in Aleppo province in 1983 and 1984, with the result that a few tractors were confiscated and sowing was delayed. Surfaces cultivated illegally between 1980 and 1985 have been estimated at varying between 200,000 and 700,000, according to rainfall in different years.[29]

From steppe conservation to the intensification of cultivation

In the absence of both means and, in all probability, the necessary political will, the measures intended to conserve the resources of the arid zones remained without effect. From 1974 on, the authorities changed course to press for an increase in production.

The clearest illustration of this new orientation can be found in the sheep-and-range co-operative programme. The second phase, begun in 1973 and funded by the World Bank, was a continuation of the World Food Programme's project. Its objective was to establish fourteen sheep-and-range and fifteen lamb-fattening co-operatives and to increase the production of forage legumes and fodder shrubs such as Atriplex. In fact the project concentrated exclusively on supplying supplemental feed.[30] A fund created for this

[26] ICARDA, 1979. [27] Thomson et al., 1989. [28] Hannoyer and Thieck, 1984.
[29] Masri, 1991. [30] FAO, 1984.

received a further allocation of $11.5 million and a (supplemental) feed bureau was set up in 1974. This organisation took charge of supplying the co-operatives and kept a permanent reserve of feed sufficient to cover animal needs for a three-month period in case of drought.[31]

The quantities of feed distributed by the co-operatives vastly exceeded objectives, or at least those that had been set by the World Bank. Quantities absorbed by the sheep-and-range and fattening co-operatives between 1980 and 1983 were between 70 per cent and 360 per cent in excess of forecasts.[32] As the supplemental feed distributed by co-operatives was highly subsidised, its cost between 1978 and 1984 was from 20 to 50 per cent below market prices.[33] The number of herding co-operatives increased rapidly, going from 117 in 1979 to 310 in 1984.[34]

At the beginning of the 1960s steppe pasturelands still supplied 70 per cent of the herds' food requirements, but this proportion had fallen to 20 per cent by the early 1980s.[35] The massive use of concentrates also led to a rapid increase in sheep numbers, going from 6 million in 1974 to 13 million in 1988. As an estimated 75 per cent of the sheep grazed part of the time on steppe pasturelands, this growth in numbers accelerated the deterioration of rangelands.

The provision of supplemental feed allowed for continuous expansion of mutton supplies at a time when market conditions were especially favourable. Starting from 1974 the effects of a growing population and higher income levels combined to increase domestic demand for meat. External demand, particularly from the Gulf countries, also shot up.[36] Saudi imports of live sheep, valued in 1974 at $30 million, rose to $300 million by the end of the 1980s, according to FAO figures. The market for locally bred Awassi sheep also benefited from a relatively protected status since this meat is preferred by regional consumers. Neither chicken, which had seen a significant boost in production, nor imported mutton was able to compete for quality. The share of live sheep sales in Syria's agricultural exports rose in value from under 1 per cent in 1976 to nearly 40 per cent of the total in the late 1980s. Sheep thus became the principal agricultural export, surpassing cotton.

It is interesting to note that the new orientation of the co-operatives' project corresponded to an administrative change in the government body responsible for them. Formerly under the Ministry of Agriculture, they passed to the control of the Peasants' Union, an organ of the ruling Baʿth Party in the rural areas.[37]

Pressure on the arid zones intensified suddenly in 1987 in the wake of a decree allowing cultivation in zones with average rainfall of under 200 mm. The abrogation of the 1970 law, which had in any case been largely ineffective, cannot by itself explain this dramatic change. However, permission to cultivate was accorded only in the autumn, following exceptionally heavy early

[31] Ibid. [32] Ibid. [33] Nygaard et al., 1982; Jaubert and Oglah, 1985. [34] Masri, 1991.
[35] FAO, 1984; Thomson et al., 1989. [36] Kaldi, 1984. [37] Masri, 1991.

rains which promised a good rainy season. As Françoise Métral indicates in her study, this encouraged many farmers or herders to try their luck at cultivation. The ploughing of nearly one million hectares could not have been possible without heavy logistical support. The authorities permitted imports of both agricultural machinery and seeds. In some regions, the equipment belonging to state irrigation projects was also used.

The following year, the rules governing use of cultivated lands were also modified. A decree passed on 20 September 1988 called for abandoning fallows in the cultivated arid zones. The extension of cultivation in the previous year, combined with exceptionally abundant rainfall, permitted the accumulation of large reserves of seeds, part of which was then distributed to farmers through the Ministry of Agriculture. The abandoning of fallows accounted for at least 50 per cent of the doubling of the surface under cultivation in the 1987–9 period.

Conclusion

The extension of cultivation, which began in the nineteenth century, has accelerated and expanded dramatically during the late 1980s. Policies initially aimed at sedentarising the bedouin populations were dropped in favour of new economic objectives. Recent changes are closely linked to a policy aimed at increasing production in the arid zones. From the mid-1970s on, in response to an increased demand for meat, the economic importance of the arid zones increased considerably. The co-operative project, intended initially to stabilise production, was set on a new course which contributed greatly to increasing the sheep population. Measures taken in 1987 and 1988 to expand the cultivated surface are at least partially a response to the economic crisis affecting the country since 1985 and the consequent need to raise export revenues. Sheep became the top agricultural export. This result has been obtained, however, at the expense of the country's long-term prospects. The increased pressure on the resources of the arid zones brought a sharp rise in production which masks the destructive effects of soil deterioration in the country's statistics. Reduced soil fertility has been more than compensated, until now, by the extension of the cultivated surface and the widespread use of concentrates for supplemental feed. The destructive effects of the extension of the cultivated area have been denounced for many years. Recent changes will make it more complex and certainly more costly to devise ways to preserve the productive potential of the arid zones of Syria.

10

Shaykhs, peasants and party comrades: political change in northern Syria

SULAYMAN N. KHALAF

Center for Middle Eastern Studies, Harvard University

In his fine study, *The Politics of Stratification*, Bujra delineates the effects of political change on local populations as basically following two directions. Either the traditionally wealthy groups are able to make greater use of new opportunities and thus continue their position of dominance, or else the poorer groups improve their economic and political conditions, thereby forcing the formerly privileged to lose their traditional high positions.

The ethnographic material from rural north Syria presented here will show that the effects of economic and political change on local groups and/or classes in a given society need not necessarily follow either of the above two patterns.[1] Processes of change are characterised by complexity, specificity and variation, so much so that it is difficult to view their overall effects on local groups in terms of strict either/or directions. Research on the topic of social/political change suggests the appearance of middle-range variations where major groups in a given community can actually experience both gains and losses.[2] The analytical description of economic and political change during the past four decades in the north Syrian Euphrates village of Hawi al-Hawa will show how the members of its dominant family, the Meshrif, first emerged as economic entrepreneurs and innovators, then after becoming victims of political change through the Ba'th Party, were in fact able to rebound from adversity, to adapt and ultimately succeed in maintaining a dominant, albeit modified, position in local society.

We should begin by considering the broad socio-economic forces that led to the birth and development of the village and the rise of the Meshrif as the village's only land-owning shayhkly family. We can then turn to the

1 This chapter is based on ethnographic material gathered in the Raqqa region of north-east Syria, specifically on the Meshrif family in their village of Hawi al-Hawa. Fieldwork research was begun in the early 1970s and formed the basis of my Ph.D. dissertation (1981). However, recent data on the topic of political change covering the past decade is incorporated and synthesised in the chapter here.

2 See, for example, contributions in Van Nieuweuhuijze, ed., 1977 and in Antoun and Harik, eds., 1972. See also other relevant studies by Peters, 1963, 1972, on Lebanon and Khuri on Lebanon, 1975 and Bahrain, 1980, Gilsenan, 1977, 1996, on Lebanon, Fernea, 1970 on southern Iraq, Salzman, 1974, on tribal chiefs and politics of encapsulation in the Middle East, Gerholm, 1977 on North Yemen, Ismael, 1982, on Kuwait, Crystal, 1990 on Kuwait and Qatar, Rabo, 1986 and Hinnebusch, 1990, on Syria, and Altorki and Cole, 1989, on Saudi Arabia.

subsequent national politico-economic transformations that the Baʿth Party brought about in rural Syria, and to the new structure and patterns of political leadership generated in this particular village.

The village of Hawi al-Hawa

The rapid development of capitalist agriculture during the late 1940s and 1950s in the Jazira–Euphrates region was followed in 1963 by socialist transformations introduced by the Baʿth as the ruling party in the country. Over the past three decades the Baʿth has restructured Syrian society according to socialist populist lines combined with the development of a capitalist sector.[3] The interplay of national and regional socio-economic and political forces, represented in this study by landed shaykhs, peasants and party comrades, can also be observed at the local village level. Thus the village of Hawi al-Hawa (located on the eastern bank of the Euphrates river 10 kilometres west of Raqqa, with a population of about 1,500) will be analysed as a small-scale arena in which changing patterns of local political leadership in the Jazira–Euphrates region may be traced in some detail. The village of Hawi al-Hawa forms a historically constructed social field. We can follow the political actions, trends and strategies of individual actors and their family groups as they move in and out of the village while pursuing their economic and political goals. By taking the village as a case study we may examine the dynamics of politico-economic change in contemporary rural Syria.

Economic transformations in the region

Capitalist penetration in the Jazira–Euphrates region began in the late 1940s when the merchants and agricultural operators of Aleppo and other urban centres introduced their money and modern agricultural machines to the Euphrates valley. These entrepreneurs not only helped in the development of the region and its integration within the larger national economy, but were also instrumental in generating broad socio-economic conditions which began undermining traditional forms of social and political relationships characteristic of tribal and/or semi-sedentary communities in the steppes and the valley. By the mid-1950s land-owning tribal chiefs, through their association with outside agricultural operators and *khanjiyya* (city merchants), had emerged as a new social class, nicknamed locally *shuyukh al-qutun*, the 'cotton shaykhs'. The members of this emerging social class were gradually able to mediate between their local communities and the larger national system, thus perpetuating their domination in their local communities.

The historical interplay of changing socio-economic and political conditions during the 1950s ultimately led to the rise of the Baʿth Party on Syria's

[3] See Hinnebusch, 1990.

political stage.[4] The Baʿth socialist revolution of 1963 brought about major changes in rural Syria. Consequently, the agrarian base of the emerging traditional 'cotton shaykhs' came to be seriously weakened, and the influential mediating roles they had manipulated to their advantage during the 1950s were contested or eliminated. This was particularly true during the short period of what is labelled as the neo-Baʿth, from 1966 to 1970.[5]

The birth of Hawi al-Hawa and the rise of the Meshrif

Members of the Meshrif family did not view themselves as shaykhs of their own *ʿashira* (sub-tribe) before the 1950s; however, it was known that the family was relatively well-off and enjoyed an influential leading position within the *ʿashira* of the Musa al-Dahir, of the larger ʿAfadla. The family's position within local society was reflected in the marriages with shaykhly families of different *ʿashira* within the larger ʿAfadla that Hajj Ibrahim had arranged for four of his sons before his death in 1949. It was also reflected in the fact that in the mid-1940s they began *daqq al-qahwa* (pounding coffee beans) in their house, thus signalling it out as an open *madafa* (guest house) for all men of their small local community.

Before 1950 the Meshrif families (Hajj Ibrahim and his five sons) were involved in both sheep-herding and farming in the steppe area of Tell al-Samin along the Balikh river on the land of Daham al-Hashim b. Muhayd. Hajj Ibrahim was very successful in sheep-raising, and when he died in 1949 at Tell al-Samin he left a sizeable fortune. In 1950 the Meshrif family bought the land of Hawi al-Hawa from an Aleppan absentee landlord for 100,000 Syrian lira, the total holding being around 400 hectares. Hajj Hamad's house was built, and then in 1951–2 a larger family house with a *madafa* was constructed. When they moved into this new house animals were slaughtered for a party to which shaykhs of the tribe, kinsmen and eminent men were invited.

The Meshrif began cultivating the land to grow wheat and cotton in 1950, initially on a small scale. Gradually they brought their relatives from various other places (such as al-Balikh, Tell al-Samin, al-Salhabiyya and al-Kassrat) to settle in the new village and work the land as sharecropping *fallahin* (peasants). During the 1950s the early settlers in the village were mostly kinsmen of the Meshrif from Dahir lineage. However, the gradual expansion of the Meshrifs' agricultural enterprise led them to recruit more *fallahin* from outside their close kin group. In 1954–5 they purchased two tractors and other modern agricultural machinery. By 1960 the Meshrif family were cultivating all the land of the village. During the late 1950s a large group of the Jhamat lineage, from the larger *ʿashira* of the Musa al-Dahir who were settled in the village of Ruwayyan, were invited to settle in Hawi al-Hawa. They constituted

[4] Seale, 1965; Al-Asad, 1973; Hinnebusch, 1989, 1990.
[5] Khalaf, 1981; Rabo, 1986; Hinnebusch, 1990.

about thirty peasant families, or about 20 per cent of the village population. Later on another fifteen families or so from Abu Saraya (non-ʿAfadla tribal peasants) were settled in the village. Thus by the late 1950s the Meshrif had about eighty sharecropping peasant families settled in their village to work the land.

Production relations within the village were representative of the wider region. As *mallak/muzariʿ* (land owner/agricultural operator), the Meshrif family was responsible for providing everything needed for cotton production: the land, seeds, water pumps, fuel, canal construction and maintenance, ploughing, supervision and so forth. The *fallah*'s share of the total annual produce of his cultivated plot was around 25 per cent where he and his family provided labour only. In situations where the *fallah* himself supplied fertiliser, his share increased to 33 per cent of the total produce. If hired labour was needed to pick the crop, the *fallah* was also responsible for this extra cost. Usually the *fallahin* sustained their simple livelihood by borrowing from the Meshrif throughout the year. In cases where the peasants borrowed far beyond the total value of their expected share, their debts would be transferred to the accounts of the following years, thus generating a structure of peasant dependence on the landlord.

During the 1950s the government did not intervene much in agriculture. Economic relations between the *mallak/muzariʿ* and the *fallahin* were based on individual personal agreements, in that there were no written contracts protecting a tenure for the *fallahin*. As Hajj Khalaf observed, 'Before, the *fallahin* were afraid of the landlord, and therefore they worked hard. If a man did not work well, there would be no work for him the following year.'[6] Production relations not only in Hawi al-Hawa but throughout the Euphrates region at large were characterised by exploitation of the *fallah* and his domination by the *mallak/muzariʿ*. As described by one *fallah*, conditions in the 1950s 'were poverty. We were only able to earn enough food to survive and it was not secured without hardship.'[7]

The marketing of cotton and other cash crops such as wheat and barley was done through the *khanjiyya* of Aleppo. These were brokers, merchants and money-lenders all in one. They supplied the landed agricultural operators of the Euphrates valley with loans on the agreement that a given *muzariʿ* took his crop to be sold for a small commission in the *khan* of his particular *khanji*.

The economic activities in which the enterprising Meshrif were involved reflect the dynamic interdependence of the steppe, the valley and the city. Their rising prosperity was not confined to cotton agriculture in the valley but was also the result of other economic enterprises located in the steppes of the Jazira, such as sheep-raising, dry farming of cereal winter crops (wheat and barley) and the rental of property in town. Many of the sharecropping peasant families who were settled in the village owned parcels of rain-fed land

[6] Khalaf, 1981, p. 245. [7] Ibid., 1981, p. 362.

in the steppes at different locations north-west of Hawi al-Hawa. Since the early 1950s the owners of such small parcels of rain-fed land usually rented them to outside agricultural operators while they themselves lived as peasants in the villages. Sometimes local entrepreneurs such as the Meshrif rented such parcels of land from their poorer kinsmen for cultivating winter cereal crops. Many peasant families were able to keep a few sheep and goats in the steppes, to supplement their livelihood, which now had come to depend essentially on cotton farming.

Leadership and domination

The rapid expansion of capitalist agriculture in the Euphrates–Jazira region generated a series of new interconnected consequences. Firstly, it produced new socio-economic 'formations' which were associated with the emergence of a combined system of *iqta*ʿ (feudal) and agrarian capitalism. Such capitalism involved the consolidation of large areas of land in the hands of a small class of land owners of shaykhly origin, who, as rising entrepreneurs, employed their tribesmen from the steppes as sedentarised sharecropping peasants. The rapid development of the village of Hawi al-Hawa exemplifies this phenomenon. Throughout the villages scattered in the Euphrates valley labour relations of capitalist agriculture superseded but also built upon kinship ideology.

Associated with this system was greater inequality in land ownership and wealth. The Meshrif, for example, established themselves in their new village/farm as a distinct local elite, and emerged as the undisputed political leaders in their village community, while in contrast the material conditions of the peasants remained underdeveloped. The second consequence was the emergence of a new outlook. The increasing association of tribal shaykhs, now agricultural entrepreneurs, with city merchants helped to widen the gap in attitudes and values between them and their fellow peasant tribesmen. The Meshrifs' emulation of the merchants and urban elite in the purchase of property in Raqqa, the education of their school-age boys, the intensification of endogamous marriage patterns as well as their increasing association in exchanges of visits and hospitality with other shaykhly families or city merchants are expressive of the new outlook and social reorientation of the 'cotton shaykhs' as an emerging social class.

The third consequence concerned the breakdown of traditional ties of economic obligation. As tribal shaykhs became large landlords in a developing capitalist economy, they were freed from their traditional ties of economic responsibility to their tribesmen. Prior to the agricultural revolution of the early 1950s, semi-sedentary tribal communities, such as the ʿAfadla, gave support to the house of the shaykh by means of a 'gift economy'. By the mid-1950s the shaykhs and sub-shaykhs, who had in part depended on the *mashyakhiyya* gifts for the upkeep of their *madafa*s, became economically independent, as their position came to rest on different bases from that of their tribesmen. The fellow tribesman became a dependent peasant.

Fourthly, the cotton shaykhs of the ʿAfadla and the wider region adopted new styles and strategies that were compatible with their rising economic–political position in society. They began driving Cadillacs and Chevrolets and also employing house servants and coffee makers. They built many large *madafa*s, each large enough for sixty to a hundred men. The expansion as well as the elaborate size and design of the *madafa* as 'strategies of accumulating capital of honour and prestige'[8] took exaggerated forms. While the *madafa* was a traditional social institution among tribesmen, the capitalisation on this social institution by the new cotton shaykhs became a conscious and elaborate strategy for achieving greater consensus for their political domination.[9] The shaykhs' behaviour in the national election of 1961 further illustrates the change in style of their domination and their quest for political power. Rather than relying basically on tribal loyalties or a distinct ideological election platform, significant portions of the votes were bought by cash.

The fifth consequence concerns the duties of the leader and the development of distinct patterns of leisure and lifestyle marking off the 'cotton shaykhs' as a distinct social class characterised by economic power, political influence and leisure. As in the case of Hajj Khalaf of Hawi al-Hawa, we see that around the late 1950s he entrusted the financial management of the family's agricultural business to his capable son Mahmud. The supervisory responsibilities over the *fallahin's* labour in the fields was assigned to Hajj Hamad, while Hajj ʿAssaf supervised the family's sheep herd in the steppes. While Hajj Khalaf supervised from a distance, as the village's leading headman, he withdrew quite early into a life of leisure, socialising with his bourgeois equals from the town and shaykhs of the region.

His son Mahmud was appointed *mukhtar* (village mayor) in 1955, while he was still in his late teens. Mahmud was the first of the family to receive modern school education, to the end of primary level. In his capacity as *mukhtar*, Mahmud performed the role of official representative of the local government as well as of the village community. Prior to the Baʿth revolution, whenever government officials came to the village, they arrived in the *madafa* and often conducted their affairs in the presence of Mukhtar Mahmud. He not only mediated in the resolution of petty problems and conflicts in the village, but also carried the stamp necessary for the official register of births, marriages, etc., in the village. He was also required to accompany the police during the arrest or interrogation of villagers. In his socialising and leisure, Mukhtar Mahmud found friends among the young men of the Meshlab, the paramount wealthy shaykhly families of the ʿAfadla. In the early 1960s he bought a large American car (Oldsmobile) and immediately hired a chauffeur. Such were the

[8] Bourdieu, 1977, p. 179. [9] Khalaf, forthcoming.

commodities of success and social distinction characteristic of the dominant class.

The Baʿth and party comrades

Three decades of Baʿth socialist rule have, in the words of Hinnebusch, left 'durable consequences' in the fabric of contemporary Syrian society. In the following section we will look at how these consequences have been mirrored at the local level in the case of the Meshrif of Hawi al-Hawa.

The political development of the Baʿth party in Syria has oscillated between what political anthropologists term 'mobilisation' and 'reconciliatory' strategies of government.[10] Confrontationist socialist moves were made against tribal shaykhs and large land owners in the Euphrates region in 1966, during the neo-Baʿth's shift towards more radical policies. The implementation of land-reform measures in the Jazira and Euphrates dispossessed or at least weakened the newly emerged class of mercantile landlords. Populist socialist policies touched the material base of cotton shaykhs and wealthy lineage heads and politically marginalised them from meaningful participation in the political process. For some shaykhly families the downfall of their position was dramatic. Former large land owners such as the Huwaydis and the Al Bu Hbal of the ʿAfadla were left with small parcels of land, while others in neighbouring areas, such as the Muhayd families of the bedouin Fidʿan in the steppes of the Jazira, were left with nothing.[11] Once, in the *madafa* of the late Shaykh Faysal al-Huwaydi, I heard Shaykh Faysal himself while playing cards with other men describe the shaykhs' condition thus: '*Bi-hal-ayyam falhit-na liʿb al-waraq*' (Nowadays, playing cards has become our cultivation, i.e. meaningless occupation).[12] Bitter statements of this kind reveal the shaykhs' realistic perception of their marginal role in society under the neo-Baʿth. It also reflects the ironical nature of the situation in which they found themselves. On the one hand wider national transformations had rendered them powerless while, on the other hand, their own perception of their shaykhly position continued to force them, as it were, to maintain the *madafa* as a politico-social institution even when it had been effectively emptied of its former role.

Events that struck at agrarian local leaders further illustrate the mobilisational politics of the neo-Baʿth during the late 1960s and their effect on the land-owning tribal shaykhs. In the Raqqa region, for example, tribal chiefs and others who were suspected of being a potential threat to the system were arrested, interrogated and on occasions jailed, including Shaykh Faysal al-Huwaydi of the larger ʿAfadla as well as Hajj Khalaf al-Meshrif of Hawi al-Hawa. As a result of such rapid and drastic changes aimed at shaykhly landlords, most if not all of the chiefs of bedouin tribes in Syria, including the Muhayd shaykhly families of the Fidʿan, who were among the largest land-

[10] Apter, 1963. [11] Khalaf, forthcoming. [12] Khalaf, 1981, p. 210.

lords in the steppes of Jazira, left the country from the late 1960s; most now live in Saudi Arabia. Many members of the shaykhly class viewed their downfall as a result of the coming of *ahl al-ittihadat* (the unionists), i.e. the Peasants' Union, Workers' Union, Women's Union, etc.

These national and regional transformations under what Hinnebusch terms the Baʿth's 'authoritarian populism' were mirrored once again at the village level.[13] After the coming of the Baʿth the village of Hawi al-Hawa went through fundamental change and socio-political polarisation. The state appropriated about two-thirds of the Meshrifs' land to be distributed later among sixty-nine village peasants, and in 1966 a peasants' co-operative was founded. Since then conflict and competition have existed within the village community. The Meshrif of the Dahir *ʿashira* were extremely dissatisfied with the appropriation and division of land by the government. At the same time, the members of the larger Dahir clan, of which the Meshrif were the single most important family and lineage, were in competition with the other non-Dahir groups in the village over the control and running of the *al-jamʿiyya* (co-operative) and the *al-naqaba* (collective). However, by virtue of their greater numbers, and most importantly, their close organisational ties with the Baʿth Party structure, the non-Dahir groups were able to take control of the affairs of the co-operative, including the elected executive council. They also gained a monopoly over the political organisation of the village peasants' collective. Similarly, there was political polarisation involving the whole community, which was mirrored in the spatial location of the two main conflicting blocs within the village. The dislocation that occurred in the fabric of village life was profound. Unlike the past, leadership in the village became fragmented, paralleling the same process in the social, political and economic structures of the village community.[14]

The peasants of Hawi al-Hawa and other villages along the Euphrates, on the other hand, gained from the reform process, and their political position as the largest class in society was given new strength. Changes occurred in the ownership of land, relations of production and political participation throughout rural Syria, all of which improved the life of the *fallahin*.[15]

Evolution of the Baʿth

Under the neo-Baʿth, the national economy came to stagnate and it proved difficult to absorb the socially and politically mobilised peasants into productive employment. The neo-Baʿth populists' methods alienated large segments of the population. The crisis was resolved by the rise of the more moderate wing within the Baʿth Party.[16]

The Asad leadership, in its quest to rebuild 'domestic unity', to preserve the

[13] Hinnebusch, 1990. [14] Khalaf, 1981. [15] Salame, 1987; Hinnebusch, 1977, 1990.
[16] Sadowski, 1978; Rabo, 1986; Hinnebusch, 1990.

party and to achieve stable development, abandoned radical mobilisation politics and the banner of social struggle that had characterised their predecessors. It opened the door to different social groups and economic sectors, as it no longer discriminated against the effective political participation of youth from rural families of the feudal/agrarian capitalists.[17] It was within this context that many of the young men of the Meshrif families, while still pursuing their education, realised the importance of joining the Ba'th Party if they were to achieve significant political careers and/or advancement through professional education. The Meshrifs' investment in the education of their youth ultimately proved to be a great asset.

Land-reform measures, state control over the production and marketing of crops, the lack of family planning and the practice of the Islamic law of inheritance all combined to reduce not only land holdings for individual Meshrif families but also their overall material well-being. However, in the light of the Ba'th shift towards more conciliatory national politics, or to borrow Hinnebusch's term, the Ba'th 'post-populist evolution',[18] the Meshrifs' early start towards giving their youth the best modern education available provided them in turn with future advantages, empowering them, as it were, to maintain for their families a privileged class position within both village and regional contexts. This fact remained true even in the face of state socialist policies carried out against landed families during the late 1960s. Education in modern societies, as Bourdieu and Boltanski argue, 'fulfils not only functions of reproducing skilled labour power (technical production) but also functions of reproducing the positions of the agents and their groups within the social structure (social reproduction)'.[19]

As late as 1991 the majority, if not all, of those from Hawi al-Hawa village who hold university degrees and have modern professional careers such as doctors, dentists, engineers, lawyers and teachers have come from the Meshrif families and/or lineage. Moreover, by the mid-1970s the leading roles of political leadership of the village and beyond it at the regional level went to the educated youth of the Meshrif. Education, as effective cultural capital in the hands of such youth, equipped them for success within a context of changing national politics and economy.

As a result of education, familiarity with urban life and membership in the ruling party in the country, the youth of the Meshrif have since the mid-1970s emerged as active, capable and articulate leaders replacing on the one hand the former traditionalist figures of Hajj Khalaf and Mukhtar Mahmud and, on the other, overshadowing the non-Meshrif members of the executive council of the peasants' co-operative, the body that had played an active though short-lived political role in the village during the late 1960s and early 1970s.

The educated *shabab* (young men) aged between twenty-five and forty-five years represent a new type of leadership. In their self-perception and in their

[17] Rabo, 1986. [18] Hinnebusch, 1990, p. 17. [19] Quoted in Harker et al., 1990, p. 103.

articulation of social and political roles they have traversed changing terrains hardly recognisable to many of their fellow villagers. In their development as local leaders, they have acquired a repertoire of experience enabling them to adjust and cope with seemingly incompatible situations and complex social and political problems.

The case of the late Husayn al-ʿAssaf al-Meshrif (the *mukhtar*'s first cousin) illustrates this new type of leader. Husayn studied the Quran in the village, went to Raqqa for his elementary and preparatory schooling, then acquired his secondary education in Aleppo. He participated there in student union activities, affiliated himself to the student ranks of the Baʿth Party, and became president of the students' union in his school. He went on to study law at Damascus University, where he became president of the students' union, confirmed his position as an active Baʿth, and established useful political ties in the capital. He then returned to Raqqa to complete his professional training as a lawyer, and became a member of the lawyers' syndicate. Later he became an attorney for the peasants' union in the Raqqa governorate, a position which his family did not expect him to occupy, as it was the peasant unionists who had only recently threatened his family, the Meshrif. In the late 1970s he was appointed as the director of a large government *mu'assasa* (establishment) for the supply of construction material in the governorate. In 1984 Husayn was elected a member of the council of local administration in the Raqqa region. He was simultaneously performing multiple roles and duties: lawyer, administrative official, *hizbi ʿamil* (active party member), family man with two children, and a member of family and tribe.

Comrade Husayn's tragic death in 1986 in a car accident at the age of thirty-nine brought a sad end to a very promising career in the Raqqa region. The large attendance at his village funeral, including the governor, top party officials, party comrades, tribal shaykhs and villagers, testified to his rising position in the region.

The case of Ustadh ʿUmar ʿAbdullah al-Meshrif (a second cousin of Husayn) also illustrates the village's emerging comrade-type of leader. ʿUmar is now in his mid-forties and works in Raqqa as a primary school education inspector. However, before his move to town he occupied an important position in village social life and in the development of its primary and preparatory schools. With limited family income derived from the rent of land inherited in the steppes, his family managed to support his secondary school education in spite of his father's early death in 1959. From 1970 to 1983 he was both a teacher and director of the village elementary and preparatory schools. He married his cousin, Husayn's sister, in 1973. He joined the party in the same year and graduated to *ʿuduw ʿamil* (active member) in 1977. He also volunteered his services as religious shaykh, when in 1978 a village mosque was built by Hajj Khalaf and his relatives, and became the *khatib* (sermon giver) of Friday prayers. In the late 1970s he participated for some years as an instructor in the summer camps which were organised along the Syrian coast for the

Baʿth political socialisation of young students. During the past two decades in his village community ʿUmar has played a number of seemingly incompatible leadership roles and activities, continually adjusting and coping with diverse demands and life pursuits.

In a similar way the case of Faris al-ʿAssaf, Husayn's younger brother, illustrates well how education provides future success and adaptation in social and political life. Through his personal influence and connections, Husayn secured for his brother Faris a government scholarship from Aleppo University to study auto-engineering in Romania. Faris himself joined the *hizb* (party) before he departed for Romania in 1976, a move which allowed him to play an active political role among the Syrian students there. Being articulate and self-confident, he eventually came to assume a leadership position in the Romanian branch of the Syrian students' national union. Faris then secured for himself a scholarship to do graduate studies in Moscow. He continued his active political role there, and in January 1990 he returned to Syria to a teaching position at Aleppo University. During his years in Moscow, Faris was able to secure scholarships or university admission for five students from the Meshrif family, including two of his brothers. These five failed to achieve admission to national universities in Syria.

The well-educated party members of the Meshrif family, such as Husayn and his cousin ʿUmar as well as others, have in their various capacities and strategies played a significant role in bringing about modern changes to their village of Hawi al-Hawa far earlier than other villages in the region. Elementary and preparatory schools, an asphalt road, electricity and a reservoir for drinking-water supplies have become conspicuous aspects of a rapidly modernising village life since the late 1970s. Husayn was instrumental in bringing the village of Hawi al-Hawa and its neighbouring village of al-Khatuniyya, both of which are close to Raqqa, under the Raqqa municipality, a move designed to secure future benefits to the village in terms of land zoning, building houses, sanitation etc. The head of the village *baladiyya* (municipal administration) is Ibrahim al-ʿAbd al-Meshrif, a first cousin of Husayn. An educated man and a party comrade, he has since the mid-1980s been emerging as one of the most vocal political figures in the village community.

As for the village peasants' co-operative, this too has undergone change in both its function and the character of its executive council. In the mid-1980s it assumed functions related to sheep-raising in addition to its services for agricultural peasants, thus expanding and diversifying its membership. The co-operative also gradually came to lose its mobilisational political role and stressed its role as an organisation to aid the peasants in farming. These functional reorientations were accompanied by political changes as well. Since the mid-1980s four of the five executive council members have been from the *ʿashira* of the Dahir, including two from the Meshrif families. Along with the evolution of Baʿth national politics towards greater reconciliation and accommodation, the village community at large came to witness a gradual erosion of the political tension it had experienced during the late 1960s and early 1970s. This was mainly due to the fact that the Meshrif, as the former dominant elite, have come to adapt to the Baʿth political-economic order over the last three decades, and to succeed in maintaining a relatively privileged position in local society, not least as many of their own educated professional men have entered this system as active participants and leaders.

Conclusion

This account suggests a number of general observations concerning political and economic change in rural north Syria. First, rural elite families have been able to survive and maintain a relatively privileged position in their societies. The account given here of the Meshrif represents a good case in point. This reflects the fact that Baʿth rule over the past three decades has aimed at implementing certain levelling reforms, not at producing radical structural transformation in society.[20] Numerous studies conducted over the past two decades on the topics of stratification, rural elites and leadership offer parallels to this generalisation.[21] For example, Leveau in his article on the rural elite in Morocco informs us that political and economic privilege has often remained with the same extended families despite great historical changes occurring over the last century.[22]

Second, land reform and the establishment of state co-operative socialist institutions did limit the control previously exercised by landlords, agricultural operators and merchants. These same measures aided the Baʿth in the expansion and consolidation of its power base as it won peasants to the party, and replaced the former structure of peasants' dependence on landlords with one of dependence on multiple Baʿth-controlled state organisations. As also noted by Hinnebusch, the consequence of Baʿth rule on both land-owning shaykhs and peasants has, from the viewpoint of the village, created a more open social structure.[23]

Third, the establishment of peasant co-operatives and populist political institutions has not only intensified the integration of village and state at multiple levels but also generated political conflicts within village life.

Finally, the evolution of Baʿth politics at the national level led to the party adopting less populist and less radical means to maintain itself. This enabled educated members of families such as the Meshrif to rise to prominence as local party comrades, in a position to offer access to government and to bring benefits to their families and village communities. The regime uses these men

[20] Hinnebusch, 1990. [21] See the studies referred to in note 2. [22] Leveau, 1977.
[23] Hinnebusch, 1990.

to extend modern services to the village, thus supporting their local influence, while at the same time reinforcing support for the regime among the rural communities. Consequently, the process of 'village urbanisation'[24] has come to be associated with the Baʿth as well as with the mediating roles performed by these local party comrades.

[24] Khalaf, 1981.

11

Managing risk: sheep-rearing and agriculture in the Syrian steppe

FRANÇOISE MÉTRAL

Centre National de la Recherche Scientifique, Lyons

Between 1982 and 1989 we witnessed, in the very heart of the Syrian steppe and well beyond the theoretical threshold limiting rain-fed cultivation to areas over the 200 mm isohyet, a large-scale expansion of barley cultivation. This expansion occurred in a region where annual rainfall averages between 90 and 120 mm, but may range locally or interannually from as little as 14 to as much as 234 mm.

This increase in barley cultivation, encroaching upon grazing lands, is both the result of and concomitant with an intensification of sheep-rearing and an increase in flock sizes. Encouraged by a growing market, this development took place in spite of the pastureland conservation programmes adopted by the Syrian government and sponsored by international organisations. The phenomenon is particularly evident in the north of the Palmyrena. We shall try to demonstrate the progress and mechanisms of this expansion by analysing the economic ventures of the residents of Sukhna, a small urban centre where we did fieldwork between 1985 and 1989.[1]

Bringing into play a variety of actors and mobilising a complex network of relations, these ventures focus our attention on pre-existing economic complementarities: those found in the steppe itself, between settled town dwellers and pastoral tribes or bedouin; those inside Syria between the Palmyrena steppe and the rich agricultural areas of the centre or the Jazira; and those that reach beyond the borders of Syria to commercial links with the Gulf countries. These same ventures bring into question the economic logic and form of risk management underlying investment in dry farming in a region where all cultivation is inherently hazardous.

[1] J. Hannoyer, J. Métral and I visited the oasis for the first time in February 1982 soon after the opening of the desert route and decided to study it because of the existing study by Boucheman, *Une petite cité caravanière: Suhné*, 1937.

In April 1985, with M. Naciri, we made a preparatory trip of several days to obtain the required authorisations. The study itself was carried out, with financial help from the MRT, IFEAD in Damascus, and the CNRS, during three fieldtrips of one month each, in November 1986, April 1988 and April–May 1989, by J. Hannoyer, J. Métral and myself with the occasional participation of B. Geyer (biogeographer) and M. Traboulsi (climatologist). We would like here to thank the Ministries of Culture and Agriculture in Syria, the Finance Administration and Antiquities Department in Palmyra for their help and understanding, as well as all the Sukhnites who generously extended their hospitality to us and patiently supported our curiosity.

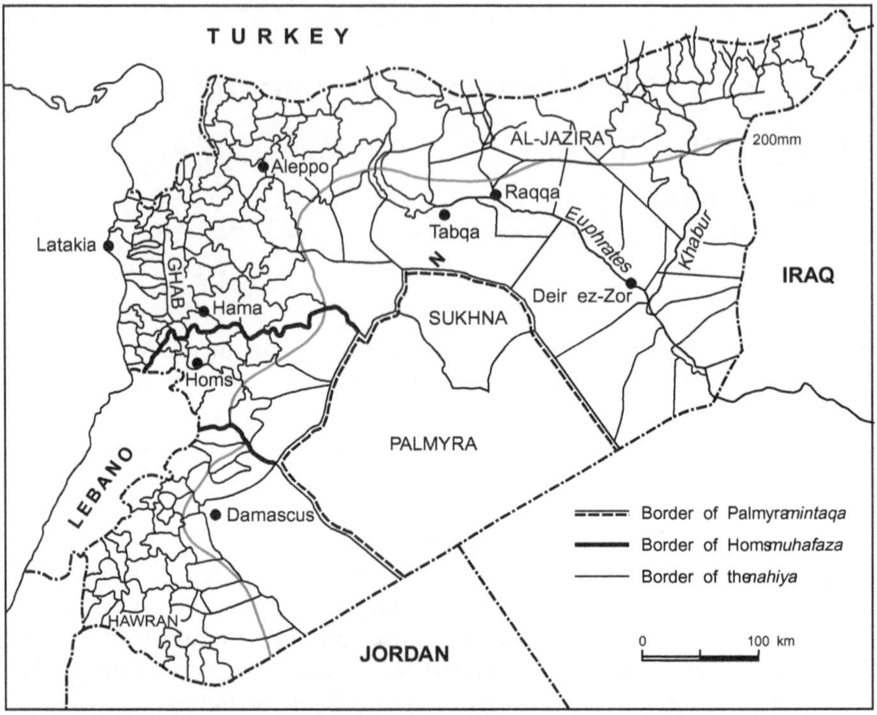

Map 11.1: The administrative divisions of the steppe in Syria

The Palmyrena steppe: townsmen and tribesmen

Since 1960 Sukhna has been the centre of a *nahiya* consisting of the northern sector of the Palmyrena, located on the eastern border of Homs *muhafaza* (See maps 11.1 and 11.2). The small trading centre, nestled at the base of a mountainous range, is at the crossroads of desert routes linking Aleppo to Baghdad, Hama to Mosul, and Damascus to the Euphrates. Today an obligatory point of passage, it was previously a place of rest and supply for caravans, notably for the great annual pilgrimage to Mecca.[2]

Badiyat Sukhna, the steppeland surrounding the city,[3] is made up of two distinct zones separated by a mountainous barrier. To the west is the *shambul*, a mountainous area intersected by depressions, with higher rainfall and more groundwater reserves than the zone to the east: the *hamad*, a plateau without water resources, which was previously the exclusive domain of camel-rearing tribes. The *hamad* turns green in autumn and spring when there is rainfall and

[2] Damascus replaced it in this function from 1870 onwards.

[3] In keeping with the tradition of writing on the caravan city (Rostovtzeff, Boucheman, Grabar, Cole and Altorki) the author has retained the term 'city' to describe the town of Sukhna so as to highlight the urban character of its society [editor's note].

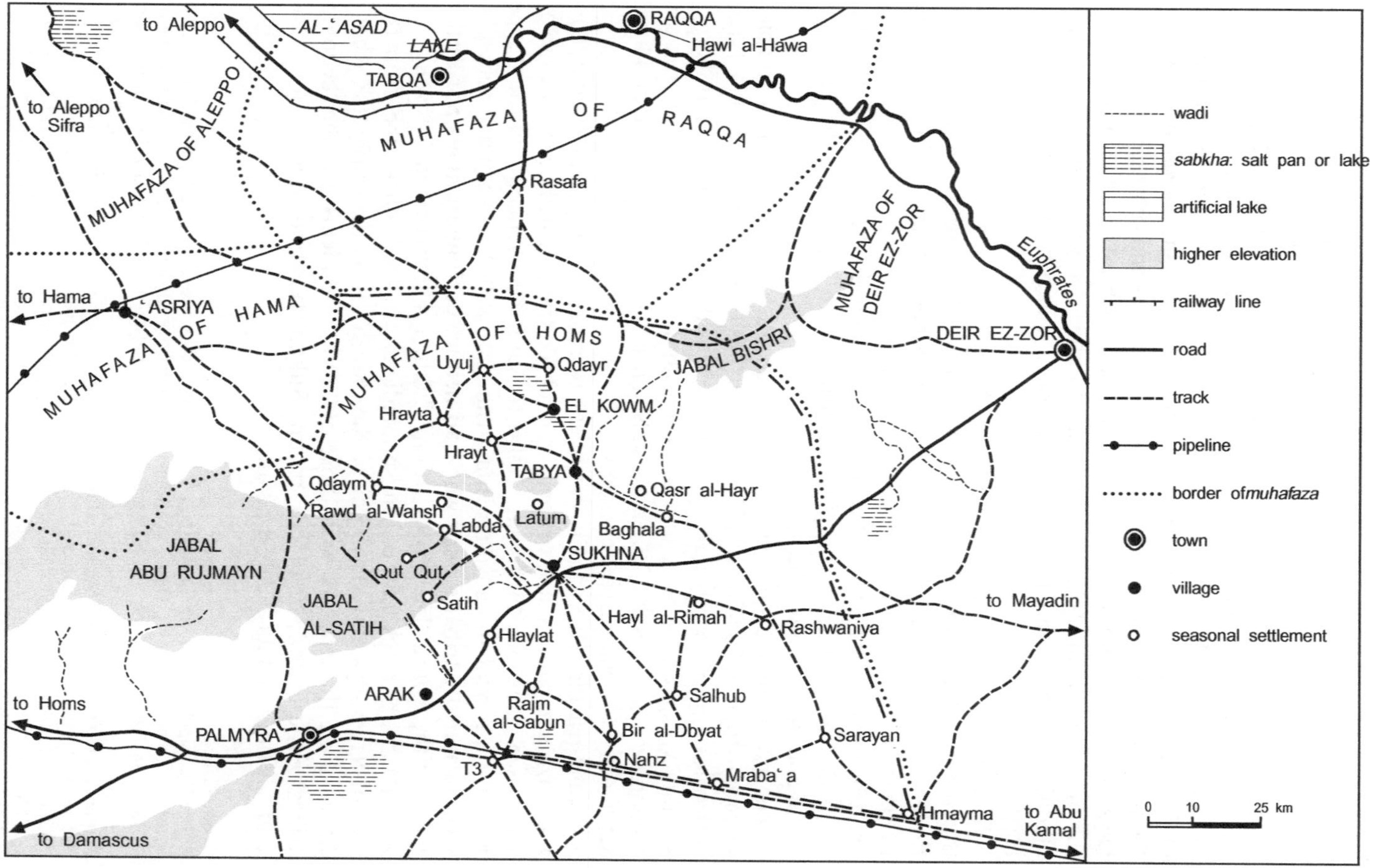

Map 11.2: The region of Sukhna in relation to the Euphrates

the mountainous zone offers pasturelands for camels until summer, making Sukhna the centre of an area of rich natural pasturelands.

Two nomadic migration routes corresponding to two different types of tribe traditionally met here. The first was that of sheep-rearing tribes known as *raʿi* or 'shepherds' or *ʿArab* or *ahl al dira*[4] who grazed their animals over distances of 300 km between west and east up to the borders of the *hamad*, between the Palmyrena and the agricultural plains of the Ghab and central Syria, nowadays irrigated. These tribes included the ʿUmur, whose home territory lies in the mountain Jabal al-Satih overlooking Sukhna, as well as the Mawali and Hadidiyin tribes, who have their sedentary villages and cultivated lands further to the west.

The second migration route was that of the great camel-rearing tribes, the Shammar and the large ʿAnayza confederation, who ranged over distances of three to four thousand km, from the Arabian Peninsula through the Palmyrena and from there to the Jazira. Among these, two branches of the great bedouin tribe Sbaʾa had their summer camps in the *badiya* of Sukhna. Their *dira* or 'grazing territory' was contiguous to that of the Rwala to the south and the Fidʿan to the north.[5]

The population of the *nahiya* of Sukhna, which (according to official records) stood at 20,000 in 1983, 26,000 in 1987, and nearly 30,000 in 1989, comprises approximately half of the settled residents of Sukhna and its two satellite villages El Kowm and al-Tayba, and another half 'tribesmen' or 'bedouin'[6] (ʿUmur, Sbaʾa Btaynat and Sbaʾa Abada) who own land and have settlements (or villages) in the *nahiya*.

Camel-rearing has virtually disappeared, replaced by sheep-herding, and the grazing territories have to some extent been transformed due to the use of motorised transport. Customary rights to water wells remain[7] but the steppe is now open to all and governmental drilling of wells has facilitated access to pasturelands by tribal groups who had neither customary rights nor settlements in the *nahiya*. The *badiya* around Sukhna is now covered, in spring and autumn, by the black tents of semi-nomadic or semi-sedentary tribes from the *dira* of Salamiyya and Manbij or of the *shawaya* from the Euphrates, whose flocks share the territory with those of Sukhna residents and the 'bedouin tribes' of the *nahiya*. For all these groups, Sukhna functions as a trading centre and has thus seen its clientele expand.

[4] Boucheman, 1934.

[5] The IPC pipeline marking the southern limit of the *nahiya* also divided it from the Rwala territory attached to Palmyra. The Fidʿan have their territory further north inside the borders of Raqqa *muhafaza*. By virtue of an agreement made between the ʿAnayza tribes through the mediation of the government, the present administrative divisions coincide with – and are intended to fix permanently – the traditional grazing territories (summer camps) of these tribes.

[6] The two terms are still registered separately in the civil register concerning 'bedouin tribes'.

[7] Out of 114 privately owned wells (for agricultural or pastoral use) registered with the *nahiya* authorities responsible for the steppe region, 51 belong to the Sbaʾa, 5 to the ʿUmur, 58 to townsmen (38 to residents of El Kowm, 12 to those of Sukhna and 6 to al-Tayba residents). The flow capacity of these, mostly artesian, wells varies from 4 to 30 cubic metres per hour. There are also 17 government-owned wells in the *badiya* of Homs *muhafaza*.

The Sukhnites were linked to these different tribes through a multitude of hierarchical economic ties. They paid the *khuwwa* (levy) on their grain harvest to the Sba'a who in return protected their trade. They consigned their flocks to the ʿUmur or Hadidiyin. To all these tribes they supplied grain, cloth, clothing and various household items and foodstuffs, buying from them their pastoral products for resale in the big cities.

Lifestyles change but identities remain. For a Sukhnite, a bedouin, even if his family spends three-quarters of the year in town, is still a bedouin, member of such-and-such a tribe. The same is true for tribesmen. Intermarriage between city and tribe is non-existent. Indeed, even neighbourly relations are absent as the bedouin do not settle permanently in Sukhna. Nevertheless, relations of complementarity and exchange are maintained between the various groups, as will be seen in our analysis of the recent developments of Sukhnite activities.

In the present as in the past, traders first

The people of Sukhna are above all traders, specialised in the purchase, sale, brokerage and transport of everything produced, consumed and handled in the steppe. For everything linked to sheep-rearing and the bedouins' everyday needs, they have for generations acted as intermediaries between the tribes and the towns within the periphery of the *badiya*.[8]

As traders they occupy a whole range of functions. These can be broken down into four categories: (1) *pedlars or itinerant traders* (or craftsmen) who follow a tribe from the Palmyrena to the Jazira, pitching their white tents near the well of the tribal chief who offers them protection. This mobile trade is usually undertaken by young men, whose time spent with the tribe is viewed as a form of apprenticeship. (2) *Semi-wholesale trade* carried out by shopkeepers in the main *suq* of Sukhna, who supply the itinerant traders and bedouin who come into town in the spring and autumn to buy stocks. According to the season, these semi-wholesalers collect truffles, *samna* (clarified butter), or wool, or store barley, wheat and fodder (or, dealing with new needs, they equip and repair trucks and tractors, sell water from their pumps etc.). (3) *Khanji*s (wholesalers) are Sukhnites settled in Aleppo or Hama, who act in relay with local traders, reselling their purchases from the bedouin or supplying goods to the traders. (4) Finally, there are the powerful *long-distance merchants* who import and export sheep between Turkey, Syria and the Gulf or, formerly, Iraq.

After a long slump due to the demise of the caravan trade,[9] which extended into the mid-1960s and led to waves of migration first towards Aleppo and then Raqqa, Sukhna's trade today has recovered some degree of prosperity.

[8] The very term Sukhnite (Sukhni in Arabic), as elsewhere that of Qubaysi or Rahjbawi (Musil, 1928b, p. 25; Boucheman, 1934, p. 11), has become synonymous with this function among the bedouin.

[9] It began its decline at the end of the nineteenth century and was so moribund that in 1939 A. de Boucheman envisaged the demise of the oasis town itself.

New public works and development of the Euphrates region, followed by job opportunities in the Gulf, helped bring about an economic revival in Sukhna. The construction of the trans-desert road linking Damascus to Deir ez-Zor completed in 1982, ended the town's isolation, and the intensification of commercial ties between Syria, Saudi Arabia and Kuwait opened up opportunities that Sukhnites were quick to seize. They bought trucks suitable for international transport and developed their role as forwarding agents and overland carriers, which they had traditionally occupied when Sukhna was a caravan city.[10] Following their forebears, the great camel and caravan traders of yore, they took again to the steppe routes, transporting goods between Aleppo, Hama, Mosul, Baghdad, Lower Iraq[11] and Kuwait or else the Hijaz and other parts of Arabia. Their knowledge of steppe tracks and their long-standing commercial ties with the bedouin allowed them, if necessary, to ignore international borders.

A few facts concerning population figures and trade expansion illustrate Sukhna's change of fortune. Until 1960, the population did not exceed 2,500 inhabitants, the same as in 1933 when Boucheman carried out his study. It then jumped rapidly: 3,550 in 1970, 6,000 in 1981, and exploded during the 1980s: 12,000 in 1985, 15,000 in 1989.

The number of licensed shops in the *suq* rose from 50 in 1978 (Boucheman counted 40) to 106 in 1982 and 161 in 1986. These figures include neither itinerant traders and craftsmen in the steppe, nor all the stores that occasionally function with semi-wholesalers, nor brokers. To these must be added about thirty workshops, three petrol stations and nearly two hundred truck drivers and persons working in transport.

Trade has diversified in accordance with needs arising from an improvement in living standards and motorised transport, but it still largely depends on the presence of tribes and on the activities and production of the steppe. Trade is marked by a pronounced seasonal rhythm and significant annual variations linked to climatic conditions. Bedouin make up over 80 per cent of the clientele of traders and craftsmen of Sukhna's *suq*. The *suq* comes to life when pasturelands turn green; commercial turnover may then grow tenfold. Business falls when the grass dries up and the flocks move off. Then Sukhna traders send their young sons and nephews to follow the tribes and their flocks in their seasonal migrations. De Boucheman described the Sukhnite as sticking to the bedouin, following him to the Jazira in summer or during dry years, and in winter to the Gulf countries or other parts of Arabia.

Today: diversified investment

The specialisation of Sukhna residents in trade, like that of the bedouin in pastoralism, is by no means exclusive of other means of livelihood. In an

[10] The relative wealth of the city formerly depended on the number of camels owned by the city dwellers (de Boucheman, 1939).
[11] Until borders between Syria and Iraq were closed.

environment governed by uncertainty, diversification is necessarily the rule. In addition to oasis gardens, dry farming of barley and wheat in the steppelands and sheep-rearing have always provided Sukhnites with the extra income essential here for the livelihood of a lineage group. These two auxiliary activities, it will be seen, are also carried out in co-operation with bedouin tribes (access to cultivable land being negotiated through the Sba'a, while the 'Umur and Hadidiyin act as shepherds for Sukhna's flocks).

Investment by Sukhna townsmen in these two sectors has grown considerably over the past fifteen years. This is both a sign of the town's gradual enrichment and an important source of it. In Sukhna alone the number of head of sheep – based on taxes paid and quantities of fodder delivered – has grown tenfold over the past fifteen years. From 7,000 in 1970, it went to 35,000 in 1980 and reached 75,000 in 1985.

Since 1985, investment has been more heavily concentrated in cultivation of the steppe. The change of scale in this activity is readily reflected in everyday language: 'In the old days of plough farming, families sowed one or two *tanaka*s (1 *tanaka* = 20 litres). Nowadays farmers sow hundreds of bags' (1 seed bag =100 kilograms). Statistical data provided by the authorities – covering only what has been declared to them and therefore giving a highly incomplete picture of real production levels – clearly show this tendency. Deliveries of barley to the Grain Administration, interrupted during dry years, have increased considerably:

5,000 metric tons	in 1980–1[12]
8,000	in 1982
zero	in 1983–4 (drought)
10,000	in 1985
30,000	in 1986
zero	in 1987 (drought)
52,000	in 1988
zero	in 1989

In 1985–6, land sown illegally in the *nahiya*, according to ministry estimates, was between 25,000 and 40,000 hectares. In 1987–8, nearly 50,000 hectares were sown. In the autumn of 1988, the Ministry of Agriculture plan provided for 40,000 hectares to be sown in the administrative region of Palmyra, but permits were finally given covering 80,000 hectares, of which 70 per cent were cultivated by Sukhnites. The activity of the Sukhnites went far beyond the limits of the *nahiya*, extending over an area with a radius of 100 kilometres from Sukhna.

The sheer scale of this phenomenon is impressive in a region where the rigours and irregularity of the climate make cultivation extremely risky, even if the rule for steppe cultivation is no longer, as we were told by officials, one good year out of ten, but rather three in ten. What process, which mechanisms

[12] In 1948, the Bread Grains Administration estimated Sukhna's production as 268 metric tons of wheat and 164 tons of barley (Naaman, 1955, p. 327).

were put to work by regional actors to achieve such a boom in agriculture and sheep-raising?

Development of barley cultivation

The oasis of Sukhna, as opposed to that of Palmyra, has very little irrigable land (120 hectares versus 1,000 hectares). Its soil, lacking Palmyra's alluvial input, is also much less fertile. The oasis today is virtually in a state of abandonment, its springs having partially dried up as a result of pumping for domestic use.

Sukhnites on the other hand do have at their disposal a steppeland more suitable for dry farming than that around Palmyra. Grain production in Sukhna was already much higher in 1948, according to estimates by the Bread Grain Administration, than was that of its neighbours in the southern zone of the Palmyrena.[13] Grain was sown over a radius of 10 kilometres around the oasis, but unevenly: at the bottom of small valleys or wadis, at the end of *sail*s or streams formed during the rainy seasons, and at the foot of the mountains. There the surface run-off water and alluvial soil made up for low rainfall levels, assuring abundant yields in good years (rainfall exceeding 150 mm),[14] but with great variations in production according to the locale. In bad years, with little rainfall in autumn, no seeds were sown; if rainfall was insufficient in winter or spring, sheep were turned onto the fields. The good plots for planting, well known to all, were shared among the town's family groups. The bedouin respected these areas, being satisfied in the past with collecting *khuwwa* on the threshing-grounds at harvest time. When this privilege was taken away from them, they contracted farmers to cultivate the lands around their wells and summer camps. In like manner they also frequently appropriated for themselves the land around wells dug by the government on their traditional grazing territories. The changeover from pulley to motor pump in the 1950s allowed them to increase substantially the areas they cultivated.

Land tenure and conditions of access: state law versus customary law

In 1948, when the French left, only land in the oasis of Palmyra had been registered by the cadastre. With two exceptions, one granting exploitation rights

[13] Naaman, 1955, p. 377.

[14] According to Naaman, in certain sites, yields from these virgin steppelands – *bur* in Arabic – were much higher than from the depleted soils of central Syria's agricultural plains (the Bread Grains Administration figures for 1948 confirm this finding): yields on *bur* land reached 20 to 25, sometimes even 30 per unit sown whereas in the western plains they could be as low as 3 or 4 per unit sown. In certain areas in the steppe – exceptionally every 10 or 20 years – yields reached the fabulous figure of 60 or even 100 per unit.

These figures appear to be part of the myth about the past and the unpredictability of steppe conditions. We heard them retold by present-day Sukhnites and they were confirmed by the Department of Agriculture in Palmyra.

(*tasarruf*) to a shaykh of the Sba'a tribe at Qdaym as a reward for his political loyalty, and the other concerning lands under irrigation around El Kowm, none of the steppeland had been officially registered as private land because cultivation there was too intermittent. Exploitation was therefore governed by customary law. This means in effect that the land belonged to those who 'grabbed' it and were able to have their rights to it recognised by others – and to those who could prevent sheep from entering the cultivated fields. To sum up, apart from the land bordering on the oases of Sukhna, El Kowm and al-Tayba, the bedouin ('Umur in the mountains and Sba'a everywhere else) considered themselves to be owners of all the lands in their *dira* and would allow no one outside their tribe to build, cultivate or settle in it without their consent. According to the Syrian constitution, however, *matruka* or *mawat* lands, such as pasturelands, fell into the category of state domain lands, and the government alone was entitled to rent or sell them.

The Agrarian Reform, the suppression of bedouin customary law in 1958, and finally the measures taken against the shaykhs of 'feudal' tribes in 1965 upset the customary situation for a number of years and led to the massive departure of the Sba'a to the Gulf states which offered them citizenship (Kuwait and Saudi Arabia). In their absence, some enterprising Sukhnites began to cultivate these 'freed' lands. With the greater flexibility of the Ba'thist regime after 1970, and especially after 1973, the bedouin returned and started negotiations at the highest state level to have their rights officially recognised. In the meantime, they took over control of the land, imposing a *de facto* recognition of their customary rights on the Sukhnites, who were glad to recover their clients and eager to remain on good terms with them.

At the same time, the government began to implement a policy of pastureland conservation.[15] In May 1970, a decree was passed outlawing ploughing in dry-farming zones where annual rainfall was less than 200 mm. The totality of the steppeland in the *nahiya* of Sukhna fell, in theory, under the domain of this law. For ten years, however, this law was in effect not applied. The local authorities, apparently recognising that it did not apply to wadi lands, shut their eyes to infringements, limiting themselves, with a notable lack of zeal, to surveillance of the interior of the steppe only. In conjunction with its conservation programme, the government sold forty parcels of land in the steppe, each covering 10 to 100 hectares. Each parcel was linked to a specific agricultural project and had its own drilled artesian well.[16]

A succession of three rainy years in 1979–81, a rise in barley (and wheat) prices, growing demand for fodder and, finally, the opening of the desert road facilitating access to the steppe for agricultural machinery – all these factors encouraged investment in dry farming. Eager to cultivate in the steppe,

[15] See the chapter by Ronald Jaubert in this volume (chap. 9).

[16] Thirty-four of these parcels, with an area of 10 to 20 hectares, are located around El Kowm and 7 per cent of their surface is devoted to tomato cultivation, which has become a specialty of that village.

Sukhnites went into partnership with bedouin shaykhs to obtain access to the land; they also came to 'informal' agreements with inspectors from the Ministry of Agriculture.

Faced with the scale of this phenomenon, the government reacted, first timidly in 1983 and then firmly in 1986, seizing the harvest of the most blatant offenders against the law.[17] The following autumn, strict directives were given and all ploughing was punishable by imprisonment, including that on privately owned land. The 1970 law was suddenly applied to the letter and no exceptions were permitted.

The Sukhnites and bedouin shaykhs then sought out the authorities to come to terms. Their efforts lasted more than a year and reached the state summit. They based their claims on two types of argument. First a technical one: it is right to protect pasturelands but outlawing cultivation should not apply to the whole region; wadi lands can be cultivated without any soil erosion and have been cultivated from time immemorial. Their second argument was a legal one: inasmuch as the law recognises rights once granted, a separate law cannot be applied to the steppe alone, since the law applies equally to all Syrian citizens. And land bordering villages in the steppe has always been cultivated.

In November 1987, an amendment to the 1970 law granted residents of built-up areas of the steppe the right, after payment of a tax, to cultivate within a limited radius around the settled areas, and rights could be granted even beyond the settled area to those who could prove they had cultivated these particular areas before 1963. With the door partially open through this law, it now became possible for farmers and investors to do almost anything, and this time (mostly) under cover of the law. Not only did they no longer risk being fined, but their registered plots gave them the right to seeds supplied by the Grain Administration at prices generally lower than those on the 'open' market.

In 1987–8, in spite of late ploughing which continued up to January, 55,000 hectares were cultivated in the *nahiya*.[18] It proved an exceptionally good year (234 mm of rain) and the results led to a veritable grain rush in the town. In the autumn of 1988, the state rented out 80,000 hectares, at 100 SL (Syrian lira) per hectare, throughout the whole *mintaqa* of Palmyra. Two-thirds of these were in the *nahiya* of Sukhna. As for the rights, 60 per cent went to the bedouin and 40 per cent to residents of Sukhna.

Until recently, the bedouin did not themselves cultivate the land. They contracted with a farmer, ceding him the land for a single season in exchange for a fixed percentage of the crop. Throughout the *nahiya* of Sukhna and even in the larger *mintaqa* of Palmyra, the farmers have usually been residents of

[17] 1986 was a good year for eastern and northern Syria but other areas faced drought. In Sukhna itself only half the lands had rainfall.

[18] Information supplied by the Ministry of Agriculture, Palmyra.

Sukhna, traders and townsmen. The radius of activity of Sukhnites now extends over more than 100 kilometres.

From cultivator to manager

How did such rapid development – in some respects comparable to that on the Euphrates in the 1950s – occur? How did residents of Sukhna manage to bring together the necessary means of production? Our answers to these questions are based partly on our own observations in November 1986, but for the most part on a comparison between 1988, an exceptionally rainy year, and 1989, a drought year.

The Sukhna cultivator often has neither land (or at most a share in a family plot of 45 hectares, the maximum allowed since the Agrarian Reform) nor agricultural machinery, aside from a pick-up truck for his own transportation. Usually he has some kind of business or various other seasonal occupations, since agriculture takes up only two months of the year (a month for ploughing and another at harvest time, when he pitches his tent near his fields). The area cultivated depends on the capital he has at his disposal and may thus double from one year to the next. In 1988, average surfaces cultivated ranged from 300 to 600 hectares and in 1989 from 600 to 1,200 hectares. The size of the 'enterprise' is expressed in the number of bags of seed: 'In 1987, I sowed 400 bags'; 'This year I sowed 800: 300 here at A's of the Sba'as at 35 per cent, 200 at B's at 20 per cent, 100 with the Rwalas in Tyas at 40 per cent . . .'

Barley makes up virtually the totality of the cultivated crop, since families plant only enough wheat for domestic consumption. No fertiliser is used except for the manure left after grazing on the stubble, and fields are rarely left fallow, especially in the depressions.

The Sukhna cultivator has a role similar to that of a promoter or manager. An entrepreneur in agriculture rather than a farmer, his tasks each season are to find the land, raise financing, purchase seeds, see that the work is done, organise transportation and sell the crop. For each of these tasks he deals with different partners. Given the competition in all these fields, whatever relations he or members of his family may have established in the course of their business activities will be of precious importance.

One of the most delicate parts of his task is to obtain good plots from landholders. Usually a Sukhnite entrepreneur enters into partnership with a tribal leader of the Sba'a who can speak for members of the sub-section of his tribe (whether present in Syria or not) whom he has had registered as landholders at the regional finance office in Palmyra. (A tribal leader may thus have at his disposal fifteen to thirty cultivation permits, each covering 45 hectares.) Depending on the number of seed bags he plans to sow, an entrepreneur enters into partnership with one, two or even three shaykhs. With no expense other than the payment of a rental tax, a landholder receives 20 to 40 per cent of the harvest – usually 30 to 35 per cent in the valleys (and just 10 per cent on land where ploughing is illegal and therefore more expensive) – and he is also entitled to stubble left in the fields.[19]

The entrepreneur is first and foremost an investor: his personal contribution may make up 40 to 50 per cent of the total capital. He may also invest the money of partners who share expenses and profits according to the proportion of capital contributed. Partners are usually family members, from the same or allied lineages, or even clients or friends who want to invest their capital. For example, Kamal puts up 50 per cent, his two brothers are partners for a further 25 per cent, and two other Sukhnites provide the remaining 25 per cent.

Often the contribution of each partner will be the result of shared capital inside one household. Young men back from a few months' work in the Gulf may put their savings to work while waiting for a longer-term project of their own. Women and even young girls may sell their gold jewellery to help increase the capital and thus the share of profits due to the head of the family, without it being known outside the family circle.

In 1988, we often heard it said: 'My brothers and I invested 100,000 SL in agriculture', giving the impression that agriculture was a strictly male affair. But in the women's quarter we heard another story: 'My mother and I, or my sister-in-law and I invested 15,000 or 25,000 pounds', with the specific aim of buying a sewing machine or a washing machine or gold from the profits. This made it easier to understand how families of apparently modest means were able to bring together very considerable amounts of money.

Seeds are purchased from the state-owned Agricultural Bank which distributes them according to a quota based on cultivation permits. The entrepreneur must nearly always supplement these purchases by buying a fourth or fifth of his seed bags on the 'open' market, at a much higher price (in 1988 a 100-kilogram barley seed bag was sold by the Grain Administration at 280 SL; the same bag on the open market went for 475 SL). The seed bags are delivered to Sukhna and the entrepreneur then contracts a (Sukhnite) transporter to truck them to the fields.

Although cultivation is completely mechanised, few Sukhnites own any agricultural machinery. They usually deal with farm machine contractors in the Jazira who do the sowing and ploughing, using tractors equipped with twenty-four to thirty-two rotary disks and a mechanical sower. When there is a real rush – as in December 1987 when ploughing started just after the decree amendment was passed – machinery is brought in from as far away as Turkey. Payment for ploughing is based on the surface sown (or the number of seed bags sown). Harvesting is again done by contractors from the Jazira or Ghab regions, depending on personal relations or availability of machinery, since

[19] The consequent returns for the bedouin are on the whole no less advantageous than what they formerly gained from the traditional *khuwwa* levied on farmers.

owners of farm machinery take advantage of the staggering of harvest seasons to move from one region to another. They arrive accompanied by a mechanic and a labourer, leave the harvest crops in sewn sacks at the edge of the fields and take 12 to 15 per cent of the harvest.

Farm machinery follows the same route but in the opposite direction to the flocks of sheep and the Sukhna traders who move in the wake of tribes. The two networks meet over the same territory. Trade, animal husbandry and, today, agriculture have woven a dense pattern over the seasons and years, linking the different groups in the Sukhna steppeland with the farmers and contractors of the two major agricultural zones. It is also to the Jazira that Sukhna traders go to buy straw (*tibin*) and winter feed for their flocks. This is because in the Palmyrena, contrary to the Jazira, crops are reaped high on the stalk, leaving the stubble for grazing.

After harvesting, the Sukhna entrepreneur again hires a truck and extra worker to load his crop and bring it into town. The government, supplier of the grain storage sacks, organises a collection centre in the town at harvest time and handles the transportation and storage of the crops at state-owned silos. Sukhna truck drivers, who by this time have finished moving the sheep flocks to their summer quarters in the Jazira or Ghab, will be busy for a good part of the summer bringing in the grain harvest. Often they cannot handle all the work: in 1988, the state was obliged to requisition trucks passing on the highways.

Calculating the risks

In good years entrepreneurs are insured against distress sales and the collapse of grain prices because the Grain Administration, to whom every producer must deliver his harvest (minus 20 to 30 per cent allowed for private consumption), buys up the entire crop at prices fixed at the beginning of the season.[20] Producers are paid in cash on delivery. Comparison with the 1950s is still present in people's minds. We were often told that if, in 1988, the state had not bought up the entire crop, barley would have been thrown into the ditches, 'like the wheat was in 1956'. If the harvest has been meagre and the state-fixed price appears too low, producers manage to avoid delivering their crops to the Grain Administration and sell it instead on the 'open' market or even abroad, where prices are not fixed.

In years when a rainy autumn is followed by a dry spring, as in 1989, the fields are not harvested. The unripe grain fields are rented out for grazing to Hadidiyin sheep-owners; the rent they pay covers expenses disbursed and may even allow a small profit. (The owner of the land also recovers the new growth.) But for those who have sown outside the valleys, barley cultivation can mean economic ruin. Nothing will come out of the soil and the topsoil

[20] Barley and wheat prices rose significantly in the 1980s.

itself will blow away with the first breeze; if drought persists over several seasons the land will be useless for both farming and grazing.

The risk for producers is then real indeed. It is known to all, but to evaluate it, other economic factors apart from climatic conditions must be taken into account, the most important being the needs of livestock. We shall return to this later. Suffice it to say that the risk is not now so great as to discourage interest in landholdings. The 1987 decree authorising cultivation on the basis of former agricultural production before the year 1963 gave a new impetus to the problem of land tenure. The possibility of acquiring rights registered with the authorities has made land an important asset and created tensions between Sukhnites and the bedouin. These tensions are all the graver because Sukhna townsmen are now conscious of the vulnerability of their own situation. On the one hand, bedouin shaykhs have taken advantage of the competition between entrepreneurs to ask for ever larger shares of the harvest, ignoring the limit fixed by the Agrarian Reform. On the other hand, some bedouin have in recent years started cultivating themselves or contracting others to cultivate for them, bypassing Sukhnite intermediaries altogether. The question is now in the hands of the state, which has become an uncircumventable referee.

Intensification of sheep-rearing

The boom in barley cultivation is closely tied to the increase of sheep production and the transformations it has brought to the region.[21] After the sheer drop in the number of sheep following the years of drought from 1958 to 1961 and again with the departure of the major pastoral tribes to the Gulf in 1965–6, sheep production improved at a slow pace. Sukhnites ventured into it, investing the capital of their wealthier relatives in Raqqa or of traders in Aleppo. In 1970, 'the year of snow', the steep rise in mutton prices encouraged investment. Within a very few years Sukhnite sheepmen were able to build up sufficient capital to make them independent of the urban traders of Raqqa and Aleppo.

Diversification in the forms of sheep-rearing

The traditional contract between sedentary populations and the sheep-herding tribes, 'Umur or Hadidiyin, to whom they consign their sheep, the 'bone' contract (50/50), is still used, but another practice has emerged alongside this, whereby townsmen manage their own flocks with the help of salaried shepherds recruited from these same tribes. The sedentary sheep-owners,

[21] This phenomenon is a general one: it has been analysed by Bonte (1987) in Mauritania at the other extreme of the Arab world.

possessing their own means of transport (pick-up trucks), no longer hesitate to set up tents in the steppe during migration periods, bringing along whatever family members are needed for the work at hand. In the spring, they camp in the *hamad*, commuting back and forth to Sukhna or the nearest well to bring water for their sheep. In May and June, when local grazing lands are exhausted, they arrange transport for the flocks by truck to the Jazira, Ghab or Hawran, where they rent pasture for the whole summer. If the sale of lambs does not cover their expenses, they sell off a few ewes.[22] In autumn they return to the Palmyrena when the steppe turns green again after the first rains and once more provides grazing. In winter the flocks are kept in the *hamad* to the south-east of Sukhna, close to a well and an enclosure built by the sheep-rearer where he relies on fodder and supplementary feedstuff to see them through until spring.[23]

As in the case of barley cultivation, sheep-rearing also involves multiple and various forms of partnership. These start from what can best be called a 'family sheep-breeders' company', made up of a small core of closely related professional breeders who share the tasks of managing the flocks. These breeders draw on capital provided by those in their enlarged family who may want to invest in the business without directly participating in management of the flocks. Whatever the type of management chosen, technical tasks such as tending the flock and health care are entrusted to the 'Umur or Hadidiyin who are experienced at this work and accept the status of 'shepherds'. The owners take charge of all commercial matters as well as the transportation of water and fodder. The formation of a flock now necessarily entails purchasing a tractor, pick-up or truck.

Sukhnite sheep-owners no longer confine themselves to open-range sheep-rearing based on herds of ewes. Since 1970 they have begun, like the urban traders of Hama and Aleppo for whom they long worked (and who often were originally from Sukhna themselves), to go into commercial sheep-raising, that is the fattening of male lambs for early marketing. Many homes in Sukhna now contain sheep enclosures built especially for this purpose in their vast courtyards. And there are recently constructed *khans* for the fattening of lambs on the main road on the outskirts of the city.

The revival of sheep-rearing began early in the Palmyrena (compared to other parts of Syria) and was accompanied by the creation of the country's first range and fattening co-operatives.[24] This gave regional sheepmen an edge

[22] In 1984, some sheep-rearers had to sell between one-fourth and one-half of their flocks to cover the costs of transportation, pastures and fodder.

[23] Sheep-rearers from some large tribes such as the Rwala and Sba'a still take their flocks towards the south-east and are to be found in winter in Jordan's Wadi Sirhan, and, until the closure of the border with Iraq, also in lower Iraq and Kuwait.

[24] For information on Syrian co-operatives see the chapter by Ronald Jaubert in this volume (chap. 9).

at the outbreak of the October 1973 war when the army put out large contracts to supply meat to the mobilised troops. Co-operatives in the Palmyrena were virtually the only ones able to supply quickly the large quantities needed. In the following years they continued to rely on army contracts as a reliable and advantageous outlet. These contracts, signed in February, specify the price paid for live animals and the quantities required for the season (a minimum of 10 metric tons). This principle has since been extended to all those who deal with the (state-owned) Meat Administration.

State encouragement of intensification

Following the 1973 drought, the authorities, with aid from the World Bank, established a programme to improve pasturelands while at the same time encouraging intensive sheep-breeding. They continued digging artesian wells, thus facilitating access of flocks to grazing areas which had previously been relatively inaccessible, such as the *hamad*, known for the high-quality meat it produced. They increased supplies of barley and other animal feedstuffs to members of co-operatives. This measure, intended to be a temporary stop-gap to diminish the catastrophic effects of the drought, continued and was extended. Breeders came to rely on it as a permanent source of feed, finding the fixed prices set at the beginning of the season by the Fodder Administration greatly to their advantage.

In 1978 the Fodder Administration built a warehouse in Sukhna, turning it into a distribution centre for the whole *mintaqa* of Palmyra. Each breeder in the co-operative is entitled to a fixed quantity of fodder and feedstuffs: 100 kilograms per ewe per annum; 60 kilograms three times a year per male lamb, though this distribution is limited to a maximum of 250 ewes per flock and to 50 male lambs per fattening cycle. In years of drought the administration may increase its quotas during the summer months and (faithful to the traditions of local merchants) it may even write off part of the breeder's debts. The sheep-owner receives his allotted feedstuff in early winter, paying only 20 per cent as down payment, with the remainder to be paid after he has sold his male lambs in spring.

The upsurge in population, urbanisation and the rapid rise in living standards in Syria since 1973, together with the opening of Gulf markets, all combined to increase demand for mutton and lamb and continuously force up prices. These favourable economic conditions and the government support for production described above led to a rapid increase in sheep numbers.

Between 1978 and 1982[25] the sheep population in Syria climbed from 8.1 million to 11.3 million, an increase equivalent to 12 per cent per year. In the Palmyra *mintaqa*, the increase was even more dramatic.[26] Sheep numbers in

[25] Al-Samman, 1985.

[26] When we visited Sukhna for the first time, in 1982, we were told that people were selling their tractors to buy sheep.

range co-operatives tripled between 1978 and 1985. Despite serious losses in 1984,[27] there were as many as 300,000 sheep in the *mintaqa* at that time.

During this period Sukhna, as well as other parts of the *mintaqa*, witnessed a significant expansion of membership in the range and fattening co-operatives: the number of sheep-owners registered rose from 150 to 290 and the size of their flocks increased as well. Today most members have flocks well over the maximum quotas: flocks of 300 to 600 head are common and several breeders own more than a thousand sheep. Fattening of male lambs, which facilitates short-term investments, has also increased, particularly in the two settlements of Sukhna and al-Tayba, where sheep-owners often belong to both range and fattening co-operatives.

Increased complementarity between sheep-rearing and agriculture

Fodder quotas allocated by the state to co-operative members, and restricted to flocks registered in local co-operatives, remain insufficient, particularly in drought years. The general increase in the sheep population and the subsequent run on steppe pasturelands in springtime by sheep-rearers in the intermediary zones (Salamiyya, Bab al-Manbij, etc.) has led to greater pressure on natural steppe vegetation and thus to a need for more cultivated pastures and barley. Sukhna acts as the market where breeders stock up on supplies for the season. Several Sukhnite traders have become specialists as wholesalers of animal feed (*'alaf*). They buy barley locally and straw and other feed from Jazira producers, supplying their bedouin clients on credit during the winter months and waiting until spring to be paid.

The ever-growing demand for supplementary pastures and barley has forced up prices on the 'open' market, thereby decreasing accordingly the risks of cultivating barley. Sukhnites are fully aware of the significance of this change and have modified their investment policies accordingly. They maintain that it is now much more profitable to invest in dry farming than in sheep: 'If we put 100 SL in agriculture we get back threefold or fourfold that amount one year out of three, covering our expenses in bad years by renting out the cultivated land as pasture, whereas with sheep alone, at best we can get double our initial outlay.' It should be added that closer surveillance of borders has cut into the profits formerly gained both by Sukhnites and bedouin from the illegal export of sheep to the Arabian Peninsula.

Sheep-raising has not however been abandoned. Few Sukhna residents put their savings in banks and Sukhnites continue to look on sheep as readily convertible capital, to be redeemed in hard times or when cash is needed quickly,

[27] In 1984 (cf. note 22 above), a drought year, prices of live animals collapsed: that of fattened lambs fell to 13 SL per kg. Two years later, in the autumn of 1986, when the Syrian pound's value had dropped dramatically, the price per kg varied between 20 and 24 SL. Between 1985 and 1986, prices rose steadily, reaching 130 SL a kg in the spring of 1988, only to fall again to 47 SL in the spring of 1989.

as for a wedding, purchase of agricultural machinery or a car, building a room onto a house, opening a workshop or retail store, buying shares in a truck or purchasing seed to invest in agriculture. Money raised from a good barley crop will thus partly be reinvested in sheep.

The wealth of the biggest traders is often measured by the number of sheep they have ranging the steppe. Popular opinion closely follows their ups and downs, ever ready to cite their gains and losses. Thus, we were told in 1986, Hajj Ahmad had 16,000 head of sheep in the steppe, Farhan M. 7,000, etc. For these urban traders, sheep is where they invest their money. Yet it requires a great deal of expertise on their part to know when to buy and sell, how best to deal with their diverse clients, from the state to Saudi Arabia, Kuwait and Qatar. These traders, who have an apartment in Raqqa or Aleppo and whose business is based on the products of the steppe, also own agricultural land and fleets of trucks, the three complementary riches of the steppe. Sukhna has five or six traders of this magnitude.

To sell or not to sell: uncertainties of the market

Sheep-raising requires constant calculations during crucial seasons. Prices must be followed daily. Sukhna may have no telephones but its residents know at all times precisely what fodder costs, how much to pay for pastures in the Palmyrena, Jazira or Ghab, the price of transportation and meat, both in Syrian pounds and dollars, in Syria and in Saudi Arabia. They anxiously await the opening of the border that will allow them to export to the Gulf, for in recent years, particularly since 1986 when economic recession caused the Syrian pound to collapse, co-operatives in the Palmyrena ceased renewing their contracts with the army, preferring the higher prices of the open market.

Sukhnites began developing commercial breeding on a large scale in response to this demand. Kamal, a trader and agricultural entrepreneur, is one example of this new trend. He paid 3,200 SL per head for 110 *dughla* year-old male lambs, purchased in Deir ez-Zor through a broker who delivered them to Sukhna. He hired the services of a bedouin shepherd from the ʿUmur tribe for three months, paying him 2,000 SL a month. The sheep were bought for purely commercial reasons, to sell at the best price. 'I buy because I have a pasture', he said. But the cultivated area was damaged by frost in February 1989 and was insufficient. So the shepherd let the lambs graze during the day and supplemented their feed with barley morning and evening. Kamal had for this purpose bought 100 sacks of barley (and other feedstuffs), purchasing half from the government stores at 400 SL per sack and the other half on the open market at 550 SL a sack. On 16 May when we saw him, Kamal's sheep weighed about 60 kilograms and he still had some fodder left so he was waiting for prices to go up. He had calculated his costs at 3,500 SL per head and wanted to sell at least at 60 SL a kilogram for live animals.

Those unable to wait because they did not have enough fodder or pasture for grazing (for which prices were rising every day) had lost nearly 1,000 SL per head. Twenty days earlier, for the feast celebrating the end of Ramadan, the price of live sheep had gone down to 47 SL a kilogram. The Syrian authorities had opened up the border to Saudi Arabia to sheep exporters a few days after the feast and prices then began to rise. When we interviewed Kamal, the price was 57 SL per kilogram. That year the Meat Administration had set the price it would pay at the beginning of the season at 72 SL a kilogram but local co-operatives had largely boycotted the public-sector buyers that year, hoping for a repeat of the previous year's windfall when prices reached 130 SL per kilogram on the open market and the state prices levelled off at 110. Ewes that had cost 5,000 SL in the spring of 1988 could not be sold in May 1989 for more than 2,000–2,500 SL. Breeders had to sell off part of their flocks at a loss in order to buy fodder, pay for transportation to the Jazira, for rent on pastures, water and perhaps supplementary feed as well. The flocks were melting away. Some breeders with very large flocks returned to the practice of moving sheep on the hoof over the steppe, in order to avoid further losses in paying for their transportation by truck. Transportation costs were rising rapidly after a sharp increase in petrol prices (200 per cent increase in May 1989).

By opening and closing borders to exporters, by setting prices for a season on its own contracts, by distributing fodder at a fixed price, the government can influence prices and exert some control over the market, preferring at times to bring in hard currency and at other times to keep local prices down to reduce inflation. The commercial breeder or contractor who invests in sheep must decide which game to play – public sector or open market – and this game is often as tricky as playing the stock market.

Logic of production or speculative game?

The extension of barley cultivation around Sukhna may appear atypical of Syria as a whole. It is nevertheless interesting to go over the conditions specific to the steppe where this cultivation occurs and look again at the socio-economic logic that is its *raison d'être.* The dominant trait that emerges from our analysis of the economic activities of Sukhna residents is the inherently hazardous nature of resources in the steppe and their strict interdependence. Whether these resources came from trade, sheep-breeding or agriculture, Sukhnites remain closely dependent on rainfall conditions in obtaining them and on the coming of the tribes, whose seasonal movement into the Palmyrena is itself dependent on the availability of natural pasturelands or sown fields.

The scarceness and the extreme irregularity of rainfall from one year to the next and from one place to another makes forecasting difficult, hampering all forms of planning for the future. In the steppe, risk is built into all activities. Tradespeople, 'wheeler-dealers', merchants used to gambling on prices varying according to seasons and markets,[28] Sukhnites deal with climate as one of the risks of the game and calculate its effects, tackling the different activities as might speculators in the stock market. They deal with risk through diversification and mobility.[29] They adopt or abandon a particular activity on the basis of probable short-term gains offered by current economic prospects. This speculative game is played by everyone with the least surplus at his disposal. Though the initiative is individual it is co-ordinated and channelled through family relations and stimulated by social rivalry between lineage groups.

As a result, investment itself is diversified, atomised and mobile, shifting from one economic domain to another, depending on what popular opinion deems to be the 'good deal' of the moment. Cultivation in the steppe is particularly suited to this kind of speculative behaviour because of the tempting experience of three profitable years out of the ten years between 1979 and 1989. Although climatic risks remain much more significant in the steppe than in the agricultural zones of western Syria and the agro-pastoral zones studied by ICARDA, the economic effects of the risks inherent in cultivation have been tempered by the conjunction of several factors: Syrian state intervention through its distribution system (sale of fodder for livestock and seeds for planting crops, purchase of cereal crops and live animals at prices fixed at the beginning of the season, thus avoiding distress sales and supporting price levels); export possibilities in the Gulf countries where there is an expanding market and in consequence 'indexing sheep to the dollar' during periods of devaluation of the Syrian pound; and finally the close integration locally of cultivation and sheep-rearing. The last two factors have brought about the development of the open market.

This so-called open or free market is at times suppressed, at times tolerated or authorised. The irregularity of government control has itself become one of the factors of speculation, making for a play between official channels and the open or black-market circuit. It should be noted that the privileged position that Sukhnites have regained in international transportation towards the Gulf and their special knowledge of steppe tracks give them an additional advantage.

Barley cultivation has normally provided a supplementary source of revenue for Sukhnite traders, but in 1988 for many traders it more than doubled incomes from their regular trade.[30] A single good year creates euphoria. The following autumn, Sukhna residents were so carried away by the prospect of a quick profit, as they themselves admitted, that they sowed double the

[28] This was one of the characteristics of the merchant – and particularly of the caravan trade merchant – in the Ottoman Empire (Inalcik, 1987). [29] Métral and Métral, 1991.

[30] Thus Kamal, who is the sole wholesaler in oil and grease for motor vehicles and supplies the twelve retailers, garages and petrol stations in the *nahiya* and whose business brings in an average of 12,000 SL a month, earned 580,000 SL in 1988 from becoming an entrepreneur in barley cultivation. His two brothers, who as state employees earn 2,000 SL a month each, joined him as partners for an eighth of the sum invested and each earned around 145,000 SL.

surface of the previous year, preferring to maximise risks and 'win big', rather than to minimise their risks by growing only on suitable land. Similarly, the high profits made from sheep-rearing in 1988 and the steep rise in meat prices led them to opt for the risks of the open market the following season rather than to play it safe by seeking advance contracts with public-sector buyers.

Severe losses, on the other hand, produce a more cautious attitude. After the 1984 drought, some Sukhnites reduced their flocks in order to invest in the only resource providing a guaranteed medium-term profit, the truck, and to go into what then seemed more profitable, barley cultivation. The forms of production in barley cultivation reflect this attitude to risk and the desire to preserve mobility in the face of uncertainty. Cultivation can be carried out without owning the means of production and without tying up one's capital, apart from the down-payment required for purchasing seed, ploughing and transportation. No land is bought or even rented on a long-term basis. The unit of production fluctuates, there is no permanent bond to the land. Neither building nor agricultural machinery is necessary. If an entrepreneur occasionally buys a tractor, this investment is itself temporary, as he can recover his costs by hiring it out for just one or two years of good rainfall. He will sell it during the first dry year. 'In bad years the price of agricultural machinery falls as much as that of sheep.' The season is always the term of reference for any deal. Though some partnerships are stable, others may be redrawn every season.

Cultivation, as it is currently practised in the region, requires little technical skill on the part of the entrepreneur since all technical tasks are carried out by external contractors. Yields depend on rainfall and where crops have been sown. Soil conservation is of no concern to the entrepreneur. The ecological effects of ploughing are only taken into account when they affect revenues gained from the land, otherwise they remain the concern of state authorities or experts. The real skill of the entrepreneur lies, on the one hand, in his ability to locate good land given his familiarity with the steppe, and, on the other, in his relations, or his ability to negotiate good terms, and his knowledge (on where there has been rainfall, on prices of goods, on the possibilities offered by the state vs. the open market, on the strictness of state controls etc.).

Agriculture and sheep-rearing are closely integrated at the local level. This integration takes the form of multiple contracts and continuous associations between settled populations, sheep-herding tribes and the Sba'a for production. It is also carried out through the intermediary of traders in the *suq* or open market and through the redistribution system of the state. The distribution of roles in the various tasks is linked to identities and individual characteristics which remain stable but adapt to new circumstances. Social identities have even tended to be reinforced through this process – for instance, that of the Sba'a who negotiate with the state on questions of land tenure and develop trade with the Gulf countries, where by virtue of their good relations they can act as intermediaries or sponsors (*kafil*) for Sukhnite traders.

However, unlike what occurs in the agro-pastoral zone, in Sukhna there has been little vertical integration at the individual or family level in agriculture or sheep-rearing. Cultivation in Sukhna, unlike that on farms in the agro-pastoral zone, does not have as its first function the provision of food for the flocks. Within the Sukhnite extended family (60 to 150 persons), each activity – agriculture or sheep-rearing – is carried out by a small number of people whom we could call specialists, while a much larger number may participate financially. Participation is voluntary for each individual. A family business consists of its capital, partnership ties and networks of relations and skills which combine for short periods and are renewed over time in varied forms and combinations. Each activity, each undertaking, calls for a new distribution of shares and has its specific accounting system, while each undertaking follows the laws of the market. This means that sheep-rearing in the steppe is not necessarily linked to sheep-fattening of lambs bought in the market, which, within the family unit, may have a totally different source of capital and set of partners from those who have flocks in the steppe. It also means that only part of a flock's requirements in barley is stocked from barley sown and this part may even be sold if prices are high enough to warrant it.

Integration between the different activities occurs only when circumstances prove it a profitable solution in a particular context. Integration depends on market conditions which themselves have local, national and international dimensions and is based on a network of personalised relations carefully nurtured by the Sukhnite traders.

12

Production and trade in north central Arabia: change and development in ʿUnayzah

DONALD P. COLE AND SORAYA ALTORKI
American University in Cairo

Focusing on the oasis city and district of ʿUnayzah, this chapter analyses change and development in an area of the Arabian Peninsula that has long been the home of both nomadic and sedentary populations.[1] Located in the Qasim region of north central Najd, the city of ʿUnayzah currently has a population of about 70,000 and is the administrative capital and market centre for a district of some 3,500 km^2 that includes both desert rangelands and cultivated areas. In addition to the city of ʿUnayzah, the district includes two small towns, twenty-two villages and five bedouin 'population centres'. The population in these communities outside the city of ʿUnayzah is estimated at about 30,000.[2] Although autonomous until 1904, the city and district now form an emirate within the local and regional administrative structures of the kingdom of Saudi Arabia.

The city's transformation is best understood in terms of three economic phases. First is that of the pre-state, pre-oil political economy that prevailed during the latter part of the nineteenth and early part of the twentieth centuries. Second is a phase of incremental, development-oriented change that began with the establishment of the new Saudi Arabian state during the first decades of the twentieth century and gathered momentum during the 1950s and 1960s as the impact of the oil industry in eastern Saudi Arabia began to be felt in other parts of the country. The third phase is associated with the oil price boom of the late 1970s and early 1980s which led to massive investments in new projects and programmes throughout the country and to a truncation of the development process that had been initiated in the 1950s and 1960s.

In the present chapter we focus on changes in production (agriculture, herding and craftwork) and in the market in ʿUnayzah. By analysing the pattern of change that has occurred in this particular case, we aim to demonstrate: (1) the basic complementarity of agricultural, pastoralist and craft production systems in the past; (2) the centrality of the market as an institution linking the various components of the local productive economy in the past;

[1] This chapter draws on fieldwork conducted by both authors in the city of ʿUnayzah in late 1986 and early 1987. For a more detailed presentation of issues presented here, see Altorki and Cole, 1989, esp. pp. 32–82; 98–113; 119–22; 140–84; and 232–48.

[2] Ibid., p. 8; al-Wasil, 1986, pp. 162–3.

and (3) how the process of developmental change associated with the state and the new oil-based economy has transformed the local economy and society. Although recent development has brought spectacular 'successes', the old integrated and self-sustaining economy has been replaced by a new system which is highly dependent on outside sources of financing, of labour, and of other production inputs.

The old order

Production in the old ʿUnayzah consisted of three separate but interrelated systems. Agriculture has been practised in the region at least since the founding, in the seventh century, of settlements that eventually grew to form the city of ʿUnayzah. Much of this agriculture was located within the confines of the walls of the city itself, but also in outlying villages in the district. Craftworkers resided mainly in the city and performed most of their work there, although some tasks were performed in villages. The third production system was that of nomadic pastoralists who herded their animals within the rangelands of the district and elsewhere and who maintained summer camps at wells located outside the settled communities of the district.

Crops cultivated in ʿUnayzah included dates, wheat, millet, barley, alfalfa, pomegranates, figs, pumpkin, squash, peppers, eggplant, okra, black-eyed peas, watercress, onions, leeks, cumin, fenugreek, melons and watermelons. Both men and women worked in agriculture, which was organised largely by domestic units but included occasional use of non-kin-based reciprocal labour parties. Wage-labour also existed for both male and female workers who tended to work on a seasonal basis on larger farms. Many farmers were peasants (*fallahin*) who worked their own land held as private property. Others worked as sharecroppers on land belonging to others, usually merchants. Irrigation was sometimes done by members of the farm-owning or sharecropper household. However, a household was often hired to do this work, especially on larger farms where the land owner could afford it.

Craft specialisations in the old ʿUnayzah include leather processing, leather working, smithery, carpentry, masonry, housebuilding, well-digging, tailoring, weapon making and repairing, and basketry – among other specialisations. Some craft occupations were organised by domestic units and involved the participation of all members of the household. Other crafts were carried out by individuals, whether in shops in the market place out of which they sold their products or at specific sites where they performed their services. Although many of the crafts were inherited within families, some individuals chose to specialise in a particular craft, such as well-digging, because of its high pay. Craftwork in the old ʿUnayzah could also entail the use of apprentices and the supervision of work by an *ustadh* or 'master craftsman'.

Although spatially separate from both the urban and village communities of ʿUnayzah, bedouin herders formed one of the production systems of the region. They raised camels, sheep, goats and horses, and produced a wide range of animal products – including ghee, dried cheese and wool. Access to rangelands in the area and use of wells within those rangelands were organised on the basis of tribal structures quite distinct from the social organisation of the village and urban communities of ʿUnayzah, although the bedouin and many of the *hadar*, 'sedentary folk', shared tribal descent status. The work of herding itself was largely organised on the basis of the household and engaged both men and women, in addition to slaves and clients.

These three production systems were interdependent, each requiring inputs from the others. The craftworker may have produced some of his own food, but generally he relied on the produce of the peasant and the bedouin as well as on the products of craftworkers of other specialisations than his own. The peasant required the services and production of all the various craft specialisations at one time or another, obtaining animals and animal products from the bedouin. With the exception of their tents, the bedouin depended on craftworkers for almost all the equipment used in daily life, herding and raiding. They also relied on peasants for most of the dates and grain that, in addition to the milk their animals produced, made up their diet.

In her discussion of the bedouin in Najd in the past, Sweet claims that 'their relations to other societies in the desert, with the possible exception of those oases cultivators who are their tenants and slaves, are managed in terms of mechanisms of interchiefdom relations, not mechanisms of state apparatus'.[3] While it is true that central state authority seldom played a significant role in Najd before the development of the present Saudi Arabian state, it is also true that the inhabitants of ʿUnayzah and its outlying villages were neither the tenants nor slaves of bedouin tribes. Although the amir of ʿUnayzah in the past sometimes engaged in 'interchiefdom relations' (including warfare) with the bedouin, most transactions took place within the context of market relations.

Soon after the founding of ʿUnayzah's first settlements in the seventh century, a market was established in an open space between them.[4] That market grew in importance and became a dominant feature of the city. Doughty described it as a major institution at the time of his visit in 1878, with well-furnished shops and streets thronged with townsmen, villagers and bedouin on the main market day.[5]

Craftworkers, peasants and bedouin exchanged their respective goods and services in the marketplace itself or, sometimes, in bedouin camps or at a work site. Some producers marketed their produce and wares directly to buyers. More commonly, the exchange of goods and services involved the mediation of merchants, who performed the key role in articulating these separate and specialised systems of production.

[3] Sweet, 1965, p. 1134. [4] Al-Wasil, 1986, pp. 205–8.
[5] Doughty, 1979 [1888], vol. II, p. 375.

Although money was commonly used, exchange via merchants sometimes took place without it. For example, bedouin brought in ghee to a merchant. The merchant then provided them with whatever they required (even if he had to obtain some items from another merchant). No money would have exchanged hands; however, all transactions were calculated in money and haggling over prices at all steps in a chain of transactions occurred, a phenomenon indicative of prices being determined by supply and demand. Out of such transactions the merchant reaped his profits.

Merchants also played a role in organising production. Some merchants, for example, used profits to purchase camels which they placed in the care of bedouin. More significantly, merchants provided credit and lent out money at interest. In the absence of specialised financial institutions such as banks, merchants provided the financial capital that was necessary for the functioning of the production systems.

The centrality of the market in the economic system of the region is further indicated by the presence of other specialists alongside the merchants, themselves specialised and differentiated in terms of size of operations. There were brokers, auctioneers and transporters who operated largely within the context of the local market for a fee. Moreover, some merchants and transporters used the market as the centre for organising long-distance trade between the region and other markets in the Arabian Peninsula and beyond.

The long-distance trade was generated by surplus production in agriculture and especially in herding. ʿUnayzah traders exported dates to the cities of the Hijaz, and dates, wheat and vegetables to Riyadh. More important (and more profitable) was the trade in camels and horses which merchants bought up from among the bedouin and sold in Iraq, greater Syria, Egypt and India. The profits generated from these sales provided the capital for the importation of coffee, cardamom, tea, sugar, spices, cloth and rice – the only significant imports into Arabia at that time. These imports, which were mainly 'luxuries', were sold in the local market in ʿUnayzah and distributed by ʿUnayzah merchants to other markets in the region.

Lastly, the old market served as a major communication centre. Men came to hear the news, to exchange views and opinions, and to debate events of interest to the community and the region at large. Moreover, the market was the centre from which political authority was administered, as it was here that the amir of ʿUnayzah held his daily *majlis* (council/court). The central mosque of the community also lay within the precincts of the main market area.

The decline of the old order and the beginning of development

This old order was gradually undermined as a result of the establishment of a new state, the creation of new international boundaries, the introduction of new technology and the development of an economy based on oil. The new state destroyed the numerous autonomous political entities of the past (of which ʿUnayzah is an example) as it forged a centralised bureaucracy which asserted its power throughout the disparate regions of the country. The creation of new state boundaries following the break-up of the Ottoman Empire severely hampered the movement of long-distance traders, whose activities ceased by the early 1940s. The introduction of motor vehicles, beginning in the 1920s, replaced camel transport locally (although some camel caravans continued to operate until the 1950s) and destroyed the distant markets for camels and horses which had been raised by local bedouin and exported by local merchants. The import of industrially manufactured goods increasingly competed with local craft manufacturing. Moreover, revenues from the sale of oil, discovered in the 1930s and mainly developed after the end of World War II, enhanced the power of the state and contributed to the expansion of its activities. Thus, as the old order continued its decline, a new phase of development led by the activities of the state and the new oil-based economy restructured economic relations in ʿUnayzah during the 1950s, 1960s and early 1970s.

People in ʿUnayzah today consider that the introduction, in 1925, of three mechanical pumps for irrigation marks the first significant technological innovation in agriculture, formerly the main productive base of the urban and village communities of the area. By 1961, ʿUnayzah had 523 mechanical pumps for irrigation. The same period saw six tractors, eighteen mechanical threshers and seventeen harrows introduced, and new fruit and vegetable crops planted.[6]

The new technology had a profound impact on agricultural production and the organisation of work, facilitating occupational mobility, which began to be especially significant in the 1950s. In the past, agriculture had been limited primarily by the cost and difficulty of irrigation. The mechanical pumps replaced the traditional *sawani* system of irrigation which had required heavy inputs of human labour, in addition to the costly use of camels. With new irrigation techniques, greater amounts of land could be cultivated with less labour. Accordingly, both the number and size of landholdings increased in the ʿUnayzah district.

Labour in agriculture was largely reorganised. The management of new mechanical pumps was restricted to males, and women no longer worked in irrigation as they had done previously on a large scale. Wage-labour replaced domestically organised labour which had prevailed in the past. By the 1950s much of the permanent and seasonal labour force in agriculture was comprised of women and older men who worked for wages. Young men began to migrate to more attractive jobs in the oil industry, in construction, and in trade and other services – especially governmental employment in the newly developing cities elsewhere in the country. Thus, while agriculture experienced a significant degree of technological development and total output increased, nevertheless it ceased during the 1950s and 1960s to be an attractive endeavour for the more ambitious and upwardly mobile young men of the community.

[6] Sharif, 1970, pp. 127–31.

A parallel process of change took place in the pastoral production of the bedouin in the region. New wells with mechanical pumps became common and motor vehicles were increasingly used. The herding of camels was replaced by sheep-raising, as the market for camels declined and the demand for mutton increased. As Cole has demonstrated elsewhere, sheep-raising with the use of motor vehicles and access to water sources with mechanical pumps required less labour than had been the case for traditional camel-herding.[7] As a result, young bedouin men, like their counterparts in the agricultural sector, began to migrate to job opportunities in the newly developing cities and left herding mainly in the hands of older men and women. Although wage-labour began to play a role in herding during this period, most labour in the pastoral sector continued to be domestically organised. However, this process of change was exacerbated by a prolonged drought in the 1960s that led to the decimation of much of the animal population and forced many bedouin to settle, at least temporarily.

The other productive sector of ʿUnayzah's old economy, the crafts, disappeared during the 1950s and early 1960s, as local products were replaced by industrially manufactured commodities, largely imported from abroad. Many of the young men from families that had previously specialised in local craft production sought jobs elsewhere in other types of occupation. Older men and women either continued to eke out a living from their work or were forced into wage-labour in agriculture or into petty trade.

When ʿAbd al-ʿAziz b. Saʿud first visited ʿUnayzah's market in 1904, he reportedly remarked that he hoped that Riyadh might one day develop and become like ʿUnayzah.[8] Philby estimated that in 1918 ʿUnayzah's market had at least a thousand shops.[9] However, as the changes discussed above took place, the market declined in size and suffered a change in function. ʿUnayzah merchants no longer organised long-distance export trade. Although they continued to market local agricultural production, for the most part they became local distributors of imported goods brought into the country by commercial establishments located in the newly expanding cities of the country such as Jedda, Riyadh and Dammam.

That the market had come to play a less active role in the organisation of the regional productive systems is attested by Sharif who shows, for example, that by the 1960s the bedouin no longer participated in the market as sellers of their own products but came there mainly as buyers. Food comprised a significant proportion of their purchases. While they continued to buy locally produced dates, much of the food they bought was imported. The same applied to the residents of the city who, like the bedouin, increasingly relied on imported food. Also by this time, all the inhabitants of the region were dependent on imported manufactured goods as local craft production had all but ceased.[10] By the 1960s not only had the market lost its pre-eminent role in

[7] See Cole, 1981a. [8] Al-Wasil, 1986, p. 112. [9] Philby, 1928, p. 174.
[10] Sharif, 1970, pp. 168–71.

the local regional economy, it had also lost its significance as a social arena, a communication centre and a political forum. Although marginalised, the ʿUnayzah market continues to exist and its present characteristics will be described below.

In part what we are describing is a process of decline and marginalisation. However, mechanisation and new crops were introduced in agriculture. New sources of water became available to pastoralists, and motor transportation became common among them and others. Modern physical infrastructure, modern education and other social services were increasingly introduced into ʿUnayzah, as elsewhere throughout the country from the mid-1950s onward. Thus, in relation to newly developing centres elsewhere in the country, ʿUnayzah was engaged in a process of gradual, incremental modernisation in the decades immediately preceding the transformational changes triggered by the oil boom of the late 1970s and early 1980s.

In the old order, the vast majority of the population had worked in production or trade. However, in 1973, just before the oil boom, a census of the city of ʿUnayzah indicated that almost half (46 per cent) of the city's work force was employed in social services, while 16.5 per cent worked in construction, 13 per cent in trade, 11.2 per cent in agriculture, 6.4 per cent in transport, 3.7 per cent in manufacturing and 3.3 per cent in 'other' occupations. According to the census of 1974, the labour force of the district as a whole had just over a third (34.5 per cent) engaged in agriculture or herding, just under a third (32.3 per cent) in social service, and the remaining third distributed among construction (11.8 per cent), trade (9.6 per cent), transport (6.5 per cent), manufacturing (3.6 per cent) and 'other' occupations (2.6 per cent).[11] Although comparable statistical data for earlier periods are not available, the large proportions engaged in the social services in both the city and the district at large can be taken as indicative of a high degree of modern occupational mobility. While some of those engaged in modern occupations in the early 1970s were expatriates, the majority were local people who came from agricultural or trading backgrounds.

Such occupational change was paralleled by the increasing involvement of the state in development-related activities from the 1950s onward. Numerous schools were established and regional offices of most national ministries were opened in the city. An office of the national Ministry of Agriculture and Water was established in ʿUnayzah in 1954, a branch of the Saudi Arabian Agricultural Bank in 1965, and an agricultural research and training centre in 1966. The work of these institutions in ʿUnayzah was modest at first; now, however, they play major roles in agriculture in the community and region.

On the national level, the Ministry of Agriculture and Water sponsored a series of intensive studies that, in the 1960s, began to explore water resources and to assess soil conditions. Significant amounts of geological water were discovered in various parts of the country, and locations for possible dams were

[11] Al-Wasil, 1986, pp. 145–6.

identified in the south-western part of the country. These studies concluded that the use of new sources of water along with improved irrigation systems could lead to substantial agricultural expansion in many parts of the country. The studies identified unclear land tenure and highly fragmented landholdings as significant obstacles to vertical intensification of existing agriculture. This led to a general focus on horizontal expansion onto new lands. The Qasim, of which ʿUnayzah is a part, was identified as one area with considerable potential for such horizontal expansion. No major government-sponsored projects were initiated in the region until after the beginning of the oil boom in the mid-1970s. However, the boom brought major changes to the region. Some of the most important of these are indicated below.

Transformation associated with the boom

In the fiscal year 1393–4 AH (1973–4), the expenditures of the government of Saudi Arabia amounted to 13.6 billion riyals. In 1401–2 AH (1981–2), expenditures reached a high of 283.3 billion riyals, after which they began to decline slightly.[12] This massive increase in expenditures is directly related to the oil-price boom (locally called the *tafrah*) that Saudi Arabia and most other oil-producing countries or regions experienced in the latter half of the 1970s and early 1980s. Changes of monumental proportions were introduced throughout the country as the government rapidly initiated numerous new development programmes and greatly increased funding for older ones. Let us briefly consider the impact of such changes on agriculture, pastoralism, and the market in ʿUnayzah city and district.

The new agriculture

In 1974, just before the boom began, there were 348 farms in the ʿUnayzah district. A decade later there were 1,112 farms.[13] Almost all the new farms have been established on newly reclaimed land. Some are located close to the urban and village areas in the district, while others are scattered across former desert rangelands of the district. Three major types of new farm are distinguished by local people: *basatin*, 'gardens', small to medium-sized farms (from about 5 to 50 hectares in size); large farms (several thousand hectares in size); and capital-intensive hot-house farms and chicken- and egg-production units.

Most of the *basatin* are found in a sandy area immediately to the west of the city of ʿUnayzah. They vary in size and produce mainly alfalfa, vegetables, citrus fruit and dates. Almost all have been developed by local investors with merchant backgrounds who are now businessmen and/or high-ranking government employees and officials. Although the soils in this area are not especially good for most crops, this area was attractive to the investors because

[12] Kingdom of Saudi Arabia, 1984, p. 152.

[13] Al-Wasil, 1986, pp. 79–80.

of its proximity to the city and government provision of piped water, paved roads and telephones. Although crops of the gardens are marketed, many of the owners note that a primary motive for developing these new *basatin* was social. Accordingly, most have houses (and many have swimming pools) that are regularly used by men, and occasionally by women and family groups, for recreation and socialising.

The new small to medium-sized farms have been developed mainly within the confines of the Wadi al-Rimmah, to the north-east of the city and in the vicinities of other towns and villages in the district. The soils are rich due to sediment built up over thousands of years, and replenishable water is relatively close to the surface (about 60 metres deep). Although Wadi al-Rimmah provided the basis for the old agriculture, these areas of the wadi had not been cultivated in the past due to malaria and to drainage problems that the traditional technology was unable to solve. These farms have largely been developed by local investors with agricultural backgrounds, although many have other primary occupations at present. Crops grown on these farms include wheat, alfalfa, vegetables, citrus fruits and dates. Owners say that they develop these farms for agricultural production and income generation.

The new large farms have been established on tracts of land at dispersed sites in the desert, remote from towns and villages. They tend to be in areas where the soil is of variable quality but not too sandy. Water in these areas is mostly non-replenishable (i.e. fossil water) and is at deep levels of between 250 and 1,000 metres. Investors come mainly from local merchant backgrounds and possess significant previous personal experience in business and contracting. The main crop cultivated is wheat. The owners say that these farms are fully commercial in orientation and that the main motive for their investments is profit.

All of the new *basatin* and farms are fully mechanised and most employ costly and highly sophisticated imported technology, imported chemicals and fertilisers. Irrigation includes drip irrigation and central pivot and stationary sprinkler systems. Although some of the larger farms employ expatriate farm managers, most of the new agriculture is managed by the local investors despite the fact that many of them have no previous background in agriculture.

The work force in the new agriculture consists almost exclusively of male expatriate labourers under contract, who come from rural areas in Egypt or, less frequently, Afghanistan, Pakistan and the Philippines. Although many of the workers have previous experience in traditional agriculture in their home countries, few of them have experience in the highly modernised and sophisticated new desert agriculture. As a result, they have to be trained on site in the new techniques. At the time of fieldwork, the turnover in agricultural labour was relatively high, with most workers staying for three or four years and then returning with their savings to their home countries. New workers then had to be recruited and trained. Thus, the new agriculture depends not only on imported technology and equipment, but also on imported labour that has to be replaced and trained anew every few years.

The new forms of agriculture described above did not grow out of the process of gradual incremental expansion described for the 1950s and 1960s, when most of the development in agriculture resulted from individual endeavours by local people investing their own personal savings. At that time, loans were few and difficult to arrange. Rather, the new agriculture of the 1970s and 1980s was made possible by national policies designed to achieve food security.

In the present case, this policy was implemented primarily though the provision of state financing to individuals. This included interest-free loans, subsidies and grants. In 1975–6 the Saudi Arabian Agricultural Bank began to increase its financing of agriculture. Between 1982 and 1986 it extended no fewer than 1,500 loans totalling 165 million riyals in ʿUnayzah. Medium-term loans were given for the purchase of irrigation equipment and other machinery. Short-term loans financed the planting of date palms. In addition, loans for special projects in ʿUnayzah (such as hot-houses and chicken and egg farms) totalled almost 57 million riyals. The requirements for loans include Saudi Arabian citizenship, proof of legal ownership of the land to be cultivated, and the provision of collateral or the support of a guarantor. If the equipment financed by the bank is put to use, the bank writes off half of the loan as a subsidy. The outstanding half of the loan has to be repaid in yearly instalments over a period of ten years.

In addition to the Saudi Arabian Agricultural Bank, other institutions of the state also support the new forms of agricultural production. For example, an agricultural research and training centre provides information about modern agricultural techniques and the requirements of the new varieties of crops being grown. The ministry of agriculture and water regulates and supervises the process of obtaining freehold ownership of public land through the process of reclaiming and developing it. The ministry organises the storage and distribution of wheat through the Grain Silos and Flour Mills Organisation, which also pays farm owners a guaranteed price for their wheat. At the time of fieldwork, the amount paid for wheat was considerably higher than the world market price. Thus, the new agriculture is dependent not only on imported technology, equipment and labour but also on state finance and subsidies – factors which ultimately depend on state revenue derived from the sale of oil in international markets.

Changes in pastoralism

As mentioned earlier, a prolonged drought during the 1960s led to the decimation of much of the livestock of the bedouin and forced many of them to settle, at least temporarily. From the mid-1970s the state initiated a programme with the aim of encouraging bedouin to rebuild their herds. This programme, administered by the Ministry of Agriculture and Water, provided cash subsidies to bedouin herders based on the number of animals they claimed to have. This subsidy programme contributed to increases in the number of animals kept on the ranges by bedouin but it did not lead to significant increases in the number of animals marketed. The bedouin had little incentive to sell animals, since the greater the number of animals kept, the greater the subsidy they could claim.

By the time of fieldwork, this programme had been curtailed, and the bedouin were widely criticised for failing to contribute to the supply of locally produced mutton. However, the practice of keeping large herds was of long standing; the bedouin sought to guard not only against the ravages of disease but also against the impact of prolonged droughts. In both cases, the bedouin reasoned that those with large herds were more likely to have some animals survive than those with small herds. Since this government programme did not lead to significant improvements in the provision of either veterinary medicine or fodder, the practice of not selling livestock can be seen as a rational decision on the part of the bedouin. The subsidy programme provides an example of non-integrated development: it focused on increasing the size of herds through cash incentives but made no provisions for the long-term maintenance, stability and improvement of herds or for the development of modern marketing mechanisms.

Although the bedouin were singled out for special consideration in Saudi Arabia's Second Development Plan for 1395–1400 AH (1975–80), aside from the subsidy programme no other programmes have specifically targeted the bedouin or pastoralist development. Nonetheless, the bedouin, like all others in the country, have been affected by the oil-price boom and the development programmes and projects associated with it.

Since the 1960s bedouin from the ʿUnayzah area (mainly from the Mutayr, Harb and Subayʿ tribes) have increasingly been engaged in processes of sedentarisation and occupational change. Thus, the nomadic population declined from an estimated 16 per cent of the total in the district in 1974 to less than 4 per cent in 1984.[14] Many bedouin settled in the city of ʿUnayzah, especially in satellite suburbs, others in other towns or villages or in new settlements (referred to earlier as 'bedouin population centres'). They live in new, permanent housing financed by a national programme of loans from the Saudi Arabian Real Estate Development Fund. On the basis of their Saudi Arabian citizenship, the bedouin qualified for subsidised loans for building houses if they so desired. Like many other Saudi Arabians, they took advantage of these loans and now live in new housing, most of which was constructed in the 1970s or 1980s.

Those who established residence in urban centres have either totally abandoned herding or entrusted their herds to the care of hired shepherds, who are

[14] Ibid., pp. 162–3.

expatriate men. Most urbanised bedouin men now work in trade and, to a lesser degree, in technical activities such as mechanical and electrical repairs, while a significant number of bedouin women are now engaged in trade. Those who opted to settle in the more rural parts of the district developed new, small to medium-sized farms with financial assistance from the Saudi Arabian Agricultural Bank, as described above. According to al-Wasil, the bedouin settled in villages as soon as they secured loans to start in agriculture. Access to government-provided services such as schools was also a motive for sedentarisation.[15]

Although our fieldwork did not directly focus on the current pastoral activities of the bedouin in the ʿUnayzah district (and more research is needed), the common view expressed by both the 'sedentary folk', *hadar*, and sedentarised bedouin in ʿUnayzah is that nomadic pastoralism as formerly practised is now part of the past. However, many of the bedouin who have developed new farms continue to raise livestock. Also, many of the *hadar* who have developed new farms, especially in the villages of the district, also keep livestock. In both cases, the livestock is grazed on nearby desert rangelands under the supervision of hired shepherds from abroad. These herds are also increasingly dependent on fodder, a phenomenon which at the time of fieldwork was being taken into account by the owners of large wheat farms in the district. Recognising the potential of profits due to a high demand for fodder, many wheat producers were planning to cultivate sorghum for fodder rather than wheat.

The market today

Al-Salman states that 2,542 commercial establishments existed in ʿUnayzah in 1988.[16] Our data, collected in 1986, show a total of about 720 shops in the old central market area, with perhaps as many more located throughout the various old and new neighbourhoods of the city. Although the figure quoted by al-Salman may be slightly inflated, trade and commerce continue to occupy an important position in the city.

Most of the largest establishments are branches of complex, modern enterprises with headquarters in Riyadh, Jedda, or one of the cities of the eastern province. Such enterprises are engaged primarily in the sale of imported agricultural and irrigation equipment and motor vehicles. They are usually managed by local men and employ expatriate men as sellers. In addition to these large establishments are eleven branches of national banks and money-exchange houses.[17] One of the bank branches is reserved for the use of women and is staffed by local women. The others are managed by local men and employ both local and expatriate men.

Numerous medium-sized enterprises employing five or more sellers exist. These are predominantly owned and managed by local men and are usually

[15] Ibid., p. 166. [16] Al-Salman, 1989, p. 145. [17] Ibid., p. 143.

staffed by expatriate men. They include supermarkets which sell a wide range of imported food products, along with shops that specialise in the sale of such consumer items as modern household utensils and furnishings, electrical appliances, video and cassette recorders and tapes, ready-made clothing, cloth and gold jewellery. Establishments of this type have modern displays of merchandise, use formal bookkeeping methods, deal with banks, and tend to have regularised and direct access to large national importers and sometimes to international suppliers.

The existence of local branches of national companies and banks and of modern medium-sized supermarkets and shops indicates that the local market in ʿUnayzah is significantly tied into the national commercial system with its headquarters in other cities. Modern business and financial institutions are important in the community. However, a very large number of essentially traditional and small-scale commercial enterprises continue to survive. These include, but are not limited to, the commercial activities of between 130 and 150 local women who are grouped together as sellers in a special section of the central market district.

Each woman runs her own business individually and does not employ others. Most of their goods are imported and include spices, nuts, biscuits, cooking utensils, flatware, perfumes, dyes, ready-made clothes, shoes and sandals. These items are obtained, usually on credit, from male itinerant wholesale traders who tend to be either of bedouin origin or from Yemen or Pakistan. The sellers are all over forty years of age, and include women who have had long careers in the market and others who have only recently begun in trade. Among the latter are women who formerly worked in agriculture or irrigation, while the latest arrivals are recently settled bedouin women. All are illiterate and do not keep records of transactions or of the multiple credit arrangements they typically engage in. They also do not use banks and are not familiar with procedures involved in setting up a modern business. Nonetheless, they report that they make significant profits.

The case of female sellers indicates that the market today, in part at least, absorbs people with few modern skills and provides them with opportunities for income generation. Traditional moneylenders, both local men and women, are also found in the market. While their importance is eclipsed by the banks and state financing and subsidies, many borrowers prefer to deal with moneylenders rather than banks, particularly borrowers who are illiterate and have little or no experience in dealing with modern bureaucratic institutions.

The continuation of traditional aspects of the market obviously serves the needs of some segments of the population. However, the lack of development of a modernised marketing and processing system for local agricultural and pastoral production is considered to be a problem by both producers and consumers.

Major increases in local agricultural production described above have not been met by development of systems of marketing. Fruits and vegetables are brought to the market daily by producers and are then sold by auction to retailing shopkeepers with stalls in the central market. Since no provisions for preservation (except for one very small cold storage facility) or for processing have been developed, excess production that does not find a consumer is dumped as waste at the end of the day. Moreover, no organised distribution network has been developed to market local farm produce in other markets in the country where significant demand may exist. What is sold elsewhere is marketed haphazardly by individual traders. This does not result in steady and regular distribution of produce even to nearby places where demand exists. Likewise, the marketing of livestock raised in the district remains traditional, as live animals (mainly sheep and goats) are sold daily in a special area of the market. No provisions have been made, for example, for feedlots for fattening or for the establishment of modern abattoirs, which together would contribute to meeting an increasingly high local demand for good quality and regularly available fresh meat.

Conclusion

We have described in this chapter, in very broad outline, major changes that occurred in the ʿUnayzah area of north central Najd over the past five decades or so. In the old order, most men and many women worked in agriculture, herding, crafts or trade. Each of these activities was specialised and formed part of a complex division of labour. The urban market of ʿUnayzah linked the separate production sectors locally and organised the export of surplus production (especially that of the pastoralists) and the distribution of imports (which were mainly 'luxury' goods).

This locally organised, self-sustaining system was undermined by exogenous factors, such as the creation and subsequent development of the present Saudi Arabian state, the introduction of imported technology and industrially manufactured goods, and the restructuring of the Arabian economy as a result of the development of the oil industry.

Local craft production and work suffered a severe decline in the 1950s and early 1960s and by now has been all but totally eliminated – with almost all locally available material goods manufactured abroad. Traditional pastoral production in the area declined significantly in the 1960s, experienced a brief revival in the 1970s, and by now has all but ceased, as most bedouin have settled and engaged in urban occupations or in the new agriculture. Livestock production is at present more an adjunct to the agricultural sector than a continuation of traditional pastoralism.

Of the three production systems of the past, only agriculture has continued as a significant and important activity in the area. Totally transformed, however, agriculture is now highly dependent on state finance and subsidies. Local men participate in agriculture mainly as investors and managers, while the agricultural labour force is imported along with most of the technology, equipment, and other production inputs. The market, too, has been transformed. Instead of playing a leading organisational role in the local regional economy, the market now provides a relatively inefficient means for the distribution of local agricultural produce, while it has also become a provincial distribution centre for goods imported by large national commercial establishments with headquarters in other cities.

In this presentation of aspects of change in an area within the steppes of Arabia, we have purposely not stressed the division between the nomadic pastoralist (*al-badw*) and the sedentary folk (*al-hadar*). By not focusing on the differences that did and do exist, we have sought to call attention to the basic interdependence and complementarity that existed between the production system associated with the *badiya* and those associated with the *hadar*. Also, we have aimed to show that the *badiya* and the *hadar* in the ʿUnayzah area have both been affected by the same set of exogenous forces that have brought about change. Because of limitations of space, we have not presented a detailed discussion of all aspects of occupational change among the two components of the local society. However, we have stressed that occupational mobility has been high, especially since the 1960s. Thus, despite some differences, people associated with both the *badiya* and the *hadar* now own and manage new farms or other commercial establishments and employ expatriate workers, while others are engaged in government or, occasionally, private-sector employment. Both categories are thus highly dependent on the wider national economy that now dominates the country at large.

13

The destruction of resources among the mountain nomads of Dhofar

JÖRG JANZEN
Freie Universität Berlin

The present social and economic situation of the oil-producing countries of the Arabian Peninsula is the result of complex and radical changes triggered by oil revenues. As well as the impressive expansion of technical and social infrastructure, described in numerous publications,[1] there have been extensive changes in the rural areas of these countries, especially among the nomadic livestock-keeping inhabitants,[2] the bedouins, Shawawis and Jabalis. This chapter will examine developments in the nomadic habitat and the possibilities of preserving it in Dhofar, the southern region of Oman.[3]

Natural conditions for livestock-keeping

The area considered here comprises the fault escarpment of the Dhofar Range and the coastal plain below it (see map 13.1). Compared with the rest of the Arabian Peninsula, this area has a unique ecosystem resulting from light rain and mist from the June–September monsoon. Because of these special climatic conditions this tropical 'mist oasis'[4] has relatively abundant flora, comparable with tropical savannah vegetation. Given these favourable physical conditions, a highland nomadism based on cattle-keeping developed. Goat and camel breeding played a secondary role, practised by only a relatively small proportion of the mountain inhabitants.[5]

The grass pastures on the monsoon-influenced southern slope of the Dhofar range have long been in danger of overstocking, because their abundant vegetation has always attracted the sedentary livestock-keepers of the coastal settlements and neighbouring bedouin tribes. Even in the late 1970s, the conspicuous degradation of the plant cover in the monsoon zone of

[1] Altorki and Cole, 1989; Janzen, 1980, 1990, 1991; Scholz, 1979, 1985, 1987, 1992, 1995; Scholz and Janzen, 1989; Zimmermann, 1981.

[2] Asche, 1981; Birks, 1978; Chatty et al., 1991; Cole, 1975; Cordes, 1981; Cordes and Scholz, 1980; Janzen, 1980, 1982, 1983, 1986; Scholz, 1975, 1981, 1987; Zimmermann, 1981.

[3] The following comments are based on the author's earlier fieldwork (Janzen, 1980, 1982, 1983, 1986) and on studies which he carried out for the FAO in Dhofar in July and August 1990.

[4] Chadwick, 1978, p. 5.

[5] In addition, north of the watershed of the Dhofar range wild frankincense trees were an important source of income for the nomads up to the late 1960s (Janzen, 1980).

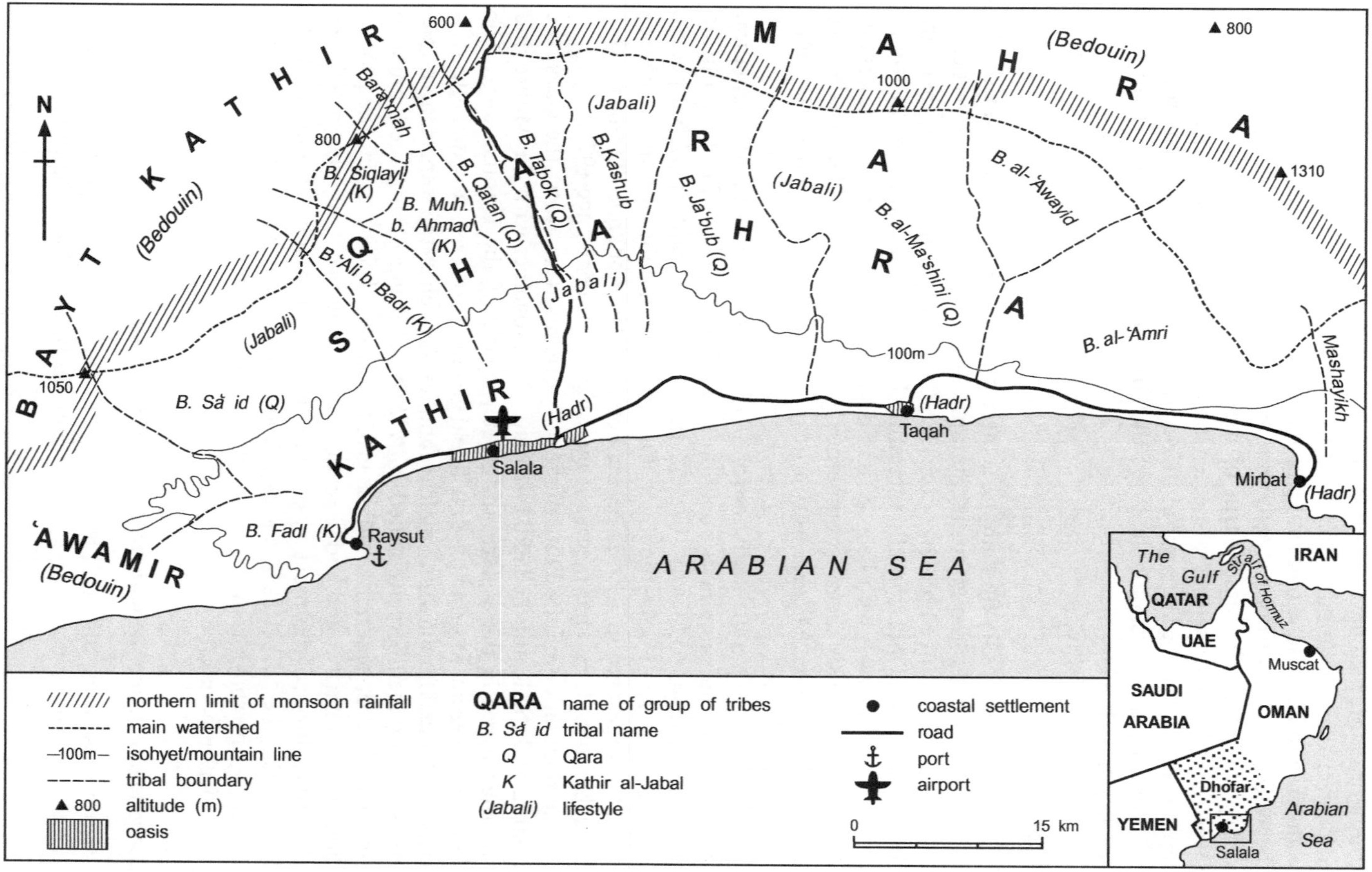

Map 13.1: South Dhofar: spatial distribution of tribes

southern Dhofar led me to the conclusion that 'the introduction of measures to protect the vegetation seems urgently necessary'.[6] Since then, damage to plant growth has reached alarming proportions. The bushes and trees outside the wadi areas have been largely eradicated and those on the wadi flanks visibly degraded. The same is true of many highly nutritious fodder grasses. Overstocked grass pastures are eaten bare before seed has been produced, rapidly impoverishing the natural fodder supply.[7] The extent of environmental problems is understandable, given the large numbers of livestock and the rise in population.

Population

The population of Dhofar comprises three groups distinct in their way of life. Besides the Jabalis (mountain inhabitants, Arab. sing. *jabali*), the vertically migrating short-range highland nomads of the Dhofar mountains, there are the less numerous, horizontally migrating long-range nomads, the bedouins (Arab. sing. *badawi*), who keep goats and camels and inhabit the deserts of inner Dhofar. Lastly the most numerous group is that of the Hadr (sedentary people, Arab. sing. *hadari*), who primarily inhabit the coastal settlements, especially Salala.

Reliable demographic statistics for 1977 and 1985 show rapid population increase. The total number of inhabitants of Dhofar rose by 67 per cent during this period, from 65,000 to 108,600. In 1985 35 per cent or 37,000 people inhabited the rural-nomadic areas. Of these, the mountain nomads constituted the largest group, with 72 per cent or 27,200 inhabitants. This means that the Jabali population has increased by some 31 per cent since 1977.[8]

The population of the Dhofar range is organised in tribes: the Qara, the Shahra and the Kathir al-Jabal (see map 13.1), together with the Mahra and the Mashayikh in the eastern and western parts of the Dhofar range. The Dhofari tribes are in principle patrilineal groups, further subdivided into subtribes, extended families and nuclear families. As well as the respected, 'noble' tribes, whose members are called *qaba'il* (Arab. sing.: *qabili*), there are also underprivileged, generally landless groups who used to be under the protection of leading tribes and had to render service in return. Until the early 1970s the tribes formed the most important political and socio-economic units. Since then the 'tribe' as a socio-political institution has lost importance. However, the shaykhs are still influential and cannot be ignored by government decision makers.

Land tenure before the nationalisation of tribal land

Before 1974, when all tribal land was nationalised, land ownership and land use were based on common law. The nomads believe that all land belongs to

[6] Janzen, 1980, p. 38. [7] According to the author's observations in July–August 1990.
[8] Oates and Ahmed, 1988, p. 2.

God. He has allowed man only the use of it. They still claim the right to use the pasture lands where their forefathers have lived and grazed their herds for generations, and they have not forgotten the exact boundaries between the different territories of the tribes and their subtribes (see map 13.1). The tribal boundaries were not closed: many inter- and intra-tribal agreements allowed neighbouring groups to use each other's areas for grazing or watering their livestock. When agreements were violated, the shaykhs of the tribes involved tried to negotiate a settlement. Particularly difficult cases were brought before a supra-tribal arbitrator, the *wali* of Dhofar, who resides in Salala, the capital of the province.[9]

With some exceptions, the traditional territories of the Jabali population were situated within a strip of land extending from the coast to the watershed of the Dhofar range (see map 13.1 and fig. 13.1). Thus each tribal area spanned all the different natural environments between the mountains and the coast. Deeply incised wadis generally formed the boundaries between the neighbouring tribal areas.

Traditional patterns of pasture land use

The different spatial requirements of the Jabali cattle-, goat- and camel-herders resulted in two different systems of pasture land use with different degrees of regional mobility (see fig. 13.1). The traditional patterns of pasture use described below have been more or less strongly modified in line with changed conditions. But knowledge of the traditional systems is of great value in the search for new, ecologically appropriate systems of pasture management.

The first type of land-use system is that of the cattle-keeping Jabalis. Their main pasture lands are situated on the south-facing plateaux of the Dhofar range (*al-khatim*). They have permanent settlements on the plateaux, where they spend the wet monsoon season and the cold winter. During the milder pre- and post-monsoon seasons, however, they move camp within that part of the plateau zone settled by the respective tribe or sub-tribe so as to use the peripheral pastures and to preserve the grassland near the main settlement for the dry winter seasons. During these periods the families live in light portable huts, and more recently in tents, a few kilometres away from the permanent settlements. Some of the Jabali families move longer distances, as far as the coastal plain (al-Jarbayb) or the watershed of the Dhofar range (al-Qatn) (see fig. 13.1).

The second type of land-use system is that of the camel- and goat-keeping Jabalis. In their spatial requirements and mobility the smaller group of camel- and goat-keeping Jabalis differs clearly from the cattle-breeders. Traditionally the camel- and goat-keepers do not possess permanent dwellings. They let their

9 It is even maintained by the local people that the *wali* issued deeds of land ownership to mountain tribes, and that the sultan's government had thus actually fixed the tribal boundaries in writing. It is now alleged that the government is concealing the existence of such documents to prevent unwanted ownership claims on pasture land.

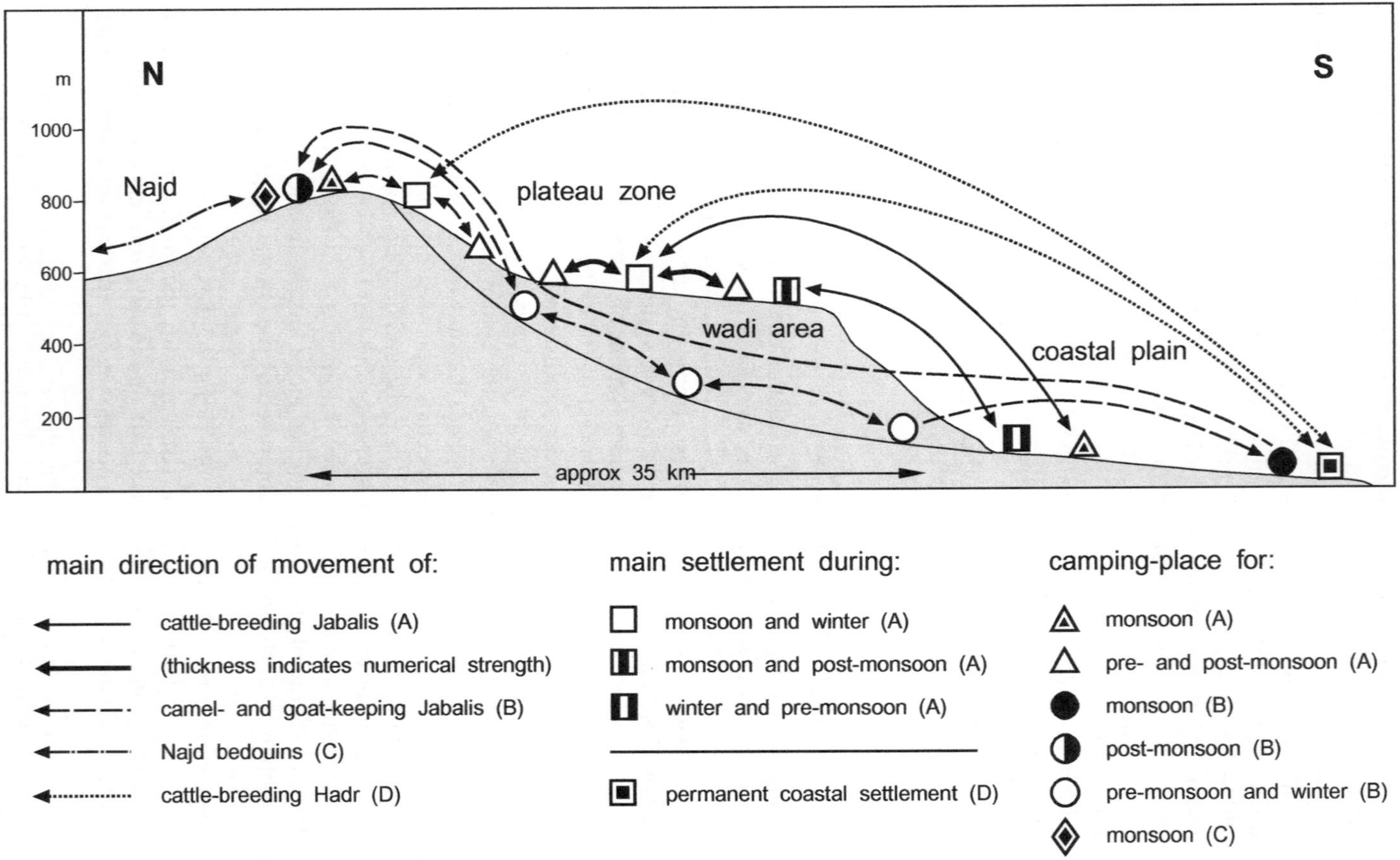

Fig. 13.1: Central Dhofar mountains: model of the traditional migration pattern of mobile livestock-keepers

camels and goats browse the trees and bushes in the wadis, and shift camp at comparatively frequent intervals. They move between the coast and the watershed of the Dhofar range. The goats graze on the steep wadi slopes, the camels prefer more gentle terrain. During the monsoon season the camels cannot graze in the mountain wadis because of the slippery ground; instead, they collect in huge camps in the coastal plain of al-Jarbayb. In the post-monsoon period the land on the watershed of the Dhofar range, al-Qatn, has always been a favourite pasture of the camel- and goat-keepers (see fig. 13.1).

The two systems of land use found among the Jabalis were adapted to the environment. Each group was responsible for a certain area. Destruction of the natural resources would have entailed an immediate threat to the Jabalis' survival. Under economic conditions offering little or no opportunity for extra-pastoral employment and no material incentives from the government, sustainable pastoral management practices were the only viable survival strategy. Various factors in the traditional system impeded a rapid increase in population and livestock numbers. For example, extreme overgrazing was prevented because the low number of waterholes in the wadis could sustain only a limited size of herd. The lack of medical and veterinary facilities resulted in a high mortality rate of humans and animals alike. Traditionally only female animals were kept for milk and rearing calves; because of the lack of marketing opportunities most of the male animals were slaughtered immediately after birth. This was a further way of preventing overstocking of the limited pastures.

The factors that previously curbed herd sizes and preserved resources are now largely a thing of the past. An ecologically inappropriate and largely abortive development policy for Dhofar has also contributed to ecological degradation in the area.

Recent changes in Dhofar and their effects on the Jabalis

In the case of Dhofar substantial material aid was provided by the Omani government to ease the hardship caused by the 1964–76 Dhofar conflict. Modern developments in the southern province of Oman began during the second half of the Dhofar war. On 18 October 1972, Sultan Qabus officially launched the 'Dhofar Development Programme'. Through free material aid and government services the young ruler hoped to win quickly the 'hearts and minds' of the nomadic population, who had backed the opposition.

One of the main aims of the programme was to develop the natural resources of Dhofar more efficiently, in order to achieve economic self-sufficiency within only a few years. An effective technical and social infrastructure was also planned, mainly in those regions inhabited by the nomadic population. Improving the difficult living and working conditions of the nomads was one of the foremost considerations here.[10]

[10] Janzen, 1980, pp. 184–286.

Within a few years this direct intervention in the nomads' regions of Dhofar resulted in all important functions – traditionally the domain of the tribes – being taken over by the government. In a very short time, immense changes occurred in the social structures of the tribes. New legal and moral concepts undermined the practices that had maintained the natural resources and guaranteed the livelihood of the tribes in their defined territories. The de facto extension of government legislation and jurisdiction into the tribal areas led to a decisive weakening of the politico-legal and socio-economic independence of the tribes. This included loss of the exclusive power of disposal over the pasture lands as a result of the nationalisation of all open, uncultivated land by the Omani government in 1974. Thus formal legal conditions were created that enabled the state to implement development measures in the lands of the nomads without obtaining the tribes' agreement and without facing claims for compensation from the nomads.

The government has not yet considered it necessary to pass a law concerning rights to forest and pasture land. The Omani Land Law regulates only questions of building, industrial and farm land.[11] According to current law, all pasture land is open to livestock regardless of ownership. After nationalisation, many nomadic families no longer kept within their old tribal boundaries, and patterns of movement came to change greatly. A particular problem has been created by the intrusion of bedouin camel-herders from inner Dhofar into the grasslands of the cattle-keepers. The traditional land claims of the Jabali cattle-keepers are no longer recognised by the camel-breeders, who maintain that 'all land is government land', and there are constant clashes, often ending in violence.

The new legal framework enabled the rapid expansion of both the administration and the technical and social infrastructure in the area inhabited by the nomads. Through the newly created system of government centres (see map 13.2) government services became available even in the most remote areas, and the nomadic population, which had largely opposed the government during the Dhofar war, was soon pacified. The various measures, such as road and well construction – more than 160 deep wells were drilled in the rural-nomadic area – the building of schools, of health-care facilities (hospitals and animal vaccination centres), of mosques and of low-cost housing, the availability of subsidies to pay for building materials, the distribution of building land, and the promotion of small-scale private trading have had a lasting effect on the nomadic economic system and lifestyle. The same is true of the many 'cash gifts' (pensions and subsidies, particularly for fodder purchases) made to the nomads by the government and the sultan.[12]

The services provided by the state have made life easier and more comfortable for both people and livestock. Improved medical care has speeded

[11] See Sultanate of Oman/Ministry of land (n.d.): Royal Decrees 5/80, 3/83 and 81/84.
[12] Janzen, 1980, 1983, 1986, 1990.

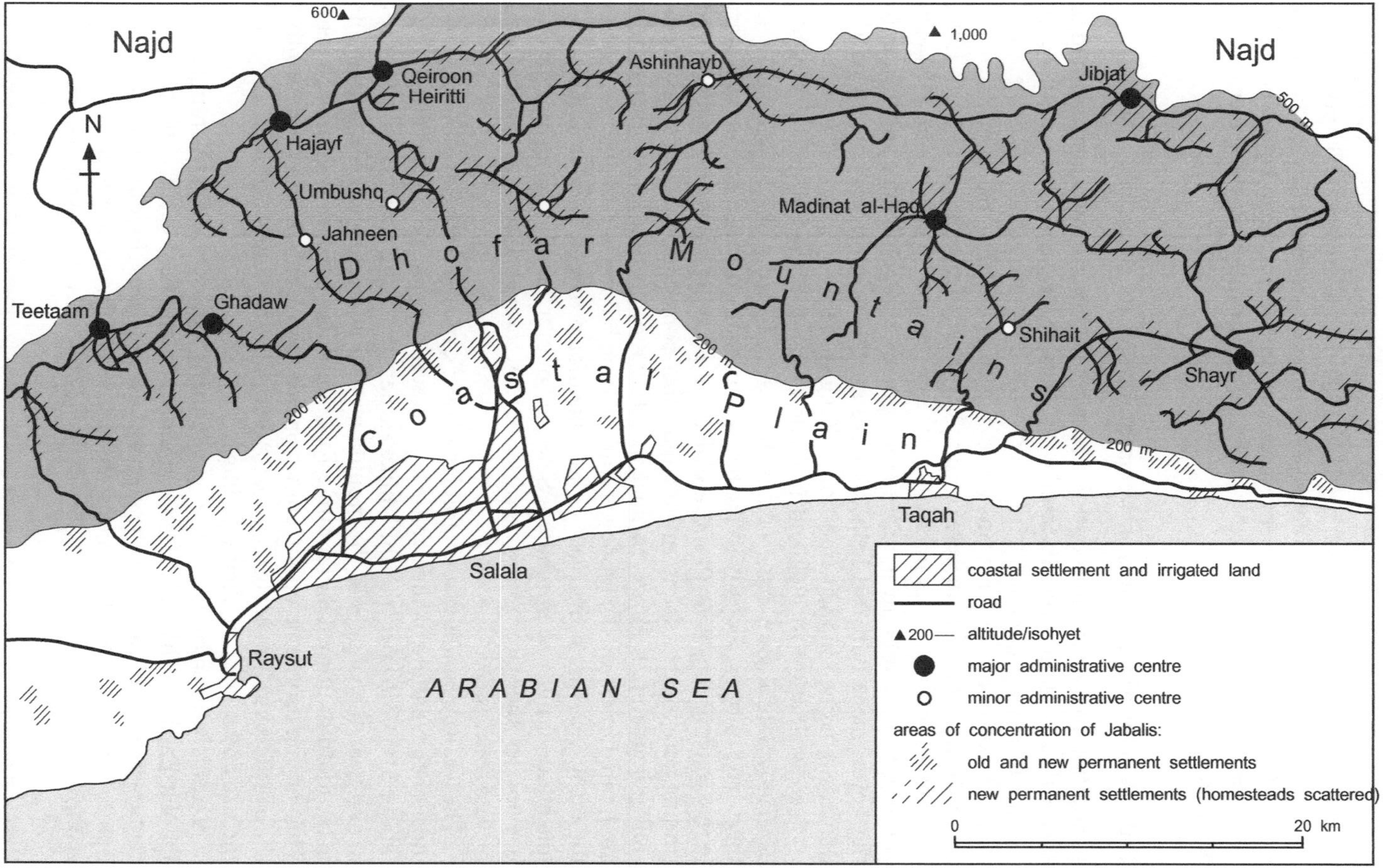

Map 13.2: South Dhofar: space utilisation and infrastructure (1990)

population growth. The size of the herds has also increased. According to official figures, about 164,000 cattle, 98,000 camels and 450,000 goats were kept in the Dhofar range in 1986.[13] These figures are much higher than those for the 1970s – the number of livestock has probably trebled. However, this is not primarily due to improved infrastructure but rather to the government's economic policy.

Failures in the economic and environmental policy for the Jabalis' habitat

In addition to the measures outlined above, the Omani government wanted to ensure that as many nomadic families as possible have a regular monthly cash income to pay for basic foodstuffs and other daily necessities. To achieve this target, a paramilitary force was created in the nomadic area. Known as the *Firqa* militia, its members were recruited primarily from the nomads. In 1990, each militia member was paid 120–140 RO (Omani riyals), about $370–430 per month. This not only increased the nomads' self-confidence and loyalty to the government but also helped to ensure that a large proportion of the nomads remained in their traditional living space.

The distribution to highland nomads of land in the coastal settlements, especially Salala, gave many Jabalis the chance to build houses and then rent them out, to open shops with the help of foreign workers, or to make a start in the transport business. Profits are often invested in further construction and trading activities, or spent on cars and other consumer goods such as television and video sets. However, since investment opportunities in other sectors are limited, most of the money is still spent on buying livestock, even though for many years now the pasture land has not provided enough fodder, and much fodder must be purchased. Since the poorer Jabali families also have to buy fodder they are often forced to borrow money from government and private sources.

The wealthy Jabalis employ foreign workers, mostly from Bangladesh, to do most of the tending of the livestock at an average wage in 1990 of 60–100 RO (about $190–310) per month. Unlike earlier times, the animals are now kept in and near the villages in the mountains, and in illegally erected settlements in the foothills of the Dhofar range, for an increasing length of time each year. The varying economic opportunities open to the Jabali families have led to a sharp differentiation according to, for example, the number of their cars, and the size and quality of their dwellings.

A decisive weakness of the government development programme for Dhofar has been the lack of an economically and ecologically effective conception of the utilisation of the nomads' living space. Undoubtedly the development efforts described above have had many positive effects on the economic system and lifestyle of the mobile livestock-keepers. However,

[13] According to information from the Department of Animal Wealth (DAW), Salala, 1990.

Table 13.1 *Animals slaughtered in the town abattoir at Salala (1988–90)*

Species	1988	1989	1990[3]
Cattle[1]	6,392	7,058	5,021
Camels[1]	1,292	1,161	761
Sheep[1]	—	33	—
Sheep[2]	9,496	11,063	6,925
Goats[1]	1,835	3,481	2,706
Total	19,015	22,796	15,413

Notes:
[1] from Dhofar; [2] from Australia and the USA;
[3] only up to and including July.

these are measures primarily aimed at improving infrastructure and services. What is lacking is a well-defined vision for the long-term integration of the Dhofari livestock-keeping nomads into the Omani economy, especially as these nomads could supply most of the meat and milk products needed in Oman.

The lack of an efficient marketing organisation to buy livestock regularly from the nomadic pastures is a serious shortcoming. The number of animals slaughtered in Salala's abattoir (see table 13.1) is relatively low compared with total Dhofar livestock. In general it is true to say that in the livestock trade the interests of influential urban businessmen are in conflict with those of the potential local producers. Because of the much higher costs of production in Dhofar the Jabali livestock cannot compete with the cheaper imported meat, mainly sheep from Australia and beef from western Europe and America.

To date, such government activities as irregular cattle-purchasing campaigns – started after Jabali protests – do not represent a viable contribution to solving the economic problems of the mobile livestock-keepers. They merely reflect the authorities' lack of overall vision. Expanding current sales of young bulls to northern Oman could increase an already lucrative source of income.

The lack of an influential lobby for the Jabalis in Salala has proved to be a great disadvantage. The wealthy businessmen and politicians in Salala have yet to show much concern for the economic development and environmental protection of the Dhofar mountains. The main reason for this is that development plans for the Dhofar range conflict with the economic interests of some influential political personalities who own several large dairy farms with more than three thousand high-yielding Friesian cows imported from Germany. These farms produce more than enough milk for Dhofar and supply even northern Oman as well. By contrast, there is no organised sales network for the milk production of the Dhofari nomads, whose excess milk has sometimes had to be destroyed.

The fodder farms on the Salala plain, which in turn belong to the big dairy farmers, rely on supplying the Dhofari nomads with hay for their livestock throughout much of the year. The Dhofar Cattle Feed Company also owns a feed factory producing cereal-based concentrates. Because of the highly degraded plant cover in their pasture lands, the Jabalis are heavily dependent on additional fodder supplies. Hence the fodder producers enjoy what is virtually a monopoly. The only serious competitors are the mainly Pakistani traders who run lorries daily transporting hay along the over 1,000-kilometre-long highway from the Batina coastal plain.[14]

Radical changes in spatial mobility with major consequences for the environment

One visible effect of these changes in the politico-legal and socio-economic framework has been a radical change in nomadic mobility patterns. Various factors are responsible. First, the spread of motor transport has increased the mobility of the mountain nomads. Necessities such as food, fodder and water are easily available at all times, making migration in search of food and water superfluous. Secondly, the installation of deep wells at easily accessible points on the plateaux has also reduced mobility. Now that the cattle no longer make the arduous journey to the springs in the wadis their reproduction rate has risen and the herds have increased in size.[15]

The considerable expansion of the road network into highland areas previously accessible only by pack animal and the construction of many new administrative centres and settlements along these roads (see map 13.2) both facilitate sedentarisation of the cattle- and even the camel-keepers. Many families keep their cattle in the vicinity of the new settlements and wells for most of the year. The resultant overgrazing is aggravated by the fact that the best pastures are also being used by non-Jabali livestock-keepers, especially camel-herders. Since camel urine makes the grass unpalatable to cattle, the cattle-herders lose even more pasture land and the pressure on the remaining pasture increases. Only a minority of Jabalis continue with the traditional pattern of movement.

However, the reduction of mountain pasture land occasioned by these changes seems slight compared with the dramatic loss of pasture land on the coastal plains. The vast tracts of building land given to the developing town of Salala and to illegal settlements at the foot of the mountains, the expansion of irrigation agriculture by urban businessmen for fodder production and, not least, the designation of large recreation areas for town-dwellers (picnic and fenced-in afforestation areas, see map 13.2) have halved the pasture lands used

[14] These Pakistani traders collaborate with Omani sponsors or act on their behalf.
[15] According to the DAW in Salala, 1990.

by the nomads during the periods before and after the monsoon season. Furthermore, the quality of the potential pasture lands on the coastal plain has been greatly reduced. Vehicle tracks criss-cross the area, causing soil compacting and impeding plant growth. Additional factors adversely affecting the coastal rangelands are the uncontrolled depositing of rubbish, the almost complete deforestation of the foothills, and the excessive pumping of groundwater to supply Salala and the irrigated farms.

The plain on the watershed of the Dhofar range, known as the Qatn zone, presents a particular type of problem. Large portions of this traditionally Jabali area are also frequented by bedouins with big camel herds. The camel keepers have already begun to erect scattered huts with shelters for the camels. Because the camel-herders remain in the area for such a long time, most of the shrubs and trees have been used for fuel and building material. This is a double loss, as the shrubs and trees also retained surface run-off which is vital for groundwater recharge in the Dhofar Range and the coastal plain.

An assessment of recent changes in the Jabali habitat

In terms of development policy the results of the changes over the past two decades in the Jabali habitat, i.e. the Dhofar range and the Jarbayb coastal plain, are in many respects negative. One of the main targets for the development programme in the nomadic areas – to bring about the economic self-sufficiency of Dhofar within a few years – has not been achieved. In spite of ample funds and the opportunity to draw on the experiences of other countries with nomadic populations, there has been little serious attempt to develop the economy and maintain the ecological equilibrium of the mountain region. The pacification policy pursued by the state and the sultan, backed up by material gifts to the Jabalis, has made the majority of the mountain population heavily dependent on the state. During the past twenty years all important decisions have been made by the state; this has encouraged the Jabalis to adopt a 'give me' attitude typical of welfare recipients. If the socio-economic situation of the mountain nomads is compared to that of the sedentary urban population of the coast, especially Salala, and the catastrophic ecological situation in the Jabali habitat is taken into account, it is clear that the mobile livestock-keepers are faring far less well, despite all the progress made in expanding the technical and social infrastructure of the Jabali living space.[16]

A development policy for the Jabali habitat

The ecological problems affecting the Dhofar range and the coastal plain could in part be solved, or at least alleviated, by a comprehensive package of

[16] An earlier prognosis which I advanced unfortunately appears on the way to being confirmed: 'If a corresponding economic development policy is not implemented . . . [it will] certainly not be possible to prevent a marginalization of large parts of the nomadic population' (Janzen, 1980, p. 286).

measures within the framework of an integrated development programme for the rural–nomadic areas of Dhofar as a whole. It should be emphasised once again that isolated measures, such as the introduction of a pastoral land-use system adapted to the changed situation, will have little chance of success if such a system does not form a part of a comprehensive conception of development that can win the backing and active participation of the mobile livestock-keepers. Such a programme could be implemented in three stages. First, excessively large herds should be rapidly reduced: by means of a livestock-purchasing campaign organised and financed by the state, the present numbers of animal stock could be halved. One way of marketing the purchased livestock would be for the state to impose measures compelling Omani livestock traders and importers to sell a proportion of the domestic livestock. Difficult to sell in Oman, camel meat could be supplied cheaply, or even free of charge, to countries such as Egypt, where the meat consumption of most poor people consists largely of camel meat.

The second stage should be the creation of a medium-term development programme for the nomadic areas in Dhofar. This programme should form part of the next five-year plan, and be closely linked with the new 'Regional Development and Land Use Plan for the Southern Region'.[17] The first priority should be the introduction of a system of pastoral land use that is ecologically sound, financially feasible and politically practicable. The proposed 'Law for Rangelands and Forestry' should be enacted as soon as possible, to provide a legal basis for implementing such a system. A further element would be the establishment of an efficient marketing system to ensure the steady withdrawal of livestock from the rangelands. It is essential to continue, as part of a long-term marketing strategy, the government programme, initiated in mid-1990, whereby about 15,000 cattle a year are bought up in the Dhofar mountains for delivery to the state's public services such as the army, militia, police, etc.

Priority should also be accorded to afforestation measures, to control of the rapid and often illegal spread of settlements in the nomadic areas, and to the spatial limitation of leisure areas.

The creation of a 'Livestock Development Company', owned and run by the Jabalis themselves on a similar pattern to a services co-operative, could help to meet the needs of the mobile livestock-keepers and to reduce their dependence on the influential merchants in the towns. Such a company would have the additional advantage of being able to play an important part in introducing a new rangeland management system, e.g. in procuring building materials, transportation, credits and fodder etc.

But the main objective of a development programme for the Dhofar range and the coastal plain should, in my opinion, be the introduction of a range-management system based on the well-tried local forms of pasture land use

[17] Atkins/WS International, 1989.

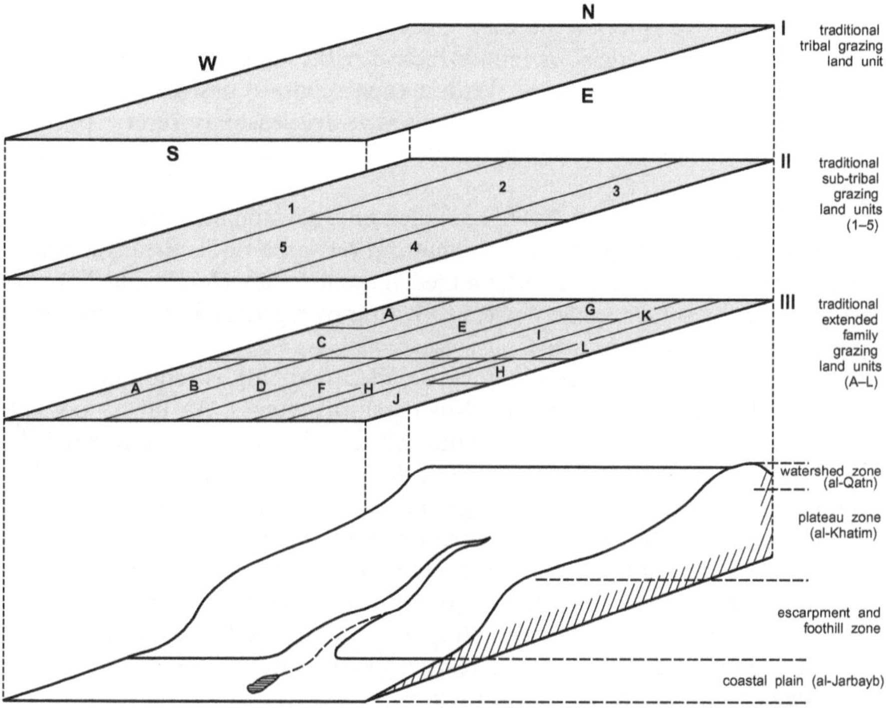

Fig. 13.2: Model of a traditional Jabali tribal grazing land unit: spatial division

(see figs. 13.1 and 13.2). The cornerstone of this system must be that the formerly tribal but now nationalised pastureland should no longer be accessible to all. Secondly, exclusive rights of use for a clearly defined area should be granted to a specific group in return for the acceptance of 'ecological responsibility' (the revival of a traditional practice). The group might be a small tribe, a sub-tribe, an extended family or simply a group of several livestock-keeping families on friendly terms with each other. The user group and their descendants should have free use of the pasture area to an environmentally tolerable degree. This right would include not only the grass, bushes and trees but also other resources such as water, wild berries, honey, wood and resin. When partitioning the pasture areas, care should be taken to ensure that the requirements of each user group are considered: wherever possible each area should span different ecological zones in order to promote maximum spatial mobility within the respective pasture area. When allocating the pasture areas to the user groups, rights of use should be assigned not only to the erstwhile land-owning tribes but also to the traditionally dependent, landless livestock-keepers. Failure to do this would mean that these groups would lose the right of free access to all pastures gained as a result of nationalisation, quickly leading to new conflicts. If necessary, the users themselves should build barriers (stone walls, hedges or fences) between the different pasture areas to prevent animals from straying. Within each separate pasture area, plateau spurs bounded by steep cliffs could be used as dry season or reserve pastures, a measure already practised in recent years by several livestock-keeping groups.

In return for exclusive rights of use, each group would be obliged to assume full responsibility for protecting the natural resources in its area. In cases of ecologically poor land use, the planned 'Law for Rangelands and Forestry' would give the state specific powers to withdraw rights of use and to impose penalties where appropriate.

Before introducing such a system, detailed mapping is required to document traditional and present land-ownership patterns. As far as possible, demarcation of the new pasture lands should follow the traditional tribal boundaries (see map 13.1 and fig. 13.2). Most mountain nomads know these boundaries well and secretly still regard them as binding. In spite of nationalisation, when conflicts arise between different livestock-keeping groups the old boundaries are still tacitly respected, even by government officials. Furthermore the administrative boundaries between the various districts of the Dhofar range generally follow the old tribal limits. Hence it would probably not cause undue difficulty to respect the majority of these old boundaries when delimiting the new pastoral areas.

An important precondition for the successful introduction of a new range-management system is the active participation of the respective livestock-keeping groups in both the planning and implementation processes. As well as the traditional tribal institutions, such as the shaykhs and councils of elders, newly formed interest groups should be included and encouraged to work closely with government bodies.

Conclusion

The various forms of mobile livestock-keeping still represent the best means of active adaptation to the specific geographical conditions prevailing in the dry belt of the Old World.[18] Given a sustainable stocking level, maximum livestock mobility is still the best way to protect the limited resources of the pasture lands of the region. Now that most of the concepts advanced by the development agencies for use of rangeland have failed, the agencies and their experts have begun to reconsider their assumptions. Currently, attention is again being paid to traditional range-management systems. The proposals advanced above to save the existing pasture land in the habitat of the mountain nomads of south Dhofar should be seen in the context of this process of rethinking.

[18] Cf. Janzen, 1988; Scholz, 1986.

The recommendation of the introduction of a range-management system in which users assume ecological responsibility is based on the hope that, because of their deep emotional ties to their own traditional tribal land, the livestock-keeping groups would be more willing to practise a resource-sustaining land-use system there than elsewhere. The introduction of such a range-management system in monsoon-influenced south Dhofar would surely help to preserve this unique and endangered ecosystem.

In other countries of the Old World dry belt, too, it is time to take a new look at the destructive land-use practices resulting from the nationalisation of pasture land and, if possible, replace them by sustainable land-use systems. It is hoped that this chapter on the habitat of the mountain nomads of Dhofar will contribute to this process.

14

Strategies for the improvement of the cultivated zone

M. J. JONES

International Center for Agricultural Research in the Dry Areas, Aleppo

The cultivated zone bordering the Syrian steppe, and closely related to the steppe historically, culturally and agriculturally, carries a dynamic and expanding economy and population. Agronomists refer to it as the barley–livestock zone and describe its farming systems as 'barley based'. Outside small areas of irrigation, barley is almost the only crop grown, and its purpose – in various forms – is to feed the flocks of sheep and goats that are the mainstay of the local agricultural economy. The nominal boundary between this zone and the steppe is usually said to be the 200 mm isohyet. Range specialists and other protectors of the steppe understandably would like to set it higher, at 220 mm, even 250 mm, but the reality that land users are already creating on the ground is of opportunistic ploughing below the 200 mm isohyet. The wetter limit of the barley zone is also diffuse. Depending on local conditions, at about 300 mm mean annual rainfall, barley-based farming merges gradually into systems in which wheat largely replaces barley, other crops are grown (lentils, chick peas and summer watermelons) and animals have a lesser importance.

Until twenty or thirty years ago wheat was also the main crop below the 300 mm isohyet,[1] but the arable area then was much smaller and limited mainly to more favourable parts of the topography. Rural communities were less integrated into the national economy, and subsistence needs had priority, the food preference being for wheat. Animals were economically important, but feed requirements were supplied largely by local grazing and transhumance. The new dominance of barley results from a shift in agricultural priority away from human food, which can easily be bought in, towards animal feed, which has become scarcer and more valuable. This shift is part of a broader syndrome encompassing rapidly rising populations (human and animal), improved communications, rapid mechanisation, an expansion of arable cropping into grazing lands, and increasing market prices for animal products.

The farmers' logic for growing barley in dry areas rather than wheat is sound. Not only is barley more versatile as a feed source, but its ability to yield more grain, more reliably, under adverse conditions becomes all the more crit-

[1] Jaubert and Oglah, 1985.

ical as cultivation is pushed on to shallower soils and into drier areas. Increasingly, the farmer's strategy seems to be to maximise animal numbers and to cover the landscape with barley, selling the surplus grain in favourable years and supplementing it in unfavourable years with transported feeds (agricultural wastes, imported barley) and by transhumance to wetter and irrigated areas. This system, which is still expanding, seems unlikely to be sustainable.

The problems for agricultural research in this zone exist at two levels:

1. Agronomic: crop yields are low and subject to large seasonal fluctuations; there is little rotation of crops, legumes are rarely grown and fallows are disappearing; fertilisers are little used.
2. Land management and sustainability: much land that is unsuitable or marginal for arable use is being brought into cultivation without any conservation measures; the alignment of land holdings often compels tillage up and down the slope; windbreaks are totally absent; the loss of nearly all crop residues to grazing, in combination with frequent tillage, is detrimental to the inherently weak soil structure; most grazing land is over-utilised and exhibits varying degrees of soil and vegetation degradation.

Underlying all the problems at the second level are the complexities of land tenure and utilisation rights and an almost total lack of central or local community control over land utilisation. Technical issues are thus heavily entangled with social, economic and, above all, political considerations. There is also a philosophical issue. Successes at the first, agronomic level resulting in the introduction of more productive techniques seem likely to fan the flames of further land exploitation: a more drought-resistant cultivar intended to help ecologically valid barley–livestock farming at, say, 250 mm rainfall also encourages an entrepreneur to try his luck ploughing up yet drier steppeland. The optimistic view sometimes expressed that increased production in relatively favourable areas will *decrease* the pressure on less favourable areas unfortunately ignores human nature.

The present chapter sets out to summarise recent research activities at the first level of agronomy and outline new initiatives and ideas relating to the second level, that of management, with references where relevant to the policy context.

Summary of recent agronomic research

Little or no agronomic research was conducted in the driest arable areas before about 1980: not unreasonably, the limited available research investment was seen as likely to yield a quicker and larger return in more favoured areas with greater potential productivity. When dry-area research did start, high priority was given to breeding barley with a greater tolerance of environmental stress, particularly drought stress. A major aim was improved stability, that is a

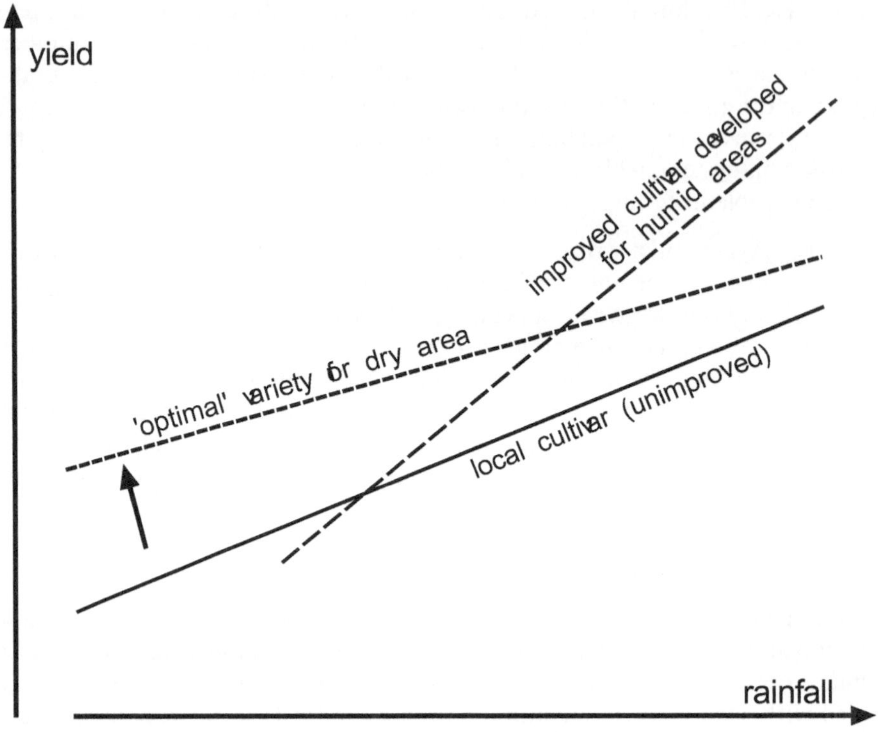

Fig. 14.1: Selection of the appropriate cultivar to help stabilise yields in dry areas

reduced weather-related variability in yield. This means raising the yield potential for very dry years without undue prejudice to the crop's capacity to respond strongly to better conditions in wet years (see fig. 14.1). Some plant characteristics favouring more efficient utilisation of low rainfall have been identified, but real progress depends on being able to exploit those characteristics under the crop-management conditions (soil type, planting times, fertility status, etc.) that obtain on farmers' fields. Improvements to germplasm and management must be co-ordinated.

Farmers currently use few inputs, and a major cause of low yields is inadequate soil fertility. Most arable soils in this zone are low in available phosphate and nitrogen. Quite small applications of fertiliser phosphate, particularly if banded with the seed, speed up barley development and growth during the cold winter period; and the earlier, more complete ground cover achieved and the earlier maturity of the crop ensure more production per unit of rainfall.[2] In a recent four-year series of seventy-five fertiliser trials conducted with the

[2] Cooper et al., 1987.

local barley landrace on farmers' fields across northern Syria, mean yield increases given by 27–40 kg per hectare were around 30 per cent for grain and 40–45 per cent for straw.[3] Rainfall ranged from 136 to 568 mm (mean, 284 mm). Under wetter conditions there were large responses to nitrogen fertiliser, but on a percentage basis the largest responses to phosphate were at the drier sites. Fairly generally, responses were economic at current costs and prices;[4] and Cooper and Bailey, working from these data, calculated that Syria has the barley-growing potential to feed its current national flock in three out of four years without ploughing up its grazing land.[5]

One continuing change in farming practices, as part of a general intensification of land use, is the elimination of fallows. This need not be regretted. In the drier arable areas fallows provide some grazing in winter and early spring but not much. After a wet year fallows store water in the soil profile for the next year's crop but, again, not much. Fallowing allows some renewal of nutrient availability, particularly of nitrogen, but the same can be achieved in other ways. The realistic question is not whether fallows should be replaced but what they should be replaced with; and the most worrying feature of current practice is the slide towards almost continuous barley cropping. Monocropping cereals is always a risky enterprise. Not only does fertility (particularly nitrogen availability) and, therefore, yield-potential decline rapidly unless fertilisers are used, but pest build-up is a serious hazard. There are already areas of northern Syria where the 'ground pearl' (*Porphyrophora tritici*), an insect that attacks the base of the cereal stem, is endemic. Control requires that cereal cropping is restricted to alternate years.

The logical replacement for fallow is a legume crop, which may be expected to improve the soil nitrogen economy and to break the cycle of most cereal pests. Grain legumes (lentils, chick peas and faba beans) are important fallow-replacing crops in wetter areas where wheat predominates; but the barley-based areas are too dry for these crops. Lentil is a potential option at the wetter fringe, and efforts are being made to develop varieties that will be productive below the 300 mm isohyet; but the most promising species at the moment are annual feed legumes and legume-based pastures. If the dominance of barley is to be moderated, other high-quality feed crops appear to offer the best chance of acceptance in a livestock-oriented farming system.

The most appropriate annual feed legumes are various species of vicia and lathyrus, which may be grazed green in spring, cut for hay or harvested mature (like lentils) for grain and straw. It should be noted that these are indigenous plants. There remain many varieties, even some whole species, that have yet to be evaluated,[6] and the process of genetic improvement has hardly begun – so the scope for future increases in yield potential is large. Even the varieties we currently have are impressive. Long-term rotations of barley with *Vicia sativa*

[3] Jones and Wahbi, 1992. [4] Mazid, 1990. [5] Cooper and Bailey 1990a.
[6] Abd El-Moneim et al., 1988.

and *Lathyrus sativus* at two sites in Syria out-produced the barley–fallow and barley–barley rotations favoured by farmers by 20–60 per cent in terms of dry matter production and by around 100 per cent or more in terms of crop protein (nitrogen) output.[7] However, farmers, though aware of these crops, rarely sow them. Major problems are the cost and restricted availability of seed and the labour costs of harvesting the mature crop. Also, it is widely believed by farmers that legumes are much less productive than barley in very dry situations; and, fairly generally, there is an inadequate appreciation of the high feed value of legumes and their major contribution, direct and indirect, to the protein output of the whole rotation.

Feed legumes can be sown and harvested like other annual crops and so do not require any new management skills of the farmers. In contrast, pasture legumes (various medicago species), grown in effect as productive fallows, need careful control of grazing to overcome winter weeds and, later, to ensure an adequate contribution of new seed to the soil 'seed bank' for subsequent re-establishment. This requires fairly sophisticated management. Currently, research is only at the stage of selecting locally adapted indigenous varieties and monitoring the productivity of barley–medicago rotations; but, in time, this system also should have the potential to out-produce monocropped barley.

One further research theme at this level is supplemental irrigation, defined as the provision of extra water to crops that could and would be grown at that site anyway – in this case, barley, or possibly wheat. The main aim is to stabilise yields from year to year, using relatively small amounts of water as efficiently as possible. For example, a yield of 1 ton per hectare from 200 mm rainfall might be boosted to, say, 2.5 tons per hectare with an addition of just 100 mm irrigation. Further increments of grain from further increments of water, though possible, would probably be less efficient in terms of water use. Efficiency is important. There are many small irrigated patches in the barley zone, but nearly everywhere the levels of the aquifers supplying them are falling. Currently, much of the water is used for the full irrigation of high-value summer crops (e.g. cotton), for which much more water is required per unit of biomass. The alternative, more efficient strategy, of supplemental irrigation to winter crops needs to be encouraged.

Land management and sustainability

The research outlined above may be expected to contribute to an increased production – of barley, of other feed crops and, therefore, of livestock – in the barley-based farming system. New barley varieties, legumes, crop rotations, fertilisers, supplemental irrigation, if all adopted, could easily double mean productivity per unit area over, say, the next ten years. However, such a success in the short term would be no guarantee of sustained output in the long term;

[7] Jones and Singh, 1995.

quite possibly the reverse. The soil cover is fragile. There is little natural vegetation to protect it, and its naturally weak structure makes it vulnerable to movement by wind and water. Almost all the innovations so far suggested involve an increased intensity of agricultural activity, especially tillage, and also provide incentives for extending the area of that tillage to land of even greater fragility.

One positive feature is that more frequent cropping and greater production by each crop should return more residues to the soil. But the potential benefit of this to the soil's structure and resistance to erosion is unlikely to be realised unless measures are adopted to moderate such negative influences as frequent tillage (which disrupts soil structure); intensive *in situ* grazing of stubble and crop residues (which reduces the amount of residue returned and tramples the soil); exposure of broad expanses of unprotected land throughout the long, arid and windy summer; and tillage of sloping land perpendicular to the contour.

Such problems are not unique to the dry areas of West Asia, and numerous technical solutions have been devised elsewhere to overcome them. In one sense, no new research is required. There is no need to re-invent the wheel. Such techniques as stubble mulching, windbreaks and contour banks are already well documented and could be technically effective; but serious problems arise locally in respect of the economic feasibility and social and political acceptability of such measures.

What is needed is much adaptive research, taking basic concepts such as stubble mulch, windbreaks and contour farming and modifying them to local circumstances. This requires technical experimentation backed up by an understanding of local society. It is essential to know the land users, their interrelationships and their objectives. A case in point: research has demonstrated that small amounts of phosphate fertiliser greatly increase the herbage, especially the legume component, of degraded hill pastures in the wheat and barley zones, resulting in large increases in animal production;[8] but transfer of this simple concept to the farming community is held back by the complexities of communal pasture management.

A strategy for future research that now seems slowly to be evolving in ICARDA comprises:

- Testing likely techniques in forms potentially amenable to local adoption;
- collecting data – scientific and technical, social and economic – for better informed decision making and implementation of new techniques;
- enhancing technical expertise for information handling and modelling back-up.

[8] Osman et al., 1991.

Already, some work has been started in relation to wind erosion, which appears to be an increasing threat in both barley zone and steppe. In the steppe, the destruction of the natural vegetation by overgrazing is a major cause, but ploughing for barley production is a hazard in both zones. Relevant research activities include:

1 *Tillage/stubble mulch trial.* At Brayda (barley zone, mean rainfall 270 mm), we are looking at no-tillage (versus normal tillage) in combination with ungrazed (versus grazed) stubble management in barley–barley and barley–vetch rotations. Although the plots are not large enough to permit any monitoring of wind erosion *per se*, they will provide hard data on the effects of these conservative treatments on soil properties and crop yields. We hope to demonstrate that tillage is not essential, that crops can be successfully established by direct drilling into the previous year's stubble, and that less frequent tillage and stubble retention improve the soil's physical condition. It is not unreasonable to suppose that direct-drill equipment might be adopted, at least by larger-scale operators, if the incentives were right. The avoidance or reduced intensity of stubble grazing presents greater difficulties.

2 *Fodder shrubs as windbreaks.* Soil conservation measures, however potentially beneficial in the long term, are acceptable to land users only if they can be seen to be profitable in the short term. Thus a project to establish windbreaks to protect exposed barley lands would succeed only if barley yields were increased appreciably and/or the windbreaks themselves were economically productive. In the steppe, schemes to improve rangeland by planting fodder shrubs such as *Atriplex spp.*[9] also control wind erosion, but shrubs may be less attractive to land users than the quick returns obtained from planting barley. The spread into the steppe of regular or seasonally opportunistic barley planting may be unstoppable, short of draconian measures by governments.

One possible compromise – with application to both steppe and barley-zone conditions – would be to grow the barley in arable strips between shrub hedges. The hedges, planted transverse to the prevailing wind direction, would (it is suggested) provide erosion control and a grazing resource, while the greater part of the land surface could still produce barley (and other feed crops). (A variant of this could be shrub planting on contour bunds for the control of water erosion on sloping land. In that case, smaller, more closely spaced shrubs (e.g. *Salsola vermiculata*) might be appropriate, since the main purpose would be to protect and stabilise the bund.)

At the present time we do not have the resources to set up the very

[9] Sankary, 1986.

large trials needed to test the effectiveness, practicability and potential acceptability of such systems; but meanwhile:

(i) We will monitor wind erosion (movement of material, windspeed, etc.) at several sites along a transect from Brayda to Mragha, a steppe station of the Syrian steppe and Range Directorate planted to atriplex. At the latter site, measurements will be made on the open rangeland and among the atriplex shrubs.

(ii) We are establishing a four-hectare trial at Gharifa (barley zone, mean rainfall 250 mm) to investigate the effects of atriplex hedges on barley and feed legumes grown in strips between them. Before testing hedges on a large scale, we need to be sure that barley yields are not depressed by competition from the bushes. The main factors tested will be width and planting density of the hedges and the width of the cultivated strips between the hedges.

3 *Dryland resource management project.* While it is essential to test the technical feasibility of new resource-management systems such as windbreaks, any large-scale implementation requires an understanding of the interrelationships between current agricultural practices (and their evolutionary trends) and their biophysical and socioeconomic context. Although there are commonalties, such relationships tend to be fairly strongly country- or location-specific. We believe it is important that the management problems of fragile agricultural resources be looked at nationally in a multidisciplinary way. A project has therefore been started to promote case studies by small national teams of specific problem areas in their countries. The general aim is to assess the impact of existing production systems on the natural resource base and, with land-users' participation, to seek safer, more sustainable farming practices.

One such study will be conducted by Jordanian scientists at Lajun in southern Jordan, along a short transect that covers several different land-use systems: open rangeland (i.e. uncontrolled grazing with barley-growing incursions), government and co-operative range reserves, and settled arable areas. It will appraise the current situation in the open range (aims and perceptions of land users; condition of soil and vegetation) and compare it with the situation in the two reserves in terms of resource degradation, current productivity and the needs of the local communities. Another case study has been started in southern Tunisia, and we expect others will soon be initiated in Libya, Yemen, Syria and, possibly, Lebanon. The findings of each study will be presented at a joint workshop. We hope this will not only serve as an exchange of experiences and ideas but will also lead to funding for more substantial research and development efforts in the future.

Modelling and information systems

The problem of location specificity underlies all the research outlined so far. In the case of agronomic trials, the relative advantages of different crop cultivars, fertiliser rates or rotations vary according to site conditions, soil type and previous utilisation, and – most especially – seasonal weather. Where the focus is on environmental problems, the site variables may be different (e.g. climate, topography, soil, vegetation cover, land use); but the problem, that the information collected pertains to an environment that is essentially unique in time and space, is the same. For the fertiliser trials on barley mentioned above, each site was carefully characterised, so that at the end we could specify likely future responses of barley to fertiliser in terms of initial soil fertility status, previous crop, rainfall receipt, etc. However, this approach is useful only for defined problems in defined areas. For more general application, a much broader reference framework is required, to which specific questions can be addressed: for example, what crops (or cultivars) will best fit a particular, defined agricultural environment; or, will the conservation measures found effective in area A be suitable in area B and, if not, what modifications are needed? And such questions may be posed at different scales, within countries or across whole regions.

Under the general label of agroecological characterisation, ICARDA is gradually developing expertise in the modelling of crop growth, weather/climate and soil erosion, and in geographic information and other data-management systems. In large part, its work consists of selecting from existing models and systems world-wide and of adapting and linking them. There are major problems in acquiring data and in validating the models. In the case of wind erosion, it seems we must start from scratch by collecting data to validate an off-the-shelf model for steppe and dry barley-area conditions. There is also the question of how to build into the model the relevant social and economic factors. The general aim is not to capture electronically the agricultural environment of the whole region but to contribute, to national governments and other users, tested systems and software for defining and matching environments, production systems and development technologies.

Discussion

In its traditional dimension, agricultural research sought – and still seeks – to resolve specific technical problems with specific technical innovations, such as improved crop varieties or fertilisers or new forages and health aids for animals. However, farmer resistance to many such innovations has slowly, over the past two decades, established the necessary complementarity of a socio-economic dimension. Research has thus expanded beyond the experimental station into various types of surveys of farmers and trials on farmers' fields, with the purpose of diagnosing more clearly the real problems and needs of practical farming and of identifying the constraints to the adoption of apparently appropriate technical innovations. The third and newest dimension is that of 'sustainability'. This takes as a premise that agricultural methods, new and old, should not only be practical and feasible economically and socially but should also conserve the long-term productive capacity of the resource base: soil, water reserves and natural vegetation.

These three dimensions are inseparable in any quest to solve the agricultural problems of the barley zone and steppe. As already mentioned, many technical solutions (or, at least, ameliorations) are potentially available for the problems of arable farming; but not all are acceptable to the farmer, and the ones that are acceptable may well be those least conducive to sustainability. Without compensating conservation measures, existing technical solutions will probably lead to an intensification of arable cropping, and also to the increasing cultivation of less suitable land. In this domain the agronomist finds himself in danger of pushing the system closer to the brink of ecological disaster.

What can be done? As long as human populations continue to increase, the process of 'development' cannot be halted in barley zone or steppe. The most we can hope to do is to understand better the forces driving it and seek ways to limit the damage. A strict conservationist position appears to be untenable. Even attempts to produce appropriate research, development initiatives and supportive (and enforced) regulations are gravely handicapped by the dearth of hard, reliable information – in three major but interdependent spheres:

1. The lands with which we are concerned are not uniform. Apart from the obvious rainfall (and temperature) gradients, there are major large- and small-scale variations in relief, topography, drainage, soil type/depth and vegetation (potential and actual), which have not been mapped with regard to their potential agricultural utilisation on a sustainable basis.
2. There are no comparative 'production' data for different forms of land use. Whether, for instance, range-grazing or arable cropping is the better way to use land on the 150 mm (or 200 mm or 250 mm) isohyet is a matter of conjecture and, in any case, depends on the basis of judgement chosen: mean annual biomass and/or its feed value (with/without consideration of its annual variability); economic return (timescale, level of investment?); or long-term effects on the resource base (soil, vegetation).
3. Land ownership and tenure systems differ between arable and grazing areas and between higher-rainfall settled areas and the drier steppe, with local differences deriving from earlier tribal boundaries and more recent settlement history. Moreover, these systems – and land users' perceptions of them – are evolving as a consequence of local and national changes in political and economic power.

Clearly, in what is already an ecological crisis, any effective action needs to be a pragmatic mix of research (information collection, environmental description and technology testing), emergency implementation of best-bet conservation measures, and land-use controls firmly policed but sympathetic to present land users' needs. Such an approach, even on a localised 'pilot scheme' basis, would require substantial funding over a long period of time. Short-term priorities ensure, however, that most government investment in agricultural development will continue to be in wetter areas where returns are more assured; and for all the western world's vocal concern for environmental conservation, most donors are as politically bound as ever to produce quick results.

It is possible to imagine the barley zone and adjacent steppe as a stable landscape, in which fields of productive barley–legume rotations lying between windbreaks and contour banks merge gradually into well-conserved pastures on the hills and into paddocks of well-managed natural range and plantations of improved range shrubs in the steppe; with, where the topography is appropriate, water harvested from rocky slopes (or pumped judiciously from aquifers) and channelled to support oases of trees and more intensive forage production. Some of the elements of this landscape exist already but are gravely threatened by uncontrolled exploitation. The massive challenge is to switch this whole zone and its people from an exploitative mode of land use to one of rational, sustainable utilisation.

15

Linkages between livestock and agricultural systems in Syria

T. T. TREACHER

International Center for Agricultural Research in the Dry Areas, Aleppo

Approximately 55 per cent (10.2 million hectares) of the total land area of Syria has rainfall below 200 mm in 50 per cent of years. In the past this area was covered by a vegetation of perennial bushes with annual plants in spring. It is called 'range' throughout this chapter, in spite of the fact that cultivation is now widespread in this rainfall zone. It is estimated that 75 per cent of Syria's sheep[1] are kept in this area for a major part of the year. In 1989 the total sheep population was 14.01 million, suggesting that 10.5 million sheep are in flocks based in the range.[2]

This chapter describes the links between the Syrian range and the cultivated land to the west and north that enable this very large number of sheep to be maintained in the Syrian range in spite of its severely degraded state. The chapter then discusses some of the research in progress that, it is hoped, may lead to modifications in farming systems to increase feed supplies. Finally, it considers some of the social and economic constraints that make it difficult to break the present cycle of expanding sheep numbers and accelerating degradation of the rangeland in Syria.

Livestock production in the range is closely linked to agricultural systems in three ways: by seasonal movements of the flocks to graze crop residues, by the transportation of feeds from the cultivated areas to the flocks whenever grazing is insufficient and, now, by the increasing cultivation of barley within the range area to provide feed for the flocks.

Movements of livestock

Traditionally, sheep flocks from the range have moved, both within the range and seasonally from the range into the cultivated areas to the west and north. Movements within the range were dependent on the seasonal or sporadic availability of both herbage to graze and water for the flocks. By the 1960s the drilling of wells by the government and the purchase of water-tankers by larger and wealthier flock-owners enabled almost any part of the range to be

[1] Syrian Arab Republic, MAAR, 1984.
[2] Syrian Arab Republic, *Statistical Yearbook*, 1990.

grazed at will. The pressure on its fragile ecosystem was increased, not only by the greater availability of water, but also by the increased availability of transport in general, with pick-up trucks being used to find good grazing areas, and lorries to transport the flocks rapidly to them.

The movement in June from the range into the areas of cultivation, to graze stubble and other by-products (e.g. irrigated cotton crops) later in the autumn, still continues, but appears to be far less regular. Studies are needed to document such changes. Probably the main factor causing the alterations to the regular movements and routes is the shift to transportation by lorry. Today flocks criss-cross the country to utilise any available grazing. For example, in 1990, with a poor cereal harvest in western Syria, the normal movement westwards in June did not occur and the flocks were taken to the north-east, where the harvest had been near average.

At present, after they return to the range in November, the flocks generally remain in one place through the winter months until March or April, when the sparse growth of annual plants occurs in the range. The main reason for this is that the degradation of the areas of *Atriplex*, *Salsola vermiculata* and *Artemisia* bushes in the range is so extensive that there is little biomass available for grazing in winter, and an extended period of feeding concentrates and straw is essential. The degradation of the range has been accompanied by a rapid increase in settlement, as almost every bedouin family now has a house, and small villages are spread throughout the range. The flocks now stay close to the owner's house where they are fed concentrates and straw and taken out to graze each day on the sparse (or non-existent) vegetation.

In addition to the movements of the ewes, there is now a major movement of weaned male lambs from the range to fattening units located close to the major towns, either privately owned units or co-operatives. The establishment of co-operative fattening units began in the 1960s, with the aim of relieving the grazing pressure on natural pastures by removing weaned lambs, and leaving only the ewes and flock replacements in the range. Some fifty fattening co-operatives were established, and these co-operatives and their members had preferential access to the government feed-purchasing organisation. Bahhady (personal communication) estimates that currently about half the lambs slaughtered, more than 2 million animals, the major part coming from the range, are fed in these units prior to slaughter.

Winter feeding

The winter feeding from November to March is based on barley, other concentrate feeds and straw. In dry years, when there is little growth of the annual plants in the range, feeding may continue for much longer. Because of the number of sheep in the range in winter large quantities of feed are transported from the areas of cultivation. It is important to quantify the amounts of feed required and their origin. The most recent detailed information on feed use in

Table 15.1 *Mean total amounts of winter feeds fed per head in flocks during three seasons (1979–81)*

		Muhasina	Bir Amala	Mean
Duration of winter feeding	days	141	148	145
Feed				
Barley	kg*	63	61	62
	MJ+	726	704	715
Other concentrate feed	kg	61	19	40
	MJ	638	208	423
tibin	kg	140	46	93
	MJ	812	169	490
Total	kg	264	126	195
	MJ	2,176	1,181	1,678

Notes:
* Air-dry feed in kg
\+ Metabolisable energy using values from Thomson et al., 1989

range flocks comes from a survey made between 1979 and 1981.[3] The information is now almost certainly out of date because of rapid changes in the range, but the differences between the villages probably give a good indication of the current level of feeding.

The survey was carried out in three villages, but only the data for the two villages where information was collected in all three years are discussed here. Muhasina, in a zone with 200–250 mm of rainfall, was settled at the edge of the range about thirty-five years before the survey was made, but, by the time of the survey, was in the barley cultivation zone. The families lived in the village most of the year and had small flocks of 20–100 sheep, except for one of 290 sheep. The other village, Bir Amala, is in an area with less than 200 mm of rainfall and was settled more recently. The families there were semi-nomadic, but grew an average of 47 hectares of barley, of which 8 hectares was in villages in wetter areas in the west. The size of surveyed flocks varied from 130 to 440 sheep.

Thomson et al. used the results of this survey to describe the feeding system in these villages.[4] Means for three years,[5] which had successively low, high and average rainfall (table 15.1) indicate that in Muhasina 55 per cent more concentrate feeds and 200 per cent more *tibin* (coarsely milled straw) was fed than in Bir Amala, where the flocks had greater access to grazing. Thomson estimated that grazing of stubble contributed 1,220 MJ of metabolisable energy to the annual feed requirements per ewe of 4,200 MJ.[6] Further calculations

[3] Thomson et al., 1989. [4] Thomson et al., 1989; Thomson, 1987.
[5] Termanini, personal communication. [6] Thomson, 1987.

suggested that grazing in the range contributed 50 per cent of the annual energy requirements in Bir Amala but only 13 per cent in Muhasina.

Data from Muhasina for the dry year of 1989, when there was little natural grazing available, indicate that the period of feeding was extended to 205 days, 50 per cent longer than in the other two years. The total amounts of concentrates and straw fed were 140 kilograms and 210 kilograms, 20 per cent and 100 per cent more than in the other years.

Over the three years of the survey, the flock-owners produced a surplus of barley grain over their requirements from the land they cultivated around the villages and in villages in the wetter areas to the west. More barley straw was purchased than was harvested in the three years, partly because the flock-owners found it cheaper to buy straw than to harvest very poor crops of barley, which they preferred to graze.

Using the mean data from this survey, the 8 million ewes in the range flocks in 1988 would have required a total of 800,000 tons of concentrate feeds and 745,000 tons of straw, most of which would have had to be transported into the range. Since the survey was made, it must be assumed that the contribution of range grazing to energy needs of the flocks has declined because the number of sheep has increased by approximately 50 per cent and the area of good range grazing has been reduced by the extension of ploughing in the rangelands. The average level of feeding of barley, straw etc. to ewes in the range is today probably closer to that in Muhasina than to that observed in Bir Amala in 1979–81.

The extension of the area of barley cultivation

The enormous expansion in the area of barley cultivation accompanying the rise in sheep population reveals the dependence of sheep production on feed from the cultivated areas. Since 1950, when the barley area was 0.3 million hectares, the area sown to barley has increased steadily, after major fluctuations between 1965 and 1975, to about 1.55 million hectares in 1986/7. In 1988 there was a further 18 per cent increase and, following the exceptionally good harvest in 1988, there was a further leap in 1989 to 2.88 million hectares.

The area under barley has increased in all areas except those with rainfall above 300 mm. Cooper and Bailey suggest that in the area with rainfall between 250 and 350 mm the increase resulted mainly from the displacement of wheat by barley, and that in the area with rainfall below 250 mm the increase was due largely to a reduction in frequency of fallows in the rotation, with a strong trend to continuous barley growing in the area with rainfall between 200 and 250 mm.[7]

Twenty-five per cent of the increase in barley area between 1950 and 1989 occurred in the range area, where rainfall is below 200 mm. The official figures

[7] Cooper and Bailey, 1990b.

show that 4–5 per cent of this area is now cultivated. The actual figure is certainly much higher, as illegal and unrecorded sowing of barley is extending further and further into the range.

Although from 1979 to 1989 the area of barley in the range averaged 15 per cent of the total barley area (ranging from 9 to 19 per cent in individual years), Cooper and Bailey estimate that the contribution of this area to total barley production is very low, a mean of 6 per cent of the total for the period.[8] The contribution in individual years ranged from 1 per cent in three years (1979, 1982, 1987) to 13 per cent in the very exceptional year of 1988, which is only likely to occur once in thirty years. These authors suggest that the growth of barley crops in the range area will only be sufficient to warrant harvesting in one out of three years and that relatively minor improvements in the management of crops grown in the wetter areas could compensate for the elimination of barley growing in the area with rainfall below 200 mm.

Implications for research and development strategies for developing more productive and stable sheep-production systems

The sheep-production system in the range has been viable for at least fifteen years, as sheep numbers have expanded steadily, with minor fluctuations, since the mid-1970s. It is clear that this expansion results from rational decisions by flock owners during a long period when the ratios between the prices they have received for slaughter sheep and the costs of purchasing or growing feeds, particularly barley, have been very favourable. The figures for sheep numbers are not available for 1990 and 1991, but two consecutive years of drought will probably have caused a substantial decrease in numbers, because the very favourable ratio between meat prices and feed costs has decreased following higher feed prices and a greater supply of meat for slaughtering.

As the sheep-production system in the range has become more and more dependent on inputs of feed from the agricultural areas, farmers in these areas have responded by substituting barley for other crops and for fallows; and flock owners, and others, have greatly extended barley-growing in the range. Even so, Syria has moved from being a frequent net exporter of barley to being a frequent net importer. This fact together with the visible degradation of the range and the drier parts of the agricultural zone, indicates that the sheep-production system in Syria is not biologically viable, even if it remains economically attractive.

Research and development clearly need to find technical innovations and development strategies to modify the sheep-production system in the Syrian range. In the long term the aim must be to restore a stable balance between the number of grazing animals and the feed grown on the range. An essential prerequisite for such changes, if animal numbers are not reduced drastically,

[8] Ibid.

is an increase in feed supplies from outside the range. If the objective is to establish a truly sustainable system within Syria, it is essential that the feed resources are produced within the country in all but the most exceptional years. In the short term the greatest improvements in the supply of feed for sheep in Syria will come from improvements in cereal growing. This is discussed in the chapter by M. J. Jones in this volume (chap. 14).

Research directed to the agricultural zones

ICARDA has programmes of research directed to increasing the overall production of sheep feed by substituting annual legume crops or pasture legumes for fallows, or by introducing them into continuous crop rotations, particularly continuous barley cropping.

The research has considered three groups of species, vetches (*Vicia sativa*, *Vicia narbonensis* and *Vicia villosa* subsp. *dasycarpa*), chicklings (*Lathyrus sativa* and *Lathyrus ochrus*) and field peas (*Pisum sativa*) as annual crops for introduction into rotations in Syria. Peas have now been discarded, mainly because of their low palatability. Selection still continues on *Vicia narbonensis* and *Vicia villosa* subsp. *dasycarpa*. Common vetch and common chickling, however, have been studied in two on-farm trials in north-west Syria.

Cocks and Thomson calculated, from data from the first trial, that replacing fallow with unfertilised forages harvested at maturity for grain and straw increased net revenue per ha by 50 per cent for vetch and by 175 per cent for chickling.[9] When 20 kilograms per hectare of phosphatic fertiliser was applied, net revenue was increased by 175 per cent for vetch and 280 per cent for chickling. Barley yields, when compared with those after fallow, were slightly higher after chickling and equal after vetch.

The current trial, unlike the earlier one, contains a continuous barley rotation, which must be considered the farmers' standard rotation now, even if the yield levels are not sustainable over many years without fertiliser inputs. Table 15.2 contains data on the yields of the crops and of sheep feed as metabolisable energy and crude protein from continuous barley (B–B) and from rotations of barley/fallow (B–F), barley/vetch (B–V) and barley/chickling (B–C).[10] The rotations that include legumes slightly reduce the production of feed metabolisable energy from barley compared with barley after fallow. The total productions of feed energy from the legume rotations, which are sustainable without inputs of N fertiliser, were about 10 per cent higher than from the continuous barley cropping. The production of feed protein from the legume rotations was 40 per cent greater than from the continuous barley cropping. Studies within both these on-farm trials, in which legumes were grazed early in the season, show that their value for feeding lactating ewes or for fattening lambs may be greater than as feed harvested at plant maturity.

[9] Cocks et al., 1988. [10] Bahhady, personal communication.

Table 15.2 *Mean yields of air dry matter and metabolisable energy per hectare of rotation for years 1988, 1989 and 1990 for four rotations at al-Bab in north-west Syria*

		B–B	B–F	B–V	B–C
Barley grain	t	0.98	0.67	0.59	0.63
	MJ*	11,270	7,705	6,840	7,190
Barley straw	t	1.54	1.13	1.01	1.09
	MJ*	8,930	6,555	5,860	6,295
Legume grain	t	–	–	0.22	0.26
	MJ+	–	–	3,036	3,484
Legume straw	t	–	–	1.00	0.78
	MJ+	–	–	6,400	5,226
Total feed ME	MJ	20,200	14,260	22,136	22,195
Total feed CP	kg	146	102	209	208

Notes:
* Calculated using values from Thomson et al.,1989.
\+ Calculated using values from Arab and Middle East Tables of Feed Composition (1979) ACSAD-AS-P1–1979.

Although rotations containing annual legumes have clear advantages for sustainability, and data from these trials show that they do not reduce the production of feed for ruminants, legume crops have the disadvantage of higher seed costs and considerably higher harvesting costs than barley growing. Availability of seed at an acceptable cost, particularly after drought years, may be a serious problem in maintaining rotations that include annual legumes. Rotations based on self-regenerating pastures of annual medics (*Medicago spp.*) with hard seed that germinate in the year following the cereal crop have been subjected to extensive research at ICARDA. Major biological constraints on the success of this system in West Asia have been overcome by selecting suitably cold-tolerant species and strains of medicagos, and sowing them with adapted rhizobia. Appropriate tillage machinery and methods have been devised. Grazing management still presents problems, especially in the establishment year and in the later part of the season, when there is the need to limit utilisation to preserve a sufficient seedbank for regeneration of pasture.

The cereal–medic rotation has serious limitations in providing feed for range flocks. In all but the most exceptional years, when conservation as hay might be possible, the medic phase will only provide grazing. Because of the need to preserve the seed bank, renting to flock owners, who are used to achieving complete utilisation of cereal stubble, presents serious problems. The system is of great potential benefit to farmers in the agricultural areas who own sheep flocks, enabling great reductions in inputs of feeds from mid-lactation and providing high-quality pasture far into the summer. It could be of benefit to flock owners in the range, who own or rent land on a long-term basis in the agricultural zones. If the cereal–medic rotation were widely adopted it would reduce requirements for barley, straw and other feeds for the flocks in the agricultural areas and increase the supply to the market, which should reduce prices for straw, but would have little effect, at least in the short term, on feeds that have government-controlled prices. But this is a highly speculative scenario and it would be very difficult to predict its full impact.

Research on marginal land within the agricultural zones

In the agricultural areas of Syria some 30 per cent of the land is not cultivated because the soil is too shallow or the land too steep. This marginal land provides a small amount of grazing, mainly in spring. Because of communal rights of access to it, this land is trapped in a cycle of excessive stocking, low plant numbers and low fertility.

Osman et al. have shown steady improvements in soil fertility, plant cover and animal performance in response to six years of applying small amounts of phosphatic fertiliser (25 or 60 kilograms P_2O_5 per hectare), when grazing was controlled using fixed annual stocking rates of 1.3 or 0.65 ewe per hectare.[11] This experiment clearly demonstrates that the potential of marginal land is much greater than its current degraded condition suggests. Nordblom and Thomson suggest that considerable increases in the profitability of flocks would result if these improvements could be achieved in marginal land grazed within the agricultural areas.[12] The problems of translating these responses into workable systems of management and utilisation within a context of communal access to marginal land will clearly be very great.

As with the introduction of medics in the rotations in the agricultural areas, improvements of marginal land in the agricultural areas with 200–250 mm of rainfall can only benefit the feed supply of flocks in the range in very indirect ways, such as reductions in feeds, or in the movement of sheep from the agricultural zones to the range.

Improvement of the range

Improvement of the range is clearly a very difficult problem. The fact that degradation of the range has continued and probably increased in intensity since a series of measures, both technical and structural, were implemented by the Syrian government, with expert international advice, is an indication of the depth of the problem.

The original ecosystem of the range consisted of perennial bushes, such as

[11] Osman et al., 1990. [12] Nordblom and Thomson, 1987.

Salsola vermiculata, *Artemisia* and *Atriplex spp.*, and annual grasses, sedges and legumes. The degradation of this vegetation is now so great that viable stands of the bush component cannot be re-established by reduction of grazing pressure, and planting or seeding of bushes is necessary. In the Mediterranean region, much research has been directed to the establishment, in degraded areas of low rainfall, of bush plantations, generally of native or exotic species of atriplex. Atriplex species have been used because of their high efficiency of use of low and irregular rainfall, tolerance of saline soils and acceptable palatability for sheep. In Syria, a number of species of atriplex and other genera have been tested[13] and plantations have been established on several government stations. In spite of all the years of research and practical experience, however, we still do not really know the patterns of utilisation and levels of stocking that can be sustained while assuring the survival of the bushes. Recently, a new study of this problem has been started by ICARDA in co-operation with ACSAD and the Syrian Ministry of Agriculture and Agrarian Reform.

Plantations of bushes appear to offer the only possibility of reversing the degradation of the range. Their potential is great, even in the driest part of Syria. Sankary for example showed that a three-year-old plantation of atriplex in a 200 mm rainfall area maintained one sheep per hectare for approximately a year.[14] If this could be achieved on three-quarters of the Syrian range, approximately 7.5 million hectares maintenance feeding could be provided for most of the 8 million ewes currently estimated to be in range flocks. As in all communal grazing areas, the problem is to devise feasible plans for establishing and, above all, for maintaining, viable plantations where free-access grazing rights exist. The potential, however, is so great that considerable effort needs to be devoted to exploring every possibility within existing, and changing, socio-economic structures. The extension of barley cultivation in the range, which gives rights to barley crops in an area, may assist in finding a solution, if planted bushes are regarded as the property of an individual or a defined group of people. Jones briefly discusses one possibility, the planting of lines of atriplex bushes with strips for the cultivation of barley between, which could allow the integration of seasonal bush grazing with barley production.[15]

Conclusion

The rapid expansion of the sheep population in the Syrian range, in a system that is primarily dependent on feeds grown in the agricultural areas, and only very secondarily on grazing in the range, is a response to a particular set of socio-economic factors. These are not unique to Syria, as similar trends have occurred in other countries in West Asia and in North Africa. Boutonnet makes a very detailed analysis of this development in Algeria.[16] Technical

[13] See Sankary, 1978. [14] Ibid. [15] See chap. 14 in this volume. [16] Boutonnet, 1989.

solutions will have little effect on the cycle of increasing sheep numbers and degradation of the environment, without change in longer term factors. As long as it is most profitable to feed high levels of purchased feed, this sheep-production system will continue. In 1989–90 severe drought in Syria narrowed the ratio between meat price and feed cost, and it is certain that sheep numbers declined as profitability has declined.

Most of the socio-economic factors are unlikely to change quickly. The strong demand for sheep meat, leading to high prices, will not change, as it results directly from the rapid rise in human population. The rapid increase in population also affects the size of the rural population, which, although declining slightly as a percentage, is still increasing in absolute terms. Sheep production remains one of the most successful of economic activities particularly in the driest areas.

Changes in government policy could influence the pattern of development of production. The government could, for example, cease to fix the prices of concentrate feeds, but even this might have only limited effects on numbers of sheep unless it were accompanied by a reduction in the subsidy on bread, which at present is cheap enough to be an alternative to cereals for feeding to sheep. Needless to say, removal of subsidies of this scale would have dramatic repercussions throughout the economy. Similarly, fuel prices have a major influence on farming and the current low price of diesel fuel favours cultivation and reduces the costs of transporting water, feed and animals.

16

International organisations and the settlement of nomads in the Arab Middle East, 1950–1990

RICCARDO BOCCO

Institut Universitaire d'Etudes du Développement, Geneva

The sedentarisation projects for pastoral nomads undertaken in the Middle East between 1950 and 1970 did not mark a departure from policies carried out during the Mandate period or in Wahhabite Arabia. Then, as earlier, the solution suggested for the nomad 'problem' was the same: sedentarisation. However, from the 1950s onwards, international organisations entered the scene as new actors setting the ideological framework for the 'new' settlement programmes. They brought along with them not only important financial means but also expertise and up-to-date technology, which aided greatly in elaborating global approaches to the sedentarisation of nomads and in legitimising the state policies adopted for the nomads of the region.

We will not attempt to establish yet another necrology of aborted or reinterpreted projects, but try, through an analysis of the logic governing development processes, to retrace the genealogy and 'philosophy' of the policies applied to the nomads. Following a brief historical presentation of the activities of international organisations from 1950 to 1965, when the 'doctrinal' basis for future projects was elaborated, we shall examine the representations underlying the work of the experts. Whether we look at western or Arab experts, we can conclude that in general their writings are not based on knowledge gained from field studies. The divide opposing western experts to bedouin populations is mirrored in the gulf separating the Arab intelligentsia from the rural people of their own countries.[1] If the experts can be criticised because of their ethnocentrism, this applies equally to Arabs and westerners: the prejudices of both are mutually reinforcing. Furthermore, the majority of

This chapter is a revised and augmented version of a paper published in French: 'La sédentarisation des pasteurs nomades: les experts internationaux face à la question bédouine au Moyen-Orient arabe (1950–1970)', published in Bernus and Pouillon, (eds.), 1990, pp. 97–117. [Editor's Note: All quotations from reports have been translated into English.]

[1] In his study covering the issues of pastoral nomadism and settlement policies in the regions included between West Africa and Turkistan, Monteil (1966) analysed almost four hundred books and articles, published between the beginning of the century and the mid-1960s. In commenting on the sources he gathered, the author stressed that 'they come either from the interested parties themselves, who lack specialised training, or from Western researchers, who can only give scant attention to these matters due to lack of time or a too brief stay. When, by chance, an Eastern researcher studies nomadism, it is a city-dweller looking at things with mistrust and from a distance' (Monteil, 1966, p. 7).

their reports have a marked ideological character, their explicit aim being to guide political action; for decision makers, the recommendations contained in these studies count more than presentation and analysis of the data. In this sense the experts enjoy the double legitimacy attached to scriptural knowledge and to their indirect political power as 'advisors to the prince'. For native-born experts, the Arab affiliation is an additional source of legitimacy.

Parallel to this question is that of the historicity of sedentarisation programmes. If westerners pretend that the projects are innovative, Arab experts want them also to mark a break with the colonial past. Our case study on Jordan shows the continuity in sedentarisation policies from the Mandate period up to the 1970s, while bringing out clearly how some texts reinterpret or even mystify certain aspects of the recent past as well as use ideological readaptations to legitimise one or another of these policies. From development programmes there emerges a vision of social change and a 'project of society' to be implemented. It should be noted that conservative or 'socialist' experts (and governments) have hardly differed in the option they favoured regarding the sedentarisation of nomads.

International organisations and sedentarisation programmes (1950–70)

The 1950s constituted a preliminary phase in the history of sedentarisation projects in the Middle East. The institutional framework set up at that time is a proof of the importance given to the problem. It is also during this period that the first research programmes were launched. The outcome of this research was presented in experts' symposia and publications that provided the scientific and technical underpinnings for the policies put into practice during the 1960s and 1970s.

Between 1949 and 1954 the League of Arab States, together with the United Nations, organised a series of seminars on the subject of 'Social Welfare in the Arab States of the Middle East'.[2] In the meetings at Beirut in 1949 and Cairo in 1950, each Arab country had been urged to set up a department whose specific task would be to 'protect' nomads, co-ordinate all actions concerning them and train indigenous experts to deal with them. Sedentarisation was adopted as an official policy at the 1952 meeting in Damascus. During the final seminar, in Baghdad in 1954, the methods to be adopted were spelled out as follows:

> We should proceed towards sedentarisation by giving a piece of land to each individual capable of engaging in agriculture, the surface area to be determined by each state and calculated in such a way as to ensure a rise in the [owner's] standard of living, and to allow him to support himself and all his dependants . . . During the redistribution of land, care should be taken to group any one family in a single area, made up of all the pieces of land given to family members, the family being defined as the parents of the first grandfather.[3]

[2] United Nations, 1956. [3] ILO, 1962, p. 80.

Thus within a relatively short time experts had moved from general resolutions to very precise recommendations leaving no doubt about the policies to be applied and the role each country was expected to play.[4]

Parallel to the Arab League meetings, in 1951 UNESCO set up a consultative committee for the 'Research on Arid Zones'. A six-year programme was launched in 1956 to study living conditions and improve soil fertility in desert areas. Comparative studies covering nomadic tribes in the Middle East and North Africa were assigned to various experts: sociologists, anthropologists, agronomists and geologists. The results, published between 1958 and 1962 as reports and conference proceedings, also favoured the settlement of nomads through the implementation of projects aimed at improving the living conditions of the steppe populations.[5]

From 1956 onwards, following a series of epidemiological studies on nomads in the Middle East, the World Health Organisation (WHO) joined in the research initiated by UNESCO. WHO's general assembly in its annual meetings in Athens in 1956 and Baghdad in 1957, after calling for various health measures and a campaign against malnutrition, also recommended the sedentarisation of nomadic populations. Its aim was to eliminate diseases (especially malaria and tuberculosis) the eradication of which would not be possible as long as nomadism continued.[6]

In 1959 the Food and Agricultural Organisation (FAO) went on record with its own series of reports on the agricultural and arboricultural situation in the Middle East and North Africa. Without questioning the imperative to settle nomads, FAO experts were, however, the first to point out the importance of maintaining and developing pasture lands and improving animal species. From the early 1960s the FAO, often in collaboration with the World Food Programme, launched a series of projects to set up agricultural colonies in the steppe areas with the declared aim of resettling nomads, developing fodder crops and encouraging sedentary animal husbandry. At the twelfth session of its general conference in 1963 the FAO passed a resolution assigning its experts the further task of studying land-tenure systems, in order to assure better integration of nomads within the regional states.

The International Labour Organisation (ILO) took the role of main coordinator for sedentarisation programmes. In 1957 the fortiethth session of the ILO (attended also by FAO, WHO and UNESCO) adopted a

[4] After the Baghdad meeting, the recommendation most debated concerned the abrogation of tribal customary law, a very sensitive issue which has known various kinds of compromises according to the political history of the different Middle Eastern states. Concerning the priorities and the objectives of settlement policies, the Syrian government did not hesitate to address them in the 'Arab Baʿth Party Constitution' of 1947. Article 6 (43) is very explicit: 'Bedouin nomadism is a primitive social state which weakens national production and makes an important part of the nation a crippled limb, and so it is a factor retarding its development and progress. The Party is therefore actively settling the bedouin, giving them land, abolishing the tribal system and applying to them the laws of the State' (Quoted in Seurat, 1980, pp. 87–142).

[5] Inside the ASFEC (Arab States Fundamental Education Centre) established under the patronage of UNESCO, a special department was created in 1959 whose main task was to deal with the educational problems of the nomadic populations.

[6] ILO, 1964b, pp. 29–34.

'Convention for the protection and integration of aboriginal and other tribal and semi-tribal populations in independent countries' (Convention no. 107). This convention states that 'governments will be principally responsible for undertaking a co-ordinated and systematic programme to protect the concerned populations and to integrate them progressively in the life of their respective countries', and 'recourse to force or coercion to integrate the concerned populations in the international community is to be excluded' (article 2). Specific articles in the convention also outline the role which the state should assume in the promotion of health, education and socio-economic development. Special attention is given to problems of land ownership and land use by nomadic groups. Recommendation 104 underlines the importance of states providing protection to the semi-nomadic tribal groups whose traditional territories are found on both sides of international boundaries.[7]

In 1958 and 1959 the ILO financed a series of studies on the conditions of nomadic tribes in several Middle Eastern countries: Saudi Arabia, Iraq, Jordan, Egypt and Iran. The research was mostly assigned to academics of Arab universities. During its sixth session in 1960 the ILO's Permanent Agricultural Commission recommended that priority be given to studies on sedentarisation in order to help the member states carry out their rural development plans. In the spring of 1962 the ILO's general director, in concert with FAO, WHO and UNESCO, formed the 'Advisors' Group on Aboriginal and Tribal Populations'; within it, a department was set up to co-ordinate the activities of international organisations and develop a programme for applied research.[8] The resulting recommendations (ILO seminars of 1962 and 1964) show clearly the orientation adopted by experts and representatives of Arab states: sedentarisation, synonymous with development and progress, is the declared objective; the state is the entity most capable of carrying out any project, and the only subject of debate concerns the strategies through which sedentarisation can best be achieved. The convergence of views among the different international organisations thus played a role in providing a transnational legitimacy to individual projects later carried out.

The views of two experts, one Arab and the other French, typify the approach dominant in the 1950s, where politics took priority over all other considerations. 'Concerning the sedentarisation of nomads,' affirmed the Egyptian researcher Muhammad Awad, 'the most important factor is the existence of a strong central government determined to maintain order and peace and to encourage the country's progress and the well-being of its inhabitants . . . Whether the motives are humanitarian, political, economic, strategic or

[7] Ibid., p. 5.

[8] The task of co-ordinating and promoting the research on nomadic pastoral populations, undertaken by the ILO, was suspended at the beginning of the 1970s, mainly because of the refusal of the Soviet Union to subscribe to the suggested recommendations and because of the veto imposed on international consultants to pursue research in Central Asia (personal communication of Dr S. Radwan, ILO, spring 1988).

administrative, it is important that this result be achieved as rapidly as possible.'[9] In spite of the sensitivity he usually displayed in analysing complex situations, Jacques Berque also affirmed: 'We can no longer see the relationship between the old and the new once a nomadic society has entered into history, once it has abandoned a cyclical world view and a conservative practice in favour of new techniques and has come to conceive of time as, so to speak, cumulative, as something which has meaning, viewed as good or bad. Is such a passage even possible outside sedentarisation?' And he continues by stressing that 'the right and indeed the imperative duty to make the nomads evolve cannot be questioned'.[10]

Experts and bedouins: representations of the 'other'

A development programme cannot be reduced to the sum of technical measures envisaged for one particular operation. It is above all an attempt to propose or impose a particular world view and praxis, and it embodies a set of values, a vision of the world, of social change and progress. The sedentarisation programmes proposed by the experts of international organisations thus reveal the representations these experts have of nomadic pastoralism. By masking their pre-established conceptions with sociological jargon, the experts transformed them into scientific postulates which were then used to justify or support development activities. The reports of international organisations which formed the basis of development programmes carried out in the 1960s and 1970s build on a core of common conceptions. Given that these reports, monographs or comparative studies all adopt a similar thematic plan – relations to the environment, economic activities, socio-political organisa-

9 Awad, 1959, pp. 37–8.

10 Berque, 1959, pp. 515, 518. Concerning the relationship between, on the one hand, the socio-geographic origin of the experts who worked for international organisations in south-west Asia and Saharan Africa during the 1950s, and, on the other, their attitudes towards sedentarisation policies, two remarks are in order. The first is that we agree with the judgement of Monteil (1966, pp. 61–8) that, in general, the experts of Arab origin, none of whom are of nomadic background, are all in favour of implementing sedentarisation programmes. Among western experts there is no such unanimity. Our second observation is that the majority of western experts opposed to sedentarisation have acquired, through their working experience, an in-depth knowledge of arid and semi-arid zones and of nomadic peoples. In this sense there is a noteworthy difference between North Africa and the Middle East. While in the Mashreq countries gained their independence before 1950, in North Africa and in the Sahara most countries won independence only at the beginning of the 1960s. Thus, during the 1950s, a number of experts for Saharan Africa were recruited from among colonial administrators still in their posts, or former colonial officials, such as Theodore Monod, director of IFAN in Dakar, Robert Capot-Rey, or the researchers of CHEAM (Centre des Hautes Etudes Administratives sur l'Afrique et l'Asie Modernes). With the exception of J. Berque, most of the western experts who had worked in French colonial administration in Saharan Africa were all extremely reticent as to the implementation of sedentarisation policies. In this respect, the Near East seems to be different and we have no knowledge of international consultants in the 1950s, whether French or English, who were recruited from among the administrators of the Mandatory period.

tion and sedentarisation problems – we shall follow the same outline to analyse the representations of nomadism they contain.

1. The ecological context is often singled out as the major constraint on pastoral societies. By presenting nomadism as a successful adaptation to a desert environment, its weakest point is effectively stressed: its dependence on the hazards of climate.[11] Perpetuating nomadism would in the best of cases represent a waste of potential agricultural land.[12] As a future Egyptian minister of agriculture also claimed: 'Nomadism and semi-nomadism are wasteful and destructive. Vast stretches of land which can be reclaimed at little cost and cultivated intensively, are simply left for grazing without any serious attempt to make better use of them.'[13]

For partisans of one particular ecological approach, nomadism is responsible for the deterioration of pasturelands and constitutes a real menace for the future of the steppe. This hypothesis is, however, not universally accepted and remains subject to debate. The land-tenure policies adopted by the states are themselves never the subject of analysis.[14] The question of territorial appropriation, though considered crucial, is approached only from the angle of land-ownership laws and ecological constraints. Only in passing is mention made of the conflicts between successive governments and nomadic and sedentary groups of a particular region, or of the socio-economic implications that the creation of international boundaries had for tribal territories. If the question of land ownership arises at all, the experts recommend that a solution to it can be found through 'equitable' agrarian reform.[15]

2. In the majority of reports, the ecological context is accorded not only a textual but also a causal priority. The economic activities of nomads are highly conditioned by the environment, forcing pastoralists to roam incessantly in search of water and pasture for their animals. As an economic activity and a pattern of land use, pastoral nomadism is reputed to be marginal and resistant to integration into the national market.[16] In most of the reports, groups are classified according to their lifestyle and economic activity: nomads, semi-nomads, semi-sedentary, sedentary. The socio-economic categories adopted by experts are never confronted with the social categories used by the interested parties themselves. Thus, when bedouin settle, experts consider them to have disappeared as a distinctive social group.[17] For the 'real' nomads, all agricultural activity is supposed to be socially degrading and wholly antithetical to their 'psychology': 'Agricultural activity is repugnant to the nomad: it deprives him of the liberty he holds so dear.'[18] Following the

[11] Yacoub, 1970, p. 109. [12] ILO, 1962, p. 15. [13] Abu Zeid, 1966, p. 280.
[14] UNESCO, 1960. [15] ILO, 1964a, pp. 96–103. [16] FAO, 1972, p. 3.
[17] Elsewhere I have outlined the different definitions of 'nomad' and 'bedouin' adopted over time by state administrations, academic researchers and development experts in Jordan, to show their implications for policy making. See Bocco, 1989b. [18] Awad, 1959, p. 36.

same perspective, a French sociologist stated: 'Used to exerting strenuous but brief efforts, [nomads] do not readily countenance the necessity of staying continuously near their cultivated plots. Furthermore, the nomad feels a certain contempt for agricultural activities, which he views as inferior tasks traditionally carried out by slaves.'[19]

Apart from some reminders of the role formerly played by nomads in caravan trade and transport – a role now eliminated due to the development of modern means of transportation – experts present nomads as wholly isolated in the desert. The myth concerning the dichotomy between nomads and sedentary groups is universally accepted, and nowhere do we find discussion of the history of interrelations between the groups, particularly ancient in the Middle East. If nomads are found practising other economic activities, it is, the experts would have us believe, due to the policies of post-independence states who have provided them with jobs in industry, technical crafts and commerce.[20]

3. Concerning the socio-political organisation of nomads we find two principal theses adopted by the experts. In the first the ecological variable is seen as determinant: 'The crucial variable of environmental uncertainty and instability at the micro-ecological level compels nomads to develop loosely organised and generally uncentralised political systems.'[21] The other interpretation makes no pretence of precise concepts and merely affirms that nomads are governed by a backward and often despotic social organisation. The terms used by Selim concerning Jordan and Iraq typify this trend:

> All political power in the tribe is centralised in the person of the sheikh – he is generally a despot with quasi-royal authority who holds in his hands the life and destiny of his subjects. The sheikh is the owner of all land, commander-in-chief and judge. He distributes the land to his subjects and can take it away from any of them. Not only can he banish any tribal member from his territory, he can also severely punish all who disobey him. It is he who imposes taxes and rights, decides the tribe's moves and conducts wars. The sheikh's executive powers are carried out through the intermediary of the heads of clans . . . as well as by his close relatives and chosen representatives.[22]

These generalised affirmations take precedence over the presentation or analysis of facts – facts so skimpy that we are entitled to wonder if in fact the expert actually knows the nomad groups he is describing. Nomadism and tribalism are always lumped together: to one type of land use there corresponds a single type of social organisation, and, apart from a few simplistic definitions, a tribal system appears inconceivable among sedentary groups. Experts also stress the consequences of tribalism, said to hamper the birth and development of a national identity,[23] to prevent the establishment of external

[19] Destrée, 1969, p. 268. [20] ILO, 1964a, pp. 27–75; Yacoub, 1970. [21] FAO, 1972, p. 5.
[22] Selim, 1959. [23] Helaissi, 1959, pp. 554–5.

authority,[24] and, in a word, to raise the problem of state control: 'Nomads are no respectors of national frontiers which they cross and recross very rapidly, evading arrest and taxation, avoiding any new modernising program . . . This elusiveness curtails the nomads' commitment to the State.'[25] In discussing relations between the communities, nomads are often presented as predators on farming societies, a veritable 'mafia' of the desert which the state alone can control.[26] The prevailing view in this respect is that tribal chiefs should be subject to strict administrative control and their powers be closely regulated. Customary law should also be abolished or at least reformed so as to be in conformity with the needs of 'modern' life.[27]

4. All the reports conclude by presenting the advantages of sedentarisation but also the problems that it raises. Defined as the process of fixing nomadic populations on the land, sedentarisation leads to the redirection of economic activity, sedentary animal husbandry, and manual skills and trade. Experts always make a distinction between the process of 'spontaneous' sedentarisation, that is, where nomads choose 'naturally' to abandon nomadism, and 'forced' sedentarisation, due either to 'direct' measures (state projects for rural development) or to the 'indirect' effects of national economic development.[28] In all forms, whether spontaneous or induced, sedentarisation is seen as a veritable cure-all. Rendered possible thanks to the control over the environment that the state is able to assure by introducing new technologies, sedentarisation also allows bedouins to benefit from health and educational facilities and their economy to be integrated into national trading networks. In other words it is synonymous with social and economic integration: 'The abolition of nomadism will lead to the regrouping of pastoral, rural and urban communities . . . into one solid whole and will bring to an end the social distance which now keeps them apart.'[29] In socio-political terms, another effect of sedentarisation of nomads will be to weaken tribalism. According to the experts, detribalisation can be attained by various means. For some experts the role of education is primordial: 'If a nomadic child has the opportunity to complete his schooling normally he will in the end be "detribalised" and lost to his family and the community to which he belongs.'[30] For other experts it is economic development that will fuel rapid emancipation: economic independence obtained by the young removes them from the authority of their elders; individualism develops proportionately to the weakening of family ties; tribal chiefs lose their power and customary law its prestige.[31] With ongoing detribalisation, a corollary to sedentarisation, socio-political organisation 'should tend to be more democratic and less prone to strife and social inequality'.[32] Another

[24] Awad, 1959, pp. 34–5. [25] FAO, 1972, p. 5. [26] ILO, 1962, p. 29.
[27] ILO, 1964a, p. 416. [28] ILO, 1962, pp. 63–9. [29] Ibid., p. 63. [30] ILO, 1964a, p. 132.
[31] ILO, 1962, p. 78. [32] FAO, 1972, p. 12.

expert views this process as replacing the trilogy 'nature–nomadism–poverty' by a new one of 'civilisation–sedentarism–prosperity'.[33]

The state is viewed as the most competent agent to effect this transformation but there is some disagreement over how it should be done. Some experts are in favour of an approach we would qualify as 'paternalistic': 'It must be understood that these nomads living outside the mainstream of modern civilisation are at present unable to perceive their real interests, nor can they find unaided the means to improve their social level. It therefore appears essential for their own good that they leave this responsibility to their own government.'[34] Other more 'alternative' experts favour less conventional development schemes but still have a very classical perspective in terms of forms of intervention: 'Successful innovation is very often best introduced by outsiders . . . It is necessary to choose appropriate innovators who are acceptable to the local community and whose presence will inspire admiration and stimulate emulation.'[35] It was only at the end of the 1970s that 'participant' approaches started to become fashionable; in earlier years communication between developers and developees was strictly from the top down: a gulf separated the two worlds. When the subject of participation was tentatively brought up, never was there any discussion as to where, when, how and by whom it should be solicited.[36]

The representations of pastoral nomads haunting the experts of international organisations during the 1950s and the 1960s contributed to the elaboration of stereotyped terms of reference and legitimised sedentarisation policies in the Middle East. The case of Jordan is an interesting example of how the rhetoric of development as applied to nomads was transposed from the international to the local level. It furthermore shows how the discourse of experts in the 1960s partially obscured the history of relations between the state and the bedouin tribes during the British Mandate. This is why it is revealing to retrace the principal stages of sedentarisation policies as they were carried out in the period preceding independence in Jordan.

Bedouin settlement policies in Trans-Jordan under the Mandate

When the Emirate of Trans-Jordan was established in 1921 it had a considerable population of nomads and semi-nomads. Estimates made by the British authorities at the end of the 1920s show that out of a total population of about 300,000, there were 120,000 semi-nomads and 50,000 nomads.[37] This significant proportion posed the problem of how the authorities were to

[33] Filali, 1966. [34] Helaissi, 1959, p. 556. [35] FAO, 1972, p. 12. [36] Leighton, 1986.

[37] For the analysis of sedentarisation policies during the Mandate period, I have relied principally on the British archives in the Public Record Office (PRO), particularly those of the Colonial Office (CO) and the Foreign Office (FO). For estimates of Jordan's population at the end of the 1920s, see PRO:CO831/8/5, Administration Report, 1929.

ensure the political allegiance of bedouin tribes, particularly those in the eastern and southern-central regions of the country. Although the Mandatory powers, France and Britain, were able to control the regions to the west of the emirate, the greater part of the desert regions to the east consisted of pasture lands of nomadic tribes, whose political loyalty was divided between Amir ʿAbdullah and ʿAbd al-ʿAziz b. Saʿud. The creation of an international border between the emirate and what was coming to be the kingdom of Saudi Arabia left the new states and bedouin groups facing the dual problems of tribes' nationality and of tribal territories' division.

The British Mandatory authorities signed an initial agreement on the emirate's north-eastern border with Ibn Saʿud – then still 'Sultan of Najd and its dependencies' – at Hadda in November 1925. The border agreed upon posed serious problems for the bedouin tribes of northern Trans-Jordan. On the one hand, the border divided in two the nomadic territories of the Bani Sakhr, Bani Khalid, Sirhan and ʿIsa tribes, whose winter grazing pastures were in the Wadi Sirhan, placed under Saʿudi jurisdiction. On the other hand, Ibn Saʿud's anti-Hashemite policy consisted of sapping the authority of Amir ʿAbdullah, considered a pawn of the British, by gaining the allegiance of 'Trans-Jordanian' tribes, and came up against article 4 of the Hadda agreement which recognised the 'traditional' rights of Trans-Jordanian tribes to grazing land and property in the Wadi Sirhan oasis.[38] In 1926, when lands belonging to the present-day governorate of Maʿan, in the south of the country, were annexed to the emirate, the question of tribal territories came up again. This time the Mandatory authorities refused to give in to Ibn Saʿud when he claimed the Jabal Tubayq region, which was the winter camping site of the Huwaytat.

Following the establishment of the northern border, and in response to the Wahhabis' expansionist ventures, the 1926–33 period was characterised by great political instability in the east of the emirate, with a rapid escalation of intertribal raids.[39] In 1924 a separate department was created to deal with tribal affairs, while Amir ʿAbdullah and the British adopted a policy of handing out subsidies to tribal shaykhs to ensure their loyalty. Later, and parallel to the periodic reorganisation of international commissions and courts to arbitrate raids across borders, the Mandatory authorities in 1929 set up a special army corps. This was the Desert Patrol Force, recruited exclusively among the bedouin, who were thus drawn into the administration of the steppe regions. Accompanying these measures was the promulgation of

[38] PRO:CO733/131/5 Annual report for Trans-Jordan, Annex 7, Hadda Agreement. See also Bocco and Tell, 1994 and 1995.

[39] Between 1926 and 1931, the period where intertribal raids reached their peak, tribes from the Hijaz and Najd were estimated to have 'stolen' about 6,700 camels and 6,200 sheep and to have killed 95 members of Trans-Jordanian tribes. The 'booty' of the latter during the same period was much less: about 3,000 camels, 950 sheep and 41 persons killed from the Hijaz and Najd tribes (PRO:CO831/12/1, McDonnell commission's report on raids' arbitration, 1931).

special legislation for the bedouin – 'Tribal Courts Laws' and 'Bedouin Control Laws' – between 1924 and 1936.

With both the Mandatory authorities and the Hashemites using diverse strategies to secure the tribes' allegiance, sedentarisation as a means of control appeared an attractive idea from the early 1930s. The economic resources of the emirate were, however, very limited: the larger part of the country's territory was made up of desert; irrigated cultivation was spread over a small area; and rain-fed agriculture was possible only on a tenth of the land. The country was also lacking in important mineral deposits. In order to develop agriculture, which remained the country's principal resource, and to reduce Britain's financial aid to the emirate's budget, the authorities decided in 1927 to reorganise the land register and to survey and evaluate land-ownership titles, with the aim of setting up a new system of land taxation.

The new Land Code and the Land Settlement Law of 1933 conceded no rights to the tribes over their traditional pasturelands. The tribes were, however, granted rights in the regions where they had summer camping grounds or where they cultivated land, either directly or via sharecroppers. From the 1930s on, several tribal shaykhs were thus given title, individually or in the name of their section, to agricultural or potentially arable land where plans were made to build villages. In the north, among the Bani Sakhr in particular, the four most important sections of the tribe acquired land near their principal summer camps, east and south-east of Amman.[40] The different sections of the Huwaytat tribe acquired similar landholding rights in the south, in the Jabal Shara' region and Wadi 'Araba. Glubb mentions the Huwaytat of Shara' engaging in plough farming from as early as 1933.[41]

The Mandatory authorities began formulating real agricultural development plans only in 1935. They set up a development department, financed by the British Colonial Development Fund, to administer and plan projects. British experts recommended a sedentarisation policy for the bedouin built around such measures as digging artesian wells, building small dams and improving old reservoirs in order to encourage the development of agriculture and the construction of villages. They planned to set up schools in the 'bedouin villages' and to teach the rudiments of health care to at least one member of each tribal section. They dug new wells and repaired old ones in the steppe region.[42] Long periods of drought in the 1930s adversely affected the pastoral economy as well as the early attempts to develop agriculture in

[40] Several shaykhs and members of different sections of the Bani Sakhr had obtained titles (*sanad tabu*) to agricultural lands during the Ottoman period (see Hamarneh, 1985; Lewis, 1987). For the bedouin tribes of southern Jordan, the situation was rather different due to the weak and sporadic presence of the Ottoman administration before World War I (see Bocco, 1989a).

[41] PRO:CO831/23/11, Glubb's report on events in southern deserts, November 1933; and PRO:CO831/41/5, Loans to Agricultural Bank, letter of high commissioner for Trans-Jordan to Colonial Office, 17/4/1937.

[42] PRO:CO831/34/8, British Resident report on the economic situation, 1935, report of the Advisory Committee to the British Colonial Development Fund, November 1934.

the steppe. Malnutrition and the epidemics consequent to it, tuberculosis in particular, brought disaster, especially to the tribes in the south.[43] In these very hard times, the army came to be the main source of livelihood for many bedouin families.

Between 1937 and 1939 the development department surveyed the emirate's hydrogeological resources. In the report written by G. Ionides, director of the department, it appeared advisable to expand irrigated cultivation in the Jordan Valley as well as on the high plateau, and to develop rain-fed agriculture on the margins of some arid zones, such as the eastern Sharaʿ areas. It was in the latter that the greatest efforts were made to settle nomads.

From the numerous reports of that period concerning sedentarisation policy, we have a series of notes written by Glubb in 1938. According to the commander of the Desert Patrol Force, it was because bedouin tribes enjoyed relative political autonomy and, in the absence of a strong state power, were able to impose a levy on peasant populations and travellers, that the stereotype of the bedouin as 'social parasite' came into being. He states that the pastoral economy is by no means an enclaved economy: the bedouin are integrated into the national market economy on which they depend to sell their goods. From an economic point of view, sedentarisation may encourage them to diversify their activities and investments. If they are not to abandon pastoralism altogether – since the national market requires meat – they should, however, take up agricultural activities to compensate the disastrous effects of the prolonged drought. On this point Glubb calls for the demystification of the image of nomads as opposed to any agricultural task, supposedly socially demeaning to bedouin. He points to the examples of the Jbur section of the Bani Sakhr at Nuqayra east of Amman, as well as that of the Matalqa, Tuwayah and Maraʿyah in the eastern region of the Sharaʿ, which contradict this myth. Glubb also stresses that, from a political point of view, sedentarisation accompanied by a redistribution of land to the nomads would permit greater control over the tribes: a nomad can take his family and

[43] An enquiry into the health conditions of the bedouin population was commissioned by the British authorities from Dr McLennan. The results of the survey were astonishing. Of 1,030 persons inspected among four main bedouin tribes (Bani Sakhr, Huwaytat, Sirhan and Bani Hasan), only 16 per cent were sufficiently nourished; 15 per cent of the adult population were suffering from advanced tuberculosis and 40 per cent of the children under 15 years of age were infected by the tuberculosis bacillus. Conscious of the close relationship between British policy towards the bedouin population in Trans-Jordan and the near starvation observed among them, Capt. Glubb did not mince his words in commenting on Dr McLennan's report:

> There can be no doubt whatever that this condition is not peculiar to all Bedouins, but to the Transjordan Bedouin alone, and that there cannot be a moment's doubt that it is primarily due directly to the diplomatic policy of His Majesty's Government in failing to protect these tribes from Ikhwan raids, and finally in failing to face up to Ibn Saoud and compel him to return the loot. The fact that bad rains and bad grazing are not primary causes is proved by the fact that . . . the Rwala and the Shararat are still prosperous, as also are the Iraq Bedouins. (PRO:CO831/29/2, Glubb's monthly reports on events in southern deserts, Enquiry into the Health Conditions of the Bedouins, report by Dr McLennan, 1934)

his herds wherever he wishes, whereas once he is a settled land owner he knows that by leaving his land he loses part of his wealth.[44]

In the last years of the Mandate sedentarisation was already well under way and the pastoral economy integrated into the national market. In socio-political terms, the bedouin were subject to special laws dating from 1924 on, had parliamentary representation since 1928, and were integrated into the army from 1929.

The emirate was not directly affected by the events of World War II, but Jordan – declared independent in 1946 – witnessed drastic upheavals as a result of the Arab–Israeli conflict that broke out in 1948. The annexation of part of Palestine and the massive influx of refugees led to serious economic and social difficulties. For the bedouin, the early and latter part of the 1950s were marked by drought so severe that the government was obliged to seek international aid. Several expert missions, mostly British and American, came to Jordan at the request of the government to define strategies for development. Two studies made by experts at the Beirut-based British Middle East Office supported the options for agricultural development of the steppe areas already adopted during the Mandate period. They maintained, however, that if agricultural development and sedentarisation of the bedouin were to be effectively carried out in the steppe regions, animal husbandry should also receive special attention.[45]

At the end of the 1950s, international and national experts could therefore draw on almost two decades of experience in the field of sedentarisation, yet the terminology and practice of planners continued to give currency to old

[44] Whether the settlement of the nomads should entail transforming their economic system into an agricultural one or maintaining a mixed agro-pastoral model was an issue debated among British authorities. Glubb sided for the second option, expressing his view in these terms: 'The breeding of livestock is as necessary and useful a profession in Transjordan as in Australia and Argentine, and half-baked statements about the value of compelling nomads to live in houses are economically unsound. For nomadism is essential to a profitable breeding of flocks under present conditions, in countries with such a sparse and uncertain grazing and rainfall' (PRO:CO831/46/9, Glubb's monthly reports on events in southern deserts, Internal Administration: Bedouin Cultivation, April 1938). The same perspective was adopted by an advisory committee composed of Trans-Jordanian and British experts:

> With regard to the recommendations made to induce the nomads to settle, it is first of all necessary to remember that the desert area will continue to hold as large a pastoral population as it can reasonably support, so that if the present nomads were to settle down, others would appear to take their place. Many of the nomads of Transjordan are already possessors of agricultural land as well, and are very anxious to obtain firm titles to such land. It is thus the duty of the Government to compel and ensure a peaceful habit amongst the Bedouin to develop the water resources of the desert so as to make available grazing areas which are at present inaccessible, and to apply the benefits of the Disposal of State Lands Law and of the Settlement Land Law to the Bedouin just as much as to the fallahin, but to ensure at the same time that they do not give up their occupation as grazers. (PRO:CO 831/34/8, British Resident report on the economic situation, 1935. Report of the Transjordan Economic Commission, para. 14)

[45] PRO:FO371/104899, Jordan's Prospects for Development, report by R. S. Porter, 1953; and PRO:FO371/104905, Agricultural Development of the Southern Districts of East Jordan, report by J. C. Eyre, 1953.

clichés.[46] Let us then analyse how the experts, by brushing away part of the recent history of development of the steppe, proposed already well-known strategies as if they were new solutions.

National and international experts in Jordan during the 1960s

At the beginning of the 1960s, sedentarisation policies took the form of projects for irrigated agriculture in the steppe areas. According to the 1961 census, the number of nomads east of the Jordan river at the time was about 80,000. Two-thirds of them were concentrated in the southern-central zone,[47] where agriculture, roads and infrastructure were the least developed. Between 1960 and 1980, with the help of international aid, the Jordanian government created eleven sedentarisation projects in these areas.

As part of an aid programme beginning in the early 1960s, the United Nations Development Programme (UNDP) carried out research on the hydrogeological resources of eastern Jordan. The Jafr basin in the south-east of the country appeared a particularly propitious site, and in 1963, with help from the World Food Programme and the UNDP, the government decided to start up a sedentarisation project for the bedouin of the region.[48]

The analyses and representations of nomads in southern Jordan published in reports of this period by Jordanian or foreign experts are virtually indistinguishable from those made in other Middle Eastern countries during the same years or earlier. Here again we find the ecological factor 'determining' the type of economic and socio-political organisation governing nomads and motivating sedentarisation policies.[49] Analysis of the socio-economic organisation of

[46] In his study on rural development studies during the Mandate period, Hamarneh (1985) supports the thesis that Britain had a purely political-strategic interest in creating a 'buffer state' in Trans-Jordan. The British lack of economic interest in the country, coupled with their desire to reduce financial aid to the emirate, thus favoured implementing agricultural policies that had the effect of reproducing underdevelopment. It is true that from a general economic viewpoint when the small kingdom became independent it was financially dependent on external aid and incapable of promoting an autonomous development. However, if we look at the plans for developing the arid regions, the results achieved during the Mandate indeed allow us to mitigate the sometimes too harsh criticism of the British authorities. Contrary to Hamarneh's thesis, the Mandatory authorities were by no means unanimous in supporting sedentarisation, a fact which reveals a less monolithic attitude than has been claimed. Furthermore, the development programmes aimed at combining agricultural and pastoral activities, which were mainly proposed by Glubb but also supported by other officers, are propositions that appeared modern in the 1980s in the course of the debate about 'sustainable development' in the arid zones.

[47] The Hashemite Kingdom of Jordan, *First Census of Population and Housing (1961: Scattered Tents Census Districts)*, interim report no. 10, Amman, Department of Statistics, October 1963.

[48] I have analysed elsewhere the institutional and legal framework of the policies of sedentarisation projects, as well as the local reinterpretations of development programmes. See Bocco, 1989a, 1990. Other settlement programmes for the southern bedouin tribes – namely the Ahaywat and the Sa'idiyin – were planned in the late 1970s by the Jordan Valley Authority in the Wadi 'Araba. See Sultat Wadi 'Araba, *Dirasat al-hajat al-tanmawiya fi qura mintaqa Wadi 'Araba*, Amman, 1987.

[49] Huneidi, 1965; Qalyoubi, 1967; UNESOB, 1973.

nomads in most of these reports is rudimentary. Opinions are sometimes contradictory concerning the chances of success of these projects: 'The nomad has neither the knowledge nor the ability to break with tradition';[50] 'The project [of al-Jafr] has shown that the Bedouin is both interested in and capable of adapting to sedentary farming life.'[51] The success of projects is supposed to result simply from detailed technical planning with a vague appeal to the 'participation' of the nomads concerned, without further specification.[52] The tribes' political organisation is analysed only in relation to changes that sedentarisation is supposed to bring about: 'For many Bedouin in the al Jafr area and elsewhere in Jordan, the lifestyles and values of sedentarisation and freedom from tribal and kinship ties are gradually replacing those of nomadism and the maintenance of strong kinship and tribal ties.'[53] In the euphoria surrounding the al-Jafr experiment, that project is perceived as wholly novel: 'The dawn of a new life started with so bold an aim as to transplant the twentieth century to where only the camels thrived . . . The project is a unique experiment';[54] 'A new community has been created at al Jafr.'[55]

If in these reports the old clichés already questioned during the Mandate period appear again, the transposition to Jordan of stereotypes fashioned elsewhere is obvious. Apart from Huneidi,[56] experts all too often ignore the historical dimension. If referred to at all, it is either to hide or to enhance some characteristics of the nomads or other actors who historically played a role in the process of sedentarisation.

Huneidi identifies the beginning of the Mandate period as a point of rupture with the Ottoman past. According to the author, bedouin tribes of northern Arabia for several centuries lived a 'natural' life based essentially on herding. This existence was broken by wars and conquests in a climate of perpetual political instability.[57] With the Mandate appeared a strong central authority capable of imposing lasting political stability, with the army permitting control and integration of the bedouin tribes. Parallel to this, economic factors paved the way for the sedentarisation process, notably the decline of the camel as a means of transportation and prolonged periods of drought.[58] For the 1946–64 period, the author stresses the role of the newly independent state as the motor for progress, through technological development in controlling the desert environment and allowing for the growth of agricultural projects, but also through the creation in 1948 of the army's cultural department, very active in developing educational facilities for the bedouin. Huneidi's report, despite its wealth of data, tends to credit the independent Jordanian state with having 'innovated' in the field of sedentarisation and development projects in the steppe areas. In his analysis, the Mandatory period appears as merely the first stage in the passage of nomadic societies to 'civilisation'.

[50] WFP, 1969a, p. 3. [51] WFP, 1969b, p. 4. [52] Qalyoubi, 1967.
[53] UNESOB, 1973, p. 32. [54] Qalyoubi, 1967, pp. 153–4. [55] UNESOB, 1973, p. 31.
[56] Huneidi, 1965. [57] Ibid., p. 1. [58] Ibid., pp. 2–3.

The experts' vision of social change (1950–70)

It is possible to deduce the vision of social change held by experts in international organisations writing between 1950 and 1970, by looking at their representations of Jordanian bedouin or nomads of surrounding countries, by reviewing their discussions concerning the role of the state, and finally by studying carefully all the ways they have hidden, manipulated and reinterpreted the history of nomadic societies. The sources for much of what has been written are simultaneously the economic and socio-political theories of 'modernisation' elaborated by the American developmentalist school and ideas born of 'Orientalist' currents specific to the Middle Eastern context.

During the 1950s and 1960s, theoreticians of modernisation of the developmentalist school elaborated models to explain development and to propose alternatives to underdevelopment.[59] They adopted a functionalist approach and worked within a comparative perspective, holding an evolutionist vision of social change. One of their principal assumptions was the idea that each society is a strongly integrated system and that any change capable of jolting the inertia of that system can only come from the outside: this postulate led them to privilege the role of the state as *the* agent in the process of modernisation. The corollary to this assumption is that social change is an irreversible, unidirectional and cumulative process. Thus sedentarisation, taken to be inevitable, seemed to be led by an almost teleological necessity: it would be the catalyst for the different 'inputs' of change.[60]

To take one example of how modernisation theories were applied in the Middle Eastern context, we may look at Lerner's *The Passing of Traditional Society*,[61] whose work often served as a reference for experts. For Lerner, western societies are the model and standard of comparison for development. Modernisation occurs through the elimination of tradition and through a process of mobilisation capable of bringing about a positive and rational mentality leading individuals to universalist behaviour patterns. According to Lerner, it is the growth of social communication that is at the origin of the process of mobilisation and that regulates the development of socio-political systems. It is thus possible to measure and to predict the progress of modernisation through a series of variables such as urbanisation ratios, literacy rates and the systems for the circulation of information.

A large number of experts found these developmentalist approaches appealing and therefore opted for an evolutionist analysis of pastoral societies in the Middle East: this one-way vision of social change has all too often ruled out any possibility of local reinterpretation or adaptation on the part of nomadic societies. Similarly, experts have often showed a lack of any sense of

[59] I refer here to such American developmentalist authors of the 1950–70 period such as W. Rostow, G. Almond, B. Powell, D. Apter and L. Pye, to mention only the most well known.
[60] Salzman, 1980. [61] Lerner, 1958.

history just as they have misappropriated sociological notions by comparing nomadic societies of different countries on the basis of typologies which take into account only the groups' mobility. The developmentalist rhetoric thus served to iron out specificities and differences and to produce veritable caricatures of pastoral societies.

Modernisation theories thus had a very significant impact on the analyses of experts between 1950 and 1970, but several 'Orientalist' currents also influenced thinking during this period. At the beginning of the 1950s the American anthropologist Coon published one of the first introductory studies of Middle Eastern and North African societies. His work, often quoted in experts' reports, was extremely popular in the Anglo-Saxon world. Coon utilised the 'mosaic' metaphor to describe the different lifestyles and physical characteristics of the population, as well as the different linguistic and religious groups or the varied systems of socio-political organisation found in the Middle East. It is possible to explain how this model functions only if what is 'modern' is separated from what is 'traditional' in the different contexts under analysis. Anything 'in transition' is eliminated: 'A culture in transition is hard to explain and harder to understand; we must find some period in history when the culture was, relatively speaking, at rest.'[62] Coon maintains that from the fifteenth to the end of the nineteenth century Middle Eastern societies lived in a state of hibernation or what might be called 'cultural rest'. From a perspective once again functionalist, in search of a golden age when societies now living the 'agony of modernisation' were in some mythical situation of equilibrium and prosperity, Coon side-steps any explanation that might take into account historical transformations of any component of the mosaic or changes in the types of interrelations between these components.

Coon's perspective is complementary to the approaches adopted by the theoreticians of modernisation and for this reason played a role in the analysis of experts. According to this perspective the history of nomadic societies in the Middle East becomes the history of societies still 'in hibernation' and sheltered from change. Following this perspective, Filali states that nomads 'continue to lead lives more or less closed to outside influences, show a high capacity for rejection and seek refuge in tradition, perhaps because they are completely unprepared to confront the impact of factors of transformation'.[63] Given this view, the history of nomads 'begins again' with the creation of independent modern nation-states.

Finally, we realise quite quickly from studying most reports that the paragraphs devoted to social factors and objectives in sedentarisation programmes are merely jargon providing a sociological 'cover'. Questions concerning the social development of nomad groups are always posed through what are called 'integrated' approaches, but the price of integration is nearly always a hierarchical cohabitation in which social factors are sacrificed to the impera-

[62] Coon, 1961, p. 8. [63] Filali, 1966, p. 72.

tives of predominant policies, to the preoccupations of immediate intervention and to the criteria of performance effectiveness. In this context it is hardly surprising to hear ILO experts define the task of sociologists as follows:

> It is necessary to make a serious effort to re-educate them [the nomads] in order to explain the real nature of these projects to them, as well as the benefits and privileges inherent in a less nomadic lifestyle. This objective can be attained with the help of a sociologist whose concern with the social aspects of sedentarisation is greater than that of the technocrat.[64]

The '*hima* system' and the rangeland development projects in the 1980s: towards a new ideology of development?

In the early 1990s the sedentarisation of nomads was no longer a priority in state policies for development in the Middle East's steppe regions. If pastoral nomadism as a means of land use had been greatly reduced, we are nevertheless justified in asking whether the effects of sedentarisation promised by the experts were actually realised. From an economic standpoint, former nomads showed a remarkable capability of adaptation to the constraints imposed by the new states, and we have seen the rise of 'multi-resource' economic systems within most bedouin families, where pastoralism is but one of the activities undertaken. Sedentarisation has contributed to the integration of local bedouin economies and has permitted access to public health and educational facilities. There has, however, been no accompanying process of detribalisation as predicted by experts. On the contrary, several recent studies have shown that the model of tribal organisation has not disappeared among sedentarised bedouin. In Jordan in particular, the term 'bedouin', once a synonym for pastoral nomad, now indicates a political identity of a tribal nature.[65]

Control of the steppe was long formulated in terms of political security, and sedentarisation of the nomads was one means of obtaining it. However, the priority given to developing agriculture in the steppe regions rather than renewing pasturelands and developing pastoralism has had other consequences. The growing ecological fragility of the steppe, due to the deterioration of its soil, linked to the rhythm and conditions of land exploitation as well as to the new pattern of management of animal and plant resources, now appears to be one of the most disturbing effects of development policies carried out over the past thirty to forty years. Modern technological assets in the hands of the state have not been sufficient by themselves to ensure control over the environment or to guarantee the success of development models. Economic and land-tenure policies contributed to the breakdown of former systems of managing steppe regions, thus leading the elites to fall back on short-term investment and speculation. In Jordan alone – though it is a regional phenomenon – local meat production in the mid-1980s was able to

[64] ILO, 1962, p. 79. [65] Bocco, 1989b; Layne, 1986.

satisfy only 25 per cent of the national market demand, and agricultural surveys have shown a dramatic reduction in soil fertility and agricultural productivity in the steppe regions.[66]

Faced with the problem of the degradation of plant resources in the steppic zones, during the 1980s a number of international organisations and state agencies from several Middle Eastern countries expressed a growing interest in pastureland conservation and development programmes. However, this important reorientation is not totally novel. During the 1960s, at a time when most studies recommended the sedentarisation of nomads and the development of agriculture in the steppe, other research carried out in Saudi Arabia under FAO auspices stressed rather the need to develop systems to regenerate natural pasturelands. Omar Draz, an official in Syria's Agricultural Ministry and an FAO consultant, was the instigator of this research by calling to the attention of planners the importance of a traditional system of range management known in the Arabian peninsula as *hima* (pl. *ahmiya*, literally 'protection' and by analogy 'reserve'). According to Draz,

> the Hema system was once common in parts of the Arabian Peninsula, and is still used in parts of Sa'udi Arabia, Yemen, Oman, Syria. It originated in the Near East and is suitable as a means for controlled grazing in selected areas in arid, semi-arid and mountain ranges, where nomadic grazing is the only system practised. Carefully protected ahmia would furnish fodder reserves essential for stability of nomadic grazing. They would also change the attitude of the people towards the range, introducing the philosophy of protection and improvement instead of exploitation.[67]

At the beginning of the 1990s, in an international context highly sensitive to environmental issues, the *hima* system has become the latest 'religion' of experts in the social and nature sciences; it is the new means of fighting against desertification and ensuring 'sustainable development' for the arid regions of the Middle East. Islamic legitimacy traced directly to the Prophet has been accorded this traditional system of resource management,[68] but no study, whether ancient or recent, has been able to provide a detailed analysis of how this system actually works in the steppic regions of the Middle East.[69]

[66] Barham and Mensching, 1988. [67] Draz, 1969, p. 8. [68] Masri, 1991; Nesheiwat, 1991.

[69] According to the examples given by Draz (1980), most of the *hima* reserves found in Syria and Saudi Arabia prior to 1960 were not located in true steppic zones, i.e. ones with less than 300 mm of annual rainfall. An American anthropologist, J. Shoup (1990), maintains that the Syrian government instituted the *hima* system at the beginning of the 1970s by setting up a network of pastoral co-operatives in the steppe areas. He is contradicted in a study by Masri, a Draz 'disciple' and his successor at the Syrian Ministry of Agriculture. Masri wrote: 'All the infrastructures (set up by the government) are meant to develop the Syrian rangelands through a revival of the Hema system, but the present situation is now analogous to the installation of a well-designed electrical circuit before the plug is inserted in the outlet, and the light is still off' (1991, p. 35). In Jordan, Nesheiwat (1991) acknowledges that there are no modern examples of the *hima* system being applied. A large-scale project, the Hamad Basin Project, launched at the beginning of the 1980s under the auspices of ACSAD (Rofail, 1984), is purportedly inspired by the *hima* 'philosophy'. However, the fact that it straddles the borders of four countries (Jordan, Saudi Arabia, Syria and Iraq) has led to its implementation proving slow indeed.

Furthermore, according to the experts who advocate it, the establishment of *hima* programmes depends on the revival of tribal landholding rights in the steppe, on a participatory approach taking into account the tribes' social organisation, and on the relative disengagement of the national authorities from the administration of these projects. This significant shift from policies advocated in the 1950s and 1960s is not only underpinned by explicit criticism of sedentarisation projects already put into effect,[70] but also implies the partial 'de-sedentarisation' of former nomads.

While we have no intention of questioning the probity of this new approach[71] – which incidentally has not yet been truly tested – we note its great popularity with a large number of experts and decision makers, a popularity we believe is closely linked to the ideologies concerning development prevalent at the end of the twentieth century. With its evocation of the principles of local participation and self-sustained development, the *hima* system cannot but appeal to the representatives of international agencies such as the World Bank or the IMF, who see in it the chance to apply their policies of economic liberalisation and promote free enterprise through the 'rediscovery' of a traditional system of resource management. If, in its socialist–Baʿthist reinterpretation, the 'philosophy' of the *hima* system has already enjoyed some success in Syria, it is no doubt destined to seduce a large number of non-governmental organisations which, while being opposed to liberal policies of structural readjustment, share the concern to take into account local models of social organisation. The consensus being formed around the *hima* programmes, however divergent the ideological positions of the experts or the institutions that advocate them, should not mislead us. Unlike forty years ago,

70 In the summing-up of a symposium on the *hima* system organised recently in Amman by the FAO, we can read: 'The man–land relationship had remained harmonious in the area until World War II. Up to this point, the range was exploited with no feed supplements, routes were agreed between tribes and range was controlled. After World War II, misdirected government efforts of modernization led to settlement, which brought further costs and no sustainable bases for production. Tribal rights were no longer recognized' (FAO, 1991, p. 3). (We might note, in passing, that the Mandatory period in the Middle East apparently had no effect on nomadic peoples and range management!) At the same symposium, the FAO representative expressed support for adopting the *hima* system in these terms: 'Traditional institutions can also become part of the modern democratic development process for range management, which requires first of all the active involvement and participation of the pastoral populations themselves' (FAO, 1991, p. 2).

71 Among the resolutions formulated by a group of experts meeting at a FAO conference in December 1990 in Amman are some which are extremely critical and innovatory in comparison to the approaches dominant from 1950 to 1970. They urge decision makers concerned only with the short-term political benefits of development projects to adopt a more far-sighted vision taking into consideration long-term effects. The experts also explicitly express their opposition to any continuation of sedentarisation projects. Finally, along with the necessity of recognising tribal land rights, they also bring up the concept of 'ecological responsibility' in resource management: 'Tribal rights should be formally respected and protected along with customary relations that exist between and among tribes . . . Rangeland and water resources should remain State property and be allocated on a long-term basis to specific local groups/associations for their exclusive pastoral use and with the responsibility of maintaining ecological equilibrium' (FAO, 1991, p. 9).

tribal organisation would now appear to be the linchpin of these new projects, but as was already the case in the past, when experts mentioned it in their reports, it is still a sort of 'black box' the workings of which are never made explicit. However, without wanting to question the importance of the ecological objectives of the *hima* programmes, it should be said that their adoption requires far more profound socio-political analyses than those we have seen so far.

Sedentarisation projects are now history, but let us hope that the accumulated experience of the past decades in development of the steppe will provide future experts with some critical abilities in elaborating projects still to come. Any development project will always be the result of a set of representations of reality and of a 'philosophy' which is the product of its time. The ability to analyse it with lucidity is thus all the more essential.

GLOSSARY

ahl al-dira	sheep-rearing tribes
ahl al-gharb	tribes of the west
amiriyya, miri	state-owned land of which the usufructory rights belong to individual owners
ʿashira	tribe, clan
badiya	open country
badw (sg. *badawi*)	bedouins
baladiyya	municipal administration, municipality
barriyya	central steppe
barwah	gifts
bur	virgin steppeland
daftar khana	government property registry
dar (or *dira*)	tribal territory, home
fallah (pl. *fallahin*)	cultivator
ghazw	razzia, raid
hadar (pl. *hadari*)	sedentary folk
hamad	plateau
hijra (sg. *hujar*)	migration; village
hima	protected pasture
imara	sovereignty
iqtaʿ	land grant, fief
jabali	mountain inhabitant
jamʿiyya	co-operative
khalya	free, empty land
khan	caravanserai, market
khuwwa	booty, levy
liwaʾ	sub-provincial administrative unit
mahlul	without owner
majlis	court, council
mallak	land owner
maʿmura	cultivated land bordering the steppe
mashyakhiyya	gift to a shaykh
matruka	(legal category) village common lands

mawat	(legal category) distant, uncultivated land
mintaqa	administrative district
mu'assasa	establishment, institution
mubah	'free land', rangeland open to all
muhafaza	administrative district, province
mukhtar	village headman or mayor
mulk/milk	privately owned property
musha'	village land held in shares, often subject to periodic redistribution
mutasarrif	administration: governor; property: holder of usufructory possession
nahiya	lowest-level administrative district
naqaba	union
qabili (pl. *qaba'il*)	noble, arms-bearing tribes
qada'	middle-level administrative district
qa'im-maqam	governor
sabkha	saltpan or lake
sanad tabu	title deeds
sawani	irrigation system
shambul	mountainous area
shawaya	sheep-herding tribes
shuyukh al-qutun	'cotton shaykhs'
suq	market
tabu (Turkish *tapu*)	Ottoman land registry title
tasarruf	usufructory possession, exploitation rights
tibin	straw
tafrah	oil-price boom
umma	the Islamic community
'ushr	tithe
ustadh	master craftsman
waqf	mortmain; charitable endowment
zakat	annual Islamic tax on wealth

Bibliographic note

The Social Sciences and Bedouin Societies in the Arabian Peninsula and the Near East, 1962–92

RICCARDO BOCCO

Institut Universitaire d'Etudes sur le Développement, Geneva

A review of collective publications or special journal issues devoted to the societies of pastoral nomads published between 1965 and 1995 in French, German or English reveals important lacunae in the analysis of regions of the Arabian Peninsula and the Near East. I have listed below the specialised journals and collective publications, usually symposium papers, that have influenced debate on pastoral nomadic societies at the international level. The emphasis is on works conceived in a comparative perspective, as against monographic studies, which are extensively cited in the contributions gathered in this volume.

It is noteworthy that whereas comparative studies of pastoral nomads in other geographic regions exist, there has been no collective publication or special issue of a journal exclusively devoted to the Arabian Peninsula and/or the Near East. This is also the case for publications in Arabic, as Ahmad Abu Bakr noted (in the journal *Etudes Orientales*, 1992, see below), the only partial exception being a collection of articles on sedentarisation problems published by the Arab League in 1966. In his annotated bibliography Abu Bakr notes that despite the acknowledged importance of the bedouin in the history of Arab societies, Arab social scientists have given little attention to the bedouin in their research. Among the favoured themes in monographic studies which have appeared in Arabic are customary law and bedouin folklore (poetry, songs, legends and genealogies), as well as socio-geographic analyses of the types of adaptation to the ecological milieu and the models of nomadism. Finally, there exists a quantitatively important number of reports and pamphlets, produced in the main by national experts, and dealing primarily with questions of sedentarisation.

It is also true, moreover, that the existing studies on pastoral nomads in the Near East and Arabian Peninsula have contributed little to theoretical debate within such disciplines as sociology, anthropology and geography. This is particularly true in comparison with the contributions made by studies on nomads of North Africa, sub-Saharan Africa and the Turko-Iranian or Central Asian regions, which are much more significant. In some ways the work of nineteenth- and early twentieth-century travellers, as well as that of the anthropologists and geographers of the colonial period, can be said to have been almost superior, both quantitatively and qualitatively, to that reviewed here.

There are a number of reasons for this. First, residence permits for academic researchers (westerners as well as Arabs) seeking to do fieldwork have been severely limited in most of the countries of the Near East. Studies of local bedouin societies carried out by nationals (especially Saudis and Jordanians) for doctoral theses are often difficult to obtain and have rarely been published as monographs. A second reason is that the weight of nationalist and anti-tribalist ideologies, espoused following independence by, among others, the different Baʿthist regimes, helped to discourage interest in studying bedouin societies, often considered 'primitive', numerically marginal and on the way to extinction.

Lastly, two recent works illustrate the small number of studies dedicated to the situation of women, in particular, in the Near East and Arabia. See M. Horowitz and F. Jowkar, *Gender Relations of Pastoral and Agropastoral Production: A Bibliography with Annotations,* Binghamton: Institute for Development Anthropology, 1991, 485 pp. See also, by the same authors, *Pastoral Women and Change in Africa, the Middle East and Central Asia,* a Report from the Gender Relations of Pastoral and Agropastoral Production Project for UNIFEM and UNDP, Binghamton: Institute for Development Anthropology, 1992, 78 pp.

This appendix therefore underlines some of the gaps in bibliographic production. The references are listed in chronological order. Following book titles we have indicated between parentheses the author's name, the country, and the subject for the articles analysing bedouin or agro-pastoral societies in the Arabian Peninsula and the Near East. Ethno-archaeological studies, studies approached exclusively from the viewpoint of the natural sciences, and studies on the bedouin of Israel and the Israeli-occupied territories have not been included in this list.

Books

Kraus, W. (ed.), *Nomadismus als Entwicklungsproblem*, Bielefeld: Bertelsmann Universitätsverlag, 1969 (E. Wirth, 'Near East, Socio-economic Integration of Nomadic Populations')

Collective, *The Study of Nomadism*, special issue of the *Anthropological Quarterly*, 44, 3, 1971 (none)

Irons, W. and Dyson-Hudson, N. (eds.), *Perspectives on Nomadism*, special issue of the *Journal of Asian and African Studies,* Leiden: Brill, 1972 (none)

Nelson, C. (ed.), *The Desert and the Sown: Nomads in the Wider Society*, Berkeley: Institute of International Studies, 1973 (D. P. Cole, 'Saudi

Arabia, Socio-economic Changes among the Al-Murrah'; T. Asad, 'Middle East, the Military Weight of the Bedouin in the History of Nomadic–Sedentary Relations')

Weissleder, W. (ed.), *The Nomadic Alternative: Modes and Models of Interaction in the African-Asian Deserts and Steppes*, The Hague: Mouton, 1978 (E. Marx, 'Middle East, Ecology and Social Organization in Pastoral Societies')

Equipe Ecologie et Anthropologie des Sociétés Pastorales, *Production pastorale et société*, Actes du colloque international de Paris, déc. 1976, Paris: Editions de la Maison des Sciences de l'Homme, 1979 (none)

Salzman, P. C., *When Nomads Settle: Processes of Sedentarisation as Adaptation and Response*, New York: Bergin, 1980 (R. Bulliet, 'Iraq, Sedentarisation of Arab Tribes in the 7th Century'; D. Chatty, 'Syria–Lebanon, Economic Development and Social Organization among the Al-Fadl and Al-Hassanna')

Galaty, J. G., Aronson, D. and Salzman, P. C. (eds.), *The Future of Pastoral Peoples*, Proceedings of the International Conference held in Nairobi, Aug. 1980, Ottawa: International Development Research Institute, 1981 (K. Abu Jaber and F. Gharaibeh, 'Jordan, Planning Programmes for Sedentarizing the Bedouin'; F. A. Bahhady, 'Syria, Animal Production Systems')

Galaty, J. G. and Salzman, P. C. (eds.), *Change and Development in Nomadic and Pastoral Societies*, Leiden: Brill, 1981 (D. P. Cole, 'Saudi Arabia, Social Change among the Al-Murrah')

Stein, L. (ed.), *Die Nomaden in Geschichte und Gegenwart*, Beiträge zu internationalen Symposium am Dezember, 1975 im Leipzig, Veröffentlichungen des Museums für Völkerkunde zu Leipzig, Heft 33, Berlin: Akademie Verlag, 1981 (H. Reintjens, 'Middle East, the Mahram'; L. Stein, 'Iraq, Middle East, Economic Changes')

Salzman, P. C. (ed.), *Contemporary Nomadic and Pastoral Peoples: Asia and the North*, Studies in Third World Societies no. 18, Williamsburg: Department of Anthropology, College of William and Mary, 1981 (D. Chatty, 'Oman, Bedouin Strategies of Economic Adaptation'; W. Lancaster, 'Jordan, Logics of Response to Economic Changes among the Ruwala'; F. Scholz, 'Middle East, Theoretical Remarks on Social Changes among Pastoral Nomads')

Scholz, F. and Janzen, J. (eds.), *Nomadismus: ein Entwicklungsproblem?* Berlin: Abhandlungen des Geographischen Instituts Anthropogeographie, Band 33, Dietrich Reimer Verlag, 1982 (G. Meyer, 'Syria'; I. Haidari, 'Iraq'; U. Fabietti, 'Saudi Arabia'; F. Scholz, 'Oman'; R. Cordes, 'United Arab Emirates'; J. Janzen, 'Dhofar, Oman')

Barfield, T. (ed.), *Nomads Stopped in their Tracks?* Special issue of the *Cultural Survival Quarterly*, 8 (1), 1984 (J. Shoup, general overview of nomadic tribes in Jordan and Syria)

Bisson, J. (ed.), *Le nomade, l'oasis et la ville*, Tours: URBAMA, 1989 (R. Bocco, Jordan, electoral laws and bedouin identity; O. D'Hont, 'Syria, Pastoral Production and Urban Consumption'; F. and J. Métral, 'Syria, Economy and Social Organization in the Oasis of Sukhneh'; M. Rasheed, 'Saudi Arabia, Political Power and Caravan Economy in the Oasis of Hail')

Baum, E. (ed.), *Nomaden und ihre Umwelt im Wandel*, special issue of *Der Tropenlandwirt*, Witzenhausen, 1989 (A. Zurek, 'Iraq, Semi-nomadic herding')

Salzman, P. C. and Galaty, J. G. (eds.), *Nomads in a Changing World* (Proceedings of the 1978 IUAES Commission of Nomadic Peoples), Naples: Istituto Universitario di Studi Orientali, 1990 (E. Marx, 'Middle East, Economic Changes among Pastoral Nomads'; D. Chatty, 'Jordan, Saudi Arabia, Syria, Comparative Perspectives of Social Changes among Bedouin Tribes')

Bernus, E. and Pouillon, F. (eds.), *Sociétés pastorales et développement*, Cahiers des Sciences Humaines No. 26, Paris: ORSTOM, 1990 (R. Bocco, 'Middle East, Jordan, International Experts and Development Programmes for the Bedouin'; U. Fabietti, 'Saudi Arabia, the Bedouin Domestic Group, Under-productivity and Development')

Galaty, J. G. and Johnson, D. L. (eds.), *The World of Pastoralism, Herding Systems in Comparative Perspective*, New York: The Guilford Press, 1990 (W. Lancaster, 'Jordan, Pastoral Production and Social Organization among the Ruwala'; J. Shoup, 'Syria, the "Hima" System')

Scholz, F. (ed.), *Nomaden mobile Tierhaltung, Zur gegenwärtigen Lage von Nomaden und zu den Problemen und Chancen mobiler Tierhaltung*, Berlin: Das Arabische Buch, 1991 (J. Janzen, 'Oman, Socio-economic Changes and Development Programmes for Pastoral Nomads in Dhofar')

Bourgeot, A. (ed.), *Etats et sociétés nomades*, special issue of *Etudes Orientales*, nos. 15–16, 1992 (Abu Bakr, annotated bibliography on bedouin societies in the Arab world based on Arabic-language sources in the social sciences)

Specialised journals

Three journals specialising in the study of pastoral societies were started in the second half of the 1970s:

Pastoral Development Network, published since 1976 in London by the Overseas Development Institute at the initiative of S. Sandford, is the only journal closely combining natural and social sciences and primarily oriented towards applied research. Since its establishment and up until March 1992, only one article has been published on the region we are concerned with: vol.

7, March 1979, paper 7c, D. P. Cole, 'Saudi Arabia, Socio-economic Changes among the Al-Murrah'.

Production Pastorale et Société, published by the Maison des Sciences de l'Homme in Paris at the initiative of the Equipe Ecologie et Anthropologie des Sociétés Pastorales, the journal gives preference to studies in the social sciences. Since its establishment in the winter of 1977–8 and up to its last issue in the spring of 1987, only four articles on pastoral societies of the Arabian Peninsula and the Syrian steppe region were published:

- No. 8, Spring 1981, P. Briant, 'Middle East, Territorial Representations of Pastoral Nomads in Ancient Times'
- No. 11, Autumn 1982, J. Wilkinson, 'South-east Arabia, the Notion of Territory among Pastoral Nomads'
- No. 13, Autumn 1983, A. Montigny, 'Qatar, the Notion of Territory among the Al-Naʿim'
- No. 14, Spring 1984, J. Hannoyer and J.-P. Thieck, 'Syria, Herding and Trading of Sheep in the Raqqa Region'

Nomadic Peoples, established by the Commission on Nomadic Peoples which is part of the International Union of Anthropological and Ethnological Sciences, the journal was published from 1978 to 1990 at the Anthropology Department of Montreal University (Canada), and since then at the Scandinavian Institute of African Studies (Uppsala, Sweden). It has always given preference to research in the social sciences, but in the years 1978–96 (nos. 1–39), it published only ten articles on the region that concerns us:

- No. 6, 1980, W. Lancaster, 'Middle East, Mutual Aid and Development in the Societies of Pastoral Nomads'
- No. 10, 1982, F. Scholz, 'Oman, Bedouin and the Oil Economy'
- No. 15, 1984, J. Hiatt, 'Jordan, State-building and "Political Encapsulation" of Bedouin Groups: the Case of the Bani Sakhr'
- No. 20, 1986, W. Lancaster, 'Jordan, the Notion of Territory among the Ruwala'; U. Fabietti, 'Saudi Arabia, the Notion of Territory among Bedouin Tribes'
- No. 24, 1987, D. Chatty, 'Oman, Bedouin and the Oil Economy'
- No. 28, 1991, U. Fabietti, 'Middle East, the Bedouin Domestic Group'; R. Webster, 'Oman, Pastoralism and the Oil Economy among the Al-Wahiba'
- No. 38, 1996, D. Chatty, 'Local Administration and Harasis' Tribal Authority in the Sultanate of Oman'; W. Lancaster and F. Lancaster, 'Nomadic Fishermen of Ja'alan, Oman'

BIBLIOGRAPHY

Abd El-Moneim, A. M., Cocks, P. S., and Swedan, Y. (1988), 'Yield Stability of Selected Forage Vetches (Vicia spp.) under Rainfed Conditions in West Asia', *Journal of Agricultural Science*, (Cambridge), 111, pp. 295–301

Abu Jaber, K. S., Gharaibeh, F. A. and Hill, A. (1987), *The Badia of Jordan: The Process of Change*, University of Jordan, Amman

Abu Jaber, R. S. (1989), *Pioneers over Jordan: The Frontier of Settlement in Transjordan, 1850–1914,* I. B. Tauris, London

Abu Zeid, A. M. (1966), 'The Changing World of the Nomads', in J. Peristiany (ed.), *Contributions to Mediterranean Sociology*, Mouton, The Hague, pp. 279–88

Achard, M. (1926) 'L'avenir de l'irrigation dans l'Etat de Syrie', *Bulletin économique trimestriel,* 1926/3, pp. 1082–8

Altorki S. and Cole, D. P. (1989), *Arabian Oasis City: The Transformation of 'Unayzah*, University of Texas Press, Austin

Ameri, A. (1982), 'Socio-Economic Development of Jordan (1950–1980)', Ph.D. Dissertation, Wayne State University

Antoun, Richard (1972), *Arab Village: A Socio-structural Study of a Transjordanian Peasant Community*, Indiana University Press, Bloomington

Antoun, Richard and Harik, Iliya (eds.) (1972), *Rural Politics and Social Change in the Middle East*, Indiana University Press, Bloomington

Apter, David (1963), 'Political Religion in the New Nations', in C. Geertz (ed.), *Old Societies and New States*, Free Press of Glencoe, New York, pp. 57–105

Al-Asad, Rifat (1973), *The Economic, Social and Political Development in the Syrian Arab Region Between the National Revolution and the Class Revolution 1946–1963* (in Arabic), Al-Dar Al-Wataniyya Distributions, Damascus

Asad, Talal (1979), 'Equality in Nomadic Social Systems? Notes towards the Dissolution of an Anthropological Category', *Pastoral Production and Society*, Cambridge University Press, Cambridge, pp. 419–28

Asche H. (1981), *Mobile Lebensformgruppen Südost-Arabiens im Wandel die Küstenprovinz Al Batinah im erdölfordernden Sultanat Oman,* Abhandlungen des Geographischen Instituts – Anthropogeographie 32, Berlin

Atkins/WS International (1989), *Regional Development Plan for the Southern Region*, Sultanate of Oman/Planning Committee for Development and Environment in the Southern Region (PCDESR)

Awad, M. (1959), 'La sédentarisation des tribus nomades et semi-nomades au Moyen-Orient', *Revue international du travail*, 79/1, pp. 27–60

Axelrod, L. W. (1978), 'Tribesmen in Uniform: the Demise of the Fidayyun in Jordan, 1970–71', *The Muslim World* (Hartford), 68/1, pp. 25–45

Bahhady, F. A. (1981), 'Recent Changes in Bedouin Systems of Livestock Production in the Syrian Steppe', in J. G. Galati et al. (eds.), *The Future of Pastoral People*, International Development Research Centre, Ottawa, pp. 258–66

Baird, D., Garrard, A., Martin. L. and Wright, K. (1992), 'Prehistoric Environment and Settlement in the Azraq Basin: An Interim Report on the 1989 Excavation Season', *Levant* (London), 24, pp. 1–32

Banks, K. M. (1984), *Climates, Cultures and Cattle. The Holocene Archaeology of the Eastern Sahara*, Department of Anthropology, Southern Methodist University, Dallas.

Barham, N. and Mensching, H. (1988), 'Pressure on the Pastureland Environment in Jordan,' *Applied Geography and Development* (Tübingen), 31, pp. 37–53

Baskin, L. M. (1974), 'Management of Ungulate Herds in Relation to Domestication', in V. Geist and F. Walther (eds.), *The Behaviour of Ungulates and its Relationship to Management*, International Union for the Conservation of Nature and Natural Resources, Morges, Switzerland, pp. 530–41

(1976), *Provedenie Kopytnykh zhirotnykh* [The Behaviour of Ungulata], Nauk, Moscow

Basson, P. (1981), 'Women and Traditional Food Technologies in Rural Jordan', mimeo, University of Yarmouk

Bates, R. (1981), *Markets and States in Tropical Africa*, University of California Press, Berkeley

Bernus, E. and Pouillon, F. (eds.), (1990), *Société Pastorales et Développement, Cahiers des Sciences Humaines* (Paris), 26/1–2

Berque, J. (1959), 'Introduction' to 'Nomades et nomadisme en zone aride', *Revue internationale des Sciences Sociales,* 11 /4, pp. 501–18

Berry, R. J. (1969), 'The Genetical Implications of Domestication', in P. J. Ucko and G. W. Dimbleby (eds.), *The Domestication of Plants and Animals*, Aldine, Chicago, pp. 207–17

Betts, A. V. G. (1992), 'Tell el-Hibr: A Rock Shelter Occupation of the Fourth Millennium BCE in the Jordanian Badiya', *BASOR* (Baltimore), 287, pp. 5–23

Betts, A., Helms, S., Lancaster, W., Jones, E., Lupton, A., Martin, L. and Matsaert, F. (1990), 'The Burqu'/Ruweishid Project: Preliminary Report on the 1988 Field Season', *Levant* (London), 22, pp. 1–20

Betts, A., Helms, S., Lancaster, W. and Lancaster, F. (1991), 'The Burqu'/ Ruweishid Project: Preliminary Report on the 1989 Field Season', *Levant* (London), 23, pp. 7–28

Birks, J. S. (1978), 'The Mountain Pastoralists of the Sultanate of Oman', *Development and Change* (London), 9, pp. 71–86

Bischoff, T. (1881), 'Reise von Palmyra durch die Wust nach Aleppo', *Globus* (Braunschweig), 40/23, pp. 303–66

Blunt, Anne (1879), *Bedouin Tribes of the Euphrates,* Harper, NY, London, 2 vols.

Bocco, R. (1985), 'Bedouin Strategies versus Sedentarisation Policies', *MESA Annual Meeting Papers*

(1987), 'La notion de dirah chez les tribus bédouines en Jordanie: le cas des Bani Sakhr', in B. Cannon, (ed.), *Terroirs et sociétés au Maghreb et au Moyen Orient*, Série Etudes sur le Monde Arabe, 2, Maison de l'Orient, Lyon, pp. 195–215

(1989a), 'Espaces étatiques et espaces tribaux dans le sud jordanien: législation foncière et redéfinition des liens sociaux', *Maghreb-Machrek*, (Paris), 123, pp. 144–63

(1989b), 'L'Etat producteur d'identités locales: lois électorales et tribus bédouines en Jordanie', in J. Bisson (ed.), *Le nomade, l'oasis et la ville*, URBAMA, Tours, pp. 271–88

(1990), 'Ingénieurs agronomes et politiques de développement dans les steppes du sud jordanien (1960–1985)', in E. Longuenesse (ed.), *Bâtisseurs et bureaucrates: ingénieurs et société au Maghreb et au Moyen-Orient*, Collection Etudes sur le Monde Arabe, 4, Maison de l'Orient, Lyons, pp. 255–80

Bocco, R. and Tell, T. (1994), 'The Pax Britannica in the Steppe: British Tribal Policy in Transjordan, 1921–1939', in E. Rogan and T. Tell (eds.), *Village, Steppe and State: The Social Origins of Modern Jordan*, British Academic Press, London, pp. 108–127

(1995), 'Frontières, tribus et états en Jordanie orientale à l'époque du Mandat', in R. Bocco and C. Velud (eds.), *Tribus, Tribalismes et Etats au Moyen-Orient,* special issue of *Maghreb-Machrek*, La Documentation Française, Paris, pp. 26–47

Boiral, P. and Olivier de Serdan, J. P. (1985), 'Introduction', in P. Boiral, J. F. Lanteri and J. P. Olivier de Serdan (eds.), *Paysans, experts et chercheurs en Afrique noire*, CIFACE-Karthala, Paris, pp. 7–23

Bökönyi, S. (1973), 'Some Problems of Animal Domestication in the Middle East', in J. Matolcsi (ed.), *Domestikationsforschung und Geschichte der Haustiere*, Academiai Kiado, Budapest, pp. 69–75

(1976), 'Development of Early Stock Rearing in the Near East', *Nature* (Munich), 264, pp. 19–23

Bonte, Pierre (1987), 'L'herbe ou le sol? L'évolution du système foncier pastoral en Mauritanie du Sud-Ouest', in Marceau Gast (ed.), *Hériter en pays musulman. Habus, lait vivant, Manyahuli*, CNRS, Paris, pp. 193–214

Boucheman, A. de (1934), 'Notes sur la rivalité de deux tribus moutonnières de Syrie: les Mawali et les Hadidiyin', *Revue des études islamiques* (Paris), 1, pp. 8–58

(1937) *Une petite cité caravanière: Suhné*, Institut Français de Damas, Damascus and Paris.

Bourdieu, Pierre (1977), *Outline of a Theory of Practice*, trans. R. Nice, Cambridge University Press, Cambridge

Boutonnet, J.-P. (1989), 'La spéculation ovine en Algérie', Institut National pour la Recherche Agronomique, Série Notes et Documents no. 90, Montpellier

Bujra, Abdalla (1971), *The Politics of Stratification*, Oxford University Press, Oxford

Bulliet, R. (1975), *The Camel and the Wheel*, Harvard University Press, Cambridge, Mass.

Burckhardt, John L. (1822), *Travels in Syria and the Holy Land,* Murray, London

(1831), *Notes on the Bedouins and Wahabys*, H. Colbum & R. Bentley, London, 2 vols.

Butler, H. C. (1919), *Syria: Publications of the Princeton Archaeological Expedition to Syria in 1904–1905 and 1909; Division 2: Architecture, Part A,* Brill, Leiden

Butler, H. C., Norris, F. A. and Stoever, E. R. (1930), *Syria: Publications of the Princeton Archaeological Expedition to Syria in 1904–1905 and 1909; Division 1: Geography and Itinerary,* Brill, Leiden

Byrd, B. F. (1989), 'The Natufian Settlement Variability and Economic Adaptations in the Levant at the End of the Pleistocene', *Journal of World Prehistory* (New York), 3, pp. 159–97

Caskel, W. (1954), 'The Bedouinisation of Arabia', in G. E. von Grunebaum (ed.), *Studies in Islamic Cultural History*, *American Anthropologist*, 56/2, Memoirs of the American Anthropological Association, 76, pp. 36–46

Cauvin, J. (1978), *Les premiers villages de Syrie-Palestine du IXe au VIIe millénaires av. J.C.*, CMO, 4, Maison de l'Orient, Lyons

(1989), 'La Néolithisation du Levant et sa première diffusion', in O. Aurenche and J. Cauvin (eds.), *Néolithisations*, BAR, int. ser. 516, Oxford, pp. 3–36

(1990), 'Les origines préhistoriques du nomadisme pastoral dans les pays du Levant', in H. P. Francfort (ed.), *Nomades et sédentaires en Asie Centrale*, Editions du CNRS, Paris, pp. 69–80

Cernik, J. (1875), 'Ingenieur Josef Cernik's Technische studien-Expedition durch die Gebiete des Euphrat und Tigris', in A. F. von Schwezer-Lerchenfeld (ed.), *Peterman's geographischen Mitteilungen, Ergänzungsheft,* Gotha

Chadwick, M. J. (1978), 'Report to Kellong International Corporation on the ecological implications of pipeline construction through Jebel Qara, Oman, for Amal/Marmu/Development Projects', unpublished report

Charles, H. (1939), *Tribus Moutonnières du Moyen-Euphrate*, Documents d'Etudes Orientales de L'Institut Français de Damas no. 8, Beirut

(1942), *La sédentarisation entre Euphrate et Balikh: notes d'ethno-sociologie*, Impr. Catholique, Beirut

Chatelus, M. (1987), 'Renter or Producer Economy in the Middle East? The Jordanian Response', in B. Khader and A. Badran (eds.), *The Economic Development of Jordan*, Croom Helm, London, pp. 204–20

Chatty, D., Zarough, M. and Osman A. (1991), 'Pastoralists of Oman. Traditional Arid Land Management and Recent Developments', unpublished report for FAO, Rome

Clutton-Brock, J. (1981), *Domesticated Animals from Early Times*, University of Texas, Austin

Cocks, P. S. (1988), 'Increasing Feed Resources for Small Ruminants in the Mediterranean Basin', in E. F. Thomson and F. S. Thomson (eds.), *Increasing Small Ruminant Productivity in Semi-arid Areas*, Kluwer, Dordrecht, pp. 51–66

Cocks, P. S., Thomson, E.F., Somel, K. and El-Moneim, A. (1988), 'Degradation and Rehabilitation of Agricultural Land in North Syria', ICARDA-119, Aleppo

Cole, D. P. (1975), *Nomads of the Nomads. The Al Murrah Beduin of the Empty Quarter*, Aldine, Chicago

(1981a), 'The Bedouin and Social Change in Saudi Arabia', *Journal of Asian and African Affairs* (Washington D.C.), 16, pp. 128–49

(1981b), 'Bedouin and Social Change in Saudi Arabia', in J. Galaty and P. C. Salzman (eds.), *Change and Development in Nomadic and Pastoral Societies,* Brill, Leiden, pp. 128–49

Compagnoni, B. and Tosi, M. (1978), 'The Camel: Its Distribution and State of Domestication in the Middle East during the Third Millennium BC in Light of Finds from Shahr-i Sokhta', in R. H. Meadows and M. A. Zeder (eds.), *Approaches to Faunal Analysis in the Middle East*, Peabody Museum Bulletin, 2, Harvard University pp. 91–103

Contenson, H. de (1971), 'Tell Ramad, a Village of Syria of the 7th and 6th Millennia BC', *Archaeology* (New York), 24/3, pp. 278–85

Coon, C. (1961), *Caravan: The Story of the Middle East*, Holt, Rinehart & Winston, New York, (1st edn 1951)

Cooper, P. C., Gregory, P. J., Tully, D. and Harris, H. C. (1987), 'Improving Water Use Efficiency of Annual Crops in the Rainfed Farming Systems of West Asia and North Africa', *Experimental Agriculture* (Cambridge), 23, pp. 113–58

Cooper, P., Jones, M. and Matar, A. (1988), 'Agroecological Constraints to Crop Production in West Asia and North Africa, and their Impact on Fertilizer Use', Countries of the Mediterranean, Middle East and North Africa, International Fertilizer Development Center, Muscle Shoals, USA

Cooper, P. and Bailey, E. (1990a), 'Livestock in Mediterranean Farming Systems: A Traditional Buffer against Uncertainty, Now a Threat to the Agricultural Resource Base', paper presented at World Bank, Risk in Agriculture symposium, January 1990, Washington, D.C.

(1990b), 'An Assessment of Risk Associated with Increasing Sheep and Feed Supplies in Syria. Current and Alternative Strategies', ICARDA, Farm Resource Management Program. Annual Report for 1989, pp. 289–316

Cordes, R. (1981), 'Wandel im nomadischen Lebensraum Abu Dhabis. Ursachen und Wirkung', in *Geographische Rundschau* (Braunschweig, Germany) 33/2, pp. 42–51

Cordes, R. and Scholz, F. (1980), *Beduins, Wealth and Change. A Study of Rural Development in the United Arab Emirates and the Sultanate of Oman*, United Nations University, Tokyo

Cowie, A. T., Forsyth, I. A. and Hart, I. C. (1980), *Hormonal Control of Lactation*, Springer Verlag, New York

Cross, B. A. (1977), 'Comparative Physiology of Milk Removal', in M. Peaker (ed.), *Comparative Aspects of Lactation*, Academic Press, London, pp. 193–210

Crystal, Jill (1990), *Oil and Politics in the Gulf: Rulers and Merchants in Kuwait and Qatar*, Cambridge University Press, Cambridge

Dann, U. (1984), *Studies in the History of Transjordan 1920–1949*, Westview, Boulder

Davis, S. J. M. (1987), *The Archaeology of Animals*, Batsford, London

Day, A. R. (1986), *East Bank/West Bank: Jordan and the Prospects for Peace*, Council on Foreign Relations, New York

Delbet, M. E. (1877), 'Paysans en communauté et en polygamie de Bousrah (Esky cham)', in F. Le Play (ed.), *Les ouvriers de l'orient*, vol. 2 of *Les ouvriers européens*, 2nd edition, 6 vols., A. Mame, Tours

Delegation Générale de la France Combattante au Levant (1943), *Les tribus nomades de l'Etat de Syrie*, Damascus

Destrée, A. (1969), 'Le développement des Etats du Moyen-Orient et la crise du nomadisme', *Revue de l'Institut de Sociologie* (Brussels), 2, pp. 263–81

Dickson, H. R. P. (1949), *The Arab of the Desert*, Allen & Unwin, London

Direction des Services du Renseignement du Levant (1930), *Les tribus nomades et semi-nomades des Etats du Levant placés sous Mandat Française*, Beirut

Dostal, W. (1967), *Die Beduinen in Südarabien. Eine ethnologische Studie zur Entwicklung der Kamelhirten in Arabien*, Wiener Beitr. zur Kulturgeschichte und Linguistik, 16, Horn, Vienna

Doughty, Charles M. (1979), *Travels in Arabia Deserta*, Dover Publications, New York, (1st publ. 1888), 2 vols.
Douwes, Dick and Lewis, Norman N. (1991), 'Taxation and Agriculture in the District of Hama, 1800–1838; New Material from the Records of the Religious Court', in T. Philipp (ed.), *The Syrian Land in the Eighteenth and Nineteenth Centuries*, Franz-Steiner-Verlag, Stuttgart, pp. 261–84
Draz, O. (1969), 'The "Hema" System of Range Reserves in the Arabian Peninsula: Its Possibilities', in *Range Improvement and Conservation Projects in the Near East*, FAO, PL:PFC/13, Rome
(1980) 'Rangeland Development in the Arabian Peninsula Based on Syrian Experience through UNDP/FAO/WFP Assistance', in *Rainfed Agriculture in the Near East and North Africa*, FAO, Rome, pp. 291–303
Eickelman, D. F. (1989), *The Middle East: An Anthropological Approach*, 2nd edn, Prentice Hall Inc., Englewood Cliffs
Elphinston, W. G. (1945), 'The Future of the Bedouin of Northern Arabia', *International Affairs* (Cambridge), 31/3, pp. 370–5
Eph'al, I. (1982), *The Ancient Arabs. Nomads on the Borders of the Fertile Crescent 9th–5th Centuries BC*, Magnes Press, Jerusalem
Epstein, E. (1938), 'The Bedouin of Transjordan: Their Social and Economic Problems', *The Journal of the Royal Central Asian Society* (London), 25, pp. 228–36
Fabietti, U. (1982), 'Sedentarisation as a Means of Detribalisation. Some Policies of the Sa'udi Arabian Government towards the Nomads', in T. Niblock, (ed.), *State, Society and Economy in Saudi Arabia*, Croom Helm, London, pp. 186–97
(1984), *Il popolo del deserto, Gli Shammar del Gran Nefud, Arabia Saudita,* Laterza, Bari
(1986), 'Control and Alienation of Territory among the Bedouin of Saudi Arabia', *Nomadic Peoples* (Montreal), 20, pp. 33–40
(1988), 'The Role Played by the Association of the "Hums" in the Evolution of Political Ideas in pre-Islamic Mecca', *Proceedings of the Seminar for Arabian Studies* (London) 18, pp. 25–33
(1990), 'Between Two Myths: Underproductivity and Development of the Bedouin Domestic Group', in E. Bernus and F. Pouillon (eds.), *Sociétés pastorales et développement*, pp. 237–253, ORSTOM, Cahiers des sciences humaines, 26 /1–2, Paris
Farra, T. O. (1973), 'The Effects of Detribalizing the Bedouin on the Internal Cohesion of an Emerging State: The Kingdom of Saudi Arabia', Ph.D. dissertation, University of Pittsburgh, Department of Geography
FAO (different years), *Production Yearbook* and *Trade Yearbook,* FAO, Rome
(1972), *Report on the FAO Expert Consultation on the Settlement of Nomads in Africa and the Near East*, FAO Regular Program n. RP 20, Rome
(1984), Syria Second Livestock Development Project: Identification Report, FAO/World Bank Cooperative Program, Investment Centre, FAO, Rome
(1991), *Workshop on Pastoral Communities in the Near East. Traditional Systems in Evolution*, FAO, Human Resources, Institutions and Agrarian Reform Division, Rome

Fernea, Robert (1970), *Shaykh and Effendi: Changing Patterns of Authority among the Shabana of Southern Iraq*, Harvard University Press, Cambridge, Mass.
(1987), 'Technological Innovation and Class Development among the Bedouin of Hail, Saudi Arabia', in B. Cannon (ed.), *Terroirs et sociétés au Maghreb et au Moyen-Orient*, EMA, 2, Maison de l'Orient, Lyons, pp. 389–405
Filali, M. (1966), 'Les structures sociales en Arabie Séoudite', *Revue Tunisienne des Sciences Sociales* (Tunis), 6, pp. 69–84
Findlay, A. (1986), 'Amman, Urbanization in a "Charity" State', *Bulletin de la Société Languedocienne de Géographie*, 109 /1–2, pp. 211–22.
Firestone, Y. (1975), 'Production and Trade in an Islamic Context: Sharika Contracts in the Transitional Economy of Northern Samaria, 1853–1943', *IJMES*, (Cambridge), 6/2, pp. 185–209
Gellner, E. (1991), 'Tribalism and the State in the Middle East', in P. S. Khoury and J. Kostner (eds.), *Tribes and State Formation in the Middle East*, I. B. Tauris, London, pp. 109–26
Gerber, H. (1987), *The Social Origins of the Middle East*, Lynne Rienner, Boulder
Gerholm, Tomas (1977), *Market, Mosque and Mafraj: Social Inequality in a Yemeni Town*, Studies in Social Anthropology, Stockholm
Gilsenan, Michael (1977), 'Against Patron–Client Relations', in E. Gellner and J. Waterbury (eds.), *Patrons and Clients in Mediterranean Society*, Duckworth, London, pp. 167–83
(1982) *Recognizing Islam, An Anthropologist's Introduction*, Croom Helm, London
(1996), *Lords of the Lebanese Marches: Violence and the Narrative in an Arab Society*, I. B. Tauris, London
Glubb, J. B. (1938), 'The Economic Situation of the Transjordan Tribes', *Journal of the Royal Central Asian Society* (London), 25/3, pp. 448–59
(1948), *The Story of the Arab Legion*, Hodder & Stoughton, London
Grosvenor, C. E. and Mena, F. (1974), 'Neural and Hormonal Control of Milk Secretion and Milk Ejection', in B. L. Larson and V. R. Smith (eds.), *Lactation: A Comprehensive Treatise*, I, Academic Press, New York, pp. 227–76
Guarmani, Carlo (1938), *Northern Najd*, Argonaut Press, London (a translation of *Il Neged Settentionale*), Jerusalem, 1866)
Guichaoua, A. and Majeres, J. (1982), 'Usage de la sociologie dans les organismes de la coopération et du développement', *Tiers monde* (Evry), 90, pp. 423–43
Habib, St J. (1978), *Ibn Sa'ud Warriors of Islam*, Brill, Leiden
Hajrah, H. H. (1982), *Public Land Distribution in Saudi Arabia*, Longman, London
Hale, E. B. (1962), 'Domestication and the Evolution of Behaviour', in E. S. E. Hafez (ed.), *The Behaviour of Domestic Animals*, Williams & Wilkins, Baltimore, pp. 21–53
Hamarneh, M. (1985), 'The Social and Economic Transformation of Transjordan, 1921–1946', Ph.D. Dissertation, Georgetown University, Washington
(1987), 'The Political Importance of the Bedouins in Jordan: Myth and Reality', Georgetown University, Department of History, research paper, mimeo
Hamidé, A.-R. (1959), *La région d'Alep, Etude de géographie rurale*, Paris University, Paris
Hannoyer, J. (1980), 'Le monde rural avant les réformes', in A. Raymond (ed.), *La Syrie d'aujourd'hui*, Editions du CNRS, Paris, pp. 273–326

Hannoyer, J. and Thieck, J.-P. (1984), 'Observations sur l'élevage et le commerce du mouton dans la région de Raqqa en Syrie', *Production Pastorale et Société* (Paris), 14, pp. 47–65

Harker, R., Mahar, C. and Wilkes, C. (1990), *An Introduction to the Work of Pierre Bourdieu*, Macmillan, London

Harris, David R. (1977), 'Alternative Pathways toward Agriculture', in C. A. Reed (ed.), *Origins of Agriculture*, Mouton, Paris, pp. 179–243

Helaissi, A. S. (1959), 'Les Bédouins et la vie tribale en Arabie Séoudite', *Revue Internationale des Sciences Sociales* (Toulouse), 11/ 4, pp. 554–60

Helmer, D. (1992), *La domestication des animaux par les hommes préhistoriques*, Masson, Paris

Helms, C. M. (1981), *The Cohesion of Saudi Arabia*, Croom Helm, London

Helms, S. W. (1990), *Early Islamic Architecture of the Desert: A Bedouin Station in Eastern Jordan*, Edinburgh University Press, Edinburgh

Hiatt, J. M. (1981), 'Between Desert and Town: A Case Study of Encapsulation and Sedentarisation among Jordanian Bedouin', Ph.D. Dissertation, University of Pennsylvania

Hill, John G. (1891), *With the Bedouins*, T. F. Unwin, London

Hinnebusch, Raymond (1977), 'Rural Politics in Baʿthist Syria: A Case Study of the Role of the Countryside in the Political Development of Arab Socialism', in S. E. Ibrahim and N. Hopkins (eds.), *Arab Society in Transition*, American University in Cairo Press, Cairo, pp. 278–96

(1989), *Peasant and Bureaucracy in Baʿthist Syria: The Political Economy of Rural Development*, Westview Press, Boulder

(1990), *Authoritarian Power and State Formation in Baʿthist Syria*, Westview Press, Boulder

Hirschman, A. (1971), *Exit, Voice and Loyalty*, Harvard University Press, Cambridge, Mass.

Hiyari, M. A. (1975), 'The Origins and Development of the Amirate of the Arabs during the 7th/13th and 8th/14th Centuries', *BSOAS* (London), 38, pp. 509–24

Hollman, K. H. (1974), 'Cytology and Fine Structure of the Mammary Gland', in B. L. Larson and V. R. Smith (eds.), *Lactation: A Comprehensive Treatise*, I, Academic Press, New York, pp. 3–95

Hopwood, D. (1988), *Syria 1945–1986: Politics and Society*, Unwin Hyman, London

Hours, F. (1985), 'L'occupation du Proche-Orient au Paléolithique', in *Le Grand Atlas de l'Archéologie*, Encyclopaedia Universalis, Paris

Horowitz, M. (1986), 'Ideology, Policy and Praxis in Pastoral Livestock Development', in M. Horowitz and T. M. Painter (eds.), *Anthropology and Rural Development in West Africa,* Westview Press, Boulder, pp. 251–72

Huneidi, M. I. (1965), 'Taqrir al mamlaka al hashimiyah al urduniyya 'an ri'ayat al badw wa tahdirihim wa tawtinihim', *Proceedings of the Ninth Congress of Experts in Social Welfare and Labour,* Jerusalem, 8–13 May 1965, II, pp. 1–26, League of Arab States, Department of Social Welfare and Labour

Hurani, H. (1976), *Al-tarkib al-iqtisadi al-ijtimaʿi fi sharq al-urdun*, PLO Research Center, Beirut

(1989) 'Intifadat Nisan 1989', *al-Urdun al-jadid* (Damascus), 5/14, pp. 7–31

IBRD (1955), *The Economic Development of Syria*, Johns Hopkins Press, Baltimore

Ibrahim, S. E. and Cole, D. P. (1978), *Saudi Arabian Bedouin: An Assessment of their Needs*, American University in Cairo Press, Cairo

ICARDA, (1979), *An Introduction to Agriculture within the Syrian Economy*, ICARDA, Aleppo

Inalcik, Halil (1987), 'Marchés et marchands dans l'empire ottoman', excerpts from the article published in English in the *Journal of Economic History* in 1969, trans. into French and published in *MAUSS* (Paris), 8/2, pp. 13–37

Ingham, B. (1986), *Bedouin of Northern Arabia. Traditions of the al-Dhafir*, Kegan Paul International, London

ILO, (1962), *Sédentarisation des tribus nomades et semi-nomades,* Rapport du groupe des conseillers en matière des populations aborigènes et tribales, PCITP/ 1962/1/3, ILO, Geneva

(1964a), *Réunion technique d'étude sur le nomadisme et la sédentarisation, Problèmes soulevés par le nomadisme et la sédentarisation*, TMNS/1964/1, ILO, Geneva

(1964b), *Coopération régionale et internationale dans le domaine de la sédentarisation*, TMNS/1964/2, ILO, Geneva

Ismael, J. S. (1982), *Kuwait: Dependency and Class in a Rentier State*. University Press of Florida, Gainesville

Janzen, J. (1980), *Die Nomaden Dhofars/Sultanate Oman. Traditionelle Lebensformen im Wandel,* Bamberger Geographische Schriften, 3, Bamberg

(1982), 'Erste Ergebnisse und Tendenzen des jungen Wandels in der Lebens und Wirtschaftsweise der Nomaden Dhofars/Sultanat Oman', in F. Scholz and J. Janzen (eds.), *Nomadismus – Ein Entwicklungsproblem?* Abhandlungen des Geographischen Instituts – Anthropogeographie, 33, Berlin, pp. 185–91

(1983), 'The Modern Development of the Nomadic Living Space in South-east Arabia – The Case of Dhofar (Sultanate of Oman)', *Geoforum* (Oxford), 14/3, pp. 289–309

(1986), 'Nomads in the Sultanate of Oman. Tradition and Development', in *Dhofar,* Westview Special Studies on the Middle East, Boulder/London

(1988), 'Mobile Viehwirtschaft – Übeliebensstrategie für die Sahelländer? Somalia als Beispiel', in: K. Fiege and L Ramalho (eds.), *Agrarkrisen. Fallstudien zur ländlichen Entwicklung in der Dritten Weit*, ASA Studien, 14, Saarbrüken/Fort Lauderdale, pp. 171–92

(1990), 'Land Tenure and Land Use in the Pastoral Living Areas of Dhofar/Sultanate of Oman – Tradition, Change and Development Perspectives', unpublished Report prepared for the FAO, Rome

(1991), 'The Revival of Traditional Pastoral Systems in the Near East. A Survival Strategy for Pasture Lands and Mobile Livestock Keeping?' Keynote address presented at the workshop on Pastoral Communities in the Near East: Traditional Systems in Evolution in Amman; publ. FAO, Rome, Annex 3, pp. 1–15

(1991), 'Sozio-ökonomischer Wandel und Ressourcenzerstörung im Lebensraum der Bergnomaden Dhofars/Sultanat Oman. Kritische Betractung der Entwicklund seit 1970 und Zukunftsperspektiven', in F. Scholz (ed.) *Nomaden-Mobile Tierhaltung*, pp. 329–54, Das Arabische Buch, Berlin

Jaradat, A. and Abu Mushrif, J. (1988), 'Soil and Water Conservation', in A. Jaradat (ed.), *An Assessment of Research Needs and Priorities for Rainfed Agriculture in Jordan*, Al-Hurria Press, Irbid, pp. 115–54

Jarman, M.R. (1969), 'The Prehistory of Upper Pleistocene and Recent Cattle, part 1: East Mediterranean, with Reference to North-West Europe', *Proceedings of the Prehistoric Society* (London), 35, pp. 236–66

Jarman, M.R. and Wilkinson, P. F. (1972), 'Criteria of Animal Domestication', in E. S. Higgs (ed.), *Papers in Economic Prehistory*, Cambridge University Press, Cambridge, pp. 83–96

Jaubert, R. (1986), 'The Semi-arid Areas of Syria: Farming Systems in Decline', in C. B. Flora and M. Tomecek, (eds.), *Selected Proceedings of the 1984 Farming Systems Symposium*, Kansas State University, Manhattan, pp. 244–57

(1987), 'Structures d'exploitation et préservation des zones sèches cultivées de Syrie', in B. Canon (ed.), *Terroirs et société au Maghreb et au Moyen-Orient*, EMA, 2, Maison de l'Orient, Lyons, pp. 233–45

Jaubert, R. and Oglah, M. (1985), 'Farming Systems Management in the Bueda/Breda Area 1983/1984', Research Report 13, Farming Systems Program, ICARDA, Aleppo

Jaussen, A. (1948), *Coutumes des Arabes au Pays de Moab*, Adrein, Paris, (1st publ. 1908)

Jones, M. J. and Singh, M. (1995), 'Yields of Crop Dry Matter and Nitrogen in Long-term Barley Rotation Trials at Two Sites in Northern Syria', *Journal of Agricultural Science* (Cambridge), 124/3, pp. 389–402

Jones, M. J. and Wahbi, A. (1992), 'Site-factor Influence on Barley Response to Fertilizer in Northern Syria: Synthesis of On-farm Trial Data into Simple Models', *Experimental Agriculture* (Cambridge), 28/1, pp. 63–87

Jureidini, P. and McLaurin, R. (1984), 'Jordan: The Impact of Social Change on the Role of the Tribes', Washington Papers Series, 108, Center for Strategic and International Studies, Washington

Kaldi, N. (1984), 'Evolving Food Gaps in the Middle East/North Africa: Prospects and Policy Implications', Research Report No. 47, International Food Policy Research Institute, Washington, D.C.

Kazziha, W. (1972), *The Social History of Southern Syria (Transjordan) in the XIXth and early XXth Century*, Arab University, Beirut

Kenyon, K. and Holland, T. (1981), *Excavations at Jericho,* III, British School of Archaeology in Jerusalem, London

Khalaf, Sulayman (1981), 'Family, Village and the Political Party: Articulation of Social Change in Contemporary Rural Syria', unpublished Ph.D. dissertation, UCLA

(forthcoming) 'Land Reform and Social Classes in Rural Syria', in R. Antoun and D. Quataert (eds.), *Syria: The Society, Polity and Culture of a Modern Nation*, SUNY University Press, New York

Khazanov, A. (1984), *Nomads and the Outside World*, Cambridge University Press, Cambridge

Khuri, Fu'ad (1975), *From Village to Suburb: Order and Change in Greater Beirut,* University of Chicago Press, Chicago

(1980), *Tribe and State in Bahrain: The Transformation of Social and Political Authority in an Arab State,* University of Chicago Press, Chicago

Kingdom of Saudi Arabia (1984), *Achievements of the Development Plans 1390–1404 (1970–1984): Facts and Figures*, Ministry of Planning, Riyadh

Knauf, A. (1985), *Ismael. Untersuchungen zur Geschichte Palästinas und Nordarabiens im 1. Jahrtausend v. Chr.* Harrassowitz, Wiesbaden

Köhler-Rollefson, I. (1988), 'The Aftermath of the Neolithic Revolution in the Light of Ecological and Ethnographic Evidence', *Paléorient* (Paris), 14/1, pp. 87–93

Konikoff, A. (1946), *Transjordan: An Economic Survey*, Economic Research Institute for the Jewish Agency, Jerusalem

Kostiner, J. (1991), 'Transforming Dualities: Tribe and State Formation in Saudi Arabia', in P. S. Khoury and J. Kostiner (eds.), *Tribes and State Formation in the Middle East*, I. B. Tauris, London, pp. 226–51

Kupper, J.-R. (1957), *Les nomades dans la Mésopotamie ancienne au temps des rois de Mari*, Les Belles Lettres, Paris

Lancaster, W. (1980a), review of *Saudi Arabian Bedouin*, by S. E. Ibrahim and D. P. Cole, in *Nomadic Peoples* (Montreal), 5, pp. 2–27

(1980b), 'Self-help for Pastoralists', *Nomadic Peoples*, (Montreal), 6, pp. 8–12

(1981), *The Rwala Bedouin Today*, Cambridge University Press, Cambridge

Lancaster, W. and Lancaster, F. (1988), 'Thoughts on the Bedouinisation of Arabia', *Proceedings of the Seminar for Arabian Studies* (London), 18, pp. 51–62

(1990), 'Desert Devices: The Pastoral System of the Rwala Bedouin', in J. G. Galaty and D. L. Johnson (eds.), *A World of Pastoralism*, Guildford Press, New York, pp. 177–94

(1991a), 'Limitations on Sheep and Goat Herding in the Eastern Badia of Jordan: An Ethnoarchaeological Enquiry', *Levant* (London), 23, pp. 125–38

(1991b), 'Modern Ar-Risha: A Permanent Address', in S. W. Helms (ed.), *Early Islamic Architecture of the Desert*, pp. 67–79

Lattimore, O. (1967), *Inner Asian Frontiers of China*, Beacon Press, Boston

Layne, L. (1986), 'The Production and Reproduction of Tribal Identity in Jordan', Ph.D. dissertation, Department of Anthropology, Princeton University

(1989), 'The Dialogics of Tribal Self-representation in Jordan', *American Ethnologist* (Washington, D.C.), 16/1, pp. 24–39

Leatherdale, C. (1983), *Britain and Saudi Arabia 1925–1939*, Frank Cass, London

Lee, S. H. and Bates, D. G. (1974), 'The Origins of Specialized Nomadic Pastoralism: A Systemic Model', *American Antiquity* (Washington, D.C.), 39/2, pp. 187–93

Lees, G. R. (1895), 'Across Southern Bashan', *Geographical Journal* (London), 1, p. 5

Leighton, C. (1986), 'How Important is Local Participation to Development Programs?', *Nomadic Peoples* (Montreal), 20, pp. 85–94

Le Mière, M. and Picon, M. (1987), 'Productions locales et circulation des céramiques au VIe millénaire au Proche-Orient', *Paléorient* (Paris), 13/2, pp. 133–47

Lent, P. C. (1974), 'Mother–Infant Relationships in Ungulates', in V. Geist and F. Walther (eds.), *The Behaviour of Ungulates and its Relationship to Management*, International Union for the Conservation of Nature and Natural Resources, Morges, Switzerland, pp. 14–53

Lerner, D. (1958), *The Passing of Traditional Society*, Free Press, Glencoe

Leveau, R. (1977), 'The Rural Elite as an Element in the Social Stratification of Morocco', in van Nieuwenhuijze (ed.), *Commoners, Climbers and Notables*, pp. 268–78

Lewis, N. (1955), 'The Frontier of Settlement in Syria, 1800–1950', *International Affairs* (Cambridge), 31/1, pp. 48–60

(1987), *Nomads and Settlers in Syria and Jordan, 1800–1980*, Cambridge University Press, Cambridge
(1988), 'The Balikh Valley and its People', in M. N. Van Loon, (ed.), *Hammam et-Turkman I, Report on the University of Amsterdam's 1981–84 Excavations in Syria*, Istanbul, Nederlands Historisch-Archaelogisch Institut Te Istanbul, pp. 683–93
(1991) 'Taibé and El Kowm, 1600–1980', *Cahiers de l'Euphrate* (Paris), 5–6, pp. 67–78
Livingstone, I. (1991), 'Livestock Management and 'Overgrazing' among Pastoralists', *AMBIO* (Norwich), 20/ 2, pp. 80–5
Luke, J. T. (1965), 'Pastoralism and Politics in the Mari Period', unpublished Ph.D. Dissertation, University of Michigan
Mahhouk, A. (1956), 'Recent Agricultural Development and Bedouin Settlement in Syria', *The Middle East Journal*, Indiana University Press, Bloomington, pp. 167–76
Malkawi, A. (1978), *Regional Development in Jordan: Some Aspects of the Urban Bias*, Royal Scientific Society, Amman
Marx, E. (1978), 'The Ecology and Politics of Nomadic Pastoralists in the Middle East', in W. Weissleder (ed.), *The Nomadic Alternative. Modes and Models of Interaction in the African-Asian Deserts and Steppes*, Mouton, Paris, pp. 41–74
Masri, A. (1991), *The Tradition of Hema as a Land Tenure Institution in Arid Land Management: the Syrian Arab Republic*, FAO, Rome
Matthews, V. H. (1978), *Pastoral Nomadism in the Mari Kingdom (ca.1830–1760 BC)*, ASOR Dissertation Series, 3, American Schools of Oriental Research, Cambridge, Mass
Mazid, A. (1990), 'Economic Analysis of Researcher Managed Trials', *Annual Report for 1989, Farm Resource Management Program*, ICARDA, Aleppo, pp. 62–7
Mazur, M. (1979), *Economic Growth and Development in Jordan*, Westview Press, Boulder
Merrill, S. (1881), *East of the Jordan*, Bentley & Son, London
Métral, F. (1980), 'Le monde rural syrien à l'ère des réformes', in A. Raymond (ed.) *La Syrie d'aujourd'hui*, Editions du CNRS, Paris, pp. 297–326
Métral, F. and Métral, J. (1991), 'Entre Palmyre et l'Euphrate: oasis et agriculture dans la Palmyrène', in M. C. Cauvin (ed.), *Rites et rythmes agraires en Méditerranée et au Proche Orient*, Travaux de la Maison de l'Orient, 20, Lyon, pp. 87–108
Métral, J. and Sanlaville, P. (eds.), (1982), *L'homme et l'eau en Méditerranée et au Proche-Orient*, TMO a 1, Maison de l'Orient, Lyons
Mitchell, M. (1986), 'Cereal Production and Risk in the Rainfed Sector', in A. Burrell (ed.), *Agricultural Policy in Jordan*, Ithaca Press, London, pp. 41–54
Montagne, R. (1932), 'Quelques aspects du peuplement de la Haute Djézire', *Bulletin des études orientales* (Damascus), 2, pp. 53–66
(1947), *La civilisation du Desert Nomades d'Orient et d'Afrique*, Hatchette, Paris
Monteil, V. (1966), *Les tribus du Fârs et la sédentarisation des nomades*, Mouton, Paris
Moore, A. (1975), 'The Excavation of Tell Abu Hureyra in Syria: A Preliminary Report', *Proceedings of the Prehistoric Society* (London), 41, pp. 50–77
Mounayer, Nassib (1929), *Le régime de la terre en Syrie*, Librairie Général de Droit et de Jurisprudence, Paris
Muller, V. (1931), *En Syrie avec les bedouins: les tribus du désert*, Leroux, Paris

Mundy, M. and Saumarez-Smith, R. (eds.), (1990), *Part-time Farming: Agricultural Development in the Zarqa River Basin,* II, Institute of Aracheology and Anthropology, Yarmouk University, Irbid

Musa, M. (1987), 'A Multi-level Analysis of the Characteristics, Determinants and Impacts of Technological Change in East Jordan Valley Agriculture', Ph.D. Dissertation, Massachusetts Institute of Technology

Musil, Alois (1927), *Arabia Deserta,* American Geographical Society, New York

(1928a) *Palmyrena,* AGS, New York

(1928b) *The Manners and Customs of the Rwala Bedouins*, AGS, New York (repr. 1978)

Naaman, Anouar (1955), 'Le pays de Homs, T. II, la zone steppique', thèse principale pour le Doctorat ès-lettres, University of the Sorbonne, Paris

Nesheiwat, K. (1991), 'Socio-economic Aspects of the Traditional Hema System of Arid Land Management in Jordan', FAO, Working Papers on Pastoral and Agro-pastoral Societies, no. 12, Rome

Niblock, T. (1982), 'Social Structure and the Development of the Saʿudi Arabian Political System', in T. Niblock (ed.), *State, Society and Economy in Saudi Arabia*, Croom Helm, London, pp. 75–105

Nordblom, T. L. and Thomson, E. F. (1987), 'A Whole-farm Model Based on Experimental Flocks and Crop Rotations in Northwest Syria', ICARDA-102, 78 pp.

Nygaard, D., Martin, A. and Bahhady, F. (1982), 'Range and Sheep and Fattening Cooperatives in Syria: Supplemental Feed Purchases and Credit Requirements', Project Report no. 4, ICARDA, Aleppo

Oates, P. M. and Ahmed A. S. (1987), 'Jerbeeb: Settlements and Seasonal Occupancy', PCDESR/Technical Working Paper (TWP) no. 3, Salala

(1988) 'Population Base Data for Southern Region', 1977 and rev. 1985, PSDESR/TWP no. 8, Salala

Oppenheim, Max F. von (1899/1900), *Vom Mittelmeer zum Persischen Golf*, D. Reimer, Berlin, 2 vols.

(1939), *Die Bedouinen*, I, Harrassowitz, Leipzig

(1943), *Die Bedouinen*, II, Harrassowitz, Leipzig

Osman, A. E., Pagnotta, M., Russi, L., Cocks, P. S. and Falcinelli, M. (1990), 'The Role of Legumes in Improving Marginal Lands', in A. E. Osman, M. H. Ibrahim and M. A. Jones (eds.), *The Role of Legumes in the Farming System of the Mediterranean Areas*, Kluwer, Dordrecht, pp. 195–204

Osman, A. E., Cocks, P. S., Russi, L. and Pagnotta, M. A. (1991), 'Responses of Mediterranean Grassland to Phosphate and Stocking Rates: Biomass Production and Botanical Composition', *Journal of Agricultural Science* (Cambridge), 116, pp. 37–46

Peake, F. G. (1958), *A History of Jordan and its Tribes*, University of Miami Press, Coral Gables

Perkins, D. (1969), 'Fauna of Çatal Hüyük: Evidence for Early Cattle Domestication in Anatolia', *Science* (Washington D.C.), 164, pp. 177–9

Peters, Emyrs (1963), 'Aspects of Rank and Status among Muslims in a Lebanese Village', in J. Pitt-Rivers (ed.), *Mediterranean Countrymen,* Mouton, Paris and The Hague

(1972), 'Shifts in Power in a Lebanese Village', in R. Antoun and I. Harik (eds.),

Rural Politics and Social Change in the Middle East, Indiana University Press, Bloomington, pp. 165–97
(1990), *The Bedouin of Cyrenaica*, ed. J. Goody and E. Marx, Cambridge Studies in Social and Cultural Anthropology, 72, Cambridge University Press, Cambridge
Philby, Harry St John (1928), *Arabia of the Wahhabis*, Constable & Co., London
(1933) *The Empty Quarter*, Constable & Co., London
Post, George E. (1891), 'Narrative of a trip to Palmyra in April, 1890', *Palestine Exploration Fund Quarterly* (London), pp. 20–40
Qalyoubi, T. A. (1967), 'Jafr Pilot Project for the Settlement of Bedouins', in A. R. Ghonemy (ed.), *Land Policy in the Near East*, FAO, Rome, pp. 152–63
Qasem, S. (1986), 'The Size of Agricultural Land Holdings', in A. Burrell (ed.), *Agricultural Policy in Jordan*, Ithaca Press, London, pp. 21–9
Rabo, Annika (1986), *Change on the Euphrates*, Studies in Social Anthropology, Stockholm
Raymond, André (ed.) (1980), *La Syrie d'aujourd'hui,* Editions du CNRS, Paris
Razzaz, U. (1989), 'Legality and Illegality as Strategies in Urban Land Conflict: The Case of Jordan', paper presented at MESA annual conference, Los Angeles
Robinson, Edward and Smith, Eli (1841), *Biblical Researches in Palestine. A Journal of Travels in the Year 1838*, 3 vols., London; repr. (1867), 3 vols., John Murray, London
Robinson, R. (1972), 'Non-European Foundations of European Imperialism: Sketch for a Theory of Collaboration', in R. Owen and B. Sutcliffe (eds.), *Studies in the Theories of Imperialism*, Longman, London, pp. 117–43
Rofail, N. (1984), *Integrated Regional Development Plan for Hamad Basin Project,* ACSAD, Damascus
Rognon, P. (1987), 'Relations entre phases climatiques et chronologies au Moyen Orient de 16.000 à 10.000 B.P.', in O. Aurenche, J. Evin and F. Hours (eds.), *Chronologies in the Near East: Relative Chronologies and Absolute Chronology 16,000–4,000* BP, BAR, int. ser. 379, Oxford, pp. 189–206
Rollefson, G. O. and Simmons, A. H. (1988), 'The Neolithic Settlement at ʿAin Ghazal', in A. N. Garrard and H. G. Gebel (eds.), *The Prehistory of Jordan. The State of Research in 1986,* BAR, int. ser. 396/1–2, Oxford, pp. 393–421
Rosenfeld, H. (1965), 'The Social Composition of the Military in the Process of State Formation in the Middle East', *Journal of the Royal Anthropological Institute,* 95, pp. 75–86 and 174–94
Russell, K. W. (1988), *After Eden: The Behavioural Ecology of Early Food Production in the Near East and North Africa,* BAR, int. ser. 391, Oxford
Ryder, M. L. (1969), 'Changes in the Fleece of Sheep Following Domestication', in P. J. Ucko and G. W. Dimbleby (eds.), *The Domestication of Plants and Animals*, Aldine, Chicago, pp. 495–521
(1973), 'The Use of the Skin and Coat in Studies of Changes Following Domestication,' in J. Matolcsi (ed.), *Domestikationsforschung und Geschichte der Haustiere*, Academiai Kiado, Budapest, pp. 163–8
(1983), *Sheep and Man*, Duckworth, London
Sadowski, Yehya (1978), 'The Knife's Edge: A Study of the Failure of Liberalization in Syria', unpublished paper, UCLA
Salame, Ghassan (1987), *State and Society in the Arab East* (in Arabic), Center of Arab Unity Studies, Beirut

al-Salman, Mahmud bin ʿAbdullah (1989), *ʿUnayzah*, Matabʿa Jamiʿat al-Malik Saʿud, Riyadh

Salzman, Philip (1974), 'Tribal Chiefs as Middlemen: The Politics of Encapsulation in the Middle East', *Anthropological Quarterly* (Washington D.C.), 47, pp. 203–10

(1980), 'Processes of Sedentarisation as Adaptation and Response', in P. C. Salzman (ed.), *When Nomads Settle*, Praeger, New York, pp. 1–20

Al-Samman, Hazem (1985), 'Sheep in the Syrian Arab Republic and the Designed Programme for Supplying their Forage Needs', Ministry of Agriculture, Damascus (report)

Sankary, M. N. (1978), 'Revegetation Trails in Three Disclimax Plant Communities of the Syrian Arid Zone with Local and Introduced Xerophytic Species', ACSAD, Damascus

(1986), 'Revegetation of the Syrian Zone', in D. J. Joss et al. (eds.), *Rangelands, a Resource under Siege: Proceedings of the Second International Rangeland Congress*, Cambridge University Press, Cambridge, pp. 303–4

Sanlaville, P. (1989), 'Considérations sur l'évolution de la basse Mésopotamie au cours des derniers millénaires', *Paléorient* (Paris), 15/2, pp. 5–27

(2000) *Le Moyen-Orient arabe: le milieu et l'homme*, A. Colin, Paris

Schilcher, Linda S. (1981), 'The Hauran Conflicts of the 1860's', *IJMES*, 13, pp. 159–79

Schofield, R. (1991), *Kuwait and Iraq: Historical Claims and Territorial Disputes*, RIIA, Chatham House, London

Scholz, F. (1975): 'Sesshaftwerdung von Beduinen in Kuwait', *Erdkunde* (Bonn), 29/3, pp. 223–34

(1979), 'Entstehung von Zentrum und Peripherie in einem "jungen" erdölfördernden Entwicklungsland', *Deutsche Gesellschaft für Friedens und Konfliktsforschung*, 12, pp. 123–44

(1981), 'Beduinen im Zeichen des Erdöls', *Tübinger Atlas des Vorderen Orients*, Series B, no. 45, Wiesbaden

(1985), *Die klienen Golfstaaten. Reichtum und Unterentwicklung-ein Widerspruch?* Klett, Stuttgart

(1986), 'Ressourcennutzung und Ressourcenerhaltung', in Deutsche Stiftung für internationale Entwicklung (ed.), *Interaktion Tier und Umwelt*, (a meeting of experts held 11–14 December 1985), Deutsche Stiftung für internationale Entwicklung, Feldfading, pp. 113–22

(1987), 'Nomaden und Erdöl. Über Lage und Rolle der Beduinen, in den Erdölförderländern der arabischen Halbinsel', *Geographische Rundschau*, (Braunschweig) 39/7–8, pp. 394–401

(1992), *Nomadismus. Bibliographie*, Das Arabische Buch, Berlin

(1995), *Nomadismus. Theorie und Wandel einer sozio-ökologischen Kulturweise, Erdkundlisches Wissen*, vol. 118, Franz Steiner Verlag, Stuttgart

Scholz, F. and Janzen, J. (eds.), (1982), *Nomadismus – Ein Entwicklungsproblem?*, Abhandlungen des Geographischen Instituts-Anthropogeographie, 33, Berlin

(1989), 'Südarabien. Traditionelle Verhältnisse und moderner Wandel im nomadischen Lebensraum/South East Arabia. AX: Wanderweidewirtschaft Beispiele', *Tübinger Atlas des Vorderen Orients*, 12/5, Wiesbaden

Schumacher, Gottlieb (1886), *Across the Jordan*, PEF, London

(1889), *Abila of the Decapolis*, PEF, London

(1893), 'Ergebnisse meiner Reise durch Hauran, Adschlun und Belka', *Zeitschrift des Deutschen Palästina-Vereins*, 16/72, pp. 67–160

(1897a), 'Das südliche Basan', *ZDPV*, 20, pp. 67–227

(1897b), 'Unser Arbeiten im Ostjordanlande', *Mittheilungen Und Nachriten Des Deutschen Palästina-Vereins*, pp. 82–4

(1913–21), *Karte des Ostjordanlandes*, Deutschen Verein zur Erforschung Palästinas, (five sheets on a scale of 1/63, 360) 163, pp. 630, Leipzig

Scott, J. C. (1976), *The Moral Economy of the Peasant: Rebellion and Subsistence in South-East Asia*, Yale University Press, New Haven

Seale, Patrick (1965), *The Struggle for Syria*, Oxford University Press, Oxford

Seccombe, I. (1987), 'Labour Migration and the Transformation of a Village Economy: A Case Study from North-West Jordan', in A. Lawless (ed.), *The Middle Eastern Village*, Croom Helm, London, pp, 115–44

Seetzen, Ulrich J. (1809), 'Mémoire pour servir à la connaissance des tribus arabes en Syrie', *Annales des Voyages*, 8, pp. 281–324

(1854), *Reisen durch Syrien, Palästina, Phönicien, die Transjordan-Länder, Arabia Petraea und Unter-Aegypten*, G. Reimer, Berlin, 3 vols.

Selim, S. M. (1959), *A Survey of Conditions and Problems of Nomadic and Semi-nomadic Tribal Populations of Jordan and Iraq*, ILO, Geneva

Service, E. P. (1989), *Origins of the State and Civilization*, Norton, New York

Seurat, M. (1980), 'Les populations, l'état et la société', in Raymond (ed.), *La Syrie d'aujourd'hui*, pp. 87–142

Sharif, ʿAbd ar-Rahman Sadiq (1970), *Mintaqat ʿUnayzah: Dirasa ʿIqlimiya*, Mathbaʿat al-Nahdat al-ʿArabiya, Cairo

Shepley, S. (1988), *Wheat Subsidy Policies in the Hashemite Kingdom of Jordan, an Economic Analysis*, USAID, Amman

Sherrat, A. (1981), 'Plough and Pastoralism: Aspects of the Secondary Products Revolution', in I. Hodder, G. Isaac and N. Hammond (eds.), *Pattern of the Past: Studies in Honor of David Clarke*, Cambridge University Press, Cambridge, pp. 261–305

(1983) 'The Secondary Exploitation of Animals in the Old World', *World Archaeology* (London), 15/1, pp. 90–104

Shoup, J. (1990), 'Middle Eastern sheep pastoralism and the Hema system', in J. C. Galaty and D. L. Johnson (eds.), *The World of Pastoralism*, Guilford Press, London, pp.195–215

Somel, K., Mazid, A. and Hallajian, M. (1984), 'Survey of Barley Producers, Northern Syria', Research Report 12, ICARDA, Aleppo

Simoons, F. J. (1979), 'Dairying, Milk Use and Lactose Malabsorption in Eurasia: A Problem in Culture History', *Anthropos* (Bonn), 74, pp. 61–80

Steuernagel, D. C. (1925), 'Der ʿAdschlun nach den Aufzeichungen vom Dr G. Schumacher', *ZDPV*, 48, pp. 1–250

Sultanate of Oman/Ministry of Land (n.d.), *Omani Land Law*, Muscat

Sultanate of Oman (SO)/Development Council Technical Secretariat (DCTS) (6/1990), *Statistical Yearbook 1989*, Muscat

Sweet, Louise E. (1965), 'Camel Raiding of North Arabian Bedouin: A Mechanism of Ecological Adaptation', *American Anthropologist* (Washington, D.C.), 67, pp. 1132–50

(1974), *Tell Toqaan: A Syrian Village*. Anthroplogical Papers 14, Museum of Anthropology, University of Michigan, Ann Arbor

Syrian Arab Republic, Ministry of Agriculture and Agrarian Reform (MAAR) (1984), Publication no. 96

Syrian Arab Republic, Central Statistical Bureau (1990), *Statistical Yearbook*, 43, Government Press, Damascus

Tadros, K. (1991), 'Changes in Livestock Systems and the Utilization of Steppe Areas in the Past Four Decades: The Case of Jordan', unpublished paper presented at the Colloque International Devenir des Steppes d'Arabie et du Bilad ach-Cham, 10–13 April 1991, Institut du Monde Arabe, Paris

Tarawneh, M. F. (1989), 'Aspects of Rural Transformation in the Jordan Valley, the Case of Deir Alla', MA thesis, Institute of Archaeology and Anthropology, Yarmouk University

Thesiger, W. (1959), *Arabian Sands*, Longmans, London

Thomas, B. S. (1932), *Arabia Felix*, Cape, London

Thomson, E. F. (1987), 'Feeding Systems and Sheep Husbandry in the Barley Belt of Syria', ICARDA 106, Aleppo

Thomson, E. F., Bahhady, F. A. and Martin, A. (1989), 'Sheep Husbandry at the Cultivated Margin of the North-West Syrian Steppe', No. 148–En., ICARDA, Aleppo

Tleimat, F. (1991), 'Livestock Development Strategies in Arid Lands: The Case of the Syrian Steppe', paper delivered at symposium Devenir des steppes d'Arabie et du Bilad ach-Cham, 10–13 April 1991, Institut du Monde Arabe, Paris

Traboulsi, Myriam (1991), 'La variabilité des précipitations dans le désert syrien', *Méditerranée* (Aix-en-Provence), 4, pp. 27–54

Tristram, H. B. (1873), *The Land of Moab*, John Murray, London

Tucker, H. A. (1974), 'General Endocrinological Control of Lactation', in B. L. Larson and V. R. Smith, (eds.), *Lactation: A Comprehensive Treatise*, I, Academic Press, New York, pp. 277–326

Tully, D. (1984), 'Land Use and Farmers' Strategies in Al Bab: The Feasibility of Forage Legumes in the Place of Fallow', Research Report 12, ICARDA, Aleppo

UNESCO (1960), *Les problèmes de la zone aride,* Imprimeries Oberthur, Paris

UNESOB (1973), *A Social and Economic Evaluation of the al Jafr Bedouin Settlement Project in East Jordan,* UNESOB/HR/73/18, Beirut

United Nations (1956), *Social Welfare Seminars for Arab States in the Middle East,* Reports on the meetings of Beirut (15.8–8.9.1949); Cairo (22.11–14.12.1950); Damascus (8–20.12.1952); Baghdad (6–21.3.1954), New York

Van Nieuweuhuijze, C. A. O. (ed.) (1977) *Commoners, Climbers and Notables: A Sampler of Studies on Social Ranking in the Middle East,* Brill, Leiden

Vatikiotis, P. J. (1967), *Politics and the Military in Jordan*, Frank Cass, London

Velud, C. (1986), 'L'émergence et l'organisation sociale des petites villes de Jazirah, en Syrie, sous le Mandat français', in P. Signoles (ed.), *Petites villes et villes moyennes dans le monde arabe*, Urbama, Tours, pp. 85–105.

(1987) 'Regime des terres et structures agraires en Jazirah syrienne durant la première moitié du vingtième siècle', in B. Canon (ed.), *Terroirs et sociétés au Maghreb et au Moyen-Orient*, EMA, 2, Maison de l'Orient, Lyon, pp. 161–94

(1991) 'Une expérience d'administration régionale en Syrie durant le Mandat français: conquête, colonisation et mise en valeur de la Jazirah, 1920–1936', unpublished dissertation, University of Lyon 2

Walpole, G. (1948), 'Land Problems in Jordan', *Journal of the Royal Central Asian Society* (London), 35, pp. 52–65

Warriner, D. (1957), *Land Reform and Development in the Middle East*, Royal Institute of International Affairs, New York

al-Wasil, 'Abd ar-Rahman bin 'Abd Allah (1986), 'Al-'Umran al-Rifi fi Mintaqat 'Unayzah', MA thesis, Imam Muhammad Ibn Sa'ud University, Saudi Arabia

Watson, A. M. (1983), *Agricultural Innovation in the Early Islamic World*, Cambridge University Press, Cambridge

Watson, P. J. (1979), *Archaeological Ethnography in Western Iran*, Viking Fund Publications in Anthropology, 57, University of Arizona, Tucson

Wendorf, F. and Schild, R. (1980), *Prehistory of the Eastern Sahara*, Academic Press, New York

Wetzstein, J. G. (1860), *Reisebericht über Hauran und die Trachonen*, Reimer, Berlin

Wilkinson, J. C. (1987), *The Imamate Tradition of Oman*, Cambridge University Press, Cambridge

(1991), *Arabia's Frontiers*, I. B. Tauris, London

Wilson, M. (1984), *King Abdullah of Jordan: A Political Biography*, Cambridge University Press, Cambridge

Wirth, Eugen (1971), *Syrien, eine geographische Landeskunde*, Darmstadt Wissenschaftliche, Darmstadt

World Bank (1989), 'Jordan: Towards an Agricultural Sector Strategy', IBRD, report 7547–JO, Washington

World Food Program (1969a), *Bedouin Settlement and Nomadic Livestock Development Projects,* WFP/IGC: 6/8, Add. 3. October, Rome

(1969b) *Jordan 036: Pilot Project for Bedouin Settlement and Improvement of Nomadic Sheep Husbandry,* WFP/IGC: 16/8, Add. 3, Annex 1, October, Rome

Yacoub, S. (1970), 'Nomadic Populations in Selected Countries in the Middle East and Related Issues of Sedentarisation and Settlement', in United Nations, *Studies on Selected Development Problems in Various Countries in the Middle East,* New York, pp. 105–17

Zakariyya, Ahmad Wasfi (1983), *'Asha'ir al-Sham* (2nd edn, 1st edn 1945), Dar al-Fikr, Damascus

Zaoual, H. (1984), 'La crise du paradigme du développement', *Tiers monde* (Evry), 100, pp. 829–36

Zeuner, F. E. (1963), *A History of Domesticated Animals*, Hutchinson, London

Zimmermann W. (1981), 'Tradition und Integration mobiler Lebensformgruppen. Eine empirische Studie über Beduinen und Fischer in Musandam/Sultanat Oman', Ph.D. dissertation, Göttingen

Zohary, D. and Hopf, M. (1988), *Domestication of Plants in the Old World,* Clarendon Press, Oxford

MAIN INDEX

INDEX OF PLACE NAMES

University of Cambridge
Oriental publications published for the
Faculty of Oriental Studies

1 *Averroes' commentary on Plato's Republic*, edited and translated by E. I. J. Rosenthal
2 *FitzGerald's 'Salaman and Absal'*, edited by A. J. Arberry
3 *Ihara Saikaku: the Japanese family storehouse*, translated and edited by G. W. Sargent
4 *The Avestan Hymn to Mithra*, edited and translated by Ilya Gershevitch
5 *The Fuṣūl al-Madanī of al-Fārābī*, edited by D. M. Dunlop (out of print)
6 *Dun Karm, poet of Malta*, texts chosen and translated by A. J. Arberry; introduction, notes and glossary by P. Grech
7 *The political writings of Ogyū Sorai*, by J. R. McEwan
8 *Financial administration under the T'ang dynasty*, by D. C. Twitchett
9 *Neolithic cattlẹ-keepers of south India: a study of the Deccan Ashmounds*, by F. R. Allchin
10 *The Japanese enlightenment: a study of the writings of Fukuzawa Yukichi*, by Carmen Blacker
11 *Records of Han administration.* Vol. I *Historical assessment*, by M. Loewe
12 *Records of Han administration.* Vol. II *Documents*, by M. Loewe
13 *The language of Indrajit of Orchā: a study of early Braj Bhāṣā prose*, by R. S. McGregor
14 *Japan's first general election, 1890*, by R. H. P. Mason
15 *A collection of tales from Uji: a study and translation of 'Uji Shūi Monogatari'* by D. E. Mills
16 *Studia semitica.* Vol. I *Jewish themes*, by E. I. J. Rosenthal
17 *Studia semitica.* Vol. II *Islamic themes*, by E. I. J. Rosenthal
18 *A Nestorian collection of Christological texts* Vol. I *Syriac text*, by Luise Abramowski and Alan E. Goodman
19 *A Nestorian collection of Christological texts* Vol. II *Introduction, translation, indexes*, by Luise Abramowski and Alan E. Goodman
20 *The Syriac version of the Pseudo-Nonnos mythological scholia*, by Sebastian Brock
21 *Water rights and irrigation practices in Lajh*, by A. M. A. Maktari
22 *The commentary of Rabbi David Kimḥi on Psalms cxx–cl*, edited and translated by Joshua Baker and Ernest W. Nicholson
23 *Jalāl al-dīn al-Suyūṭī.* Vol. I *Biography and background*, by E. M. Sartain
24 *Jalāl al-dīn al-Suyūṭī.* Vol. II *'Al-Tahadduth bini'mat allāh'*, Arabic text, by E. M. Sartain
25 *Origen and the Jews: studies in Jewish–Christian relations in third-century Palestine*, by N. R. M. de Lange
26 *The Vīsaḷadevarāsa': a restoration of the text*, by John D. Smith

27 *Shabbethai Sofer and his prayer-book*, by Stefan C. Reif

28 *Mori Ōgai and the modernization of Japanese culture*, by Richard John Bowring

29 *The rebel lands: an investigation into the origins of early Mesopotamian mythology*, by J. V. Kinnier Wilson

30 *Saladin: the politics of the holy war*, by Malcolm C. Lyons and David Jackson

31 *Khotanese Buddhist texts* (revised edition), edited by H. W. Bailey

32 *Interpreting the Hebrew Bible: essays in honour of E. I. J. Rosenthal*, edited by J. A. Emerton and Stefan C. Reif

33 *The traditional interpretation of the Apocalypse of St John in the Ethiopian orthodox church*, by Roger W. Cowley

34 *South Asian archaeology 1981: proceedings of the sixth international conference of South Asian archaeologists in western Europe*, edited by Bridget Allchin (with assistance from Raymond Allchin and Miriam Sidell)

35 *God's conflict with the dragon and the sea. Echoes of a Canaanite myth in the Old Testament*, by John Day

36 *Land and sovereignty in India. Agrarian society and politics under the eighteenth-century Maratha Svarājya*, by André Wink

37 *God's caliph: religious authority in the first centuries of Islam*, by Patricia Crone and Martin Hinds

38 *Ethiopian Biblical interpretation: a study in exegetical tradition and hermeneutics*, by Roger W. Cowley

39 *Monk and mason on the Tigris frontier: the early history of Ṭur ʿAbdin*, by Andrew Palmer

40 *Early Japanese books in Cambridge University Library: a catalogue of the Aston, Satow and Von Siebold collections*, by Nozomu Hayashi and Peter Kornicki

41 *Molech: a god of human sacrifice in the Old Testament*, by John Day

42 *Arabian studies*, edited by R. B. Serjeant and R. L. Bidwell

43 *Naukar, Rajput and Sepoy: the ethnohistory of the military labour market in Hindustan, 1450–1850*, by Dirk H. A. Kolff

44 *The epic of Pābūjī: a study, transcription and translation*, by John D. Smith

45 *Anti-Christian polemic in early Islam: Abū ʿĪsa al-Warrāq's 'Against the Trinity'*, by David Thomas

46 *Devotional literature in South Asia: current research, 1985–8. Papers of the fourth conference on devotional literature in new Indo-Aryan languages*, edited by R. S. McGregor

47 *Genizah research after ninety years: the case of Judaeo-Arabic. Papers read at the third congress of the Society for Judaeo-Arabic Studies*, edited by Joshua Blau and Stefan C. Reif

48 *Divination, mythology and monarchy in Han China*, by Michael Loewe

49 *The Arabian epic: heroic and oral storytelling*, volumes I–III, by M. C. Lyons

50 *Religion in Japan: arrows to heaven and earth*, edited by P. F. Kornicki and I. J. McMullen

51 *Kingship and political practice in colonial India*, by Pamela G. Price

52 *Hebrew manuscripts at Cambridge University Library: a description and introduction*, by Stefan C. Reif

53 *Selected letters of Rabindranath Tagore*, edited by Krishna Dutta and Andrew Robinson

54 *State and court ritual in China*, edited by Joseph P. McDermott

55 *Indian semantic analysis: the* nirvacana *tradition*, by Eivind Kahrs

56 *The Syriac version of the Old Testament: an introduction*, by M. P. Weitzman

57 *The cult of Asharah in ancient Israel and Judah: evidence for a Hebrew goddess*, by Judith M. Hadley